CORPUS APPROACHES TO DISCOURSE

'In this welcome new contribution to the emerging field of meta-reflection on corpus linguistic methodology, the editors expertly bring together a range of studies that address "dusty corners" (for example, neglected aspects such as similarity and absence) and "blind spots" (for example, the omission of non-verbal elements) as well as the pitfalls of research design. A convincing argument for accountability, self-reflexivity and triangulation, this volume is a must-read for any researcher in corpus-based discourse analysis and corpus linguistics more generally.'

Monika Bednarek, University of Sydney, Australia

'Readers interested in corpora and discourse will find that this book is a new departure. Insightful and thought-provoking, each chapter deals with a key methodological issue. Under the headings of "dusty corners", "blind spots" and "pitfalls", the volume addresses under-researched topics, genres and analytical tools. It is a prime example of self-reflexive research.'

Gerlinde Mautner, Vienna University of Economics and Business, Austria

Corpus linguistics has now come of age and *Corpus Approaches to Discourse* equips students with the means to question, defend and refine the methodology. Looking at corpus linguistics in discourse research from a critical perspective, this volume is a call for greater reflexivity in the field. The chapters, each written by leading authorities, contain an overview of an emerging area and a case-study, presenting practical advice alongside theoretical reflection. Carefully structured with an introduction by the editors and a conclusion by leading researcher, Paul Baker, this is key reading for advanced students and researchers of corpus linguistics and discourse analysis.

Charlotte Taylor is Senior Lecturer at the University of Sussex. She is author of *Mock Politeness in English and Italian* (2016), co-author of *Patterns and Meanings in Discourse* (with Alan Partington and Alison Duguid, 2013) and *The Language of Persuasion in Politics* (with Alan Partington, 2017) and co-editor of *Exploring Silence and Absence in Discourse* (with Melani Schroeter, 2018).

Anna Marchi is an Adjunct Lecturer at the University of Bologna She is the author of *Self-reflexive Journalism: A Corpus Study of Journalistic Culture and Community in The Guardian* (Routledge, forthcoming).

CORPUS APPROACHES TO DISCOURSE

A Critical Review

Edited by Charlotte Taylor and Anna Marchi

Routledge
Taylor & Francis Group
LONDON AND NEW YORK

First published 2018
by Routledge
2 Park Square, Milton Park, Abingdon, Oxon OX14 4RN

and by Routledge
711 Third Avenue, New York, NY 10017

Routledge is an imprint of the Taylor & Francis Group, an informa business

British Library Cataloguing-in-Publication Data
A catalogue record for this book is available from the British Library

Library of Congress Cataloging-in-Publication Data
Names: Taylor, Charlotte, 1977- editor. | Marchi, Anna, (Professor of linguistics) editor.
Title: Corpus approaches to discourse: a critical review / Charlotte Taylor and Anna Marchi [editors].
Description: Milton Park, Abingdon, Oxon; New York: Routledge, 2018. | Includes index.
Identifiers: LCCN 2017043814| ISBN 9781138895782 (hardback) | ISBN 9781138895805 (pbk.)
Subjects: LCSH: Corpora (Linguistics) | Discourse analysis.
Classification: LCC P128.C68 C655 2018 | DDC 410.1/88–dc23
LC record available at https://lccn.loc.gov/2017043814

ISBN: 978-1-138-89578-2 (hbk)
ISBN: 978-1-138-89580-5 (pbk)
ISBN: 978-1-315-17934-6 (ebk)

Typeset in Bembo
by Deanta Global Publishing Services, Chennai, India

CONTENTS

FIGURES

TABLES

CONTRIBUTORS

Clyde Ancarno is Lecturer in Applied Linguistics at King's College London. Her current research interests include inter-religious relations in multi-religious contexts and discourses about the natural world. She was a researcher on the three-year project entitled 'People', 'Products', 'Pets' and 'Pests': the discursive representation of Animals, funded by the Leverhulme Trust.

Laurence Anthony is Professor of Applied Linguistics at the Faculty of Science and Engineering, Waseda University, Japan. His main research interests are in corpus linguistics, educational technology, and English for Specific Purposes (ESP) program design and teaching methodologies. He received the National Prize of the Japan Association for English Corpus Studies (JAECS) in 2012 for his work in corpus software tools design. He is the developer of various corpus tools including *AntConc*, *AntWordProfiler*, *AntMover*, *FireAnt*, *ProtAnt* and *TagAnt*.

Paul Baker is Professor of English Language at Lancaster University. His research interests include language, gender and sexuality, discourse analysis and corpus linguistics. He has published 14 books, including *Using Corpora to Analyse Gender* (2014), *Sexed Texts: Language, Gender and Sexuality* (2008), *Using Corpora in Discourse Analysis* (2006), *Public Discourses of Gay Men* (2005) and *Polari: The Lost Language of Gay Men* (2002). He is commissioning editor of the journal *Corpora*.

Vaclav Brezina is a Research Fellow/Lecturer at the Department of Linguistics and English Language, Lancaster University. His research interests are in the areas of corpus design and methodology, statistics and applied linguistics. He is a co-author of the New General Service List (Applied Linguistics 2015). He has also designed a number of different tools for corpus analysis such as #LancsBox, BNC64, Lancaster Vocab Tool and Lancaster Statistical Tools online. He is involved in corpus building projects such as the BNC2014, Trinity Lancaster Corpus and Guangwai Lancaster Corpus of L2 Mandarin Chinese.

Helen Caple is an Australian Research Council DECRA Fellow and Senior Lecturer in Journalism at the University of New South Wales, Australia. Her research interests centre on news photography, text-image relations and discursive news values analysis. She is currently exploring the role of citizen photography in contemporary journalism. Helen has published in the area of photojournalism and social semiotics, including *Photojournalism: A Social Semiotic Approach* (2013, Palgrave Macmillan), *News Discourse* (2012, Continuum, with M. Bednarek), and *The Discourse of News Values* (2017, Oxford University Press, with M. Bednarek), which explores corpus-assisted multimodal discourse analysis in the context of news media.

Alison Duguid is Associate Professor of English Language and Linguistics at the University of Siena. Her recent publications include (with Alan Partington and Charlotte Taylor) *Patterns and Meanings in Discourse*, John Benjamins 2013; Class distinctions: a corpus study, in Duguid, Marchi and Partington (eds.) *Gentle Obsessions*, Artemide editori 2014; Evaluation as positioning in English language world news channels in Piazza, in Haarman, Caborn (eds.) *Ideological Positioning in the Linguistic and Semiotic Discourse of Television*, Palgrave Macmillan 2015; and (forthcoming 2017 with Alan Partington) Forced lexical primings in political discourse in *Lexical Priming advances and applications*, John Benjamins.

Jesse Egbert is Assistant Professor in the Applied Linguistics program at Northern Arizona University. He specialises in corpus-based research on register variation, particularly academic writing and online language, and methodological issues in quantitative linguistic research. His research has been published in journals such as *Journal of English Linguistics*, *International Journal of Corpus Linguistics*, *Corpus Linguistics and Linguistic Theory* and *Journal of Research Design and Statistics in Linguistics and Communication Science*. His books include a volume titled *Triangulating Methodological Approaches in Corpus Linguistic Research*, and a forthcoming book titled *Register Variation Online*.

Costas Gabrielatos is Senior Lecturer in English Language at Edge Hill University. His research combines the following areas: corpus linguistics methodology (compilation of topic-specific corpora, metrics, annotation techniques), lexicogrammar (conditionals, modality, tense-aspect, construction grammar, lexical grammar), language education (pedagogical lexicogrammar, learner language) and (critical) discourse studies.

Sylvia Jaworska (PhD) is an Associate Professor in Applied Linguistics in the Department of English Language and Applied Linguistics at the University of Reading. Her main research interests are discourse analysis and corpus linguistics and the application of both methods to study (new) media, health and business communication. She has published widely on these topics in *Applied Linguistics*, *Journal of Pragmatics*, *International Journal of Corpus Linguistics*, *Corpora*, *Discourse & Society* and *Language in Society*.

Karen Kinloch is a Researcher in Health Communication and Corpus Linguistics at Lancaster University and Edge Hill University. Following on from an ESRC funded PhD on the comparative discourses around infertility across a range of text types, her research interests are in Corpus-Assisted Discourse Studies, health and identity, human reproduction, health and science communication and perinatal mental health.

Alon Lischinsky is Senior Lecturer in Communication and Discourse at Oxford Brookes University. His main scholarly interest lies in the discursive construction of knowledgeable experts and legitimate identities in a range of fields, from the steamy – such as normative patterns of sexual agency and amatory ability – to the utterly staid – such as corporate reporting and branding as discursive activities, including questions of sustainability and greenwash. He is currently working on an introductory volume to corpus linguistic applications in scholarly and professional settings (with Sylvia Jaworska and Rachelle Vessey).

Anna Marchi is an Adjunct Lecturer at the University of Bologna. and has collaborated with the Universities of Siena, Cardiff, Swansea and Lancaster. Her research interests are in the area of methodology of corpus linguistics and discourse analysis, news discourse and linguistic approaches to journalism studies.

Alan Partington is Associate Professor of English Linguistics at Bologna University. His research interests include corpus research methodology, Corpus-Assisted Discourse Studies, particularly into political discourses, modern diachronic language studies, evaluation and evaluative prosody, corpus-assisted stylistics, irony, wordplay and metaphor.

Erin Schnur is a doctoral candidate at Northern Arizona University. Her work focuses on corpus-based investigation of spoken academic language. Her research has been published in the *International Journal of Corpus Linguistics* and the *Yearbook of Phraseology*.

Charlotte Taylor is Senior Lecturer in English Language and Linguistics at the University of Sussex. She is co-author of *Patterns and Meanings in Discourse* (with Alan Partington and Alison Duguid 2013) and co-editor of *Exploring Silence and Absence in Discourse* (with Melani Schroeter 2018).

ACKNOWLEDGEMENTS

This volume was the result of much discussion and collaboration and we are grateful to all those who were part of the process. In many ways, the conversations leading to this volume started as soon as Anna and Charlotte began working together nearly 10 years ago, and continued from there as we discussed and developed these ideas with our colleagues and peers. The Corpus & Discourse Conference hosted at the University of Siena in 2016 proved to be particularly influential in identifying key areas for attention and we are grateful to Alison Duguid for organising an event with space for reflection and discussion.

We would like to thank our contributors for reviewing one another's papers. To reflect the audience of our book we also asked external reviewers from across the academic career spectrum to read chapters. We would like to thank the following for giving up their precious time to help us all:

Guy Aston, Andrew Brindle, Gavin Brooks, Dario Del Fante, Matteo Di Cristofaro, Adriano Ferraresi, Heather Froehlich, Antonio Fruttaldo, Elvis Gomes, Nuria Lorenzo-Dus, Gerlinde Mautner, Lee Oakley, Daniella Samos, Rachelle Vessey.

1

INTRODUCTION

Partiality and reflexivity

Anna Marchi and Charlotte Taylor

1.1 Aims

Corpus linguistics and the analysis of discourse are described by Sinclair (2004: 11) as 'the twin pillars of language research' and, in his words, 'what unites them is [...] they both encourage the formulation of radically new hypotheses [and] the dimensions of pattern that they deal with are, on the whole, larger than linguistics is accustomed to.' Thus we have a long-standing and natural synergy between the two, based on their individual goals and foundations. This combination has become increasingly popular over the past decade in which we have seen a dedicated conference series emerge (Bologna 2012; Siena 2016; Lancaster 2018) and in 2017 the *Journal of Corpora and Discourse Studies* was established. The increased prominence of the combination may also be seen if we look at articles published in the journals *Corpora* and *International Journal of Corpus Linguistics*; in the period from 2015 to the time of writing, over 40 per cent referred to discourse in the title, keywords or abstract. This interest is also matched by scholars coming from a primarily (critical) discourse studies background who are moving into corpus analysis. Thus we have a situation where corpus & discourse methodologies are being combined and, while some researchers are doing both from the beginning of their career, many are incorporating one or the other approaches into their existing research repertoire. As Mautner (2016: 171) points out: 'as a junior researcher you are likely to be socialized into the one methodology or the other, but rarely into both.' Therefore, this book is aimed at a large family of scholars who use corpora to study how social realities are constructed, represented and transmitted linguistically, in other words, people who work with corpora 'to make sense of the ways that language is used in the construction of discourses' (Baker 2006: 1).

There have been a number of publications explicitly addressing this relatively new audience (such as Baker 2006; Charles, Hunston & Pecorari 2009; Partington,

Duguid & Taylor 2013; Baker & McEnery 2015, *inter alia*). However, to date there has been relatively little dedicated space for reflective or reflexive work on what the combination of corpus linguistics and (critical) discourse analysis can achieve and what kinds of theoretical assumptions are embedded into the methodological choices (with some notable exceptions, discussed below). What we want to argue here is that as corpus & discourse research has come of age, the time has come to pause and reflect on what it is we do. As the editors and contributors are practitioners of this methodological combination, we aim to look at our practices critically and reflexively. This is not intended as an assault on the exciting work which is emerging, but a recognition of the maturity of the methodology which is now robust enough to withstand, and indeed demand, close scrutiny.

One of the key assumptions regarding added values in corpus & discourse work is that corpus linguistics can provide greater objectivity to (critical) discourse analysis.[1] However, at least in part, this assumption is based on the misapprehension that the latter is purely qualitative and the former purely quantitative. And this in turn seems to be based on a misreading of what each of these terms involves, as we discuss in Section 1.2. The role of discourse analysis cannot simply be reduced to close reading. If we recognise, instead, that the various toolkits employed within (critical) discourse analysis offer a highly structured set of resources for classifying and interpreting language features, which gain salience against a pattern of (un)usuality, then it is easy to see that discourse analysis inherently has quantitative potential. No pattern can be identified unless its components are quantifiable. Similarly, as corpus linguistics is the use of corpus tools by researchers who themselves determine which linguistic questions are worth posing, and who interpret the findings at each stage, it too necessarily invokes a qualitative dimension. In this regard, another key similarity between corpus linguistics and discourse studies is that neither is a standardised set of approaches to data and therefore any combination involves selection from a range of resources. Just as McEnery and Hardie argue that corpus linguistics 'is not a monolithic, consensually agreed set of methods and procedures for the exploration of language' (2012: 1), so van Dijk (2013, no page) asserts that 'contrary to popular belief and the unfortunate claims of many papers submitted to discourse journals, CDA is not a method of critical discourse analysis' because the methodologies employed are so diverse.

Mautner (2016: 171–176) identifies six potential areas of concern in combining corpus linguistics and critical discourse analysis: skills gap and lack of standardisation, institutional barriers, resisting temptation in data collection, decontextualised data, language innovation and epistemological issues. It is principally to this last point which we dedicate our attention. This volume systematically questions assumptions of guaranteed 'objectivity' as a result of the combination of corpus linguistics and (critical) discourse analysis and addresses the theme of *partiality* in this research. By partiality (discussed further in Section 1.3) we mean both the potential *incompleteness* of research (for instance, focussing on difference at the expense of similarity) and potential *bias* or influence (for example, the influence of the individual researcher, or of individual research techniques).

We aim to cast light on the ways in which methodological choices affect the outcome of the research and to use case studies to show how researchers may enhance the completeness ('non-partiality') of their analysis. Thus, we may summarise the main objectives of the work collected in this volume as:

1 Greater awareness of the implications of methodological choices.
2 Exploration of neglected or under-studied areas.
3 Improved toolkit for carrying out research combining corpus linguistics and discourse analysis.

In the remainder of this introductory chapter, we discuss the concept of the qualitative/quantitative relationship which underpins so much discussion of the combination of corpus & discourse analysis and the different kinds of partiality that may affect the direction and interpretation of our research.

1.2 Qualitative and quantitative

A fantasy dialogue circulates amongst social scientists staging an exchange between the American sociologists Charles Wright Mills, heir of the critical school, and Paul Felix Lazarsfeld, founder of empirical sociology, taking the famous incipit of Wright Mill's *Sociological Imagination*:

C. W. M.: 'Nowadays men often feel that their private lives are a series of traps.'
P. F. L.: 'How many men, which men, how long have they felt that way, which aspects of their private lives bother them, when do they feel free rather than trapped, what kinds of traps do they experience, etc.?'

(Elcock 1976: 13)

Quantitative and qualitative purists have long been in opposition, they have conceived quantitative and qualitative research as incommensurable paradigms, and their results as incomparable (Howe 1988). Paradigms are 'universally recognised scientific achievements that for a time provide model problems and solutions to a community of practitioners' (Kuhn 1970: viii); in time a paradigm exhausts its explanatory power and it is surpassed by a new paradigm. By definition, then, paradigms are in competition with one another and conceptualising qualitative and quantitative research in these terms makes the two appear mutually exclusive: We can shift from one to the other but we cannot merge them (Guba 1990). In the context of the 30-year 'paradigm wars' (see Tashakkori & Teddlie 1998), mixed methods emerged as a 'third way' (Johnson & Onwuegbuzie 2004), following the idea that research should combine methodologies in order to suit the matter under investigation.

The principle behind a non-paradigmatic view of methodologies is that methods should derive from the research question and follow its needs. Wright Mills (1959), who famously criticised the twin evils of 'grand theory' and 'abstracted empiricism', warns that methods should suit the social problem and not the other way around. *Qualitative* and *quantitative* are labels we attach to what we do and methods should be tools, not schools. Therefore, our conceptualisations and identifications should be instrumental rather than deterministic:

> I have never presented myself as a single-minded advocate either of 'qualitative' or 'quantitative' methods. I have certainly stressed the need for adopting methods appropriate to research questions.
>
> *(Oakley 1999: 252)*

It is in this instrumental perspective that the discussion about combining the quantitative rigour of corpus linguistics with the social perspective of qualitative approaches to discourse analysis finds its frame.

In her seminal 1995 paper Hardt-Mautner speaks of the integration of corpus linguistics and critical discourse analysis in terms of the selection of the best tools available from the two approaches. She discusses the benefits of integrating them, presenting a win–win situation where the methodological mix allows the researcher to overcome the limitations of the individual methods, while benefiting from their respective qualities. On one side we have the 'greater precision and richness' of qualitative analysis; on the other we are also granted the 'statistically reliable and generalizable results' (McEnery & Wilson 1996: 77) of quantitative studies. Corpus linguists often complain that discourse analysts rarely use quantitative tools to describe the extent to which their findings are generalisable. Discourse analysts, on the other hand, criticise corpus linguists for mainly focusing on individual words and lacking insight into the various dimensions of discourse structure and into the extralinguistic knowledge needed to get to the 'hidden story' of meaning (Cameron 1997: 45). Seen from the point of view of their complementary qualities and limitations the combination of the two approaches has been favourably described as a 'natural match' (Mautner 2009: 33) and 'useful methodological synergy' (Baker et al. 2008). Most literature discussing the synergy between CDA and corpus linguistics focuses on how quantitative methods can help the soundness of qualitative interpretations[2] and contribute to the analysis by making it possible to handle larger amounts of texts (Orpin 2005) and by 'checking overinterpretation and underinterpretation' (O'Halloran & Coffin 2004). Referring to Corpus-Assisted Discourse Studies (CADS), Vessey describes it as 'a useful framework because of the ways it addresses some of the weaknesses and exploits the strength of its constituent parts' (Vessey 2013: 3), namely corpus linguistics and 'traditional discourse analysis' (Partington & Marchi 2015: 216). Corpus linguistics is ultimately seen as improving the analysis by providing more neutral starting points and generalisability, i.e. accounting for the scale of phenomena. At the same time the overall 'qualitative' nature of the analysis guards against the commonly lamented trouble with quantitative studies, that is, their disregard for context(s). Mixing the two should bring together social relevance and statistical relevance, thus overcoming the peril of quantitative studies 'counting only what is easy to count' (Stubbs &

Gerbig 1993: 78) and of qualitative studies 'find[ing] what they expect to find' (Stubbs 1997: 2).

As mentioned above, this kind of mixed approach has seen increasing popularity and vitality over the past 20 years, and, rather than one approach there is, in fact, a diverse range of kin approaches that go under different names, such as *corpus-based CDA* (e.g. Baker et al. 2008), *CADS* (e.g. Partington 2004), *discourse-oriented corpus studies* (Gabrielatos, private conversation), *corpora and discourse studies* (Baker & McEnery 2015) or under no particular label. Furthermore, much work that prefers the names *corpus stylistics* (e.g. Mahlberg & McIntyre 2011) or *corpus pragmatics* (e.g. Aijmer & Ruhlemann 2015) and some *corpus-based sociolinguistics* (e.g. Friginal & Hardy 2014) will be very similar in scope and tools to projects using the 'discourse' range of labels. This book wishes to overstep disciplinary barriers and avoid pigeon-holing or branding, and addresses the integration of (critical) discourse analysis and corpus linguistics in the full range of forms and combinations. As will be seen, contributors in different chapters adopt different terms to describe their methodology and we have deliberately chosen not to standardise such usages as to do so would erect barriers where we want to see them fall. Following Mautner (2016), what we would really like to see is a reduction in 'academic tribalism' and we hope that the work collected here will be useful to the full spectrum of users interested in using corpora to investigate discourse. The end goal is, after all, a shared one. As Johansson (1991: 6) reminds us, in discussing corpus linguistics more generally:

> The ultimate aim is the study of language(s), through corpora and other means. Linguists who neglect corpora do so at their own peril, but so do those who limit themselves to corpora. In practice there will often be a division of work, with some linguists focussing on theory building and others on corpus work. This is not a problem as long as we realise the limits of our approach and respect other lines of investigation. An open mind is the best guide in linguistics, as in research in general and indeed in life itself.

Independently from the denomination they choose (or refuse to adopt) the reason that drives researchers to work with corpora and discourse is epistemological in nature and their goal is achieving greater soundness and greater breadth in their research. As Hardt-Mautner (1995: 22) summarises: '[d]rawing on corpus evidence fundamentally redefines the nature of "interpretation", turning it from an introspective undertaking into an empirical one.' Having access to large amounts of data not only grants greater representativeness to our findings, but it also 'allows a greater distance to be preserved between observer and the data' (Partington 2006: 268). While this may not be a safeguard against subconscious bias, nor an impediment to a conscious one, it leaves room for the unexpected to be discovered and it gives us the opportunity to be surprised by the data. Rather than searching for evidence fitting pre-determined categories, new categories can emerge bottom-up from our repeated encounters with a specific pattern (see Baker et al. 2008). This means new ideas are stimulated, in a logic of discovery that does not contradict or interfere with in-depth contextual understanding. Partington (2009: 286) talks of the exploratory nature of CADS and describes the explorer's activity as 'serendipitous journeys' playing around with the data, organising them in new ways and finding new ways of looking at them. A corpus & discourse approach is, in other words, about releasing creativity.

1.3 Triangulation

Mixing methods is a form of triangulation and all forms of triangulation hold creative power (Marchi & Taylor 2009), because they allow the researcher to look onto the data from many different windows, they account for complexity and help us in dealing with it. Recently Baker and Egbert (2016) edited a remarkable volume collecting 10 different ways of addressing the same research question working on the same corpus; in the final part of the book the editors assess the outcome with a comparative meta-analysis of the different analyses. The methods included in the experiment covered the quantitative–qualitative spectrum ranging from so-called corpus-driven techniques, through so-called more corpus-based (or more targeted/hypothesis-based) ones, to closer analysis of small samples of text in the corpus. In this way the project accounts for the non-homogeneous practices of corpus work and reflects corpus approaches as 'falling between two end points of a continuum, rather than belonging to one of two polar extremes' (McEnery & Gabrielatos 2006: 36). Indirectly, the project then also challenges the dualistic view of qualitative and quantitative as polar opposites and allows for a more fluid and flexible view of methodology, which we strongly endorse. Rather than conceptualising approaches as a binary system, we should see them as positioned along a continuum. Baker points out that there are 'fuzzy boundaries' (Baker et al. 2008: 296) between what we identify as quantitative and qualitative and that 'corpus analysis shares much in common with forms of analysis thought to be qualitative' (Baker 2005: 36).

What we do when we analyse discourse using corpora 'is a qualitative analysis of quantifiable patterns' (Marchi, forthcoming). Because of the fuzziness of boundaries, triangulation is not an anchor that guarantees validity, 'nor can it be used to make claims for "scientific" neutrality' (Marchi & Taylor 2009: 19); it is rather a means of achieving greater precision, richness as well as awareness.

The term *triangulation* was originally imported into social research from navigation and land surveying (Layder 1993) – where it indicates the trigonometric operation for finding a position or location by means of bearings from two fixed points a known distance apart. But triangulation goes beyond the correct identification of a result:

> The idea underlying triangulation is that a researcher observing an object from two different perspectives will obtain a three dimensional representation of this object by combining the two complementary two dimensional images.
>
> *(Erzberger & Prein 1997: 146)*

There can be different types of triangulation (see Denzin 1970): the triangulation of *methods*, of *tools* within a methodological approach, of *investigators* and of *data*, and there is room for combinations of different kinds of triangulation. There can also be different outcomes of triangulation: results can *converge*, which means that they corroborate the same conclusion; this kind of outcome is a classic form of cross-validation. Results can be *complementary*, thus offering a thicker description of the problem matter than if just one method had been adopted; Ezerberger and Prein (1997) conceptualise this complementary relation as a 'jigsaw puzzle', where different approaches add different pieces to the picture's completeness. In their extensive experiment, Baker and Egbert (2016) found evidence of both types of results. Finally, results can *diverge*, contradicting each other. Dissonance, far from being daunting, holds great creative potential, as it 'suggests areas for further analysis' (Rossman & Wilson 1985: 633) and ultimately is a barometer of complexity of the topic/research question(s).

In this sense there is more to triangulation than mixing methods, but there is also more to both triangulation and to mixed method approaches than validation. The idea of validating findings by combining methods is something to be rather cautious with. Mixing methods does not eliminate bias; while complementing methodological limitations (complementarity, as discussed earlier, being seen as the dominant advantage of combining corpus linguistics and CDA) indubitably improves the soundness and the reach of analysis, it does not guarantee a solution to the vexed problem of validity and reliability, and much less objectivity. All methods have inherent biases and limitations; by combining methods we sum their strengths, we compensate some of their limitations, but we might also be combining other respective flaws. In any combination, the researcher has to be aware and guard against the 'corroboration drive' (Marchi & Taylor 2009), or 'confirmation bias' (Wason 1960), that is, the tendency to reinforce existing beliefs by selecting confirmatory evidence, while disregarding alternatives, supported by converging findings. We should be particularly careful about the conclusions we derive from corroboration and '[w]e should combine theories and methods carefully and purposefully with the intention of adding breadth and depth to our analysis but not for the purpose of pursuing "objective" truth' (Fielding & Fielding 1986: 33). The positivistic idea of 'objective truth' appears to be impractical the moment we acknowledge the fact that all science is primarily and necessarily *researcher-driven*, the very object of research depends on a subjective sense of significance: '[a] "disinterested" social science has never existed and, for logical reasons, can never exist' (Myrdal 1970: 55). On this matter Stubbs (2007) borrows an effective summary from McGuire (1999: 399): 'knowledge is always an underrepresentation (since there is always selective attention to data), a misrepresentation (since it is influenced by the knower), and an overrepresentation (since it is based on inferences that go beyond the given data).'

Relying on large amounts of data and computer-aided techniques does not bring objectivity, but it can provide greater accuracy and accountability. Our interpretations are not replicable, but the process that has brought us to them is reproducible, and if we systematically account for the process we can check on our (or others') findings and conclusions: using the same set of data, asking the same questions, possibly arriving at different answers.

1.4 Partiality

Having established that a quantitative/qualitative mix cannot in and of itself bring greater objectivity, in this section we introduce the kinds of *partiality* that we may encounter (or create) and counter. As discussed at the beginning of this chapter, we do this against a backdrop of relative paucity of research to date into the effects of methodological choices on the direction of the research in corpus & discourse studies. Understandably, most people just get on with the task of doing their research, rather than discussing what didn't work and how they balanced it. However, this then means that any newcomers to the area, or colleagues starting out on a new project, have to reinvent those checks and balances anew each time. What we attempt to do here is to draw together those threads to create a kind of contact point for current and future researchers. And we should note that while some of the effects may appear 'obvious' to an expert in the field, it is certainly not the case that these effects are understood and recognised more generally.

Areas of methodological interest which have received attention include the need to pay attention to both reliability of corpora (e.g. Miller & Biber 2015), the need for corpus linguists generally to understand and expand the range of statistical measures which they use (e.g. Gries 2010, 2015), the need for total accountability in analysis (e.g. Leech 1992; McEnery & Hardie 2012). Biber and Gray (2013: 369, our numbering) reflecting on methodological issues for corpus linguists more generally, identify the following considerations:

1 registering differences should be an essential component of any investigation of language use;
2 critical evaluation of the corpora that we use;
3 more awareness of research design considerations;
4 more accountability in the reporting of quantitative findings;
5 more accountability in the linguistic interpretation of quantitative findings;
6 the development of new methods for the comparison of type distributions across corpora.

Although, as Biber and Gray wonder, it may be that 'those considerations might all boil down to the need for greater awareness of the foundations of quantitative (social) science research' (2013: 369). Such re-examination of the foundations is an important part of what we hope to enable with this volume. We see our contribution as part of that same drive to increase reflexivity across the field and, more specifically, to aid newcomers to the combination of corpus & discourse analysis. Thus, in the following section we have attempted to sketch out the kinds of issues we feel that we need to be aware of when designing, conducting and evaluating our research. As will be seen, these three aspects constitute the framework for this volume.

1.4.1 Dusty corners

The *dusty corners* of research are both the neglected aspects of analysis and under-researched topics or text types. If we consider the first type, these are overlooked features such as similarity (Chapter 2) and absence (Chapter 3). These areas have often been neglected for both theoretical and practical reasons. If we take the case of absence, knowledge of the frames for carrying out (critical) discourse analysis would lead us to expect any systematic corpus and discourse study to account for both what is present and what is not present in the discourse. For instance, Van Leeuwen's (1996) seminal work on social actors guides us to ask as our first question in the investigation 'who is included and who is excluded?'. Thus, in combining corpus & discourse work we might expect that exclusion or absence would be accounted for. In reality, it is rarely integrated for a number of more practical reasons such as the difficulties of defining which absences are meaningful, the lack of integrated corpus software to aid identification of absence and the dilemma of what to do, say or analyse once the absent has been identified. Thus, the researcher is guided by the software that is available initially and asks questions (quite sensibly) which may be answered. However, at a later stage, as they realise that their account is only of the visible and not of the potentialities, they have to develop a system for accounting for such features. Exactly the same occurs with the analysis or identification of similarity, in which we have a drive to look at what is there and what is interesting, and that is usually what is *different*. By neglecting absence we may lose half the object of study; by neglecting similarity we may lose half the analytic capacity.

The second kind of dusty corner refers to under-researched content, both in terms of topics and text types. This aspect is addressed in Chapter 4, which discusses overlooked text types of various kinds. In this case then we are switching the attention not from the process of conducting corpus & discourse research, but to an even earlier stage of deciding which texts are worthy of analysis. A criticism of corpus & discourse work has been that it relies (understandably) on texts which may easily be converted into corpora. As a consequence, work on media discourse has been dominated by newspaper discourse and yet, if we purport to combine corpus linguistics and (critical) discourse analysis, we need ways to incorporate the non-dominant voices too. Within this category of under-researched content, we might also consider languages which are under-researched, often due to lack of resources at the level of both corpora and expertise. Similarly, we might think about the relative lack of studies on multilingual corpora. Again, if we look outside at the wider arena of sociolinguistics, there are convincing challenges to the notion of language boundaries, such as translanguaging (e.g. Garcia & Wei 2014) and superdiversity (e.g. Vertovec 2007) yet the multilingual corpora we use in our work are often conceived as presenting genres subdivided by language, which excludes many language practices.

Lastly, we might consider the role of *positive* discourse analysis which holds potential to address the tendency for corpus & discourse work, like critical discourse studies more generally, to focus on negative discourses, rather than on positive change.

1.4.2 Blind spots

Blind spots refer to the aspects that remain necessarily undetected or under-analysed in research that tackles complex communicative events when limiting itself to text-only corpora (mono-modal datasets), to corpora of just one text type or to just corpora at large. One of the key ways to identify such blind spots is triangulation (whether of texts, methods, disciplines or researchers, as discussed above). As so convincingly illustrated in Baker and Egbert (2016), and discussed previously in Marchi and Taylor (2009), triangulation is a rich means of completing the analysis because it tends to provide complementary findings which broaden our picture of the data. Recent research has drawn attention to the different kinds of triangulation which may be employed, such as Römer (2016) on cross-disciplinary investigation of phraseology, and multichannel analysis for the identification of deception (Archer & Lansley 2015).

The contributions in this section show how the various articulations of multiplicity can make corpus-assisted discourse analysis richer and more complete, thus overcoming, or at least addressing, a host of possible blind spots. Areas which are covered here include employing triangulation of data in two distinct ways. In Chapter 5 this takes the form of the construction and analysis of multimodal corpora to capture the entirety of the discourse under study and eliminate the blind spots created by the omission of non-verbal elements. Following Van Leeuwen (2011: 668), who states that 'many forms of contemporary written language cannot be adequately understood unless we look, not just at language, but also at images, layout, typography and colour', the chapter sets out to show how multimodal features can be systematically accounted for through the development of corpus-assisted multimodal discourse analysis (CAMDA). Chapter 6 also draws on triangulation of data and develops an eight-step framework for CADS with multiple data sets. As the authors argue, this becomes a means of accounting for and investigating the influence of context on discursive phenomena, avoiding the blind spots introduced by a single subject. In Chapter 7, the contributors show how triangulation of method may be employed. This involves integrating different disciplinary approaches as well as multiple methods, which becomes a means of broadening the scope of any research investigation and thus seeing further into the data and analysis.

Alongside these, other potential rich sources for triangulation which are not explored here are cross-cultural and cross-linguistic studies. If we consider one goal of critical discourse studies to involve interrogating naturalised discourses (e.g. Fairclough 1985), then comparative tools of all kinds are key to this endeavour because they show us that other options are available. However, to date, the difficulties of making truly comparable corpora, and perhaps limitations in language expertise, have often led to the neglect of cross-linguistic comparison at the discourse level (for exceptions and further discussion see Vessey 2013, Taylor 2014).

1.4.3 Research design (avoiding pitfalls/re-examining the foundations)

The third category of factors that might lead to the research being partial in either sense regards those structural aspects that may inadvertently impact on the results. The contributions in this section raise awareness of how specific methodological choices influence the direction the analysis will take and affect the results. Initial steps of research such as the segmentation and the (automatic or manual) handling of the data, or the choice of tools and metrics have an impact on the steps that follow, and this effect needs to be acknowledged and accounted for. At the most fundamental level, given that we are talking about *discourse*, we have to consider what we actually have as the basic unit of analysis – in other words, what is the text? (Chapter 8). Although not covered in this volume, the ways in which we prepare our data through markup and annotation will also affect both what can be searched for and thus the kinds of questions which can be posed. This area of potential partiality has been more thoroughly documented partly because it was addressed by Sinclair, who argued against the use of grammatical part-of-speech tagging because 'the system that produces the tags in the first place is not challenged' (2004: 191). As researchers expand the use of corpora into discourse and pragmatic levels, the use of annotation becomes increasingly important and, concurrently, so does the need for transparency about the origins of those tags.

At the level of analysis, the ways in which we segment our data will also change the story the data will tell. For example, using time divisions of different length in analysing diachronic data makes some features very salient while others will become invisible (Chapter 9). Similarly, the choices of techniques for visualisation of the data will both lead the research in particular directions by foregrounding and making visible certain connections, and lead the reader of the research to understand the data in particular ways (Chapter 10). These are all areas that are often overlooked, or assumed to be straightforward until we look a little more closely and experiment with moving those segmentations in order to see how our view is being altered or biased. As Chapter 10 shows us, even the heart of corpus linguistic work, the KWIC (key word in context) concordance line, is not unproblematic. This theme is continued in Chapter 11, which addresses another core of much corpus & discourse work: keywords. Many of us use them, but how many are aware of exactly what the outputs mean and how they are affected by the different statistical measures available? Finally, in Chapter 12, this question is opened out more broadly by casting light on the influence of preliminary choices of metrics in determining what the researcher will pursue in the analysis. It shows how the use of different statistical measures, ranking and cut-off points lead the research in different directions and ultimately produce different results.

1.5 Looking forwards

In light of this discussion, the question arises of what we, as researchers, can do? What we want to initiate with this book is a greater awareness of the range of possible levels at which partiality may come into play. Bednarek and Caple (2017: 23, our italics) propose that 'to manage subjectivity, researchers can adopt the principles of *transparency* and *consistency*'. This is a research agenda with which we would certainly want to align ourselves, but we might go further to suggest that we can actually replace the goal of increased objectivity with more achievable ones of greater *accountability* (including those key values of transparency and consistency) and *self-reflexivity*. Each of the following chapters will tackle a different aspect of this. However, no single volume can reach for a totally comprehensive view of what factors might impact on any given project. As we have indicated in the discussion above, there are areas that we have not been able to include here, and there are also certainly areas that we have not yet thought of. What we need, then, is a more general set of principles which can guide our work and be employed alongside the specific issues discussed here. In this way, the research choices and impacts are monitored throughout the process, the researcher becomes more sensitive to the impact of decisions taken, and the research is presented in ways that are sufficiently clear to allow for replication, one of the cornerstones of sound research (e.g. as discussed in McEnery & Hardie 2012).

Furthermore, an increased self-awareness regarding the impact of the researcher on the researched may also be something that we actively try and pass on, not just through sharing experiences in volumes such as this one, but in teaching, by giving students the experience of playing with their data, parameters and processes, and observing the effects. As Gabrielatos (2013) so persuasively puts it, 'corpus linguistics is very easy to do badly' and so we need to incorporate more ways of checking and evaluating what it is we are doing when we do corpus & discourse analysis.

Notes

1 The term *(critical) discourse analysis* is used to encompass both research that identifies as *discourse analysis* and that which identifies as *critical discourse analysis*.
2 Gabrielatos and Duguid (2014) criticise as a misrepresentation the idea that 'the sole contribution of CL in CDA is in the quantification of patterns'.

References

Aijmer, K. & Rühlemann, C. 2015. *Corpus Pragmatics: A Handbook*. Cambridge: Cambridge University Press.

Archer, D. & Lansley, C. 2015. Public appeals, news interviews and crocodile tears: An argument for multi-channel analysis. *Corpora*, 10(2), 231–258.

Baker, P. 2005. *The Public Discourses of Gay Men*. London: Routledge.

Baker, P. 2006. *Using Corpora in Discourse Analysis*. London: Continuum.

Baker, P. and Egbert, J. 2016. *Triangulating Methodological Approaches in Corpus-Linguistic Research*. London: Routledge.

Baker, P. & McEnery, T. 2015. *Corpora and Discourse Studies: Integrating Discourse and Corpora.* Basingstoke: Palgrave Macmillan.

Baker, P., Gabrielatos, C., Khosravinik, M., Krzyzanowski, M., McEnery, T. & Wodak, R. 2008. A useful methodological synergy? Combining critical discourse analysis and corpus linguistics to examine discourses of refugees and asylum seekers in the UK press. *Discourse & Society*, 19(3), 273–305.

Bednarek, M. & Caple, H. 2017. *The Discourse of News Values: How News Organizations Create 'Newsworthiness'*. New York: Oxford University Press.

Cameron, D. 1997. Dreaming the dictionary: Keywords and corpus linguistics. *KeyWords*, 1, 35–45.

Charles, M., Hunston, S. & Pecorari, D. (eds.) 2009. *Academic Writing: At the Interface of Corpus and Discourse*. London: Bloomsbury.

Denzin, N. K. 1970. *The Research Act in Sociology*. Chicago: Aldine.

Elcock, H. J. 1976. *Political Behaviour*. London: Methuen.

Erzberger, C. & Prein, G. 1997. Triangulation: Validity and empirically-based hypothesis construction. *Quality and Quantity*, 31(2), 141–154.

Fairclough, N. L. 1985. Critical and descriptive goals in discourse analysis. *Journal of Pragmatics*, 9(6), 739–763.

Fielding, N. G. & Fielding, J. L. 1986. *Linking Data*. London: Sage.

Friginal, E. & Hardy, J. 2014. *Corpus-Based Sociolinguistics: A Guide for Students*. London/New York: Routledge.

Gabrielatos, C. [@congabonga]. (2013, September 13). The allure of #corpuslinguistics: it's quite easy to do badly [Tweet]. Available online at: https://twitter.com/congabonga/status/377331048448671744

Gabrielatos, C. & Duguid, A. 2014. 'Corpus Linguistics and CDA: A critical look at synergy'. CDA20+ Symposium, University of Amsterdam, 9 September 2014.

García, O. & Wei, L. 2014. *Translanguaging: Language, Bilingualism and Education*. Basingstoke: Palgrave Macmillan.

Gray, B. 2013. Interview with Douglas Biber. *Journal of English Linguistics*, 41(4), 359–379.

Gries, S. 2015. The most under-used statistical method in corpus linguistics: Multi-level (and mixed-effects) models. *Corpora*, 10(1), 95–125.

Gries, S. T. 2010. Methodological skills in corpus linguistics: A polemic and some pointers towards quantitative methods. *Corpus Linguistics in Language Teaching*, 121–146.

Guba, E. G. 1990. The alternative paradigm dialog. In E. G. Guba (ed.), *The Paradigm Dialog*. Newbury Park, CA: Sage. pp. 17–27.

Hardt-Mautner, G. 1995. 'Only connect': Critical discourse analysis and corpus linguistics. *UCREL Technical Paper 6*. Lancaster: University of Lancaster.

Howe, K. R. 1988. Against the qualitative-quantitative incompatibility thesis or dogmas die hard. *Educational Researcher* 17(8), 10–6.

Johansson, S. 1991. Computer corpora in English language research. In S. Johansson & A. Stenström (eds.) *English Computer Corpora: Selected Papers and Research Guide*. Berlin: Mouton de Gruyter. pp.3–6.

Johnson, R. B. & Onwuegbuzie, A. J. 2004. Mixed methods research: A Research paradigm whose time has come. *Educational Researcher*, 33(7), 14–26.

Kuhn, T. 1970. *The Structure of Scientific Revolutions*. Chicago: University of Chicago Press.

Layder, D. 1993. *New Strategies in Social Research*. Cambridge: Polity Press.

Leech, G. 1992. Corpora and theories of linguistic performance. In J. Svartvik (ed.) *Directions in Corpus Linguistics*. Berlin: Walter de Gruyter. pp. 105–122.

McEnery, T. & Gabrielatos, C. 2006. English Corpus Linguistics. In B. Aarts & A. M. S. McMahon (eds.) *The Handbook of English Linguistics*. Oxford: Blackwell. pp. 33–71.

McEnery, T. & Hardie, A. 2012. *Corpus Linguistics: Method, Theory and Practice*. Cambridge: Cambridge University Press.

McEnery, T. & Wilson, A. 1996. *Corpus Linguistics*. Edinburgh: Edinburgh University Press.

McGuire, W. J. 1999. *Constructing Social Psychology*. Cambridge: Cambridge University Press.

Mahlberg, M. & McIntyre, D. 2011. A case for corpus stylistics: Ian Fleming's *Casino Royale*. *English Text Construction*, 4 (2), 204–227.

Marchi, A. in preparation. *Self-Reflexive Journalism: A Corpus Study of Journalistic Culture and Community in the Guardian*. London/New York: Routledge.

Marchi, A. & Taylor, C. 2009. 'If on a winter night two researchers': A challenge to assumptions of soundness of interpretation. *Critical Approaches to Discourse Analysis across Disciplines*, 3(1), 1–20.

Mautner, G. 2009. Corpora and critical discourse analysis. In P. Baker (ed.) *Contemporary Approaches to Corpus Linguistics*. London: Continuum. pp. 32–46.

Mautner, G. 2016. Checks and balances: how corpus linguistics can contribute to CDA. In R. Wodak & M. Meyer. *Methods of Critical Discourse Studies* (3rd edition). London: Sage. pp. 154–179.

Miller, D. & Biber, D. 2015. Evaluating reliability in quantitative vocabulary studies: The influence of corpus design and composition. *International Journal of Corpus Linguistics*, 20(1), 30–53.

Mills, C-W. 1959. *The Sociological Imagination*. Oxford: Oxford University Press.

Myrdal, G. 1970. *Objectivity in Social Research*. London: Gerald Duckworth & Company Ltd.

Oakley, A. 1999. Paradigm wars: some thoughts on a personal and public trajectory. *International Journal of Social Research Methodology*, 2(3), 247–254.

O'Halloran, K. A. & Coffin, C. 2004. Checking overinterpretation and underinterpretation: help from corpora in critical linguistics. In C. Coffin, A. Hewings & K. A. O'Halloran (eds.) *Applying English Grammar: Functional and Corpus Approaches*. London: Hodder Arnold. pp. 275–297.

Orpin, D. 2005. Corpus linguistics and critical discourse analysis. Examining the ideology of sleaze. *International Journal of Corpus Linguistics*, 10(1), 37–61.

Partington, A. 2004. Corpora and discourse, a most congruous beast. In A. Partington, J. Morley & L. Haarman (eds.) *Corpora and Discourse*. Bern: Peter Lang. pp. 11–20.

Partington, A. 2006. Metaphors, motifs and similes across discourse types: Corpus-Assisted Discourse Studies (CADS) at work. In A. Stefanowitsch & S. T. Gries (eds.) *Corpus-Based Approaches to Metaphor and Metonymy*. Berlin: Mouton de Gruyter. pp. 267–304.

Partington, A. 2009. Evaluating evaluation and some concluding thoughts on CADS. In J. Morley & P. Bayley (eds.) *Corpus-Assisted Discourse Studies on the Iraq Conflict. Wording the War*. London/New York: Routledge. pp. 261–303.

Partington, A. & Marchi, A. 2015. Using corpora in discourse analysis. In D. Biber & R. Reppen (eds.) *Cambridge Handbook of English Corpus Linguistics*. Cambridge: Cambridge University Press. pp. 216–234.

Partington, A., Duguid, A. & Taylor, C. 2013. *Patterns and Meanings in Discourse: Theory and Practice in Corpus-Assisted Discourse Studies (CADS)*. Amsterdam: John Benjamins Publishing.

Römer, U. 2016. Teaming up and mixing methods: collaborative and cross-disciplinary work in corpus research on phraseology. *Corpora*, 11(1), 113–129.

Rossman, G. & Wilson, B. L. 1985. Numbers and words. Combining quantitative and qualitative methods in a single large-scale evaluation study. *Evaluation Review*, 9(5), 627–643.

Sinclair, J. 2004. *Trust the Text*. London: Routledge.

Stubbs, M. 1997. Whorf's children: critical comments on critical discourse analysis. In A. Wray & A. Ryan (eds.) *Evolving Models of Language*. Clevedon: Multilingual Matters.

pp. 100–16 [Reprinted in M. Toolan. 2002. *Critical Discourse Analysis*. London: Routledge. pp. 202–18].

Stubbs, M. 2007. Text, Technology and the Question of Induction. *Studies in Fuzziness and Soft Computing* 209: 233–254.

Stubbs, M. & Gerbig, A. 1993. Human and Inhuman Geography: On the Computer-Assisted Analysis of Long Texts. In M. Hoey (ed.) *Data, Description, Discourse. Papers on the English Language in Honour of John McH Sinclair on his Sixtieth Birthday*. London: Harper Collins. pp. 64–85.

Tashakkori, A. & Teddle, C. 1998. *Mixed Methodology: Combining Qualitative and Quantitative Approaches*. London: Sage.

Taylor, C. 2014. Investigating the representation of migrants in the UK and Italian press: A cross-linguistic corpus-assisted discourse analysis. *International journal of corpus linguistics*, 19(3), 368–400.

Van Dijk, T. 2013. CDA is NOT a method of critical discourse analysis. *EDISO website*. Available online at: www.edisoportal.org/debate/115-cda-not-method-critical-discourse-analysis

Van Leeuwen, T. 1996. The representation of social actors. Texts and Practices: *Readings in Critical Discourse Analysis*, 1, 32–70.

Van Leeuwen, T. 2014. Critical discourse analysis and multimodality. In C. Hart & P. Cap (eds.) *Contemporary Critical Discourse Studies*. London: Bloomsbury Publishing. pp. 281–296.

Vessey, R. 2013. Challenges in cross-linguistic corpus-assisted discourse studies. *Corpora*, 8(1), 1–26.

Vertovec, S. 2007. Super-diversity and its implications. *Ethnic and Racial Studies*, 30(6), 1024–1054.

Wason, P. C. 1960. On the failure to eliminate hypotheses in a conceptual task. *Quarterly Journal of Experimental Psychology*, 12(3), 129–140.

PART A

Overlooked areas (checking the dusty corners)

2

SIMILARITY[1]

Charlotte Taylor

2.1 Introduction

The aim of this chapter is to raise the methodological importance of searching for similarity and stasis, as well as difference and change, in corpus and discourse analysis. I outline some of the possible methods for searching for similarity in corpus studies of discourse, and, more specifically, I look at methods which are accessible to language researchers who may not have a strong background in programming and/or statistics.

In the first section, a 'toolkit' is presented of the resources available to researchers looking for similarity. In the second section, a case study is reported which employs some of the tools discussed in the previous section to investigate the similarity and stasis in the representation of *refugees* in British parliamentary and media discourse over the last 200 years.

In many ways, of course, corpus linguistics is founded on similarity, because it involves the search for 'usuality' and repeated patterns of behaviour. However, we are generally most used to focussing explicitly on similarity and comparability as key concepts at the stage where we are selecting or creating comparable corpora or reference/comparator corpora. For instance, Kilgarriff (2001) shows the importance of identifying similarity between and within corpora in order to assess the extent to which grammars or other tools may usefully be extended from one to another. Likewise, Gries and Hilpert (2008) address similarity between corpus segments as a way of creating meaningful divisions in diachronic corpora (see also Chapter 9 of this volume).

In this chapter, I argue that the analysis for similarity can also be profitably expanded beyond the corpus selection/creation stage into the discourse analysis. Thus, this will be the kind of similarity which interests us here. Furthermore, I argue that this aspect is somewhat neglected within corpus and discourse studies (and indeed more generally but that is beyond the scope of this chapter). To take a brief snapshot of some recent work in corpus and discourse studies, I identified all articles published in *Corpora* and *International Journal of Corpus Linguistics* since 2015 which referred to discourse or stylistics in the title, keywords or abstract (28 out of a total of 55 published papers) and concordanced them for references to *same/similar** and *differen**. There were 784 occurrences of *differen** across the 28 texts, compared to 499 for *same/similar** across all 28 texts. This is a rather rough measure as it does not tell us the context of use, but it certainly points towards a concentration of attention on what is different. For a more accurate estimate, we could look at the research aims and what are presented as the key findings. In this case, the pattern was stronger with none exclusively focussing on similarity and eight only addressing difference. Although not represented in the journals examined here, one exception to this general pattern of backgrounding of similarity at the level of analysis is the area of authorship studies which systematically addresses similarity across texts for the purposes of attribution of texts to a particular author (mainly within forensic linguistics) and description of the style of a particular author (mainly within stylistics).

2.2 Why is similarity important for corpus and discourse work?

There are research questions we might want to pose which are entirely driven by an interest in similarity. For instance, in response to claims about the shifting of the centre ground to the right in British politics, we might want to investigate whether political manifestos show an increasing amount of similarity over time, converging towards the right-wing discourses. In addition, there are a set of reasons why looking at similarity can help us in more open questions posed as part of a project. For instance, if we were asking 'how is immigration represented in the British press?', rather than only looking at how it differs according to political orientation or newspaper type (broadsheet or tabloid) we might want to try and get a sense of any shared discourse patterns that characterise the UK press. Even with a difference-oriented starting point, such as 'how do student apology emails to female and male lecturers differ?', as I will argue below, there is some benefit from deliberately addressing the opposite question 'and how are they the same?'.

I would like to suggest that there are several principal, interrelated reasons why we might also want to focus on similarity in corpus approaches to discourse studies. The first is simply that, by focussing on difference, we effectively create a 'blind spot'; this means that, rather than aiming for a 360-degree perspective of our data, we are actually starting out with the goal of achieving only a 180-degree visualisation. Therefore, the search for similarity can add a new range of starting points into our data and allow us to begin with a more ambitious aim regarding the 'completeness' of the analysis. In contrast, the potential neglect of patterns of similarities in the data leads to another significant threat to the balance of the analysis, which is that by setting out to look at difference, the analyst is likely to find and report on difference. No matter how arbitrary the construction of two corpora, if you carefully searched for differences between them, it is highly likely that you would be able to find some. Any such difference-oriented findings are potentially highly misleading as it may be that in quantitative terms the similarities between two corpora or topics considerably outweigh the differences. As Baker (2010: 83) notes:

> [N]ot publishing or sharing such findings can result in what has been called 'bottom drawer syndrome'. For example, imagine that ten sets of researchers, working independently from each other, all build a corpus of Singapore English and compare it to a similar British corpus, looking at the same linguistic feature. In nine cases the researchers find that there are no significant differences, decide that the study is therefore uninteresting and assign the research to the bottom drawer of their filing cabinet rather than publishing it. However, the tenth researcher does find a difference and publishes the research, resulting in an inaccurate picture of what the general trend is when such a comparison is undertaken.

This, then, leads on to the second major motivation for highlighting the role of similarity, which is that the deliberate and systematic 'looking in both directions' may offer some kind of counterbalance to the issues of cognitive bias or corroboration drive. As Scott and Tribble (2006: 6) have argued, we are pattern perceivers; indeed, 'it seems to be a characteristic of the homo sapiens [sic] mind that it is often unable to see things "as they are" but imposes on them a tendency, a trend, a pattern.' As they say, this insight and imagination has positive implications when manifested in our ability to identify patterns and is essential for discourse work, but there is also the risk of perceiving tendencies where there are none, or where they are the result of ignoring much of the data, as mentioned under the first point. The reporting of both difference and similarity could allow us, therefore, to check on unintentional bias and provide some evidence to counter any suspicions of intentional bias. Furthermore, there is the issue of the 'corroboration drive' (Marchi & Taylor 2009), that is to say, the systematic search for elements that validate previous findings which is a variant of the more general confirmation bias. As researchers, we naturally tend towards building on our work; we look for corroboration that what we have found is valid and less frequently do we think to look for falsification or contrasting findings. Thus, a 'push' towards also looking for what we are not expecting – similarity– may serve as a valuable check on that (natural) researcher instinct to focus on change and corroboration.

This is not an argument that difference and similarity will always be of equal importance, or that paying equal amounts of attention to each will automatically confer balance. But, at least, checking for both will offer a more rounded view of the data. So, the search for similarity may help us to achieve a more complete picture of our data and, cumulatively, of our field of study; it helps counterbalance the issues of cognitive bias, and the reporting of similarity data provides robustness to the analysis. This search for similarity cannot, of course, remove the researcher from the research process, nor can it guarantee objectivity any more than any other form of triangulation; our corpus and discourse research will, therefore, naturally continue to be 'researcher-driven' (Taylor 2010). As Stubbs reminds us, with reference to corpus stylistics, a purely automatic analysis is not possible because 'the linguist selects which features to study, the corpus linguist is restricted to features which the software can find, and these features still require a literary interpretation' (Stubbs 2005: 6). However, along with the key components of *transparency* and *replicability*, the search for similarity can help us to achieve a more methodologically sound analysis, not least because it pushes the software to find new features.

2.3 Similarity and the tools of corpus and discourse research

The combination of corpus linguistics and (critical) discourse analysis provides the researcher with two potential macro starting points. In the first, the analyst may start from the corpus, making use of corpus software to access the data and identify for further exploration any areas of interest, as may occur in an analysis which is driven by a keyword comparison. In the second, the analyst may start with a discourse-analytical frame and then use the corpus to collect data which is interpreted and categorised through that frame. In reality, of course, we are most likely to move or cycle between these different positions and perspectives at various points in our research. However, for the purposes of this paper, I am primarily focussing on corpus analysis as the main entry point into the data.

The classic corpus linguistic entry points would include the analysis of concordances, collocates and keywords/key clusters and key semantic domains. In particular, I would argue that it is the popularity of the concept of keyness, and the provision of user-friendly software that can calculate keyness (e.g. AntConc, CQPWeb, Sketch Engine, WordSmith Tools), which has facilitated the analysis of difference. There are also tools which facilitate the comparison of collocates, such as Sketch Engines' Sketch Difference (discussed below) and the 'compare' function in the BYU interface (http://corpus.byu.edu). Both of these also allow for comparison across different corpora; for instance, it is noted on the BYU BNC page that, 'you can compare between registers – for example, verbs that are more common in legal or medical texts' (Davies 2004), and this illustrates the (natural) emphasis on using the tools to search for difference.

Since these tools are accessible and very user-friendly, they constitute a prime example of how the tools which are available shape and form the type of research which may be carried out.[2] This is particularly the case for new researchers to an area, where they tend to start by learning the tools and then investigating questions which the tools facilitate. As McEnery and Hardie (2012: 42) note, 'if the toolset does not expand, then neither will the range of research questions that may be reasonably addressed using a corpus.' Thus it is hoped that the overt discussion of similarity in this chapter, like the topics in other chapters in this volume, may increase awareness both of the presence of these aspects and ways of looking into them from a corpus and discourse perspective. And, who knows, even to developments in the software to aid future investigations.

2.3.1 The habit of looking both ways

Although the focus here will be on the tools that can aid accounting for similarity in corpus and discourse work, it should be noted that a fundamental aspect of looking for similarity is by implementing the procedure of 'looking both ways' as a standard practice and methodological principle. For instance Seale et al. (2007: 422) carry out a keyword comparison of broadsheet and tabloid corpora containing articles referring to sleep, and note that:

> A disadvantage lies in the fact that the method identifies differences between texts rather than similarities or overlaps which could be relevant. It was therefore important also to read and become familiar with the content of the articles and to use this knowledge to influence our interpretations.

Indeed, even if we think of *keyness* which is most often used to investigate difference, comparing two or more corpora against a reference corpus (rather than each other) would allow the researcher to identify similarities too.

In the following sub-sections, I start by considering what similarity-oriented analytical tools are embedded within existing software and then focus mainly on notions or procedures that have been developed within corpus linguistics for this purpose.

2.3.2 Collocate comparison

One of the tools mentioned in the previous section, Sketch Difference, allows us to analyse similarity as well as difference in collocational patterns because it includes shared collocates. For instance, Bednarek and Caple (2017) employ it to identify overlap in the use of *cyclist* and *cyclists* in the press and find that negativity is a shared news value associated with both forms. Sketch Difference can be used either to compare two words in the same corpus (as in the cyclist example), or the same word in two different (sub)corpora. This latter form of comparison is illustrated in Figure 2.1, which displays part of the output for a comparison of *immigrant* in the 2005 and 2010 sub-corpora of the SiBol British press corpus.[3]

The words which are coloured in grey (in colour originally) at the top of the image are those which are stronger collocates for the 2010 corpus, and those at the bottom in grey were strongest for the 2005 corpus. Those which are unshaded in the middle, are the shared collocates, thus they are the target for any study of similarity.

However, although there is this option of examining similarity at the same time, most research using Sketch Difference has so far focussed on the differences between items. As Pearce (2008: 21) notes in his study of the collocational behaviour of MAN

immigrant Sketch diff for subcorpora **2005/2010**

2005	6.0	4.0	2.0	0	-2.0	-4.0	-6.0	2010

verbs with "%w" as object	720	568	0.20	0.24
assimilate	6	0	7.3	--
repatriate	5	0	6.6	--
integrate	4	0	4.8	--
detain	6	0	4.7	--
deter	5	0	4.6	--
encourage	9	0	2.6	--
treat	6	0	2.5	--
hire	4	0	2.4	--
return	5	0	2.2	--
require	13	5	2.4	1.0
allow	20	8	2.3	0.9
deport	12	5	7.1	5.9
attract	10	5	2.9	1.9
arrive	13	7	5.0	4.1
employ	16	10	4.3	3.7
catch	6	5	2.1	1.9
welcome	6	5	3.0	2.7
blame	5	5	2.5	2.5
expel	4	6	5.2	5.8
describe	0	7	--	1.9
target	0	7	--	3.4
recruit	0	4	--	3.4
estimate	0	13	--	4.7
smuggle	0	4	--	5.1
scapegoat	0	4	--	7.7

FIGURE 2.1 Comparison of *immigrant*.

and WOMAN, there is a risk that 'inevitably, with a tool (Sketch Difference) that is designed, as its name suggests, to reveal contrasts, the analyst is in danger of exaggerating the differences and overlooking similarities'.

Another Sketch Engine tool which can facilitate the analysis of similarity in terms of collocational patterns is the Thesaurus. The Sketch Engine Thesaurus is a distributional thesaurus which works by identifying the collocates of a word, and then, in the second stage, identifies which other words share similar collocates term (see Rychlý & Kilgarriff 2007 for more detail on the algorithm used). So, for instance, if you were to look up *hot* in a general corpus, one of the highest ranking items the thesaurus is likely to produce is its antonym *cold*, because they occur

FIGURE 2.2 Sketch Thesaurus for *immigrant*.

in similar kinds of contexts (e.g. premodifying *water*, *weather* and so on). Figure 2.2 shows the findings for the Sketch Thesaurus for *immigrant* in EnTenTen13 (a 22-billion word web-based corpus collected in 2013). The size of the word in the visualisation corresponds to its ranking: the more similar the collocational patterns, the larger it is shown. Here we might note that the apparent relational antonym of *emigrant* is not prominent while a semantic set relating to crime (*criminal*, *prisoner*, *offender*, *terrorist*) suggests similar lexical company is used.

2.3.3 Consistent collocates

Consistent collocates (or c-collocates) may be defined as 'words that stably collocate with the node in multiple datasets and are to be viewed as indicating core elements of meaning, semantic associations and semantic prosodies' (Germond, McEnery & Marchi 2016). The identification of consistent collocates seems to draw on Scott's (e.g. 1997) notion of consistency and the use of key-keywords (both discussed below), and was developed during work on the ESRC-funded project 'Discourses of refugees and asylum seekers in the UK press, 1996–2006' at Lancaster University, which was led by Paul Baker. The research team introduced this concept of c-collocates to describe the lexical items which collocated with *refugees / asylum seekers / immigrants / migrants* (RASIM) in at least seven out of the 10 annual sub-corpora which they had collected (described in Gabrielatos & Baker 2008). The consistent collocates were calculated in order to exclude *seasonal collocates* – that is, words which may have been triggered by particular events, rather than being representative of newspaper discourse across the extended time period. Once again, to date, there seems to have been relatively little uptake of this notion, although it has been more popular in diachronic studies (e.g. McEnery & Baker 2017).

2.3.4 Consistency analysis

WordSmith Tools allows for the creation of consistency lists when producing word lists, which will identify words which are shared across a number of texts. These consistency lists are useful when working with several corpora, or corpora containing multiple files. According to Scott and Tribble (2006: 39), the main uses are:

> First, in a general corpus like the BNC, to distinguish between wordtypes in terms of how consistently they get used in a mass of texts in the language. Second, if the scope of the research is the genre, to be able to locate lexical items which characterise certain genres or sub-genres. Third, to be able to study text variants (e.g., alternative translations or editions).

Like keyword analysis, it requires the researcher to be working on a set of (sub)corpora. Scott (2001) employs the function in illustrating how a teacher of English for Specific Purposes (ESP) might identify core lexis by looking for items which occur across a number of relevant sub-corpora. A brief review of recent work suggests that this function is significantly underused compared to more popular tools such as keywords and collocates.

2.3.5 Key keywords

Key keywords are introduced in Scott (1997) and defined in the WordSmith Tools guide as follows: 'A "key key-word" is one which is "key" in more than one of a number of related texts. The more texts it is "key" in, the more "key key" it is' (Scott 2016). Thus, while keywords identify what is different about one corpus compared with another, the analysis of key keywords allows the analyst to go on to identify how those differences and characterising features may be shared by other corpora – that is, to focus on similarity. Rather like the procedure for consistency analysis, key keywords are particularly useful when looking for repeated patterns across large numbers of sub-corpora. In Scott's (1997: 238) model, the calculation of key keywords subsequently allows for the identification of associates, that is 'words found to be key in the same texts as a given key key word,' which form an alternative means of calculating collocation in the wider sense.

Although used more frequently than some other tools discussed here, as Bachmann (2011) notes there is still a scarcity of studies employing this procedure (Bachmann 2011: 83). Bachmann draws on McEnery's (2009: 169) use of keywords to identify transient and permanent key keywords in moral panic discourse and applies them to his analysis of parliamentary debates in order to identify 'a list of concepts that are representative of the debates as a whole' (Bachmann 2011: 87). In other words, it becomes a method for identifying concepts which are similar across the sub-corpora and is a means of avoiding isolated spikes of data. A similar notion is used by Fitzsimmons-Doolan (2009) in a study which functions as a model for this chapter as it both sets out to look for similarity and falsifies its own hypothesis – the hypothesis being that there would be similarities in the lexical patterns of newspaper discourse about language policies, and newspaper discourse about immigration. Fitzsimmons-Doolan uses WordSmith Tools for the calculation of keywords but adopts a manual analysis of what she calls the keyest keywords by counting: how many of the top 10 keywords from each corpus were (a) in the top 20 and (b) in the top 500 keywords lists for each of the other corpora. These measures show the distribution of the "keyest" keywords from one corpus within each of the other corpora. (Fitzsimmons-Doolan 2009: 392) After the key keyword analysis, she found little similarity in terms of what characterised the sub-corpora of articles on language policies and articles on immigration.

2.3.6 Lockwords

Baker (2011) further addresses the issue of search for similarity by introducing the concept of *lockwords* which was designed to complement the existing notion of keywords by focussing on similarity in frequencies of lexical items across corpora. This notion, and the procedure used for determining them, was conceived as a result of his observations of stasis in the BLOB, LOB, FLOB and BE06 corpora. He notes that certain words 'were so consistent in their frequencies that they appeared to be the opposite of Scott's (2000) concept of keywords – words which are highly frequent in one corpus when compared against another' (Baker 2011:73). Secondly, the notion of lockwords was conceived by Baker as a means of taking a more corpus-driven approach to diachronic language study, so that, rather than starting with a specific item or set of items to investigate, the researcher may start with lists of items that have or have not changed over the time period under study. One of the qualities of lockwords is that they may be used in conjunction with keywords as part of that principle of 'looking both ways', thus increasing the researcher's general awareness of patterns of both similarity and difference in two or more sets of corpora.

As the counterpart to keywords, lockwords may be relevant in most places that keywords are used, and yet they have seen surprisingly little uptake since 2011, both in terms of application and integration into existing software packages. At the time of writing, the lockword calculation is only available with CQPWeb (Hardie 2012) which calculates them using the log ratio method which is also applied to keywords and collocation.[4] Researchers using other software packages can calculate them manually, as detailed in Baker's (2011) original paper. In order to identify change in the corpora, Baker used the *WordSmith Tools* detailed consistency list (discussed above) to create lists of items for analysis and then calculated the coefficient of variance which is the ratio of the sample standard deviation to the sample mean. Baker (2011: 72) notes that this 'is easily calculated by dividing the standard deviation by the mean and then multiplying by 100'. This measure does not specify whether the change is an increase or decline, so in the final stage, the results need to be sorted manually.

2.3.7 Identifying the typical: ProtAnt

We might also consider *prototypicality* to be a measure of similarity. That is to say, the most prototypical text in a corpus is in some way the one that is most like the others. The identification of the most typical texts in a corpus is an important one for (critical) discourse studies. As researchers who combine both corpus linguistics and discourse analysis, we often need ways of identifying key texts for in-depth analysis. Although we often 'shunt' between the text and corpus level, entry point at text level can be, in itself, a form of methodological triangulation. The problem, as Anthony and Baker (2015) discuss in their presentation of a new software tool, ProtAnt (Anthony & Baker 2017) is how to identify texts for a (critical) discourse analysis starting point in a balanced and replicable way. They operationalise the concept of protypicality through ProtAnt which 'analyses the texts, generates a ranked list of keywords based on statistical significance and effect size, and then orders the texts by the number of keywords in them' (Anthony & Baker 2015: 274). Thus, the texts which are highest ranked are those with the highest number of keywords in them (compared to a reference corpus).

The concept of prototypicality may also be used, like keyness itself, to get a sense of 'aboutness' (Scott & Tribble 2006) regarding the texts in a corpus. For instance, Bednarek and Caple's (2017) investigation of news values around cycling uses ProtAnt to identify the 'typical' values in each sub-corpus of newspapers from different countries. By focussing on the newspaper articles which were identified as most prototypical, they were able to look at which news values characterised the reporting across their sub-corpora. And, once again, they found that negativity was the key news value associated with cycling in the press. Thus we can see how tools not necessarily designed for investigating similarity may be 'repurposed' to fit this aim.

From this brief overview, we can see that, although they are not as prominent as the tools for searching for difference, we have access to a range of techniques for turning our focus towards similarity. In the following case study, I will explore what results and picture may emerge when we focus on the search for similarity.

2.4 Case study: representation of refugees in political and media discourse

In this case study I set out to see what happens when we (re)focus our attention entirely towards similarity. Thus, this study is not intended to be representative of an entire research process, but rather a stage within a corpus and discourse analysis. The example on which I will concentrate is how the term *refugees* is used in the *Times* newspaper and British parliamentary debates over the last two hundred years.[5] In many diachronic corpus and discourse studies, the tendency is naturally to look at what changed over the time period and thus the risk is that we lose sight of what has remained constant over time. The example discussed here forms part of a wider project which sets out to address this imbalance and identify continuity in discourses of migration (understood as including both immigration and emigration) over the same time period. These two sources were chosen as they provide two potential avenues for similarity: 1) Are there consistent patterns of representation in each corpus over time? 2) How similar are the representations in the law-making and reporting corpora, and does this relationship change over time?

2.4.1 The data

The two corpora used for this case study are:

Times Online. This corpus was created at University of Lancaster, using the OCR (optical character recognition) files made available by the British Library. The corpus covers the period 1785–2011. The current size is c. 10.5 billion words and it was analysed through CQPWeb. The scanned articles are also available to view as images through the *Times Digital Archive* to which many UK libraries subscribe.

Hansard Corpus. This resource was created by the SAMUELS consortium and hosted on the Brigham Young University corpus interface.[6] The corpus contains approximately 7.6 million parliamentary speeches from the period 1803–2005 and covers both the House of Commons and the House of Lords (overall size c.1.6 billion words). Access is available through the BYU corpus interface.

These two corpora represent an incredible resource for diachronic corpus-assisted discourse studies. However, there are also some challenges involved in using such huge resources hosted on (different) external websites. Namely, as they are discourse-complete corpora, and search-term specific, sub-corpora made up of meaningful text units cannot be extracted in equivalent ways, which means that keywords and lockwords cannot be employed here. Thus, the main measure of similarity used in this study will be c-collocates. Furthermore, as the start and end dates do not match up precisely, for the purposes of comparison, only whole decades are included, thus the analysis covers 1810–2000.

2.4.2 Refugees

Of the many terms available for describing people who move across national boundaries (see, for instance, Gabrielatos & Baker 2008) *refugee* is perhaps one of the more sympathetic terms available, at least in the UK context. Indeed, if we consider recent debate about naming choices, much of it has centred around the apparent avoidance of the term *refugee* where it would be applicable, at least partly triggered by change in *Al Jazeera* editorial policy, which made news in the article 'Why Al Jazeera will not say Mediterranean "migrants"' (Malone 2015). The fact that it is a more sympathetic term should also alert us to the fact that when we look at representation of *refugees*, we are not necessarily looking at the representation of the group of people who have the status of refugee according to the UN 1951 Refugee Convention. Indeed, in earlier work (Taylor 2014), I found that the contemporary British press tended to use *refugee* to refer to people who were forced to move elsewhere in the world. Those forced to move to the UK were either not discussed frequently or were described using another naming choice with a different set of connotations (e.g. *immigrant*).

Another feature that makes *refugees* an interesting lexical item for analysis in a study of similarity, is that it is a term that shows a high degree of similarity in frequency trends across the two corpora used here (discussed in the following section). Figure 2.3 shows a sample of possible naming choices that occur across the whole time period

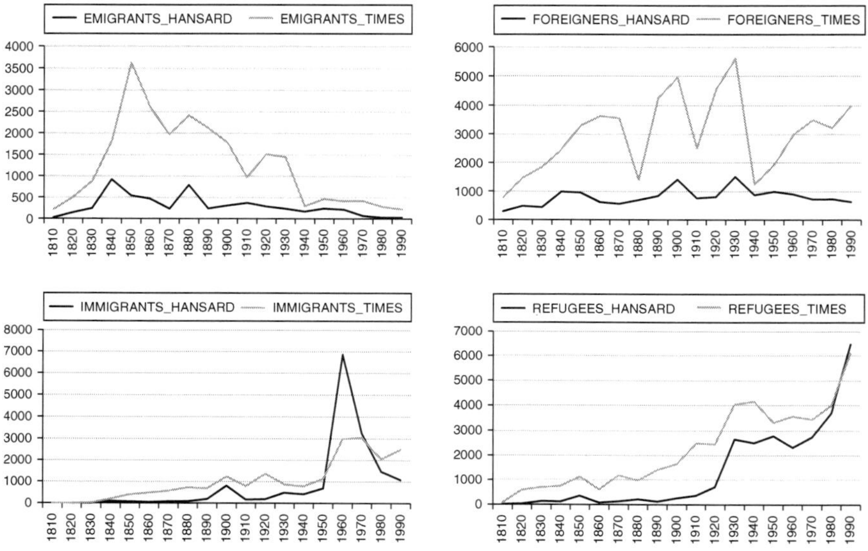

FIGURE 2.3 Naming choices.

(thus excluding more recent names like *asylum seekers* or now archaic names like *aliens*). The naming choices tracked are: *immigrants*, *emigrants*, *foreigners* and *refugees*.

As can be seen, *emigrants* occurs much more frequently in the *Times* than in parliamentary discourse in the earlier stages, but both sources show a steep decline in more recent times (which does not reflect a simple absence of movement out of the UK). *Foreigners* shows a similar mismatch at the level of interest, which we could just attribute to size differences in the corpora, but this is not borne out by the closer frequencies in Hansard and *Times* for *immigrants* and *refugees* (both in the bottom half of the figure). For both *foreigners* and *immigrants*, we see a divergence between the sources in the trend towards more recent times, with the frequency of occurrence in the *Times* newspaper increasing while the frequency in parliamentary discourse decreases. In contrast, *refugees* shows a closer pattern between the two sources although once again it is more frequent in the *Times* than Hansard up to the most recent sub-corpus when we actually see a small inversion. We may hypothesise that the incipient decrease in the *Times* reflects changing attitudes towards forced migration, but this requires a closer examination of the data.

2.4.3 Identifying c-collocates

In order to identify the c-collocates, in the first stage collocates were calculated for *refugees* in each decade in each of the two sub-corpora. Regarding the measure of collocation, it was essential to keep this the same for the two corpora and so the measure used had to be mutual information because this is what is available within the BYU interface. The span was set at 5L/R, the minimum frequency for collocates was set at five for both corpora and the minimum MI score was above zero. It should be noted that these are both relatively arbitrary measures, but for the purposes of comparison the key factor was that they were kept constant.

In the second stage, Excel was used to modify the lists as there is currently no dedicated tool for identifying c-collocates across corpora and the lists were too long to make manual matching time-efficient. I chose Excel for this case study as it is relatively widely available and so I hope detailing the process may help others. Consistent collocates may be identified across two long lists by using the conditional formatting function to highlight duplicate texts between columns (assuming that columns correspond to collocates found in different sub-corpora). When looking at corpora where the size of the sub-corpora changes substantially over time, the shared collocates should be reported as a proportion of the collocates in the paired lists because we can expect that larger sub-corpora will yield greater numbers of shared collocates simply because there are more available, thus the comparison across time loses meaning if they are reported as raw figures. In order to track c-collocates across multiple lists, the COUNTIF function may be used to identify in how many columns (which in this case study corresponds to collocates for decades) each term occurs.

There are two interrelated questions that we might pose regarding the consistency reference to *refugees* across time and discourse type:

1. To what extent are discourses consistent within one discourse type over a historical period? If present, what are these shared discourses?
2. To what extent are discourses shared between press and parliament? If present, what are these shared discourses?

These will be tackled briefly in the following two sections.

2.4.4 Investigating c-collocates

The first question we might ask is to what extent are collocates shared over time? The percentage of collocates of *refugees* which were shared between pairs of decades were calculated and are shown in Figure 2.4. What the sharing of collocates can tell us is whether the discourse/s surrounding *refugees* remain relatively stable and/or develop gradually over time. If there is a sudden drop in the number of shared collocates, then we would expect that to correspond to a marked shift in the discourse (although, as always, this would only be an indicator and we would then need to delve into the corpus to analyse the texts).

The frequencies in Figure 2.4 suggest that the collocates were relatively stable over time. For both the *Times* and Hansard we see an increase in the proportion of shared collocates (note the trendlines – labelled as 'Linear' in the legend – go up), though this was more marked for Hansard. Shifting to difference, we might note that the *Times* consistently shows a larger number of shared collocates between years. This may be attributed to the fact that Hansard is more subject to variation as different political parties gain larger number of seats and therefore have more representation in the discourse overall.

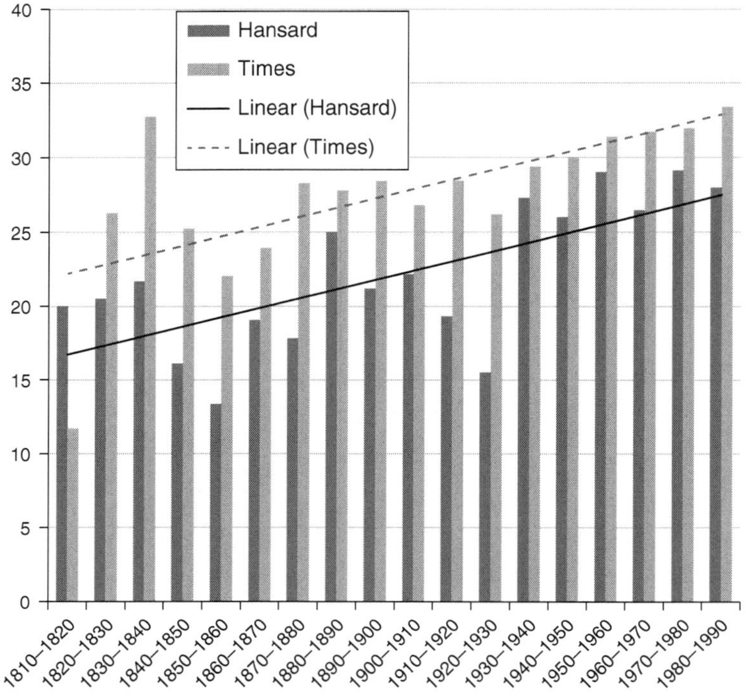

FIGURE 2.4 Percentage of collocates of *refugees*.

To turn towards the second question posed above, the shared collocates between the *Times* and Hansard for each decade were then identified and are reported in Figure 2.5 (the same vertical axis is maintained to ease comparison).

In Figure 2.5 we see a more marked shift over time. The trendline here is somewhat misleading because there is not a gradual increase, but it appears that the proportion of shared collocates increases substantially from 1930. It is likely that a year-by-year plot would help uncover more precise shifts in the conformity of discourses (see also Chapter 9, this volume on the importance of time periods). In the period from 1930 to 1999, the proportion of shared collocates then remains stable, suggesting that there is a consistent shared discourse between press and parliament.

However, it should still be noted that, overall, the greatest cohesion lies between the paired *Times* decades, followed by the Hansard decades, followed by each Hansard and *Times* pair for the same decade. Thus, overall, we can report that there is greater similarity within discourse types than across them. However, there is a flattening of difference between discourse types in the more recent time period and this would be an interesting focus for further investigation.

2.4.5 Patterns in the shared discourses

In the next stage, we move from the patterns of sharing, to illustrating how the shared items may be used as the basis for further similarity work. McEnery and

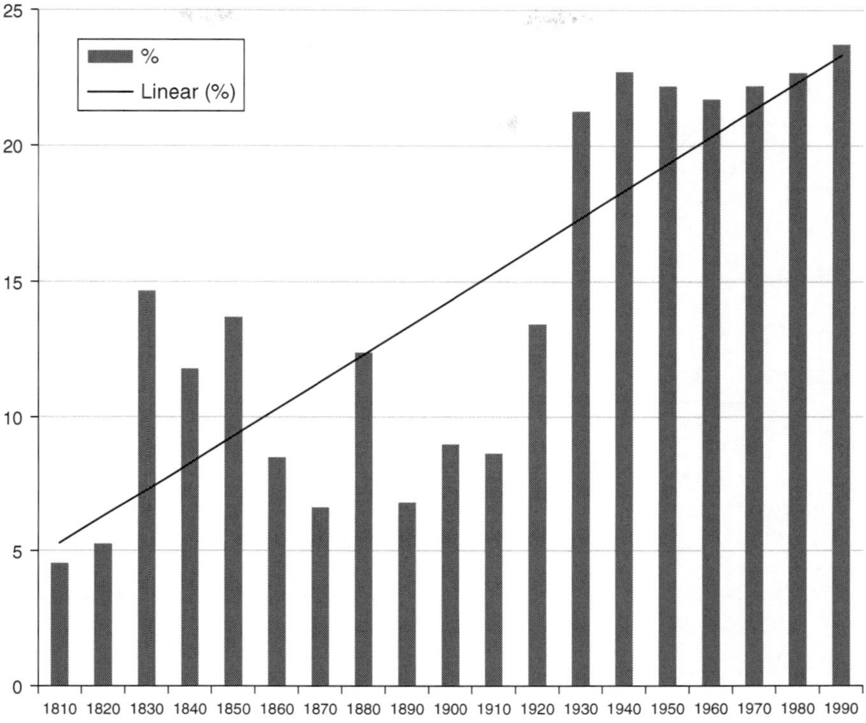

FIGURE 2.5 Shared collocates between the *Times* and Hansard.

Baker's (2017) study of prostitution in the seventeenth century pre-empted many of the issues involved in working with historical data found in this study. Like Gabrielatos and Baker (2008) they operationalised consistent collocates as those which occurred in seven of the 10 decades under analysis. However, for the purposes of this study, the lower numbers of collocates for *refugees* in the early nineteenth century data and the missing decades in the *Times* data meant that this had to be modified further. Thus the items which were identified for further analysis in this case study were those which occurred in at least 50 per cent of the decades. It should be clear that this proportion may be too low to talk about consistency and so the actual distribution is discussed further below.

Table 2.1 shows the collocates of *refugees* which occurred in at least half the decades analysed for Hansard. They have been grouped according to semantic themes which is a researcher-driven interpretation of what they are doing in the discourse (based on checking concordance lines, not abstracted dictionary-style meanings). For reasons of space, grammatical collocates (prepositions, determiners, auxiliaries, conjunctions, modals) have not been included here.

Table 2.1 shows that the semantic preference for quantification, as documented in contemporary migration discourse (e.g. Baker 2006) is strong over at least five decades of parliamentary discourse. We also see a pattern of deictic references to

TABLE 2.1 Shared collocates of *refugees* from Hansard

quantification	*number, numbers, large, many, thousands, total*
movement	*back, came, come, coming, return, left, towards*
nationality	*British, Polish, French, countries, country*
aid	*assistance, asylum, given, relief*
discussion	*problem, question*
people	*persons, refugees*
places	*camps, settlement*
description	*unfortunate, voluntary*
misc.	*behalf, dealing, parts, regard*

TABLE 2.2 Shared collocates of *refugees* from the *Times*

movement	*arrival, arrive, arrived, arriving, back, came, come, coming, expelled, fled, influx, land, landed, leave, left, reached, repatriation, return, returned, returning, sent, settled, towards*
nationality	*British, countries, country, Eastern, England, foreign, France, French, frontier, German, Greek, Italian, Paris, Polish, Russian, Spanish, States, Turkey, Turkish, territory*
quantification	*200, 300, 1000, 2000, great, hundred, hundreds, large, majority, many, more, most, nearly, number, numbers, Several, thousand, thousands, total, two*
people	*authorities, children, Committee, families, Government, men, persons, prisoners, soldiers, troops, women*
aid	*aid, assistance, asylum, benefit, help, home, homes, protection, Relief, shelter*
description	*crowded, destitute, poor, starving, wounded*
exchange of goods/ services	*brought, give, given, receive, received, take, taken*
religion	*Jewish, Christian*
discussion	*question*
places	*villages, town*
misc.	*allow, allowed, become, behalf, board, cause, certain, condition, continue, driven, expected, found, fund, last, living, made, place, political, present, regard, remain, reported, reports, sought, state, treatment, war*

movement, and mentions of geographical locations at a national level. Alongside this, we have a concentration of items relating to assistance that may be offered to the people involved. In terms of problematizing and/or topicalizing *refugees*, we also see *problem* and *question* occurring repeatedly.

Table 2.2 shows the same data for the *Times*. As can be seen, there are a larger number of collocates here, partly because there was more similarity across the decades within the *Times* corpus (as shown above). The collocates were classified and the larger number led to a wider range of categories.

As in Table 2.1, in this table we see the dominance of semantic fields relating to quantification, movement and nationality. We also see expansion of the people category to institutions who may be reacting to *refugees*. The items from the description category indicate the suffering of those described as *refugees*, pointing towards a continuous sympathetic stance taken with this term. We might note that here the meta-reference to the problematisation is not expanded as a category, and only *question* occurs. Similarly, the 'places' category remains relatively underpopulated and does not indicate temporary locations (such as *camp* for instance).

Each of these groupings may constitute an avenue for further investigation in building up a picture of how *refugees* are positioned in discourse over time and across discourse types, as a way to understand the reflexivity between press and parliament.

2.5 Conclusions

In this chapter, I have tried to show both why we should consider similarity if we want to try and account fully for the discourses that we are analysing, and how we might approach it both with the tools available and various 'work arounds'. In the case study examining collocates of the lexical item *refugees* over time, we have seen that looking at what is shared has confirmed the long-standing sympathetic stance of this lexical item. This continuous evaluation may account for the decline in use in the *Times*, given that the UK press has been increasing in its anti-immigration sentiment.

Through raising the topic of similarity and illustrating some of the methods we have available, I hope to place it into the standard set of practices with which we engage when doing discourse analysis using corpora. In future, it may be that software packages will integrate features such as c-collocates and lockwords as standard tools which will help cement the relevance of similarity in research.

Although the case study here has focused on similarity, the argument I wish to put forward is not just that we should have more research looking at what is shared but that the simple practice of 'looking both ways' will help us reflect on where our research direction is taking us, and to achieve a more 360 degree view of the discourse/s we are investigating.

Indeed, a singular focus on similarity may be counterproductive. As Bednarek and Caple (2017: 165) reflexively conclude after employing ProtAnt to investigate the discourses around cycling 'a focus on prototypicality and range may background variety to some extent', for instance, submerging differences between the newspapers in their corpora. As they go on, 'in the same way in which a focus on differences (which is generally more common in corpus linguistics) may create a "blind spot" (Taylor 2013: 83) a focus on similarities may do so, too' (Bednarek & Caple 2017: 165–166).

Acknowledgements

I am very grateful to the University of Lancaster-based ESRC Centre for Corpus Approaches to Social Science (CASS) for allowing me access to the magnificent *Times* corpora while I was a visiting researcher there in 2016–2017.

Notes

1 Parts of the overview presented in Sections 2.1–2.3 were first published in Taylor (2013).

2 For more on the relationship between tools and objects of observation see Partington (2009).
3 More information is available here: http://www.lilec.it/clb/?page_id=8.
4 See http://cass.lancs.ac.uk/?tag=cqpweb.
5 The plural term was preferred because I was interested in collectivised representations.
6 For more on the SAMUELS consortium see http://www.gla.ac.uk/schools/critical/research/fundedresearchprojects/samuels/.For access to the corpus via the BYU interface see http://www.hansard-corpus.org/. Basic level access is free at the time of writing.

References

Anthony, L. & Baker, P. 2015. ProtAnt: A tool for analysing the prototypicality of texts. *International Journal of Corpus Linguistics*, 20(3), 273–292.

Anthony, L. & Baker, P. 2017. ProtAnt (Version 1.2.1) [Computer Software]. Tokyo, Japan: Waseda University. Available online at: http://www.laurenceanthony.net/

Bachmann, I. 2011. Civil partnership – 'Gay marriage in all but name': A corpus-driven analysis of discourses of same-sex relationships in the UK Parliament. *Corpora*, 6(1), 77–105.

Baker, P. 2006. *Using Corpora in Discourse Analysis*. London: Continuum.

Baker, P. 2010. *Sociolinguistics and Corpus Linguistics*. Edinburgh: Edinburgh University Press.

Baker, P. 2011. Times may change but we'll always have money: A corpus driven examination of vocabulary change in four diachronic corpora. *Journal of English Linguistics*, 39, 65–88.

Bednarek, M. & Caple, H. 2017. *The Discourse of News Values: How News Organizations Create Newsworthiness*. Oxford: Oxford University Press.

Davies, M. 2004. *BYU-BNC: The British National Corpus*. Available online at: http://corpus.byu.edu/bnc/

Fitzsimmons-Doolan, S. 2009. Is public discourse about language policy really public discourse about immigration? A corpus-based study. *Language Policy*, 8, 377–402.

Gabrielatos, C. & Baker, P. 2008. Fleeing, sneaking, flooding: A corpus analysis of discursive constructions of refugees and asylum seekers in the UK Press 1996–2005. *Journal of English Linguistics*, 36 (1), 5–38.

Germond, B., McEnery, T. & Marchi, A. 2016. The EU's comprehensive approach as the dominant discourse: A corpus-linguistics analysis of the EU's counter-piracy narrative. *European Foreign Affairs Review*, 21(1), 137–156.

Gries, S. Th. & Hilpert, M. 2008. The identification of stages in diachronic data: Variability-based neighbour clustering. *Corpora*, 3(1), 59–81.

Hardie, A. 2012. CQPweb – combining power, flexibility and usability in a corpus analysis tool. *International Journal of Corpus Linguistics*, 17 (3), 380–409.

Kilgarriff, A. 2001. Comparing corpora. *International Journal of Corpus Linguistics*, 6(1), 97–133.

McEnery, A. & Baker, H. 2017. *Corpus Linguistics and 17th-century Prostitution: Computational Linguistics and History*. London and New York: Bloomsbury.

McEnery, T. 2009. Keywords and moral panics: Mary Whitehouse and media censorship. In D. Archer (ed.) *What's in a Word: Investigating Word Frequency and Keyword Extraction*. Farnham: Ashgate. pp. 93–124.

McEnery, T. & A. Hardie. 2012. *Corpus Linguistics: Method, Theory and Practice*. Cambridge: Cambridge University Press.

Malone, B. 2015. 'Why Al Jazeera will not say Mediterranean 'migrants'. *Al Jazeera*, 20 August. Available online at: http://www.aljazeera.com/blogs/editors-blog/2015/08/al-jazeera-mediterranean-migrants-150820082226309.html

Marchi, A. & C. Taylor. 2009. If on a winter's night two researchers … A challenge to assumptions of soundness of interpretation. *CADAAD Journal*, 3(1): 1–20.

Partington, A. 2009. Evaluating evaluation and some concluding thoughts on CADS' in J. Morley & P. Bayley (eds.) *Corpus-assisted Discourse Studies on the Iraq Conflict: Wording the War*. London: Routledge. pp. 261–304.

Pearce, M. 2008. Investigating the collocational behaviour of MAN and WOMAN in the BNC using Sketch Engine, *Corpora*, 3 (1), 1–29.

Rychly, P. & Kilgarriff, A. 2007. An efficient algorithm for building a distributional thesaurus. *Proc ACL*. Prague Czech Republic. Available online at: http://www.kilgarriff.co.uk/Publications/2007-RychlyKilg-ACL-thesauruses.pdf

Scott, M. 1997. PC analysis of key words – and key key words. *System*, 25(2), 233–45.

Scott, M. 2000. Focusing on the text and its key words. In L. Burnard & T. McEnery (eds.) *Rethinking Language Pedagogy from a Corpus Perspective*, volume 2. Frankfurt: Peter Lang. pp. 103–22.

Scott, M. 2001. Comparing corpora and identifying key words, collocations, frequency distributions through the WordSmith Tools suite of computer programs. In M. Ghadessy, A. Henry & R.J. Roseberry (eds.) *Small Corpus Studies and ELT: Theory and Practice*. Amsterdam and Philadelphia: John Benjamins.

Scott, M. 2016. *WordSmith Tools version* 7, Stroud: Lexical Analysis Software.

Scott, M. & C. Tribble. 2006. *Textual Patterns: Key Words and Corpus Analysis in Language Education*. Amsterdam and Philadelphia: John Benjamins.

Seale, C., Boden, S., Williams, S., Lowe, P. & Steinberg, D. 2007. Media constructions of sleep and sleep disorders: A study of UK national newspapers. *Social Science and Medicine*, 65, 418–430.

Stubbs, M. 2005. Conrad in the computer: Examples of quantitative stylistic methods. *Language and Literature*, 14(1): 5–24.

Taylor, C. 2010. Science in the news: A diachronic perspective. *Corpora*, 5(2), 221–50.

Taylor, C. 2013. Searching for similarity using corpus-assisted discourse studies. *Corpora*, 8(1), 81–113.

Taylor, C. 2014. Investigating the representation of migrants in the UK and Italian press: A cross-linguistic corpus-assisted discourse analysis. *International Journal of Corpus Linguistics*, 19(3), 368–400.

3

ABSENCE

You don't know what you're missing. Or do you?

Alison Duguid and Alan Partington

3.1 Introduction: is there something missing from corpus linguistics?

Since the inception of corpus linguistics (CL) the issue of absence has preoccupied both its practitioners and its detractors. To the latter it is self-evident, a truism, that a corpus can yield no information about phenomena it does not contain, a criticism which we hope to demonstrate is based on a failure to grasp the complexity of the notion of absences and an underestimation of the flexibility of corpus techniques. However, the former, the exponents of CL, have also worried greatly about the significance of *not* finding something, say, a particular set of lexical items or a certain syntactic structure in their corpus. Is this (non) discovery telling me something about the discourse type(s) under study or about what is usually termed the 'representativity' of the corpus (i.e. how typical of the discourse type is the subset of it contained in the corpus)? And the CL literature is replete with warnings to 'not confuse corpus data with language itself' (McEnery & Hardie 2012: 26), to which we would add that observations arising from corpus data can only be generalised with the utmost care. Following Plato and Kant, we must not confuse the tangible, the *phenomenal* (corpus) with the intangible *noumenal* (language).[1]

In this chapter we will discuss, on the basis of a number of case studies, what can reasonably be inferred about discourses from corpus analysis, with regards to absences. Along with Scott (2004), we maintain that 'much can be inferred from what is absent' and, following Taylor (2012), we will argue that corpus tools provide an 'armoury' for locating and verifying absence. In particular, the comparison and contrast across different corpora can firstly *reveal* absences, both those being searched for and others accidentally stumbled upon, and then allow the analyst to *track* the appearance and disappearance of linguistic elements or discoursal notions once they have come in some way to the analyst's attention.

Since most things are absent from most places most of the time, we need to decide the parameters of *relevant* or *salient* or *meaningful* absence/s – those which are worth either looking for if somehow suspected or instead, if stumbled upon, are worthy of further investigation. One indication could be unexpectedness or non-obviousness, that is, discovering absence when a presence is expected. This however raises the question of expected by whom and why, especially since researchers have their own unique past primings (Hoey 2005) which influence expectations in the present. And then, when an absence is discovered, how does one decide whether the absence is intentional or otherwise, especially given, as already stated, that absence is the norm? Far too often, particularly in the field of critical discourse analysis, it is taken for granted that a silence or absent message or voice must have been deliberately *suppressed* with little evidence of intentionality (for a discussion of some examples, see Breeze 2011).

Finally, once an absence is judged relevant and worthy of investigation, do we attempt to *explain* it? If so, what kinds of explanations are valid and interesting and in what ways? Which are trivial and which non-trivial, that is, are themselves non-obvious and unexpected?

3.2 What is absence?

At first sight, then, looking at *absence* would seem both a paradoxical and hopelessly wide-ranging endeavour. Paradoxical because, by definition, it cannot really be said to be anywhere, wide-ranging because it is everywhere; as we say above, most things are absent from most places most of the time. And in effect, very little attention has been paid to it in corpus linguistics literature. Taylor (2012) addresses the question of both absence from a corpus and absence from the discourse, pointing out how absence is not an issue for corpus linguistics alone but for all text linguistics, including discourse analysis. In the framework of a case study on discourses around immigration, she surveys the ways in which absence – defined as discourses, information or roles which might be expected to be present but which are not – may be identified when combining corpus linguistics and discourse analysis. She focuses on ways in which expectations of presence may be generated in systematic and replicable ways, employing corpus linguistics tools such as collocation and keywords, discourse analytic tools such as transitivity and semantic frames, and external data such as population statistics and meta-discussion of what is absent.

Partington (2014) follows this up by breaking down the notion of absence into a number of different sorts, and we expand here his classification definitions to include:

i 'known' – or suspected, or 'searchable' – 'absence', you already know which linguistic feature you are searching for and simply want to know whether or not it is in the corpus;

ii 'unknown absence', an absence stumbled upon serendipitously in the course of a piece of research;

iii relative absence and absolute absence;
iv unexpected absence from a sizeable corpus, which may raise questions about the representativeness of the corpus;
v absence from a limited set of texts, including from a specific portion of a corpus;
vi absence from a position in a single text, including from a location in a phrase;
vii absence defined as 'hidden from open view', that is, hidden meaning.

These are not meant to be necessarily mutually excluding categories; for instance, one might be studying absolute and relative absences (type iii) from a specific portion of a corpus (type v), say, in the utterances of one particular type of speaker.

However, there are two more types of absence not included in Partington (2014):

viii the somewhat paradoxical absence of something because it is too obvious to mention and taken for granted

and

ix the absence of something which is hidden from the search due to the method of analysis adopted.

A good example of this second type was shown in Partington (2012) when two corpora on the representation of anti-Semitism in UK broadsheets from different time periods (1993 and 2005) were each compared against the same reference corpus, namely the BNC Sampler, written. Keywords such as *rightwing*, *Nazi*, *Hitler*, *Holocaust*, *racist-racism* appeared high in the lists for both periods. But when the two corpora containing representations of anti-Semitism were compared to each other, these keywords no longer appeared. The keywords relating to the later period included instead *attacks*, *incidents*, *levels*, *highest*, *rise-rose*; *Britain*, *UK*, *London*, *Manchester*; *Muslim**[2] and *Labour (party)*, *Livingstone* (a British politician), which was interpreted as a worrying indication that anti-Semitism was being discussed as resurgent in UK domestic contexts. However, we cannot conclude that rightwing anti-Semitism had disappeared from either the corpora or from the real world being represented in it; its disappearance was due solely to the different kind of comparison employed. Searching for similarities naturally produces different data from searching for differences (Taylor this volume), but this also implies that one sort of search will actually hide what another might reveal.

Our sense of the relevance of absences is strongly connected, as Taylor (2012) first indicated, to our *expectations* of what should be present. For instance, Duguid's (2015) analysis of English-language transnational news programmes, namely *Russia Today* (*RT*), *France 24* (*F24*), *Al Jazeera* (*AJ*) and *China Central Television* (*CCTV*), found that in a corpus of 107,619 tokens *Russia Today* had only two references to President Putin, despite being set up, according to its mission statement[3], to provide news 'from a Russian perspective' from which one might expect that mentions of the Russian president would be considered relevant.[4] What makes the absence still more relevant is finding it alongside a concurrent interest in the people and places of what is known as the Anglosphere[5] (42 per cent of Anglosphere mentions were from *RT* compared with 11 per cent from *F24*, 12 per cent from *AJ* and 35 per cent from *CCTV*). We can contrast this with the data from *CCTV* (conceived as a way of broadcasting the Chinese voice to the rest of the world) and *F24* (whose mission statement includes 'to cover international news with a French perspective')[6] both of which showed a high proportion of 'own nation' references. In the same study, it was found that *AJ*, based in Doha, makes no mention of its owner nation, Qatar, whose ruling royal family fund the network. *AJ*'s mission statement includes the aim of strengthening 'the values of tolerance, democracy and the respect of liberties and human rights'[7] and the data does include references to campaigns decrying the situation of migrants in Europe. However, in this dataset the channel makes no mention of the situation of migrant workers in Qatar or the harsh working conditions and many work-related deaths in Qatar during preparations for the 2022 World Cup. These matters have been widely reported elsewhere, as indeed has the broader controversy of Qatar itself as a venue. Such topics are apparently not considered by *AJ* to be part of their mission of supporting the values of tolerance and the respect of liberties and human rights. In a sense, it is our expectations, created by our knowledge of the world and primed by the *AJ* mission statement, which have 'created' an absence.

3.3 What is the impact of overlooking absence/s?

Various studies have dealt with the problem and the consequences of only dealing with what is present, including Baker et al. (2008: 296), who note that 'the corpus-based analysis tends to focus on what has been explicitly written, rather than what could have been written but was not or what is implied, inferred, insinuated or latently hinted at.' As a consequence, it has been claimed that 'pragmatic devices and subtle, coded strategies or concepts cannot be readily analysed through corpus linguistic means' (Wodak 2007, quoted in Baker et al. 2008: 296). But such statements, as Partington (2014) contends, would seem to undervalue the growing body of corpus work on pragmatic devices (Adolphs 2008), not to mention that on subtle strategies and concepts such as metaphor (Stefanowitsch & Gries 2006), irony (Louw 1993; Partington 2007, 2011) and im/politeness (Culpeper 2011, Taylor 2016). He takes issue with two separate arguments purportedly explaining why corpus techniques cannot handle absence. The first is that the corpus linguist cannot describe the behaviour of any item or set of items which are not found in his or her corpus. The other is that corpus techniques can provide no insight into why particular choices were made at any point in a text and why other choices were not made. In this chapter we hope to show why these objections are unsustained.

There are many vitally important aspects of language which would be precluded if implication and inference, pragmatic devices and coded strategies are to be removed from a study of discourse and the studies cited proved that they need not be. Like the importance of silence in a speech community highlighted by Dell Hymes (1972) (see also Schröter 2013; Schröter & Taylor forthcoming), absence can have significant meaning and must be considered even by an approach which usually starts from what is present in the discourse. An important caveat also needs mentioning, however: not all absences are necessarily meaningful, or at least not in the way we might first think. In a comparative study into EU-scepticism in UK newspapers before the 2016 EU referendum vote, we discovered that the item *democratic deficit* was absent from the EU-sceptic *Daily Mail's* key clusters, but present in that of the pro-EU *Guardian*. Are we to conclude that the latter admits to a democratic deficit in EU institutions while the former has not noticed it? The explanation is rather more straightforward and a question of stylistic choice. The *Guardian* chooses the rather more formal expression, sometimes averring a *democratic deficit*, but often claiming it is a false perception. The *Daily Mail* preferred to use expressions like *unaccountability* and *faceless bureaucrats*. The absence, then, is not meaningful politically, though it does tell us something about the styles of the two newspapers.

3.4 Approaching absence through corpus-assisted discourse studies

Corpus work and corpus tools focus on what is in the corpus. We interrogate a corpus and the answers come in the form of items in the corpus. Lexis and structures are considered in concordance lines along with the company they keep. The software can identify collocates and clusters and we can examine occurrence through dispersion plots. We can also discern patterns of co-occurrence. Criteria for analysing the items are discussed in terms of word lists and keyword lists, the boiled-down (Scott & Tribble 2006: 6) rendering of the texts in numerical terms of occurrence. Non-occurrence, or absence, then, seems a difficult object for corpus study. How can we use corpus tools which are mainly designed to reveal what is *there* to treat rather than uncover what is *not*? Taylor (2012) outlined a number of tools in the corpus linguist's armoury which can be used to deal with absence, some of which will be expanded on in the following section. The standard corpus linguistic starting points of keywords, key clusters and key semantic domains, the process of comparison and the consideration of expectation all expose absences, both relative and absolute. From such absences much can be inferred.

Collocation comparison can reveal both differences but also absences (see Marchi 2011 for an account). Sketch Engine's Sketch Difference tool is an extremely useful resource for revealing absence of this kind, indicating the strength of different collocations or comparing the behaviour of the same item in two different subcorpora. While a Word Sketch will indicate the company the item keeps, i.e. its collocates, and list the presences, it is when comparison comes into play through the Sketch Difference tool that absences will appear. So, for example, we used Sketch Difference to examine an item in two comparable corpora: the 2010 SiBol newspaper data (see Section 3.5 below) and the 1993 SiBol newspaper corpus. We chose for our search the item *immigrant*, and the resulting Sketch Difference profile showed that in 1993 there were no occurrences of *hostility toward* immigrants, no occurrences of *the invasion of* immigrants, or *scapegoating, targeting, deporting, blaming* or *stopping*. This group of absences says a great deal about the discourse of immigration in 2010 and changes in newspaper representations of the issue. It is the comparative element which allows us to identify relative absence.

As well as using other corpora to bring absences into focus, other sources can be brought into play to provide a comparative element. Taylor (2012) highlighted various sources which can be used for comparison, which include external 'real world' data, previous research and metalinguistic data (see also Schröter 2013 on silence in German political discourse), but also the role of internal or introspective inquiry whereby we examine the data in the light of what may be our expectations, another key factor in identifying absence or pointing to further comparative resources:

> Prior awareness or intuition about what is possible in language should help to make us aware of [...] absences, and often comparison with a larger normative corpus will reveal what they are.
>
> *(Baker 2005: 35)*

In the following case studies we outline some of the techniques that can be used to illustrate the role of both comparison and expectation. An example of modern-diachronic corpus-assisted discourse analysis is used to illustrate where presence in the keywords of one corpus implies absence in the other, reference corpus. Such a diachronic study of a particular item illustrates how the presence and absence of trends over time can be identified. Presences and absences are then analysed in cross-cultural comparisons of similar corpora in a study of press briefings in the US and China and a third study illustrates the way absences can highlight matters of im/politeness in political discourse through the comparison of candidates' speeches in the 2016 US presidential campaign, where traditional expectations were disrupted by the absence of mitigation (see also Partington & Marchi 2015; Partington forthcoming).

3.5 Case studies

One main reason for the current rise in interest in absence in corpus linguistics research is the arrival on the scene of systematically designed diachronic corpora which make it possible to compare and contrast both the linguistic features of, and the social and political issues present or absent in, specific discourse types of a language from different periods of time. The Corpus of Historical American English (COHA, Davies 2012), which contains more than 400 million words of text from the 1810s–2000s, appeared online in 2010. In the same year, the term 'Modern diachronic corpus-assisted discourse studies' (MD-CADS) was coined in a set of papers on the subject, prepared by the SiBol group, to describe research on corpora from different recent time periods (Partington ed. 2010). Researchers at Lancaster University have produced versions of both the Brown family of corpora and of the British National Corpus containing more recent texts, part of whose *raison d'être* is for comparison purposes with the older corpora (Baker 2009; Potts & Baker 2012).

The SiBol project work mentioned above (Partington ed. 2010) sheds a considerable amount of light on how diachronic corpora can be used to study both presences and their converse, absences and the significance of each. Indeed, this work underlined how presences and absences are complimentary in comparative work, the one implies the other, and in a sense, they are the same phenomena just seen from a different perspective, forward or backward in time, keyness in the earlier dataset automatically means absence in the later dataset, and vice versa. For example, when comparing UK newspaper discourse from 2005 with that from 1993, Duguid (2010) discovered a large number and variety of keywords in the 2005 data marking extreme importance – for example, *pivotal*, *key*, *huge* – or expressing hyperbolic evaluation, almost always positive, such as *amazing*, *inspired*, *stunning*, *gorgeous* and many more. At first blush, this seemed to run counter to the much discussed news value of negativity (Galtung & Ruge 1981; Bednarek & Caple 2012). The question 'why are these items much more present in the later data-set?' is the same question as 'why are they relatively absent from the earlier data-set?'

3.5.1 Presence and absence of trends: problems in the Arab world?

In this section we wish to examine a particular form of presence and absence, that of a trend over time (see Marchi, this volume). The particular trend we wanted to examine was the media news reporting of the Arab Middle East and North Africa (MENA) in 2010, the year leading up to the uprisings which began in the region at the very end of that year. We wanted to check whether there was any awareness, any inkling of what was about to happen, simply by investigating whether reporting of events in the region increased over the year. Put another way, to check whether the trend in frequency of reporting was upwards, downwards or flatlining. We looked at two sets of newspapers, firstly two of the most prominent US papers, the *New York Times* and the *Washington Post* and two UK papers, the left-leaning *Guardian* and the right-leaning *Telegraph*. All articles containing the items *Middle East** or *North Africa** were downloaded from the Lexis Nexis database in four three-monthly, that is quarterly, batches. Occurrences of the items were then counted, and the counts are displayed in Figures 3.1 and 3.2 below.

These two figures show a similar picture. Although there is a small peak of reporting in the third quarter, mainly due – we discovered by concordancing the relevant files – to reports of *Middle East peace talks* between the Israelis and the Palestinians, there is no trend of increased media interest in the region; in fact, the final quarter registers a fall in reporting. We then concordanced in each quarterly file of the two US newspapers, the items *protest**, *revolt** and *uprising* and were surprised by a sharp *fall* in occurrences of these items collectively from 382, 431, 273 and 130 respectively. The protests were also not necessarily anti-government, though two major such protests occurred in Iran and Afghanistan. But there were also, *inter alia*, protests at suggestions to burn a copy of the Koran, the perennial anti-Israel protests and a protest in Yemen against child marriage.

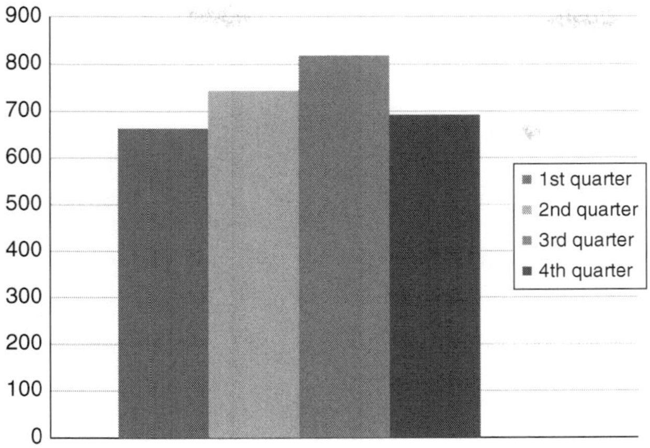

FIGURE 3.1 Mentions of the items *Middle East** and *North Africa** quarter-yearly in 2010 in the US newspapers *New York Times* and *Washington Post*.

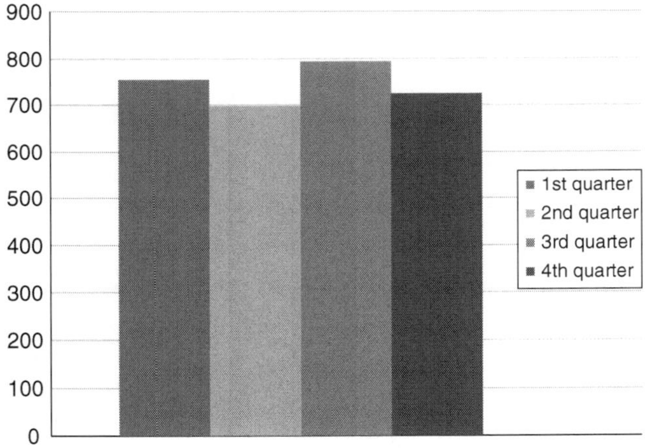

FIGURE 3.2 Mentions of the items *Middle East** and *North Africa** quarter-yearly in 2010 in the UK newspapers the *Guardian* and the *Telegraph*.

However, from the overall statistics, which reveal no trend of rising interest, and an examination of concordances from which specific discussions of anti-government sentiments are absent, we can reasonably infer a complete absence on the part of these highly resourceful and influential Western news-workers at least of any inkling of the devastating events that were about to unfold in the region (see also Partington forthcoming).

3.5.2 US and Chinese press briefings: presences and absences

In this section we make a comparative analysis between press briefings held at the White House and the Chinese Ministry of Foreign Affairs, noting various presences/absences at both the interpersonal and the diplomatic levels. Both the White House and the Chinese Foreign Ministry hold press briefings or conferences on a regular basis, in normal times, daily. They are a particular type of *institutional talk* (Drew & Heritage eds. 1992), which is defined as talk between professionals and lay people, but the definition can be stretched, as here, to include talk between two groups of professionals with an audience of lay persons (the TV and Internet audience). But a further audience is constituted by the representatives of other nations and so the stakes can be very high. Not only are the various US or Chinese podiums' words interpreted by the press as government policy, but they are also interpreted by foreign administrations as official US or Chinese policy. Since they are broadcast both on television and on the Internet, 'any misstep can be beamed instantaneously around the world' (*CNN-allpolitics*).

Two corpora of briefings are employed here. The first is called WH-2011, and contains all the briefings of the Obama administration in the year from December 2010 to the end of November 2011, a total of 239, comprising around 1,300,000 words,[8] which was created to study the reactions to the Arab uprisings. The second is CFA-2016, a corpus consisting of all the conferences, a total of 236 and comprising 270,000 words, conducted at the Chinese Ministry of Foreign Affairs, held over the course of 2016 to study China's intricate relations with its near neighbours (Marakhovskaiia 2017). Official translations of the original Chinese language versions are available in Arabic, English, French, Russian and Spanish. The English language versions were examined for this research, although the original Chinese versions were also consulted if we felt there were any linguistic ambiguities.

3.5.3 Comparison and contrast: the absence of negotiation in the CFA conferences

To analyse the content – and what was missing from the content – concordances of the CFA conferences we prepared word and cluster (up to 4-gram) frequency lists, followed up by concordancing, often 'chain-concordancing' – that is, noting an interesting item in one concordance leading to its being concordanced in turn and so on, often involving several rounds, and close reading of a sample of the conferences.

The most immediately striking feature of the CFA conferences, compared to the White House press briefings, is their apparent formal and formulaic nature. The questions, for example, often take the form of a statement on some foreign policy issue, followed by a formally interrogative locution, such as 'what is your/China's comment on that?' (390 occurrences in the 1,542 questions in the corpus), 'Do you have any comment (on this/that)' (63 occurrences), 'What is your/China's response (to that/this)?' (148 occurrences). Just occasionally the question opens with 'Can you give us more details/information on' followed by the statement of an issue (27 occurrences). Moreover, there are no first names used, the podium much prefers to use *we* (1,891 occurrences) rather than *I* (834), stressing their role as representative rather than individual human interlocutor. There are no hesitation fillers, except formal ones such as *what is more*, and follow-up clarification questions, so frequent in the White House briefings, such as,

1 Q: Jay, I want to understand. Are you saying that the President will not support […],

are entirely absent from the CFA questioning, and so is the banter which permeates the White House exchanges (Partington 2006). Jiang (2006: 244) conducted a comparative study of CFA and US Department of State briefings, noting how speakers in the latter:

> may integrate other communicative functions into their main task, such as criticizing, clarifying, joking, repeating, negotiating, apologizing, complaining, justifying, commenting, inferring, and disagreeing.

However, Jiang notices also that these speech acts are all almost entirely absent from the CFA discourse. Indeed, the kind of multiple-turn interaction, that is, question–response, then potential multiple follow-ups and clarification requests, in which meaning is negotiated and a response is agreed that partially at least satisfies both sides, all of which is typical of US briefings, is absent:

> The back-and-forth negotiation of meaning seems to be unavoidable at press conferences in order for the journalists to get the exact information they want and for the spokespersons to do a good job in keeping a balance between what they know and what they should say. However, this kind of multiple-turn interaction does not happen in the Chinese press conferences.
> *(Jiang 2006: 245)*

What this concentration on the transactional business in hand and the absence of interpersonal interaction (Brown & Yule 1983) really reveals is that the nature of the two discourse events is very different. From the point of view of the White House or the Chinese Foreign Office, the whole *raison d'être* of briefings, the reason they were instituted in the first place, is to affirm the administration's favoured view of events to the press and through them to the public and to the outside world. But while this favoured view can meet quite detailed and even hostile scrutiny in the US data, the Chinese journalists are, as Jiang (2006: 245) points out, more 'compliant'. This is confirmed by close reading of a sample of the questions in the CFA data, the majority of which are barely questions in any real sense and are more like platforms to enable the podium to enhance China's and the government's positive image:

2 Q: Russian President Vladimir Putin stressed in the recently-signed new national security strategy to 2020 that Russia is developing the comprehensive strategic partnership of coordination with China, which is a key factor for regional and world stability. What is China's response?

Or to provide the podium with an invitation from which to launch a face-threatening rebuke, in this case to the US administration (our emphasis):

3 Q: While giving a speech at the US Naval Academy, US Defense Secretary Ashton Carter mentioned China 22 times, saying that China could be erecting 'a Great Wall of self-isolation'. Some US media said **that the US is good at weaving a story, turning daytime into night**. What is your comment?

A: We have noted US Defense Secretary Carter's remarks on China, which reflect **the typical American thinking and hegemony**. Some from the US side, while living in the 21th century, are **still thinking with the Cold War mentality** [...].

3.5.4 Presences and absences in the CFA conferences

It was apparent from the word and cluster frequency lists that a great deal of attention is paid to China's 'inner circle', that is, its close regional neighbours, namely *Taiwan, North and South Korea, Hong Kong* and *Japan*, and so we decided to examine what was said about these, mainly by concordancing followed by close reading.

The year 2016 saw China involved in various territorial disputes with neighbouring powers over ownership and access to various parts of the *South China Sea* (mentioned 742 times in the CFA conferences). One of the most striking presences in the CFA corpus is the degree and type of vituperation reserved for Japan and the Japanese government (*Japan** occurs 304 times). The main strategy of the various podiums is 'historical shaming', the delegitimisation of Japan by constant reference to its behaviour towards its neighbours and China in particular in the 1930s and 1940s. Japan is mentioned repeatedly in conjunction with items such as *Japanese war crimes* (18), *Japanese militarism* (12), *Japan's war of aggression* (10), *Nanjing massacre* (of 1937, eight occurrences), *China's war of resistance* (4), and *comfort women* (20), that is, non-Japanese women forced into prostitution by the Japanese military in that period. Admonishments, such as 'not to ... whitewash or deny the history', 'make a break with militarism', 'win back the trust of international community', all attempt to identify modern Japan with the militarist empire of its past. Any protests about China are said to only 'make people more suspicious of Japan's real intentions', the podiums claiming to speak for the whole of South East Asia. They also back the historical admonishments with demands for an apology (12 instances):

4 Q: The Japanese Prime Minister is on a visit to the Pearl Harbor. Do you think it is now time for him to come to Nanjing and apologize to the Chinese people?

A: I noticed that media from both China and the west are following closely Japanese Prime Minister Shinzo Abe's visit to the Pearl Harbor. We have also taken note of reports saying that this visit is only about offering prayers to the victims and does not include an apology, and that the visit is highly likely to be a publicity stunt aimed at China. Also, over 50 historians from Japan and the US have reportedly sent an 'inquiry letter' to Abe, stating that Abe needs to offer prayers to war victims from China, the ROK and other Asian countries and it is the Chinese people that Japan should apologize to first.

This aggressive stance is in stark contrast to the absence of any sort of negative evaluation of other near neighbours, the Democratic People's Republic of Korea (*DPRK, North Korea,* 375 occurrences) and the Republic of Korea (*ROK; South Korea,* 301 occurrences). There were two nuclear tests carried out by the Democratic People's Republic of Korea in 2016 and so the Korean peninsula and relations with the Republic of Korea are a frequent topic of questioning. These tests drew condemnation from many bodies including the United Nations (UN), but not from the CFA. In fact, the CFA podiums refrain from criticising either North or South Korea, and the language used is distinctly more restrained with locutions such as 'it is hoped that all parties will refrain …' and 'it is hoped that all parties will work in tandem to create conditions for the peaceful settlement of the Korean nuclear issue through dialogue'.

Instead of criticism, condemnation or demands for an apology, the podiums use the situation to enhance China's own positive image and present the state as a cooperative and responsible party committed to peaceful settlement of disputes:

5 A: Denuclearization, **peace and stability** of the Korean Peninsula are in the best interests of China and all relevant parties. To make that happen, the Chinese side has been working for the proper settlement of relevant issues through **dialogue and negotiation** … to bring the Korean nuclear issue back to the track of **dialogue and consultation** and explore ways to achieve lasting **peace and order**.

6 A: The Chinese side has been striving to promote denuclearization on the Peninsula both in words, policies and in actions. Denuclearization on the Peninsula as well as **peace and stability** of Northeast Asia serves the **common interests** of all parties and calls for their concerted efforts as well.

The official Chinese position is constructed by the repeated use of *dialogue*, *consultation* and *negotiation*, as well as other notions with positive connotation such as *peace*, *order* and *stability*.

Another sensitive regional issue is *Taiwan* (295 mentions), where elections were held in 2016, provoking a number of questions, for instance:

7 Q: Tsai Ing-wen, candidate of the Democratic Progressive Party (DPP) won the election in Taiwan. How will it impact the cross-Straits relations? How would the mainland react if Tsai Ing-wen pursued 'Taiwan Independence' after taking office?

A: **The Taiwan question falls within China's internal affairs**. There is **only one China** in the world. Both the mainland and Taiwan belong to **one China**. China's sovereignty and territorial integrity **brook no division**. This basic fact and consensus of the international community will not be changed by the result of the election in Taiwan. The Chinese government sticks to the **one-China** principle and opposes 'Taiwan independence', 'two Chinas' and 'one China, one Taiwan'. This position remains unchanged and **will not change** regardless of what happens in Taiwan.

Critical comments are strikingly absent from the podiums' responses. The Taiwanese government and people are neither blamed nor praised, they are ignored. The podiums typically resort to evasion, preferring to repeat China's official 'one-China policy' often, as above, using strongly affirmative language, with the distinct absence of any hedging (Marakhovskaiia 2017).

It should come as no surprise that in the world of diplomacy and *realpolitik*, both the US and Chinese podiums lay into perceived unfriendly nations and refrain from criticism of friendlier ones. However, the strategies used to criticise differ from situation to situation, form outright denunciation, to delegitimisation, to historical shaming. And so do the strategies of absence of criticism, which range from praise, to implicit respectfulness, to appeals for restraint 'on both sides', to appeals for dialogue and consultation to complete evasion, absence of comment or opinion.

3.5.5 The 2016 US presidential campaign: expectations, face threats and the absence of mitigation

We have seen above how presence and absences are complementary in comparative work which looks at different points of time – absence in one data set is contrasted with presence in the other and in a sense, they are the same phenomena just seen from different perspectives. Similar results are observable in other kinds of comparable corpora with the same communicative purpose, such as in presidential campaigns, that of persuading voters of the reasons to vote for a particular candidate. In a corpus of candidates' campaign speeches, we can compare the different perspectives, in the different candidates' representations of the world. Furthermore, when one campaign is compared to other previous campaigns then the perspective of different time frames can also be observed. This case study shows how the total absence of a keyword (or more precisely several keywords which can be seen to make up a set) points us to peculiarities of the discourse which have both sociolinguistic and political implications.

We usually have the expectation that different candidates in a political campaign will produce some differentiating features in their discourse. When we find keywords, calculated to be salient by our software, that correspond to a total absence in the reference corpus we might find, on examination, that such expectations are reset by further considerations. Expectations, of course, play a large part generally in interpersonal communication. Goffman's (1955) concept of face as something which can be lost, maintained or enhanced involves a tacit acceptance that we all have the same vulnerabilities and it is as well to speak as we would be spoken to. When someone transgresses and performs in a way which upsets such expectations the clash is noticed. This can happen inadvertently when a person is not used to the conventions of maintaining other peoples' face, or it can be done deliberately to disrupt a situation. The concept was then taken up by Brown and Levinson for their theory of linguistic politeness (Brown & Levinson 1987). Cooperative face-work usually involves polite language, perhaps used tactically, to avoid a breakdown of communication and ensure a smooth exchange of ideas or transactions; markedly aggressive face-work can be seen as inappropriate in a context of cooperation and shared roles. In the recent American election campaigns the debates and campaign speeches represent a particular type of *institutional talk* with an audience of lay persons (the audience on site and TV and Internet audiences). Participant roles in such institutional talk carry with them certain expectations and when such roles are performed in public the beneficiaries, the various audiences, have much the same expectations as the active participants. Not only are the different candidates' words examined as to intentions for future government policy, but they are also interpreted by the public as evidence of character or leadership qualities.

Public debates, interviews and campaign speeches are promotional exercises with a persuasive purpose. Since they are broadcast and reported on by all political editors, soundbites can be chosen by the campaign teams, and by the media, to exemplify both policy and personality; both *competence* face and *affective* face are at issue (Partington 2006: 97–98, 170) and the way a participant interacts with interviewers, other politicians in a debate or with the public are all scrutinised by the media. The image of a politician as well-informed, in control and authoritative will contribute to competence face, while the image of being good-humoured, likeable, affable and easy-going has in the past been considered to be a part of affective face. We also have some expectations that people share our primings; we expect to be speaking the same language, to have a common vocabulary. An example of a clash of expectations came when an MSNBC reporter interviewing libertarian presidential candidate Gary Johnson in the 2016 election, was clearly shocked to find that the word *Aleppo* was not in his lexicon, his personal corpus. It was clearly not part of his primings so that, when asked if elected what he would do about Aleppo, he responded 'What's a leppo?', showing he had no mental concordance for the word. This brought the response 'you're kidding, right?' It is clear that the reporter felt that a candidate for president should have the place name as part of his receptive primings at least in the context of a position on foreign policy. He went on:

> Aleppo is the center of a lot of people's concerns across the planet about the terrible humanitarian crisis that is unfolding not only in Syria, but especially in Aleppo. You asked, 'What is Aleppo?' Do you really think that foreign policy is so insignificant that somebody who is running for president of the

United States shouldn't even know what Aleppo is, where Aleppo is, and why it is so important?

It was the absence of *Aleppo* as an immediately recoverable item with the meaning 'second city of Syria which has been so much in the news as the site of geopolitical conflict and thus an important issue for foreign policy', from his lexicon that created a loss of the candidate's competence-face. The reporter clearly had expected the candidate's mental corpus to correspond more closely to their own; the press coverage suggested that many shared this expectation; the candidate withdrew after the incident. In general, the 2016 presidential election in America was treated in the press as being most singular, and coverage indicated that expectations were being confounded on a regular basis.

As an investigation of the different discourses involved in the campaign, we compiled a set of corpora consisting of campaign speeches from the two outlier populist candidates, one Democrat, one Republican, who were presenting themselves as an antidote to the status quo: Donald Trump (171,000 tokens) and Bernie Sanders (137,526 tokens). Further reference corpora were provided by the presidential debates of 2016 (50,539 tokens) and previous presidential debates (2008 and 2012, 258,157 tokens), all gathered from the excellent American Presidency project website.[9] Another corpus of coverage of the elections, from the '*G & T*' corpus, consisting of all the articles from two UK papers, the left-leaning *Guardian* and the right-leaning *Telegraph*, throughout 2016 was compiled (305,151 tokens). This was employed as a means of accessing the reception of the candidates' speeches and debate performances.[10] This commentary corpus revealed a strong interest in Trump's language which was perceived as being anomalous, as we can see from press commentary where Trump's language was a key target of opinion pieces:

8 His **stump oratory** – especially his convention speech, delivered from a preposterous mock-Grecian stage set in Denver – was vacuous. He is clever and **has a way with words**: but his **words** contained little. (*Telegraph* 2016)

9 He overwhelmed his interviewer with such **a profusion of misstatements, half-truths, dodges and red herrings** that one grows dizzy trying to untangle it all. Our first impulse might be to run **this verbal stew** through a fact-checking rinse. (*Guardian* 2016)

However, even comments which were described by press and other politicians as *vulgar, rude, inflammatory, reprehensible, inappropriate and offensive* did not seem to ruffle the Trump supporters who appeared not to have the same expectations about the pragmatic delicacy necessary in a presidential candidate and indeed to have strong feelings about freedom of speech:

10 Tuesday's event was notable for a child heckler who twice shouted 'take the bitch down' about the former secretary of state. The adult who accompanied the heckler, who was roughly 10 years old, told reporters who asked about the

coarse language afterwards:'I think he has **a right to speak what he wants to**.' (*Guardian* 2016)

Our first step was to compare the keyword lists of Sanders' and Trump's campaign speeches and interviews, observing those items which did not occur at all in the corpus of the other candidate's speeches. Some items reflect political positions and are to be expected in a campaign of this kind. When Sanders's campaign speeches were compared with those of Trump, we discovered a series of items related to the economy, a semantic set which is absent from Trump's speeches: *billionaire/s, wealthiest, inequality, greed, austerity, profits, speculation* and *childhood* (of which 16 out of 17 occurrences collocate with *poverty*). These are content-related absences which reveal stark differences in the way in which the debate is being framed and the way reality is being represented, highlighting problems of a gap between the rich and the poor and vulnerable. Another two items are *socialist* and *socialism*.

When we reverse the procedure, and search the Trump keywords for items which are absent from the Sanders corpus we find a different kind of item, which form not so much a semantic set of policy-related items but more a set of rhetorical devices. Interestingly, these items are absent from the discourse of the other candidate, in the corpus of debates after Trump's official nomination as Republican candidate. Indeed on further comparison with the debates of 2012 and 2008, we see they are also absent there; in other words, they only appear in the discourse of the Trump campaign. In both sets of keywords, we find the absolute absentees from the reference corpora are: *disaster, lie, fake, theft, rigged, disastrous, bitter, arrogance, failed, righteous, tremendous, stamina, unfit*. These items, all evaluative, help perform the speech acts of attacks, accusations and general negative campaigning. We will examine a small selection.

Explicitly accusing someone of being a liar is highly face-threatening, and is often considered out of bounds (for instance, in the UK parliament). But the keyword *liar* is used by Trump to attack without mitigation and is reinforced by repetition:

11 Look, she's been proven to be a **liar** on so many different ways. This is just another **lie**. (debate 2016 10 19)
12 The establishment and their media enablers wield control over this nation through means that are well known … They will attack you, they will slander you, they will seek to destroy your career and reputation. And they will **lie, lie and lie** even more. The Clintons are criminals. (debate 2016 10 13)
13 Clinton and her cronies will say anything, do anything, **lie** about anything to keep their grip on power – to keep their control over this country. (debate 2016 09 30)
14 One more Hillary Clinton **lie**. Lie after **lie** after **lie**. Hillary Clinton is unfit to hold public office. (2016 08 23)

Another item in which there is a distinct lack of mitigation of a face-threatening attack is *disaster*; indeed it is intensified through repetition:

15 Look, Hillary Clinton's a **disaster**. I'd love to see a woman become president and it'll happen, absolutely. But I think it would be bad for women if it were Hillary Clinton. (2016 07 27)

16 He has been a **disaster** as a president. He will go down as one of the worst presidents in the history of our country. It is a mess. (2016 07 27)

17 I challenge anyone to explain the strategic foreign policy vision of Obama–Clinton – it has been a complete and total **disaster**. (2106 04 26)

The issue of fake news came to the fore in this presidential campaign (see Section 6 below) in attacks on the media, again we see how this keyword is reinforced by repetition:

18 Some of the **fake news** said, I don't think Donald Trump wants to build the wall. Can you imagine if I said we're not going to build a wall? **Fake news. Fake, fake news. Fake news**, folks. A lot of **fake**. (2017 03 15)

19 But I want to just tell you, the false reporting by the media, by you people – the false, horrible, **fake** reporting makes it much harder to make a deal with Russia. (2017 02 16)

This kind of insistent message repetition is a clear and dramatic instance of what Duguid calls 'forced lexical priming' (Duguid 2009; Duguid & Partington 2017).

Other unadorned, unvarnished and unmitigated attacks contain on-record accusations of illegality, usually avoided in the presidential campaigns, as we see from the absence in the reference corpora:

20 Remember, we are competing in a **rigged** election – the media is trying to **rig** the election by giving credence to false stories that have no validity and making it front page news, only to poison the minds of the American voters. (2016 10 17)

21 Hillary is running for President in what looks like a **rigged** election. The election is being **rigged** by corrupt media, pushing false allegations and outright **lies**, in an effort to elect her President. (2016 10 15)

As regards foreign policy, the criticisms are equally direct and devoid of diplomatic wording; China in particular came in for attacks:

22 This includes stopping China's **outrageous theft** of intellectual property, along with their illegal product dumping, and their devastating currency manipulation. They are the greatest that ever came about; they are the greatest currency manipulators ever! (2016 07 21)

23 **Predatory trade practices**, product dumping, currency manipulation and intellectual property **theft** have taken millions of jobs and trillions in wealth from our country. (2016 09 15)

Nearly all these keywords, which are totally absent from all the reference corpora, contribute to face-threatening acts lacking any mitigation and are a characteristic of Trump's campaign style. We might say he displays an absence of any conventional politeness techniques, indeed, he adopts a strategy of deliberate *im*politeness (Bousfield 2008; Taylor 2016).

We expect participants in institutional discourse to use hedging to tone down the illocutionary force of an utterance, by verbal restraint, to avoid unadorned aggression or unvarnished violent emotions. This is seen as part of both affective and competence face in a politician. We expect negative evaluations to be mitigated or hedged in the interests of restraint, maintaining communication and avoiding aggressively conflictual interaction. However, the fortunes of the Trump campaign indicate that maintaining politeness strategies was not necessarily a winning tactic, or a positive value, as witnessed in the following exchange:

24 Trump: Somebody said to me the other day, a reporter, a very nice reporter, 'But, Mr. Trump, you're not a nice person.'

Audience Member: **We don't need nice**.

3.5.6 The limits of corpus evidence in investigating absence: the case of fake news

We saw in examples (18) and (19) how the notion *fake news* entered the 2016 US presidential election discourse. The item is absent from COHA from 1810 right up to the 1980s. It is also absent from the Hansard corpus of UK parliamentary discourse.

In COHA it appears just four times between 1980 and 2009. In contrast, it occurs 831 times (including the hyphenated *fake-news*) in the *New York Times* between January 2016 and January 2017. It co-occurs with *Facebook* (65 occurrences), *social media* (22) and *websites* (19), testifying to a perceived ease of dissemination of fabricated news.

But again we have to ask whether or not there was a relative absence of fake news in the past compared to today. Nothing occurred in 2016 to match the Pulitzer Prize hoax of 1980 or the invented Jenin 'massacre' of 2002, and certainly nothing to match William Randolph Hearst's use of false news in his *Morning Journal* to help spark the Spanish-American War in the 1890s. This is a timely warning that absence from a corpus does not equate to absence from the real world, a reminder that the corpus consists of and reveals *phenomena*, not *noumena*.

3.6 Evaluations and conclusions

In this chapter we have attempted to illustrate some of the different types of absence and ways in which looking for absences in corpus work can be revealing and also how corpus work can deal with absence to answer past criticisms that it cannot. Taylor (2012) spoke of an impressive armoury of tools for uncovering absences.

A key element is that of comparison. We can compare corpora, sub-corpora and reference corpora, but also make use of other sources such as corpus-based grammars, dictionaries and real-world data to confirm our introspections and intuitions based on our expectations (hence our preference for the term corpus-*assisted* discourse studies; the corpus is not the only resource available).

Taylor (2012) also poses the question, once an absence has been identified, how do we interpret it? In other words, we may well have a list of items found to be absent, but what kind of significant generalisations about language phenomena can we go on to make about these disparate absences? We have shown here how individual lexical items or grammatical structures can often be grouped into sets which reveal particular language behaviours. A list of lexical items can together form part of a group of features related to a particular linguistic phenomenon such as face threatening acts or politeness, or to features of modality which relate to subjective attitudes, such as necessity and desirability. Absences can be not just of lexical items but also, say, speech acts such as criticism or praise. They can reveal regularities which reflect relationships and interpersonal interaction.

Comparison and contrast, then, have been key in all these studies, but this should be no surprise. As Partington, Duguid and Taylor (2013: 12) observe:

> all discourse analysis [...] is properly comparative; it is only possible to both uncover and evaluate the particular features of a discourse type by comparing it with others. We are not deontologically justified in making statements about the relevance of a phenomenon observed to occur in one discourse type unless, where it is possible, we compare how the phenomenon behaves elsewhere.

Here, we have tried to show how, by contrastive analysis of different sets of text, absences can first be located and then their significance appraised. We have encountered absences of many different sorts, some deliberate and strategic, and some almost accidental; some expected and some surprising; some content-related and others stylistic; some highly meaningful and some less so. We noted how important the choice and design of comparison corpora need to be and that different methodological approaches can reveal – and hide – different things. But what all the case studies here have in common is that, without the use of contrastive corpus techniques, very little could have been gleaned on what was absent, where it was absent from and, by incorporating inferences from the analysts' knowledge of the world, why it was absent.

Notes

1 The dichotomy between *phenomena* and *noumena*, literally 'things that appear' to our perception and 'things that are (capable of being) thought', is discussed by Plato in the *Republic* and is his principal legacy to western philosophy and, indeed, religion. It was taken up and discussed at length by Kant, firstly in *On the Form and Principles of the Sensible and Insensible World* (1770) and then in the *Critique of Pure Reason* (1787). The relevance to

science in general and corpus linguistics in particular is clear: we can only get to know, or better, to model language via the instruments we have to observe – or *perceive* – it.

2 Muslims were discussed as both perpetrators of anti-Semitic acts and also as fellow victims of prejudice.

3 Visit to Russia Today television channel, Kremlin.ru website, June 11, 2013, Max Fisher, In case you weren't clear on Russia Today's relationship to Moscow, Putin clears it up, Washington Post, June 13, 2013.

4 In 2006, the director stated 'We would like to present a more complete picture of life in our country'.

5 A group of English speaking countries which share a cultural heritage and maintain cooperation through military, political, intelligence, communication and technology programmes and where transnational news programmes first started.

6 http://news.bbc.co.uk/2/hi/europe/6215170.stm.

7 http://aib.org.uk/al-jazeera-to-launch-ethics-code/ 10 july 2004.

8 Compiled by Franconi, 2011.

9 The American Presidency Project (APP), is the leading source of presidential documents on the internet. The archives contain 124,763 documents and are growing rapidly. It is hosted at the University of California, Santa Barbara© 1999-2017 - Gerhard Peters and John T. Woolley - The American Presidency Project ™

10 Corpus work has sometimes been criticised for lack of attention to the reception of discourses. Notable exceptions are Taylor (2009), who used a corpus of newspaper comments to track the reception of face-work in the Hutton inquiry and Duguid and Partington (2017) on the efficacy of political message repetition on media audiences.

References

Adolphs, S. 2008. *Corpus and Context: Investigating Pragmatic Functions in Spoken Discourse.* Amsterdam: John Benjamins.

Baker, P. 2005. *Public Discourses of Gay Men.* London: Routledge.

Baker, P. 2009. The BE06 Corpus of British English and recent language change. *International Journal of Corpus Linguistics*, 14(3), 312–37.

Baker, P., Gabrielatos, C., Khosravinik, M., Krzyzanowski, M., McEnery, A. & Wodak, R. 2008. A useful methodological synergy? Combining critical discourse analysis and corpus linguistics to examine discourses of refugees and asylum seekers in the UK press. *Discourse and Society*, 19(3), 273–305.

Bednarek, M. & Caple, H. 2012. *News Discourse.* London: Continuum.

Bousfield, D. 2008. *Impoliteness in Interaction.* Amsterdam: John Benjamins.

Breeze, R. 2011. Critical discourse analysis and its critics. *Pragmatics*, 21(4), 493–525.

Brown, G. & Yule, G. 1983. *Discourse Analysis.* Cambridge: Cambridge University Press.

Brown, G. & Levinson, P. 1987. *Politeness: Some Universals in Language Usage.* Cambridge: Cambridge University Press.

Culpeper, J. 2011. *Impoliteness: Using Language to Cause Offense.* Cambridge: Cambridge University Press.

Davies, M. 2012. Expanding horizons in historical linguistics with the 400-million word Corpus of Historical American English. *Corpora*, 7(2), 121–157.

Drew, P. & Heritage J. (eds.) 1992. *Talk at Work.* Cambridge: Cambridge University Press.

Duguid, A. 2009. Insistent voices, government messages. In J. Morley & P. Bayley (eds.) *Corpus-Assisted Discourse Studies on the Iraq Conflict: Wording the War.* London: Routledge. pp. 234–260.

Duguid, A. 2010. Newspaper discourse informalisation: A diachronic comparison from keywords. *Corpora*, 5(2), 109–138.

Duguid, A. 2015. Evaluation as positioning in English language news channels. In R. Piazza, L. Haarman & A. Caborn (eds.) *Values and Choices in Television Discourse: A View from Both Sides of the Screen*. London: Palgrave Macmillan. pp. 75–92.

Duguid, A. & Partington, A. 2017. Forced lexical priming in political discourse: how they are produced and how they are received. In M. Pace-Sigge & K. Patterson (eds.) *Lexical Priming: Advances and Applications*. Amsterdam: John Benjamins. pp. 67–92.

Galtung, J. & Ruge, M. 1981. Structuring and selecting news. In S. Cohen & J. Young (eds.) *The Manufacture of News: Social Problems, Deviance and the Mass Media*, 2nd edn. London: Constable. pp. 52–63.

Goffman, E. 1955. On face-work: An analysis of ritual elements of social interaction. *Psychiatry; Journal for the Study of Interpersonal Processes*, 18(3), 213–231.

Hoey, M. 2005. *Lexical Priming: A New Theory of Words and Language*. London and New York: Routledge.

Hymes, D. H. 1972. Models of the interaction of language and social life. In J. J. Gumperz & D. Hymes (eds.) *Directions in Sociolinguistics: The Ethnography of Communication*. New York: Holt, Rinehart & Winston. pp. 35–71.

Jiang, X. 2006. Cross-cultural pragmatic differences in US and Chinese press conferences: The case of the North Korea nuclear crisis. *Discourse & Society*, 17(2), 237–257.

Louw, W. 1993. Irony in the text or insincerity in the writer? – The diagnostic potential of semantic prosodies. In M. Baker, G. Francis & E. Tognini-Bonelli (eds.) *Text and Technology: In Honour of John Sinclair*. Amsterdam: John Benjamins. pp. 157–176.

McEnery, T. & Hardie, A. 2012. *Corpus Linguistics: Method, Theory and Practice*. Cambridge: Cambridge University Press.

Marakhovskaiia, M. 2017. *National Face as a Factor Shaping China's International Relations*. Unpublished M.A. thesis, Bologna University.

Marchi, A. between journalists and reporters – A CADS analysis of occupational representations within journalism. Paper given at Corpus Linguistics 2011. Birmingham UK.

Partington, A. 2006. *The Linguistics of Laughter*. London: Routledge.

Partington, A. 2007. Irony and reversal of evaluation. *Journal of Pragmatics,* 39, 1547–1569.

Partington, A. (ed.) 2010. Modern Diachronic Corpus-Assisted Discourse Studies (MD-CADS). *Corpora*, 5(2), Special edition.

Partington, A. 2011. Phrasal irony, its form, function and exploitation. *Journal of Pragmatics*, 43(6), 1786–1800.

Partington, A. 2012. The changing discourses on antisemitism in the UK press from 1993 to 2009: A modern-diachronic corpus-assisted discourse study. *Journal of Language and Politics*, 11(1), 51–76.

Partington, A. 2014. Mind the gaps. The role of corpus linguistics in researching absences. *International Journal of Corpus Linguistics*, 19(1), 118–146.

Partington, A. Forthcoming. Intimations of 'Spring'? What got said and what didn't get said about the start of the Middle Eastern/North African uprisings: A corpus-assisted discourse study of a historical event. In M. Schröter & C. Taylor (eds.) *Exploring Silence and Absence in Discourse*. Basingstoke: Palgrave Macmillan.

Partington, A. & Marchi, A. 2015. Using corpora in discourse analysis. In D. Biber & R. Reppen (eds.) *The Cambridge Handbook of Corpus Linguistics*. Cambridge: Cambridge University Press. pp. 216–234.

Partington, A., Duguid, A. & Taylor, C. 2013. *Patterns and Meanings in Discourse*: Amsterdam: John Benjamins.

Potts, A. & Baker, P. 2012. Does semantic tagging identify cultural change in British and American English?. *International Journal of Corpus Linguistics*, 17(3), 295–324.

Schröter, M. 2013. *Silence and Concealment in Political Discourse*. Amsterdam: John Benjamins.

Scott, M. 2004. *WordSmith Tools version 4*. Oxford: Oxford University Press.
Stefanowitsch, A. & Gries, S. (eds.) 2006. *Corpus-Based Approaches to Metaphor and Metonymy*. Berlin & New York: Mouton de Gruyter.
Taylor, C. 2009. Interacting with conflicting goals: Facework and impoliteness in hostile cross-examination. In J. Morley & P. Bayley (eds.) *Corpus-Assisted Discourse Studies on the Iraq Conflict: Wording the War*. London: Routledge. pp. 208–233.
Taylor, C. 2012. 'And there it isn't: (how) can we access the absent using CADS?' Talk given at *CADSConf 2012*, September 13–14, University of Bologna.
Taylor, C. 2013. Searching for similarity using corpus-assisted discourse studies. *Corpora*, 8(2), 81–113.
Taylor, C. 2016. *Mock Politeness in English and Italian*. Amsterdam: John Benjamins.
Wodak, R. 2007. Pragmatics and Critical Discourse Analysis. A Cross-disciplinary Inquiry. *Journal of Pragmatics and Cognition*, 15(1), 203–227.

4

OVERLOOKED TEXT TYPES

From fictional texts to real-world discourses[1]

Alon Lischinsky

4.1 Introduction

Behind the enthusiastic adoption of corpus-based approaches in discourse research lies the promise of an ability to explore data more completely and representatively. Traditional methods in discourse studies were primarily designed for delicacy and richness; given the complexity of the links between language use and its social context, and the wide range of linguistic features in which these links are expressed, research tended to focus on the 'detailed analysis of a small number of discourse samples' (Fairclough 1992: 230). But the depth afforded by such approaches places corresponding limits on breadth of coverage: examining particular excerpts in such detail is only possible at the expense of overlooking everything else that goes on in a given discursive practice. The 'fragmentary [and] exemplificatory' nature of the evidence that can be thus gathered poses considerable problems for generalisation (Fowler 1996: 8). When texts and features for analysis are selected on the basis of the researcher's intuitive judgement (Marchi & Taylor 2009: 3), there is no guarantee that they truly represent the distinctive patterns that characterise a discourse (Stubbs 1997).

Corpus approaches have been instrumental in providing scholars with the tools to go beyond such partial examinations, and obtain reliable evidence of typical patterns of description, evaluation and argumentation across large bodies of text. These advances have been, for the most part, conceptualised in terms of size: using computer-assisted tools allows researchers to identify and retrieve relevant linguistic features in datasets large enough to provide more than a selective characterisation. However, quantity by itself is not a sufficient guarantee of representativeness; however large it may be, a sample will remain partial and incomplete unless it adequately covers the range of genres and contexts in which a given discourse circulates.

Especially for the scholar whose interest lies in the varied ways in which language is used to accomplish particular functions (Partington et al. 2013: 4), making inferences from linguistic evidence to social and cultural practices demands acknowledgement of the diversity and complexity of such practices. In this chapter, I focus on the ways in which corpus-assisted discourse studies (CADS) have sometimes failed to address this complexity 'as seriously as it should' (Leech 2007: 134). In particular, I argue that overlooking fictional and imaginative genres limits the ability of CADS to explore how individuals are motivated and seduced by the meanings and ideological assumptions of discourse. The following section discusses the difficulties involved in determining representativeness in language data, and illustrates the issues raised by the bias of CADS towards particular genres – typically official, public and factual ones. Section 4.3 discusses how fiction and imagination are central to our understanding of the real world and sketches some of the complex ways in which readers' affect and attention are engaged by imaginative discourses, while Section 4.4 addresses disciplinary divides about fiction and outlines some of the particular interpretive caveats required to deal with such materials. Finally, Section 4.5 offers an example of how these limitations can be addressed by exploring the role of erotic fiction in the circulation of discourses about gender and sexuality.

4.2 The salient and the overlooked in CADS

In the sense I am using the term here, discourse studies is concerned with how language features in the performance of social action, and especially with its role in structuring the conduct of communicative activities and shaping interactions between individuals and groups (cf. Partington et al. 2013: 3). The language employed in a given context is studied as a tangible trace of the ways in which speakers engage with one another – harmoniously or contentiously – for the purpose of coordinating their beliefs and behaviours. CADS in particular seeks to capture the recurring traces left by social routines, 'the ways in which society creates itself' (Mahlberg 2007: 196) by discursively producing and reproducing habitual patterns of understanding and acting. From this point of view, the starting point of the analysis is not linguistic but social (Biber 1993: 244): what CADS seeks to characterise is not a particular language or linguistic variety, but rather a particular situation, purpose or function repeatedly enacted within a speech community. Assessing the representativeness and completeness of this characterisation therefore requires understanding the complex and messy ways in which texts are linked to the circumstances of their production, circulation and use (Maingueneau 2010: 150).

It is important to note that, despite the air of mathematical rigour carried by the term, representativeness in corpus linguistics invariably involves messy decisions. In the simplest definition, a sample is representative of a broader population if it shares its characteristics at a smaller scale: for each of the dimensions across which the population varies, the sample should show a distribution similar to that of the whole (Moessner 2009: 223). However, a precise and principled measurement of this similarity is impracticable in linguistics for two reasons. In the first place, one of the terms of comparison is unmeasurable: the textual universe of a language or linguistic variety as a whole is so large that its actual proportions can never be estimated with certainty (Hunston 2002: 28). Furthermore, the parameters of variation (from participant demographics to topic, medium, purpose and participation framework) are so many that ensuring that a sample remains representative along all of them would be infeasible (Nelson 2010: 60). In consequence, attempts to design representative corpora are never accurate in statistical terms. That does not mean, however, that the notion is without value: perfect representativeness may not be attainable, but it can be approximated (Leech 2007: 140). Even if conceptualised more modestly in terms of balance, it provides a useful regulative ideal for scholars seeking a more comprehensive and less biased image of discursive action.

The choice of variables regarding which representativeness should be prioritised depends, ultimately, on the research question that the evidence intends to answer (Kilgarriff & Grefenstette 2003: 340–342). In an ambitious proposal for best practices in corpus design, Biber (1993: 245) observes that one particularly relevant factor is how 'important [a given genre is] in defining a culture', and his argument seems especially apposite for CADS. While no corpus can fully capture a discursive formation – understood as 'all the things that are said about a given topic at a given historical period' (Stubbs 2001: 165) – it is important to approximate the full range of variation that can be found in this textual universe. Crucially, this entails keeping in view that any specific domain of social life involves many different discursive activities, enacted through a variety of genres in complex assemblages: sequential chains, hierarchies of prestige, repertoires defining specific communities, etc. (Prior 2009: 17). Ädel (2010) offers the example of political discourse: while executive speeches and parliamentary debates are prototypical exemplars, the means used to make sense of and take positions towards political issues are much broader, from manifestos and pamphlets to media interviews and editorials, bumper stickers and lapel buttons. In a similar manner, discourses of sexuality and gender circulate in a wide range of forms: biology handbooks, reproductive health advice materials, legislation on sexual assault and harassment, dating tips in lifestyle magazines, water-cooler gossip, hallway taunts, etc. Yet only few of these genres are covered in general-purpose corpora, and even custom-built ones are rarely comprehensive. Instead of 'considering the whole network [of genres] to understand the functioning' of a specific discourse domain (Maingueneau 2010: 153), much CADS work is limited to snapshots of particularly salient junctures (Stubbs 2001: 149).

The temptation to adopt such an approach is understandable, in that it simplifies the interpretive work required to make sense of the evidence. Ensuring that textual data can provide insight into a 'discursive event as social practice' (Fairclough 1995: 134) requires taking into account their context of production and use. In monogeneric corpora, no situational variations complicate interpretation: corpus composition acts as a proxy for the relevant contextual information (Thornbury 2010: 276). However, snapshots offer only limited possibilities for the comparative analysis that is intrinsic to discourse studies (Partington et al. 2013: 12). Of the three levels that Fairclough identifies for categorising discursive practices – the local context of specific discursive exchanges, the institutional context of a whole organisation or domain, and the wider context of culture – only the first can be appropriately tackled through the analysis of a single genre; institutions and *a fortiori* cultures can only be captured by exploring broader assemblages.

This exploration can in principle be accomplished incrementally, but CADS has shown a persistent bias towards a restricted set of genres. While committed in theory to a more democratic notion of importance, in practice the majority of work in the field focuses on discourse practices made 'sexy' by their public or official nature (Lee 2008: 92), such as news reporting, political speech, public and corporate policy or courtroom discourse. Doubtlessly, there are reasons for this bias: the size of the readership or audience is often a useful proxy for cultural salience, since a text engaged with by an audience of millions – such as mainstream print or broadcast media content – will exert a larger influence than one restricted to a narrow segment of the population (Leech 2007: 138).[2] Texts intended for widespread consumption may also be particularly useful for CADS because in order to be accessible and understandable to a wide audience they must reproduce – or at least acknowledge – mainstream common-sense assumptions (Baker 2005: 18). Nonetheless, the disproportionate prevalence of work on such materials leaves open important gaps in our understanding of the way in which discourses circulate in society. Just like traditional approaches in discourse studies were limited by addressing only the highest-profile exemplars, CADS is often partial to the highest-profile genres. This forecloses the possibility of a more dynamic and socially embedded model of how meanings and attitudes are disseminated, taken up and recontextualised.

An important step towards representativeness would be to reduce the gaps caused by the bias towards the factual and the official. In particular, I would like to argue that fictional genres have rarely been accorded a space commensurate with their cultural salience.

4.3 Fiction, fact and meaning

The corpus linguist seeking to model a particular linguistic variety readily acknowledges fiction as one of the important registers that must be included for a balanced portrayal. The CADS scholar – like the critical discourse analyst more generally (Gupta 2015: 197) – tends to be less willing; being interested primarily in texts as tangible traces of social action, the relevance of genres that make no claims to actuality seems in principle limited (Maingueneau 2010: 148). Paradoxically, it is the frequent emphasis on social critique what makes CADS uncritically accept the common-sense principle that 'pre-assigns a low modality' to non-factual texts (Hodge 1990: 166). But this attitude unfairly marginalises forms of discourse that are essential to the way in which meaning circulates within a society.

Taking his lead from recent work in cultural studies, Richardson (2016) argues that attempts to capture social and political reality must not privilege the actual over the fantastic. The manner in which agents make sense of aspects of the real world – whether nation or anorexia, security or sexual fulfilment – is never built solely on the discourses that (claim to) report the *facts* about it; rather, these factual claims are interlocked in multiple and complex ways with discourses in which imagination plays a central role. Thus, for example, understandings of politics do not draw only on government budgets, population censuses or unemployment figures, but also on narratives that articulate utopian projects of the just (or prosperous, or strong) society that is to be achieved, as well as dystopian visions of the decline and degeneracy that we risk (Glynos et al. 2009: 11–12).

The importance of such fantasies in organising and shaping social action is underscored by Fairclough and Fairclough (2012: 103, emphasis mine), who point out that 'discourses as ways of representing the world do not only describe what social reality *is* but also what it *should* be'. The world, both in its natural and human dimensions, is too complex to be fully apprehended; discursive sense-making reduces the interpretative effort that this complexity requires by selectively drawing attention to specific features and aspects of this world, and especially by defining the situation that the individual occupies and the possibilities for agency that are open within it. Within the interlocking of the actual and the fictional that makes up social life, *imaginaries* thus 'have a central role in the struggle [...] for "hearts and minds"' by orienting decision and inspiring action (Sum & Jessop 2013: 165). The ability of imaginative narratives to 'absorb a reader's full attention, to the point that real-time obligations and concerns are temporarily forgotten' (Toolan 2009: 195) allows them to engage readers' affect in ways that factual discourses can only rarely achieve.

Imaginaries can grip subjects in two different but connected forms. When explicitly construed not as actual, but rather as possible, imaginative discourses operate as projects or visions: they function as goal premises in processes of practical reasoning (Fairclough & Fairclough 2012: 107), which in turn recommend specific courses of action. But imaginaries can also gain performative power through institutionalisation and naturalisation; being collectively recognised and embedded in the norms and expectations that govern a given social domain, fantasies gain deontic actuality in that they can effectively constrain or enable specific forms of social agency. A growing body of literature suggests that the distinction between the fictional and the factual is not always reflected in audiences' sense-making: information and evaluations gleaned from fictional media can blend with non-fictional ones in their general knowledge (Marsh et al. 2003). The importance accorded to specific social issues within dramatic plots, for example, can affect audience beliefs about their social salience and significance in the real world even if the fictional nature of these narratives is recognised (Mulligan & Habel 2013); the ideational dimension of discourse comprehension is largely identical regardless of the modality value assigned to the genre (Jeffries 2015: 163).

The likelihood of this slippage between the imagined and the actual seems especially great regarding those domains where first-hand knowledge is limited. There are numerous aspects of social life that are rarely open to unmediated encounters, either because of geographical, temporal or social distance, or because they are surrounded by privacy, stigma and taboo. In such cases, it is almost impossible to disentangle the object itself from the skein of narratives and imaginings that preform it in our experience. Phenomena as varied as crime, bereavement, romantic love or sexual passion are not only experienced first, but also more frequently and with greater variety in fiction than in real life; while we have little opportunity to observe them directly and systematically (or perhaps *because* we have little opportunity to observe them), they feature prominently in imaginative discourses such as popular fiction or music lyrics (Edwards 1994: 242). Attention to such genres, then, can 'stretch critical discourse studies in ways that better reflect the ways that meanings circulate in societies' (Richardson 2016).

4.4 Literature, style and discourse

Though literature has long played a central role in enquiry into language, it has traditionally been conducted under a separate disciplinary aegis, and the relationship between linguistic and literary research has not always been cordial (Fialho & Zyngier 2014; Gupta 2015; Maingueneau 2010). Nevertheless, the intersection of these interests has received considerable attention since the 1960s under the banner of stylistics.

We can distinguish two ways in which an understanding of literature as discourse has informed this field of research. The first involves adopting the methodological repertoire of discourse studies to address questions of literary criticism, such as the work of Fowler (1989), who employs register analysis to explore characterisation. Such techniques have proved useful to describe various aspects of prose and drama, from speech acts and face threats to the management of dialogic interaction. Though corpus-based approaches remain under-represented in literary stylistics (Fialho & Zyngier 2014: 331), there is growing interest in these methods, sometimes under other disciplinary labels like digital humanities or computational analysis of style (Biber 2011: 16; Hoover et al. 2014: 3; Toolan 2009: 4). The focus of analysis in such cases, however, is framed in traditional literary terms, as 'the provision of a basis for fuller understanding, appreciation and interpretation of avowedly literary and author-centred texts' (Carter & Simpson 1989: 6). Questions of social function and impact remain marginal.

A different approach is to adopt literary or (more broadly) fictional materials as data for enquiry into language in use. Explorations of literature as a locus of social action were important in early discourse studies; the same Fowler (1981: 80) encouraged treating 'literature as discourse [...] to see the text as mediating relationships between language-users: not only relationships of speech, but also of consciousness, ideology, role and class'. Other authors such as van Dijk (1977) or Hodge (1990) embarked on similar arguments. But engagement with fiction became progressively rarer as the articulation of discourse studies with the social increasingly focused on everyday genres and their common-sense assumptions.

Gupta (2015: 200) examines how this elision of 'the literariness of the social and the socialness of the literary' was related to the contested constitution of discourse studies as separate from literary criticism. Stylisticians justified the social component of their analyses by challenging the idea of *literaturnost*, the distinctive uniqueness of literary language; if the same linguistic features that characterise literature can be found elsewhere as well, there is no principled reason for separate treatment (Fowler 1981: 21; Jeffries & McIntyre 2010: 2; Simpson 1993: 2). Critical discourse scholars, on the other hand, founded the relevance of their discipline on a socio-political engagement that excluded the more rarefied and aesthetically oriented domain of the literary. An aspect downplayed in Gupta's account, however, concerns the particular methodological and epistemological complexities posed by treating fiction as discourse while acknowledging its fictional nature (Talbot 1995: 28; Sunderland 2004: 60; Sunderland 2010: 35). Three important features that make it difficult to draw inferences about real-world discourse practices from fictional materials are the indirect and unusual nature of literary meaning-making; the multiplicity of levels and voices in fiction; and the temporal, local and even ontological dislocation that fiction allows.

The first of these issues is closely connected with the traditional conception of *literaturnost*: literary texts are characterised by the poetic drawing attention to the act of linguistic engagement rather than its function. Through the calculated use of expressions that deviate from conventional linguistic and discursive expectations, literature 'makes form palpable' in order to enhance the enjoyment of perceptual and interpretive activity (Sotirova 2015: 6). Such foregrounding is, of course, hardly limited to literature, and 'discourse can be norm-breaking in everyday usage for everyday reasons' (Toolan 2009: 25). But while non-fictional genres typically employ deviation to emphasise certain aspects of the force or sense of the message, literature is often interested in challenging expectations about the functional structure of language itself (Cook 1994: 197). This drawing of attention to the constructed nature of the text makes problematic one of the typical assumptions in discourse work: that the process of ideation is downplayed or naturalised so as to make its results uncritically acceptable to readers (Fairclough & Fairclough 2012: 121).

At the same time, the comparatively greater singularity of literary texts makes it difficult to treat them, in corpus linguistic fashion, as samples from which generalisable patterns can be drawn (Mahlberg 2015: 144). Even for analysts that do not share the literary critic's interest in the uniqueness of individual texts, the literary is methodologically challenging simply because it is less predictable and more variable than other forms of text. Nevertheless, it is important to remember that not all fiction is *literary* fiction, and in fact the kind of high literature characterised by conspicuous linguistic foregrounding is the exception rather than the norm both in terms of production and of audience. Not only modern popular genres such as chick lit or detective fiction, but also traditional narrative forms in the oral tradition, follow much stricter (if implicit) rules of composition (Opas & Tweedie 1999: 89; Semino & Short 2004: 25). There is no principled reason to assume that the range of variation is so significantly greater than in non-fictional genres that generalisations about fiction are impossible.

Even in forms characterised by predictable narrative formulae there is space for innovation; Leech (1985: 48) conceptualises these as secondary deviations from the reader's expectations about the genre, which informs savvy readers' interpretation and enjoyment of the text (Walsh, 2015: 125). This multiplication of the layers that must be considered to make sense of fiction represents a second challenge for the discourse analyst. At the most obvious level, fiction tends to be polyphonic: rather than consistently expressing a single point of view, it refracts ideas, attitudes and beliefs through a plurality of protagonists and narrative voices that may be in tension or outright conflict with one another (Toolan 2009: 193–194). In consequence, it is impossible to draw direct links between the presence of a certain representation or propositional content within the discourse and the writer's commitment to its truth. Even beyond the dialogue explicitly attributed to characters, their perspectives can colour the narrative through a variety of indirect features (Semino & Short 2004: 10ff), and carefully contextualised analysis may be necessary to identify whose point of view is being represented.

Not only variation between texts, but also within them, becomes then a critical factor in analysis. The first-order meaning created through the actions and utterances of protagonists – the *fabula* in traditional narratological terms – is never conveyed fully or directly; even if presented by an allegedly omniscient narrator, the selection of what is to be told and from whose perspective – the *syuzhet* – represents a second order of meaning that may differ from or even contradict the first through ironic, humorous or satirical presentation. Once again, none of these aspects is categorically exclusive to fiction; multi-voicedness is conspicuous in news discourse, and ironic detachment has long been prominent in advertising. But while CADS work on other genres can hope to smooth out occurrences of these phenomena within a larger body of monologic text, in fiction the refracted form of representation must be taken as the default (Sunderland 2010: 74).

A final issue when seeking to identify traces of real-world actions and attitudes in fiction is that the latter, by definition, does not deal with the real world. Fiction writers have discretion not only to set their narratives in places and times removed from that of composition – a decision that will colour readers' evaluation and interpretation of the events – but also to choose a setting that differs in important ways from reality (Sunderland 2010: 51): one in which magic exists, for example, or in which humans are hermaphroditic, or in which the Axis powers won World War 2. The distinction is not, however, absolute. Whether a story is realistic or fantastic, the events and characters it portrays must remain intelligible to readers who will interpret them on the basis of background knowledge drawn from the real world, and the default assumption will be that narrative and reality are congruent unless specific information to the contrary is provided (Tabbert 2016: 29). Fantasy thus gives the author greater scope for imagination, but the ultimate background for these fabulous elements remains the external reality that readers inhabit (Sunderland 2004: 61).

Departures from realism are nevertheless of particular interest: like stylistic norm-breaking, deviation 'on the plane of fiction-building' (Leech & Short 2007: 128) highlights aspects of the narrative that will be of significance for its interpretation. A typical way in which such deviations are employed is for allegorical or metaphorical purposes (Stephens 1992: 248): unrealistic elements in the story must be interpreted as stand-ins for aspects of the real world. Treating fiction as fiction requires then considering the choice of a specific setting – realistic or fantastic – and of the particular generic norms attached to such settings as a potentially significant aspect of the way in which a particular perspective is conveyed.

4.5 Case study: discourses of gender and sexuality in erotic writing

This case study focuses on what the analysis of erotic fiction can contribute to our understanding of discourses about gender and sexuality. As the enormous popular success of E.L. James' *Fifty Shades* trilogy illustrates, such fiction – like other forms of pornography – is an increasingly salient part of contemporary cultural life, where explicit representations of sexual activity have become staples of a range of media forms, from print to photography, film and animation (Attwood 2011). But while the fictional and unrealistic nature of pornographic narratives is readily apparent to their audiences (McKee 2010), both scholarly and popular debates about the 'pornification of society' have been quick to fixate on the impact they may have on real-world behaviours, attitudes and beliefs about sexuality and gender roles. Critical voices have claimed that pornographic discourses contribute to normalising sexual permissiveness, both in terms of increased interest in sexual matters and of acceptance of casual sex and sexual experimentation (e.g. Zillmann 2000); a more favourable take is that pornography plays an educational role, serving not only to inform about sexual anatomy and mechanics but also to destigmatise sexual desire and curiosity, especially when other sources of information are lacking, incomplete or perceived as judgemental (Albury 2014).

4.5.1 Fragmentation and stereotyping in the porn debates

One particularly contentious topic has been the relationship between pornographic discourses and issues of power in sexual relations. Porn has been criticised for 'eroticising inequality', denying female sexual agency in line with conventional ideologies and structuring its representation of women in terms of their attractiveness to men (Crabbe & Corlett 2010; Gill 2003). But for all the heat in these debates there has been a surprising scarcity of evidence; more than 25 years after Williams' (1989: 29) complaint that 'so much has been written about the issue of pornography and so little about its actual texts', there is still considerable uncertainty about the range of discourses articulated even in its mainstream varieties (for some valuable exceptions, see Baker 2005; Bolton 1995; Koller 2015; Marko 2008; Morrish & Sauntson 2007; Motschenbacher 2010).

In particular, I focus on two questions raised in critiques of gendered representation. The first is that of *fragmentation*. Analyses of sexualisation in media discourse have highlighted how bodies can be dehumanised by dismantling them into disjointed anatomical elements (Caldas-Coulthard 2008: 465): using body parts as meronymic stand-ins for the whole person dissolves our perception of a unified and conscious subject, so that they appear 'not as whole people but as fetishized, dismembered "bits", as objects' whose volition and humanity are elided (Gill 2009a: 96). A corpus approach allows us to assess whether such representations are, as is often claimed, especially characteristic of pornography as opposed to other forms of fictional or informative discourse.

The second is that of the discursive construction of *gendered bodies*. Other than those for primary – and, to some extent, secondary – sexual characteristics, terms for body parts do not directly index biological sex; there is nothing in the core semantics of lexemes such as 'nipple', 'thigh', 'belly' or 'chest' that limits their reference to either the male or female body. Nevertheless, they may acquire gendered associations on the basis of their typical contexts of appearance (Hellinger & Bußmann 2001: 11). Recurring practices of reference and description can provide insights on the social or covert gendering that colours stereotypical body talk.

4.5.2 The L1K corpus of erotic fiction

The data analysed here were collected from *Literotica.com* (2016), one of the oldest, largest and most widely read erotic fiction repositories online, archiving more than 1.5 million user-contributed stories. Though the writing advice available to contributors 'represents a normative model of a "good story" as one involving plot and character development, complexity, and non-explicit elements' (Paasonen 2010: 144), in practice texts range from elaborate novellas to wall-to-wall sexual accounts. *Literotica* imposes few restrictions on the content it will publish: only bestiality, mutilation, snuff and underage sexual encounters are banned. Within these limits taboo subjects are an 'object of emotional investment' (Paasonen 2011: 109), and some of the most popular categories concern incest, swinging, bondage and sadomasochism. The corpus analysed here comprises the top-rated 39 stories from 26 categories in the archive (excluding texts other than short stories to maintain generic consistency), totalling approximately 10 million word-tokens tagged for part of speech using the NLTK averaged perceptron tagger (Bird et al. 2009);[3] see Table 4.1 for details.

4.5.3 Fragmented bodies vs. whole subjects

Fragmentation has been observed in factual genres such as news and advertising (Attenborough 2011; Caldas-Coulthard 2008), as well as literature. After illustrating how female bodies are 'dismembered' in both traditional poetry and modern thriller fiction, Mills (1995: 133–135) suggests that this convention is so deeply gendered that it would be 'very difficult to imagine the same process being applied to the depiction of male characters'. From a corpus perspective, this hypothesis can be conceptualised by comparing the frequency of references to characters by a proper

TABLE 4.1 Corpus composition

Category	*Word count*		
	Total	*Mean*	*StDev*
Anal	315651	7915.33	7299.89
BDSM	698121	17900.54	25461.25
Celebrities	320317	8213.26	11622.66
Chain stories	255606	6554.00	6140.24
Erotic couplings	600327	15393.00	10959.56
Exhibitionist & voyeur	448255	11493.72	7848.65
Fetish	174206	4466.82	3815.70
First time	445747	11429.41	7842.80
Gay male	127106	3259.13	2344.76
Group sex	460154	11798.82	8107.83
Horror	255990	6563.85	9524.50
Humour & satire	216654	5555.23	4829.16
Illustrated	556629	14272.54	60616.45
Incest & taboo	677955	17383.46	28879.54
Interracial love	332696	8530.67	8099.91
Lesbian sex	536667	13760.69	13423.54
Letters & transcripts	81128	2080.21	1296.33
Loving wives	539128	13823.79	13255.51
Mature	308020	7897.95	6178.77
Mind control	291407	7471.97	4700.21
Nonconsent & reluctance	291595	7476.79	6671.59
Nonhuman	291778	7481.49	9336.43
Romance	553880	14202.05	7915.92
Sci-fi & fantasy	530861	13611.82	28498.40
Toys & masturbation	205513	5269.56	4205.85
Transexuals & crossdressers	258939	6639.46	6582.08
Total	**9767376**	**9632.52**	**17177.83**

name or a personal pronoun (*holonymic* references) with those in which a body part stands in for the whole person (*meronymic* references). Figure 4.1 shows that across the corpus the frequency of each type of reference varies quite widely and that each type is used largely independent of the other.

Body part terms in erotic narratives are generally overlexicalised (Marko 2008), showing the norm-breaking typically associated with literature, but their frequencies follow a typically Zipfian distribution and most occurrences are captured by a relatively limited set of terms. Table 4.2 lists the 50 most frequent ones. Many of these are immediate indicators of the *aboutness* of the corpus – making reference to male and female genitalia, breasts and nipples, buttocks and the anus, and other erogenous zones – though other anatomical terms are frequent as well; as Figure 4.2 shows, both types appear more frequently in *Literotica* stories than in general fiction as represented by the imaginative writing sections of three large reference corpora.

At first blush, such evidence seems to support the fragmentation hypothesis: participants in erotic stories are reduced to their parts – especially their private parts

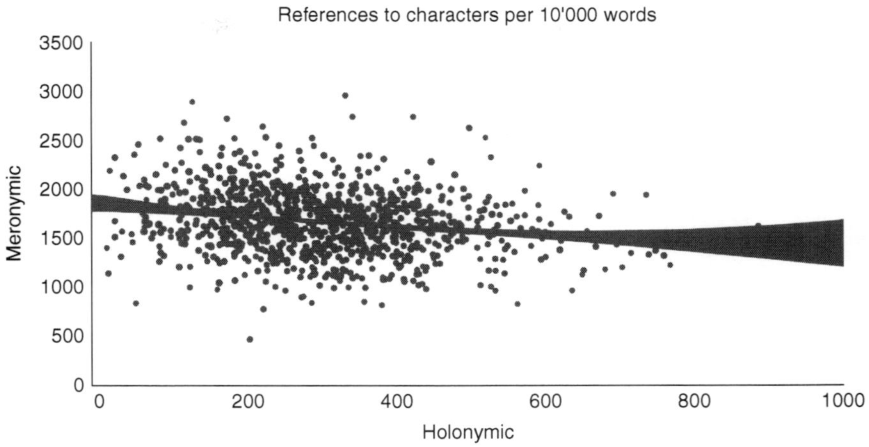

FIGURE 4.1 References to characters per 10,000 words.

– much more frequently than in other forms of writing. Nevertheless, pornographic representations do not only capture their characters in extreme close-ups of bodily action, but also frequently talk about the person as a whole. Holonymic references are in fact more common in L1K than in the reference corpora (Figure 4.3),[4] and they frequently addresses emotional, volitional and epistemic dimensions that unequivocally involve the characters' subjectivity. Their most frequent right-hand verbal collocates included terms denoting mental (WANT, WONDER, UNDERSTAND, WISH), behavioural (WATCH) and verbal processes (TELL, WHISPER, YELL), together with the more predictable material ones (TAKE, TURN, GO, WALK, WEAR). Even if these actions are less prominent in porn than in other genres (being negative keywords in comparison to the imaginative section of the BNC), they are far from absent. This suggests that the pervasive attention to bodily action and sensation does not come *at the expense* of attention to the subjects' individuality, but appears *in addition* to it. Issues of 'character motivation, desire, and sexual build-up' (Paasonen 2010: 151) provide a sustained counterpoint to the fleshy details of body part talk.

In addition, a closer look at meronymic references shows that they are not always or necessarily depersonalising. Kuhn (1985: 36) points out that Western cultural norms recognise the face as 'stand[ing] in for the person's whole being', and other forms of partial physical framing have the same effect: eyes are frequently called 'windows to the soul', and the heart is often used to refer specifically to the emotional and personal dimensions of subjectivity (Niemeier 2000). Significantly, these three meronyms occur in *Literotica* stories no less frequently than in other fiction. The narrative gaze does thus not only linger on the naughty bits; its focus on characters' physical presence is often used to provide evidence of their emotions, attitudes and reactions in the form of grinning faces, wide-open eyes or pounding heartbeats. Attention to such aspects is necessary in order to avoid the temptation of a 'paranoid reading' (Paasonen 2011: 134) that simply confirms pre-existing assumptions and criticisms of pornography as dehumanising.

TABLE 4.2 Most frequent body part terms

Lemma	*Frequency per 10,000 words*
hand	32.1690
cock	29.8498
eye	19.0423
pussy	18.7130
mouth	16.6413
body	16.4102
face	15.5727
finger	14.2311
ass	13.9417
leg	13.4345
lip	13.3589
breast	10.0222
tongue	9.7901
nipple	7.7051
hair	6.7316
hip	6.5189
thigh	5.4022
tit	4.5279
dick	4.3531
knee	4.2927
chest	4.2539
clit	4.2355
ball	4.0627
cunt	3.8203
penis	3.7518
skin	3.5442
neck	3.1137
shaft	3.0023
hole	2.7180
ear	2.5759
heart	2.5002
stomach	2.4583
butt	2.0748
asshole	2.0124
crotch	1.7108
erection	1.7056
vagina	1.5267
belly	1.3079
slit	1.2445
thumb	1.1095
chin	0.9551
ankle	0.9510
anus	0.9489
wrist	0.9142
palm	0.8947
pubic	0.8845
mound	0.8375
brain	0.7587
buttock	0.7352
clitoris	0.6698
fist	0.5757

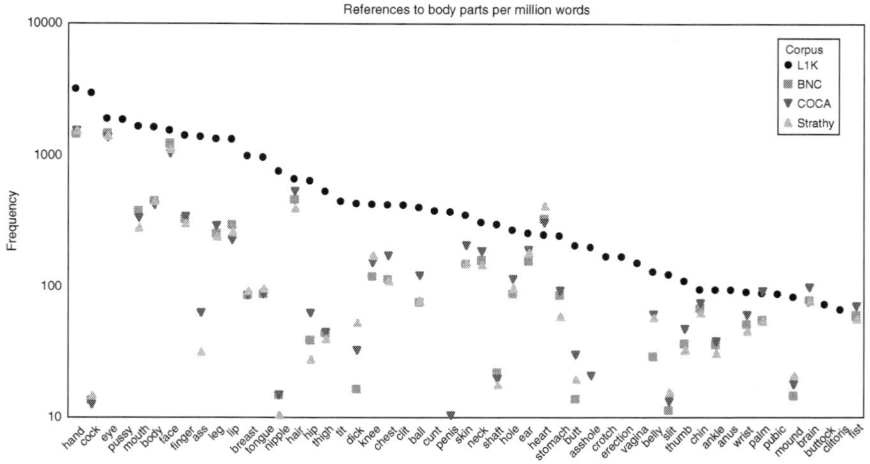

FIGURE 4.2 References to body parts per million words.

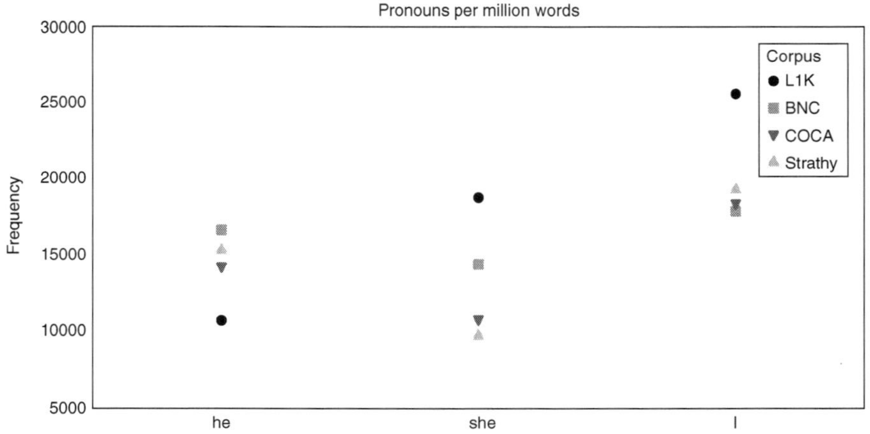

FIGURE 4.3 Pronouns per million words.

4.5.4 Gendered ideals in body talk

However, this does not mean that such criticisms can be simply ignored. Gill (2009b: 153–154, emphasis mine) argues that 'claims about the "sexualization of culture" have paid insufficient attention to the *different* ways in which different bodies are represented erotically'. Rather than taking sexualisation as an undifferentiated monolith, analysis must consider how the patterns and modes it adopts intersect with axes of social difference. Though race, class and age are all important in mediating sexualisation, I focus here on the crucial role of gender.

Figure 4.4 shows that the hyperbolic carnality of Literotica stories is unequally distributed across this axis. Other than terms for male genitalia, only a few body parts – CHEST, HAND, FINGER, CROTCH – are more characteristic of

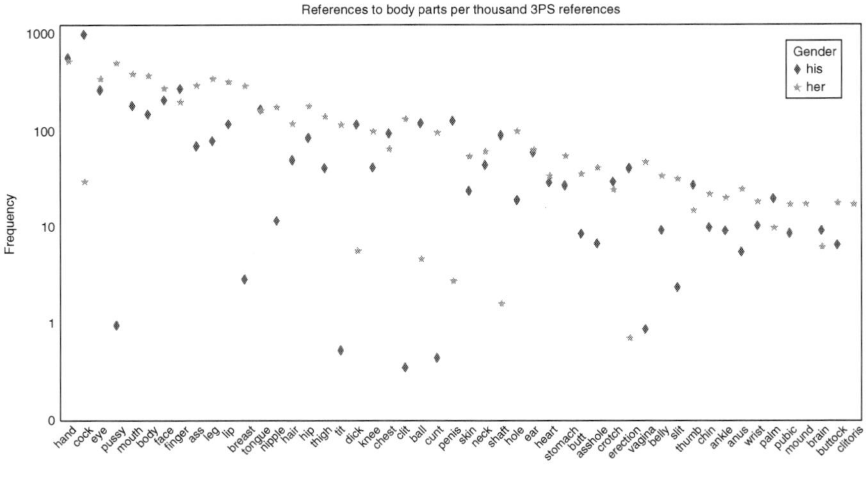

FIGURE 4.4 References to body parts per thousand 3PS references.

male representations, and even in such cases the difference is relatively minor, with log ratios ranging from 0.5 to 0.75. Facial features (FACE, EYE, EAR, TONGUE) are mentioned with roughly similar frequency regardless of gender (log ratios between -0.5 and 0.5). All other terms in the list – including references to the lower limbs, buttocks, abdomen, nipples, hair and mouth – are more frequently used to refer to female than to male characters, even if the higher overall frequency of female mentions is factored out. Body talk overall, then, seems to be stereotypically associated with a focus on women; even if most of this vocabulary has a gender-neutral core meaning, the patterns in which it routinely appears associate its semantics with femininity.

One way to explore in more detail the nuances that the discursive construction of gender superimposes over biological difference is to focus on terms that are intrinsically gendered by denoting sexually dimorphic aspects: the labelling, description and evaluation of primary and secondary sexual characteristics can illustrate normative ideals of the male and female body. Table 4.3 shows the adjectival collocates most strongly associated with terms for male and female genitalia. Though anatomical differences mean that direct lexical overlaps are unlikely, the most frequent terms on both lists focus on the visible physiological signals of arousal and orgasm. Talk about females shows greater lexical diversity, but sexual anticipation, readiness and pleasure seem to be important in characterisation regardless of gender.

Other aspects such as size, however, show sharp contrasts: male genitalia are hyperbolically large, whereas female genitalia are described as 'tiny' or 'tight' following the logic of 'heterosexual structuralism' that presents male and female bodies in binary opposition (Paasonen 2011: 125–126). Also noticeable is the importance of the lexical field of grooming in the construction of the feminine sexual ideal: while there is occasional mention of male genital shaving, it is over 40 times more frequent in talk about females. Such representational practices indicate different

TABLE 4.3 Top 25 adjectival collocates of terms for genitalia

cock			*pussy*		
Frequency	*PMI*	*Collocate*	*Frequency*	*PMI*	*Collocate*
70	7.46241	softening	154	8.29553	bald
80	7.04607	hardening	228	7.73834	shaved
40	6.78531	flaccid	84	7.72434	sopping
319	6.68866	throbbing	59	7.68823	shaven
37	6.67284	pulsating	50	7.18182	hairless
78	6.63944	twitching	84	7.10882	soaking
57	6.62675	spurting	37	7.04287	wetter
157	6.42476	stiff	54	7.01589	drenched
86	6.3587	rigid	55	6.91002	hairy
90	6.33659	engorged	46	6.80359	gaping
277	6.25406	erect	1006	6.70257	wet
197	6.23807	massive	212	6.67838	dripping
47	6.23187	impaled	41	6.63758	juicy
105	6.15508	monster	40	6.54561	oozing
204	6.15008	rock	42	6.47015	trimmed
49	6.11841	fake	90	6.31129	soaked
137	6.11756	fat	80	6.27747	glistening
80	6.10157	enormous	36	6.23671	clenching
81	5.94957	limp	97	6.23047	slick
74	5.92005	giant	37	6.22219	leaking
58	5.89642	biggest	40	6.1002	quivering
81	5.89407	aching	66	6.1002	moist
444	5.86494	huge	158	5.8873	swollen
1158	5.79897	big	513	5.86282	tight
353	5.74254	thick	238	5.84909	sweet

normative relationships towards the body: while the ideal COCK is born 'huge' or 'massive', the ideal PUSSY is achieved through extensive investment in womanscaping labour.

A second approach involves exploring the purely social gendering discursively applied to parts that are biologically and functionally equivalent in healthy human bodies. The example of EYE, salient in both male and female characterisation, is instructive (Table 4.4). Closing the eyes and opening them widely are frequent indices of emotion without a specific gender association, but other routine formulae are strikingly different. Males' eyes are primarily defined by the direction and manner of their looking: they STARE fixedly at their target, BORE through it, ROAM over it or LINGER on its sexual characteristics. Sometimes this is a result of overpowering attraction, when men can't KEEP their eyes away from the curves of a partner, sometimes deliberate, when they STRAIN their gaze to watch. Discussion of emotional expression – whether gentle or predatory – is much less common. In contrast, women's eyes are more frequently described in terms of appearance or emotion than gaze. Most of their characteristic actions are involuntary: they ROLL in

TABLE 4.4 Key collocates of eye by gender of referent, with up to three intervening words

Left of the node		*Right of the node*	
Category	*Collocate (f)*	*Category*	*Collocate (f)*
Terms associated with male referents			
expression	predatory (6)	*expression*	feeling (12), gentle (5)
gaze	keep (32), staring (28), feel (23), meet (20), let (18), strained (7)	*gaze*	leaving (20), followed (19), roamed, (16), roaming (9), bore (7), linger (6)
		target	body (40), breasts (12), ass (9), wife (9), mother (9)
Terms with similar frequency for female and male referents			
gaze	into (244 m, 342 f)	*gaze*	closed (119 m, 484 f), wide (59 m, 267 f), widened (23 m, 105 f)
Terms associated with female referents			
description	green (47), blue (24), beautiful (29)	*description*	green (53)
expression	tears (184), smile (42), wiped (33), pleading (13), welling (10)	*expression*	rolled (78), glazed (49), tears (48), fluttered (30), sparkling (29), sparkled (27), fire (13), dancing (11), cheeks (10)
gaze	opening (49), paused (10)	*action*	kissed (18), parted (10)
		target	cock (38)

annoyance, FLUTTER in abandon, SPARKLE with excitement or GLAZE with tears, often in the company of other displays of feeling such as parted lips. Emotional distress seems to be a distinctly female condition in the corpus, with collocates related to crying appearing much more frequently in references to women. A binary opposition seems at play here as well: men's eyes are presented as a site of agency and volition, whereas those of women reflect the uncontrollable welling of supervening emotion.

4.6 Evaluation: fictional stories and their real consequences

What then can we learn about the discursive construction of the gendered body from an examination of erotic fiction? The patterns of reference and description found in this corpus are in many cases congruent with those observed in other, more factual and mainstream, discourses. Rather than the misogynistic reduction of women to 'anonymous, panting playthings, adult toys, dehumanized objects to be used, abused, broken and discarded' (Brownmiller 1975: 394) suggested by anti-pornography criticism, the portrayal of female characters in porn is no more extreme in its fragmentation than that of advertising or journalism. The lavish attention devoted to the details of bodily actions and reactions is doubtlessly a significant aspect of these narratives, but interpreting it as a denial of the humanity and subjectivity of characters would be a distorting oversimplification.

The construction of the protagonists involves not just such fleshy details, but also addresses their emotional moods and responses, their cognitive capacities and their communicative engagements. Rather than being elided, as critics have argued, these dimensions appear refracted through the point of view of the narrator and presented primarily through their visible signs; though a systematic examination of the modulation of narrative point of view was beyond the remit of this chapter, corpus methods can reveal the traces of internal focalisation that provide the appearance of first-person witnessing that characterises the genre. Body talk in pornographic narratives is thus overdetermined: a good deal of it functions, in fact, as the main means of conveying the inner life of characters. If anything is neglected in porn, it is not the actions, thoughts and feelings of protagonists, but the details of the background against which they are set. Pornography is, after all, about the graphic representation of sexual activity, and the prominence of body part terms is an obvious reflection of this subject matter.

The need to take into account such contextual factors as the purpose and uses of a genre is, of course, not new to discourse analysts, but it comes into a sharper relief when fictional materials are concerned. Far too often, analyses assume that the gendered scripts present in pornographic materials are internalised by their users (e.g. Vannier et al. 2014: 254); though it is easy to recognise that erotic narratives are not intended as realistic accounts of actual sexual encounters (Baker 2005: 154), the temptation remains to interpret them as idealised versions of the sexual activities that authors and readers would like to participate in. However, such interpretations fail to address pornographic fiction as *fiction*. Erotic stories are made tellable – and therefore enjoyable – precisely by the spectacular character of the events and participants they portray, and the often-conspicuous lack of realism of their scenarios has to be understood in terms of this specific context of production and use.

From this point of view, the hyperbolic binarism with which porn portrays physical sexual characteristics is more closely linked to its appetite for transgression (Paasonen 2011) than it is to normative discourses of the properly gendered body; the profusion of massive cocks and tiny pussies is one of the ways in which pornography attempts to make engrossing the ultimately repetitive and predictable dynamics of sexual encounters. Without considering such narrative constraints, ideological interpretations are unreliable. Common-sense interpretations that explain audiences' relationship to porn in terms of identification or ideological reproduction miss the fact that their reactions are often ambivalent, and can involve as much disturbed or confused fascination as outright appeal (Paasonen 2011: 182). If the study of fiction can stretch our comprehension of the social circulation of discourses, it also requires the analysis to stretch its understanding of how these discourses are used and engaged with, recognising the complexity of attachments that go beyond the tired binary of hegemony and resistance.

Of course, acknowledging the diversity of possible engagements with fiction does not entail denying that the discourses it contains can be naïvely reproduced, but this possibility must be assessed against the background of the other sites and genres in which these discourses circulate. Erotic fiction can certainly function as an 'instructional discourse' providing audiences with normative ideas about the characteristics and dispositions they should find desirable in partners – or should adopt themselves in order to be found desirable (Baker 2005: 190). But such readings are all the more likely because of the absence of alternative spaces where open and non-judgemental discussion of sexual activities can be found. It is the existence of ill-informed – and therefore vulnerable – audiences that underscores the ideological dimension of porn, though it is equally important to bear in mind that even such audiences are equipped with critical literacies developed in their engagement with other genres. Even to relatively naïve readers the hyperbolic excess of pornographic representations may suggest their transgressive and even camp nature. For the critical analyst, perhaps the most problematic aspects of pornography – in terms of reinforcing social norms and expectations – are not the spectacular displays that have attracted critical attention, but rather those features it borrows seamlessly from factual discourses: one of the main contributions that the analysis of fiction can make to CADS is shedding light on the ways in which even our fantasies often remain bound by the assumptions and preconceptions of the society we live in.

Notes

1 I would like to thank Juliet Henderson, Elvis C. Gomes and an anonymous reviewer for invaluable feedback.
2 Texts that have a restricted circulation may still have broader indirect effects if they are taken up and reproduced by other, wider-reaching voices; political manifestos, for example, are read far less often than the media reports on their content. Nevertheless, this uptake should leave its own tangible traces in a well-designed corpus.
3 The author is grateful to Mark Allen Thornton, Princeton University, for scraping the materials and metadata.
4 For ease of visualisation I present only pronominal data in the following analyses, but the inclusion of nominal references does not introduce any significant differences.

References

Ädel, A. 2010. How to use corpus linguistics in the study of political discourse. In A. O'Keeffe & M. McCarthy (eds.) *The Routledge Handbook of Corpus Linguistics*. London: Routledge. pp. 591–604.

Albury, K. 2014. Porn and sex education, porn as sex education. *Porn Studies*, 1(1–2), 172–181.

Attenborough, F. T. 2011. Complicating the sexualization thesis: The media, gender and 'sci-candy'. *Discourse & Society*, 22(6), 659–676.

Attwood, F. 2011. Sex and the media. In K. Ross (ed.) *The Handbook of Gender, Sex, and Media*. Oxford: Wiley-Blackwell. pp. 455–469.

Baker, P. 2005. *Public Discourses of Gay Men*. London: Routledge.

Bolton, R. 1995. Sex talk: Bodies and behaviors in gay erotica. In W. Leap (ed.) *Beyond The Lavender Lexicon: Authenticity, Imagination, and Appropriation in Lesbian and Gay Languages*. Luxembourg: Gordon and Breach. pp. 173–206.

Biber, D. 1993. Representativeness in corpus design. *Literary and Linguistic Computing*, 8(4), 243–257.

Biber, D. 2011. Corpus linguistics and the study of literature: Back to the future? *Scientific Study of Literature*, 1(1), 15–23.

Bird, S., Klein, E. & Loper, E. 2009. *Natural Language Processing with Python: Analyzing Text with the Natural Language Toolkit*. Sebastopol, CA: O'Reilly.

Brownmiller, S. 1975. *Against Our Will: Men, Women and Rape*. New York: Simon and Schuster.

Caldas-Coulthard, C. R. 2008. Body branded: Multimodal identities in tourism advertising. *Journal of Language and Politics*, 7(3), 451–470.

Carter, R. & Simpson, P. 1989. Introduction. In R. Carter & P. Simpson (eds.) *Language, Discourse and Literature: An Introductory Reader in Discourse Stylistics*. London: Unwin Hyman. pp. 1–18.

Cook, G. 1994, *Discourse and Literature*. Oxford: Oxford University Press.

Crabbe, M. & Corlett, D. 2010. Eroticising inequality: Technology, pornography and young people. *Domestic Violence Resource Centre Victoria Quarterly*, 3(Spring), 1–6.

van Dijk, T. 1977. The pragmatics of literary communication. In E. Forastieri-Braschi, G. Guinness & H. López-Morales (eds.) *On Text and Context: Papers of the International Conference on Literary Communication*. Río Piedras: Editorial Universitaria. pp. 3–16.

Edwards, E. D. 1994. Does love really stink? The 'mean world' of love and sex in popular music of the 1980s. In J. Epstein (ed.) *Adolescents and Their Music: If It's Too Loud, You're Too Old*. New York: Garland. pp. 225–250.

Fairclough, N. 1992. *Discourse and Social Change*. Cambridge: Polity.

Fairclough, N. 1995. *Critical Discourse Analysis: The Critical Study of Language*. London: Routledge.

Fairclough, I. & Fairclough, N. 2012. *Political Discourse Analysis: A Method for Advanced Students*. London: Routledge.

Fialho, O. & Zyngier, S. 2014. Quantitative methodological approaches to stylistics. In M. Burke, (ed.) *The Routledge Handbook of Stylistics*. London: Routledge. pp. 329–345.

Fowler, R. 1981. *Literature as Social Discourse: The Practice of Linguistic Criticism*. London: Batsford.

Fowler, R. 1989. Polyphony in *Hard Times*. In R. Carter & P. Simpson (eds.) *Language, Discourse and Literature: An Introductory Reader in Discourse Stylistics*. London: Unwin Hyman. pp. 77–94.

Fowler, R. 1996. On critical linguistics. In R. Caldas-Coulthard & M. Coulthard (eds.) *Texts and Practices: Readings in Critical Discourse Analysis*. London: Routledge. pp. 3–14.

Gill, R. 2003. From sexual objectification to sexual subjectification: The resexualisation of women's bodies in the media. *Feminist Media Studies*, 3(1), 100–106.

Gill, R. 2009a. Beyond the 'sexualization of culture' thesis: An intersectional analysis of 'sixpacks', 'midriffs' and 'hot lesbians' in advertising. *Sexualities*, 12(2), 137–160.

Gill, R. 2009b. Supersexualize me! Advertising and the mid-riffs. In F. Attwood (ed.) *The Sexualization of Western Culture: Mainstreaming Sex*. London: I.B. Taurus. pp. 93–111.

Glynos, J., Howarth, D., Norval, A. & Speed, E. 2009. *Discourse Analysis: Varieties and Methods*. ESRC National Centre for Research Methods review paper 14. Southampton: National Centre for Research Methods. Available online at: http://eprints.ncrm.ac.uk/796/

Gupta, S. 2015. *Philology and Global English Studies: Retracings*. Basingstoke: Palgrave Macmillan.

Hellinger, M. & Bußmann, H. 2001. The linguistic representation of women and men. In M. Hellinger & H. Bußmann (eds.) *Gender Across Languages: The Linguistic Representation of Women and Men*. Amsterdam & Philadelphia, PA: John Benjamins. pp. 1–26.

Hodge, R. 1990. *Literature as Discourse*. Cambridge: Polity Press.

Hoover, D. L., Culpeper, J. & O'Halloran, K. 2014. *Digital Literary Studies: Corpus Approaches to Poetry, Prose, and Drama*. London: Routledge.

Hunston, S. 2002. *Corpora in Applied Linguistics*. Cambridge: Cambridge University Press.

Jeffries, L. 2015. Critical stylistics. In V. Sotirova (ed.) *The Bloomsbury Companion to Stylistics*. London & New York: Bloomsbury. pp. 157–176.

Jeffries, L. & McIntyre, D. 2010. *Stylistics*. Cambridge: Cambridge University Press.

Kilgarriff, A. & Grefenstette, G. 2003. Introduction to the special issue on the web as corpus. *Computational Linguistics*, 29(3), 333–347.

Koller, V. 2015. The subversive potential of queer pornography. A systemic-functional analysis of a written online text. *Journal of Language and Sexuality*, 4(2), 254–271.

Kuhn, A. 1985. *The Power of the Image: Essays on Representation and Sexuality*. London: Routledge & Kegan Paul.

Lee, D.Y.W. 2008. Corpora and discourse analysis: new ways of doing old things. In V. Bhatia, J. Flowerdew & R.H. Jones (eds.) *Advances in Discourse Studies*. London: Routledge. pp. 86–99.

Leech, G. N. 1985. Stylistics. In T.A. van Dijk (ed.) *Discourse and Literature*. Amsterdam & Philadelphia, PA: John Benjamins. pp. 39–57.

Leech, G. N. 2007. New resources, or just better old ones? The Holy Grail of representativeness. In M. Hundt, N. Nesselhauf, & C. Biewer (eds.) *Corpus Linguistics and the Web*. Amsterdam & New York: Rodopi. pp. 133–149.

Leech, G. N. & Short, M. 2007. *Style in Fiction: A Linguistic Introduction to English Fictional Prose*. 2nd ed. Harlow: Pearson Education.

McKee, A. 2010. Does pornography harm young people? *Australian Journal of Communication*, 37(1), 17–36.

Mahlberg, M. 2007. Lexical items in discourse: Identifying local textual functions of sustainable development. In M. Hoey, M. Mahlberg, M. Stubbs & W. Teubert (eds.) *Text, Discourse and Corpora: Theory and Analysis*. London: Continuum. pp. 191–218.

Mahlberg, M. 2015. Corpus stylistics. In V. Sotirova (ed.) *The Bloomsbury Companion to Stylistics*. London & New York: Bloomsbury. pp. 139–156.

Maingueneau, D. 2010. Literature and discourse analysis. *Acta Linguistica Hafniensia*, 42(S1), 147–158.

Marchi, A. & Taylor, C. 2009. If on a winter's night two researchers …: A challenge to assumptions of soundness of interpretation. *Critical Approaches to Discourse Analysis across Disciplines,* 3(1), 1–20.

Marko, G. 2008. *Penetrating Language: A Critical Discourse Analysis of Pornography*. Tübingen: Narr.

Marsh, E. J., Meade, M. L. & Roediger III, H. L. 2003. Learning facts from fiction. *Journal of Memory and Language*, 49(4), 519–536.

Mills, S. 1995. *Feminist stylistics*. London: Routledge.

Moessner, L. 2009. How representative are the *Philosophical Transactions of the Royal Society* of 17th-century scientific writing? In A. Renouf & A. Kehoe (eds.) *Corpus Linguistics: Refinements and Reassessments*. Amsterdam: Rodopi. pp. 221–238.

Morrish, E. & Sauntson, H. 2007. *New Perspectives on Language and Sexual Identity*. Basingstoke & New York: Palgrave Macmillan.

Motschenbacher, H. 2010. *Language, Gender and Sexual Identity: Poststructuralist Perspectives*. Amsterdam & Philadelphia, PA: John Benjamins.

Mulligan, K. & Habel, P. 2013. The implications of fictional media for political beliefs. *American Politics Research*, 41(1), 122–146.

Nelson, M. 2010. Building a written corpus. In A. O'Keeffe & M. McCarthy (eds.) *The Routledge Handbook of Corpus Linguistics*. London & New York: Routledge. pp. 53–65.

Niemeier, S. 2000. Straight from the heart: Metonymic and metaphorical explorations. In A. Barcelona (ed.) *Metaphor and Metonymy at the Crossroads. A Cognitive Perspective*. Berlin: Mouton de Gruyter. pp. 195–211.

Opas, L. L. & Tweedie, F. 1999. The magic carpet Ride: reader involvement in romantic fiction. *Literary and Linguistic Computing*, 14(1), 89–101.

Paasonen, S. 2010. Good amateurs: Erotica writing and notions of quality. In F. Attwood (ed.) *Porn.com: Making Sense of Online Pornography*. New York: Peter Lang. pp. 138–154.

Paasonen, S. 2011. *Carnal Resonance. Affect and Online Pornography*. Cambridge, MA & London: The MIT Press.

Partington, A., Duguid, A. & Taylor, C. 2013. *Patterns and Meanings in Discourse: Theory and Practice in Corpus-Assisted Discourse Studies (CADS)*. Amsterdam & Philadelphia, PA: John Benjamins.

Prior, P. 2009. From speech genres to mediated multimodal genre systems: Bakhtin, Voloshinov, and the question of writing. In C. Bazerman, A. Bonini & D. Figueiredo (eds.) *Genre in a Changing World*. Fort Collins, CO & West Lafayette, IA: WAC Clearinghouse & Parlor Press. pp.17–34.

Richardson, J. E. 2016. Culture, British fascism and Critical Discourse Studies. Paper presented at the CADAAD 2016 conference. Catania: Università degli Studi di Catania.

Semino, E. & Short, M. 2004. *Corpus Stylistics: Speech, Writing and Thought Presentation in a Corpus of English Writing*. London: Routledge.

Simpson, P. 1993. *Language, Ideology, and Point of View*. London: Routledge.

Sotirova, V. 2015. Introduction. In V. Sotirova (ed.) *The Bloomsbury Companion to Stylistics*. London & New York: Bloomsbury. pp. 3–18.

Stephens, J. 1992. *Language and Ideology in Children's Fiction*. London & New York: Longman.

Stubbs, M. 1997. Whorf's children: Critical comments on Critical Discourse Analysis (CDA). In A Ryan & A. Wray (eds.) *Evolving Models of Language: Papers from the Annual Meeting of the British Association for Applied Linguistic Held at the University of Wales, Swansea, September 1996*. Clevedon: BAAL. pp. 110–116.

Stubbs, M. 2001. *Words and Phrases: Corpus Studies of Lexical Semantics*. Oxford: Blackwell.

Sum, N.-L. & Jessop, B. 2013. *Towards a Cultural Political Economy. Putting Culture in its Place in Political Economy*. Cheltenham & Northampton, MA: Edward Elgar.

Sunderland, J. 2004. Gendered discourses in children's literature. *Gender Studies*, 1(3), 60–84.

Sunderland, J. 2010. *Language, Gender and Children's Fiction*. London & New York: Continuum.

Tabbert, U. 2016. *Crime and Corpus: The Linguistic Representation of Crime in the Press*. Amsterdam & Philadelphia, PA: John Benjamins.

Talbot, M. 1995. *Fictions at Work: Language and Social Practice in Fiction*. London: Longman.

Thornbury, S. 2010. What can a corpus tell us about discourse? In A. O'Keeffe & M. McCarthy (eds.) *The Routledge Handbook of Corpus Linguistics*. London: Routledge. pp. 270–287.

Toolan, M. J. 2009. *Narrative Progression in the Short Story: A Corpus Stylistic Approach*. Amsterdam & Philadelphia, PA: John Benjamins Publishing.

Vannier, S. A., Currie, A. B. & O'Sullivan, L. F. 2014. Schoolgirls and soccer moms: a content analysis of free 'teen' and 'MILF' online pornography. *The Journal of Sex Research*, 51(3), 253–264.

Walsh, C. 2015. Feminist stylistics. In V. Sotirova (ed.) *The Bloomsbury Companion to Stylistics*. London & New York: Bloomsbury. pp. 122–138.

Williams, L. 1989. *Hard Core: Power, Pleasure, and the Frenzy of the Visible*. Berkeley, CA: University of California Press.

Zillmann, D. 2000. Influence of unrestrained access to erotica on adolescents' and young adults' dispositions toward sexuality. *Journal of Adolescent Health* 27, 41–44.

PART B

Triangulation (identifying blind spots)

5

ANALYSING THE MULTIMODAL TEXT

Helen Caple

5.1 Introduction

One of the most obvious blind spots in corpus approaches to discourse studies is the fact that communication is multimodal. Language-only corpora will tell us some of the story, but they will not tell us the whole story, as confirmed by van Leeuwen (2011: 668), who states that 'many forms of contemporary written language cannot be adequately understood unless we look, not just at language, but also at images, layout, typography and colour'. Here van Leeuwen is talking about examining the distinct potential for meaning of each semiotic mode (image, gesture, speech, architecture) involved in a communicative artefact or event, or, as Kress (2010: 28) calls it, a modal ensemble. This is a complex task, and one that involves multiple methods (e.g. corpus linguistics plus multimodal discourse analysis) and careful sampling techniques. It also requires agility: in finding researchers with the necessary expertise for collaboration; compatibility and communication across various software for analysis; sufficient time to conduct analyses; and space (in publications) to be able to explicate the complexity of the findings. These are points already noted by other scholars, for example Egbert and Baker (2016: 204) in relation to triangulation, and Adolphs and Carter (2013: 178), who note that size remains a particular limitation of multimodal corpora given the time and effort involved in aligning different streams of data.

This chapter engages with the issues surrounding large-scale analyses of the modal ensemble through a case study that focuses on one form of contemporary written communication, the Instagram post (consisting of a photograph and caption), and demonstrates an analytical approach that takes into account the whole text, including non-verbal elements. It makes use of corpus-assisted multimodal discourse analysis or CAMDA (an approach developed by Bednarek & Caple 2014: 151), which entails the triangulation of corpus methods with multimodal discourse analysis. The aim of the chapter is to demonstrate the complementarity of the triangulated findings revealed through CAMDA, 'which when put together may offer a more complete view of the construct which is being investigated' (Marchi & Taylor 2009: 7).

5.2 Key terms and definitions

Since this chapter focuses on the multimodal text, it is important to be clear from the outset what is meant by the terms *multimodal*, *multisemiotic* and *multimodality*. Strictly speaking, a multimodal text combines two or more modalities, e.g. visual and aural in filmic text, and multisemiotic texts combine two or more semiotic systems such as image and language (O'Halloran 2008), e.g. a newspaper article. However, the term *multimodal* is typically used as a cover term for both multimodal and multisemiotic texts, and I do the same in this chapter. Further, I use the term *semiotic mode* to refer to meaning-making systems (image, language, gesture), and *semiotic resource* to refer to linguistic devices (e.g. temporal reference, intensifiers) and visual devices and techniques (e.g. attributes, setting, camera angle) that constitute a semiotic mode. I follow van Leeuwen (2005: 281) in defining multimodality as 'the combination of different semiotic modes – for example, language and music – in a communicative artefact or event'. However, Kress (2010: 28) uses the term 'modal ensemble' to capture the fact that this communicative event/artefact is the result of the process of '*assembling/organizing/designing* a plurality of signs in different modes into a particular configuration to form a coherent arrangement' (Kress 2010: 162, italics in original). I find the term 'modal ensemble' useful for this project, since it will be demonstrated later that key meaning potential is to be discovered in Instagram posts precisely because of the particular configurations of different semiotic modes to form a coherent arrangement.

5.3 (Corpus) linguistics and 'new' media

Much is changing in the contemporary mediated landscape of the modal ensemble. The 'pictorial turn' of the 1990s signalled both the use and study of pictures, images and iconic signs (Mitchell 2011: 69). The 2000s saw the digitization of the mass media and in the 2010s we have witnessed the dominance of select social media corporations along with their pictorial-based platforms such as Instagram that broadcast everyday micro-moments to the world. Such contemporary written communication along with blog posts, tweets, Facebook posts, etc. make use of a range of semiotic modes (still and moving images, emoticons, typography, layout and so on) that all contribute to the construction of the modal ensemble and one can only access the full meaning-potential of the text by engaging with the whole text in this multimodal richness.

While corpus linguistic studies have investigated communication in the 'new' media, including social media posts, such research has typically focused only on the language component, often with a particular linguistic feature as the object of study. Knight (2015: 21), for example, examines e-language, including blogs and tweets, but focuses specifically on the incidence and frequency of modal verb usage in order to investigate (in)directness and (im)politeness in the CANELC (1 million word) corpus of e-based communication. Hardaker and McGlashan (2016) examine the construction of identity in a corpus of tweets (912,901 words) focusing on the language of sexual aggression directed at feminist campaigner Caroline Criado-Perez. While they acknowledge the multimodal nature of computer-mediated communication, their study focuses only on the textual (typed words) component of tweets (Hardaker & McGlashan 2016: 81). Page (2014) examines corporate apologies in a dataset of 1,183 apologies that were made via Twitter, again, focusing on linguistic features and practices/strategies that establish social distance (Page 2014: 43).

As social networks, Twitter, Facebook and Instagram are formed and maintained largely through interpersonal meanings; thus there is an emerging field of research on evaluative meaning and social media. Zappavigna (2011, 2012, 2014, 2015), for example, has conducted a number of corpus studies focusing on interpersonal meaning, affiliation and the typographic convention, the hashtag, on the social media platform Twitter. The hashtag is a method of discourse tagging and a form of searchable talk (Zappavigna 2011: 799). More than just searchable talk, Zappavigna's various studies have uncovered further, mainly interpersonal, functions for the hashtag. Her 2011 study, for example, examined a Twitter corpus of over 45,000 tweets (813,310 words) collected in the 24 hours after Barack Obama's victory in the 2008 US presidential election and demonstrated how the hashtag has 'extended its meaning potential to operate as a linguistic marker referencing the target of evaluation in a tweet' (Zappavigna 2011: 788). In addition, by using the HERMES corpus of over 100 million words and close to 7 million tweets, her 2012 study asserts that 'it is interpersonal meaning that builds and sustains online social networks' (Zappavigna 2012: 11).[1]

While the verbal components of social media posts have thus been analysed by corpus linguists, the non-verbal components of new media communication have yet to attract the attention of large-scale studies in linguistics or social semiotics (but see Caple in preparation). However, a number of 'big data' studies in media, cultural studies and sociology have begun to map space, time and movement using the linguistic metadata (e.g. geotag, user information, time) associated with Instagram posts (Hochman & Manovich 2013; Highfield & Leaver 2014). Such information is obtained by querying the platform's Application Programming Interface (API) and returns a wealth of linguistic information, e.g. time and place of creation, caption, comments, hashtags, likes etc. that can be explored both quantitatively and qualitatively. Social media researchers are also starting to produce direct visualisations of 'visual characteristics', like hue, brightness and saturation in Instagram images (Manovich 2016: 3).[2] Visual analytical categories that have the capacity to be automated to a certain degree are also emerging for large-scale studies of image data. The selfie-city project, for example, uses face analysis software to analyse pose (angle, eye-contact and facial affect) in 3,840 single selfies (self-portraits taken with the front-facing camera of a smartphone) shared on Instagram (see selfiecity.net; Manovich 2016: 2).

In linguistics, the development of analytical frameworks for the qualitative analysis of meanings in images, e.g. the system of subjectification (Zhao & Zappavigna 2015), have been applied to small scale analyses of images posted to Instagram. Zappavigna (2016: 277) claims that 'the essential principle behind a user's Instagram stream is an ongoing display of self to the ambient audience' and suggests therefore that 'a new description is needed to explain the relationship construed in social photographs between the *photographer* and the viewer where the subjectivity of the photographer is signalled either by compositional choices or through inclusion of parts of the photographer's body within the frame' (p. 277, italics in original). Also focusing on the selfie image, Zappavigna demonstrates the relationship of 'imagining oneself as being' or 'being in fusion with' the image producer, and concludes that the viewer is invited to 'approach the image as if they were sharing in the photographer's subjective experience' (2016: 289).

To conclude this section, while it is now widely acknowledged that the visual content in contemporary written (and spoken) communication is an important aspect of meaning-making (Hjorth & Burgess 2014; Highfield & Leaver 2014; see Hutchby 2014 and Adolphs et al. 2015 in relation to spoken discourse), research engaging fully with the multimodal aspects of social media texts is still in its infancy. Large-scale studies tend to focus on the linguistic metadata only, ignoring the visual (Manikonda et al. 2014; Highfield & Leaver 2014), and qualitative studies have so far focused on one aspect of meaning-making in the image and ignored the verbal (Zappavigna 2016). Research examining the whole text as a modal ensemble, i.e. bringing analyses of both the verbal and visual elements of a social media post together, and on a large scale, are still rare. However, a new approach combining corpus linguistic methods with multimodal discourse analysis (CAMDA) is a first step in addressing the complex issues surrounding such analyses, and is an attempt at reducing the partiality of corpus and discourse analysis, as exemplified in the next section.

5.4 The contribution of CAMDA to reducing partiality

CAMDA combines corpus linguistic analysis with qualitative multimodal discourse analysis and is the approach that will be employed in the case study in this chapter. To date it has been applied to relatively small multimodal corpora, but has demonstrated the value in bringing these different methods together. Bednarek (2015) reviews how multimodal analysis can be and has been incorporated into corpus linguistic research (e.g. designing and interrogating multimodal corpora; combining corpus linguistic and multimodal discourse analysis in various ways), but her focus is on film and TV series, and she only undertakes a small case study. Nevertheless, the multimodal analysis undertaken in the study adds insights into affective meaning, personality and how characters relate to each other (Bednarek 2015: 82) – aspects of meaning-making that cannot be gleaned from the verbal text alone.

In a more comprehensive study, Bednarek and Caple (2017a) use CAMDA to investigate the construction of news values in a small corpus of 99 online news items whose URLs were shared many times among users via Facebook. They found that the establishment of news values conforms to the strengths of each semiotic mode. However, by aligning the verbal and visual streams of analyses using a relational database, they further demonstrate how the construction of multiple news values accumulates across semiotic modes (Bednarek & Caple 2017a: 219). This suggests that both semiotic modes are important in establishing newsworthiness, since they each construe different, complementary aspects of an event as newsworthy.

As the large-scale analysis of multimodal texts is very complex, it requires triangulation on multiple levels and the bringing together of expertise in: linguistic and multimodal/semiotic analysis; corpus linguistic and multimodal analysis software and their integration with each other; and the development of tools for presenting or visualising the results of such analyses in a way that is meaningful to readers. Inroads have already been made into some of these areas (Bednarek 2015: 67–68), and this chapter aims to contribute further to this body of work.

5.5 Case study: the Australian federal election and Instagram

The remainder of this chapter presents a case study investigating Instagram posts (consisting of a photograph and caption) made in relation to the Australian federal election in July 2016 (for a very different view of how the 2016 election played out on social media (Twitter) see Bruns 2016). It makes use of CAMDA to explore the contributions of both corpus methods and multimodal discourse analysis to our understanding of how Australians responded to the election through their posts to this social media platform. The research question posed is both a simple and ambitious one: Can CAMDA shine a light on the blind spots of corpus approaches to discourse analysis and thereby tell us the whole story?

5.5.1 Brief background to the Australian federal election

The 2016 Australian federal election, held on 2 July, was a double-dissolution election, which meant that members from both houses (Senate and House of Representatives) were up for re-election. The double-dissolution was triggered by the inability of the government to pass three bills: Building and Construction Industry (Consequential and Transitional Provisions) Bill 2013; Building and Construction Industry (Improving Productivity) Bill 2013; and the Fair Work (Registered Organisations) Amendment Bill 2014. On 7 May, incumbent (conservative) Prime Minister Malcolm Turnbull asked the governor-general of Australia to dissolve parliament and set the election date to 2 July. Both houses were duly dissolved on 9 May resulting in one of the longest campaign periods (56 days) since the 1960s. With all members of parliament up for election, there were 994 nominees in the lower house and 631 in the Senate (AEC 2017). Since all states and territories have different numbers of seats allocated, the ballot papers are all slightly different from each other. The white Senate paper in the state of New South Wales, for example, had 12 seats, 42 columns and 151 individual candidates listed. The subsequent size of the Senate ballot paper attracted several comments (realised both verbally and visually) on Instagram, as exemplified in Figure 5.1.

EXAMPLE A

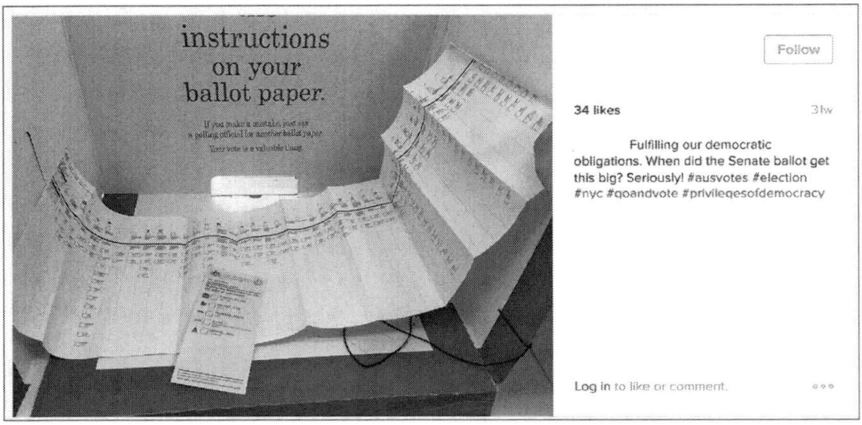

EXAMPLE B

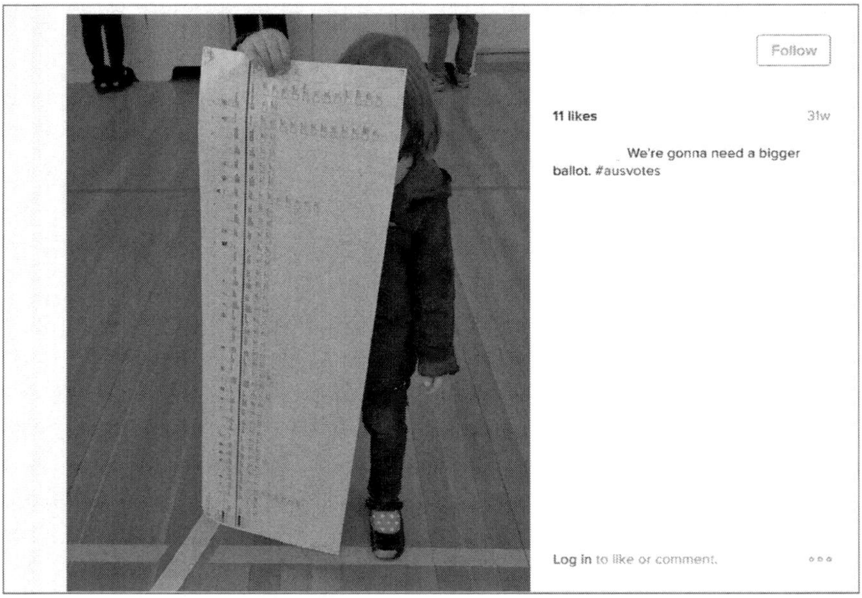

FIGURE 5.1 Instagram posts commenting multimodally on the size of the ballot paper.

The major political parties (according to the percentage of votes won in previous elections) contesting the 2016 federal election were the incumbent Liberal/National Coalition (conservative), the Australian Labor Party and the Australian Greens (commonly known as the Greens).

Since this case study is attempting to gauge the response to the election, it is necessary to explain some of the distinctive features of Australian elections to better account for the sentiments expressed in the posts to Instagram. Australia has compulsory voting, and some Australians see voting as participation in a democratic process, a civic duty that can be demonstrated by voting below the line (i.e. numbering all 151 boxes in order of preference on the white Senate paper shown in Figure 5.1). Voting takes place at polling places, located at primary schools and town halls, and at peak times during voting hours can see queues snaking through playgrounds and along the street. Polling stations also often set up baked goods stalls, which sell cakes and cookies as fundraisers for community/school events, and a BBQ stand for a sausage sizzle. This is where the uniquely Australian 'democracy sausage' comes from. In its truest form, it consists of a sausage or 'snag' in Australian English (with fried onions and various sauces optional) encased in a slice of white bread (Example A, Figure 5.2), and deviations from this form are met with derision (Example B, Figure 5.2; see Zappavigna 2014 for a linguistic study of the hashtag *#democracysausage* on Twitter). The sausage sizzle is also cited on social media as the key incentive for participating in the voting process, over and above the $20 fine one receives for failing to vote.

5.5.2 Collecting Instagram posts relating to the 2016 Australian federal election

Like the social media platform Twitter, posts to Instagram often include hashtags: discourse co-ordinators that serve many functions including to signal the topic of the post, to create humour, to signal the target of evaluation, and to convene with other Instagrammers (people who post to Instagram), often emotionally, around a theme or event (Zappavigna 2011; Bruns & Burgess 2015). As this case study will demonstrate, Instagram users posting in relation to the Australian federal election are well-versed in the multiple functions of hashtags.

A hashtag was used as the search term for collecting posts relating to the 2016 federal election, and the data collection period was five days: two days before the election, the day of the election (2 July) and two days after the election.[3] Deciding which hashtags to search for and collect was based on examination of previous research on Australian elections, hashtags and social media, and through observation of Instagram during the campaign period, before the data collection period began. Two enduring or established hashtags *#auspol* and *#ausvotes* have been used on Twitter for a number of years (Zappavigna 2014; Bruns & Burgess 2015). *#auspol* (Australian politics) emerged on Twitter in early 2010 (Bogle 2016) and is widely held to be the co-ordinator of general discussion of everyday political events in Australia (Zappavigna 2014; Bruns & Burgess 2015; Bogle 2016) and

EXAMPLE A

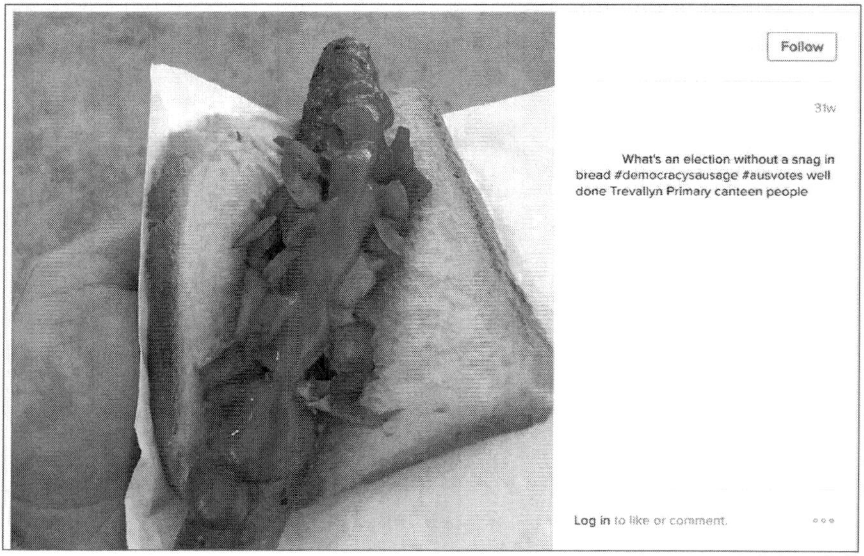

EXAMPLE B

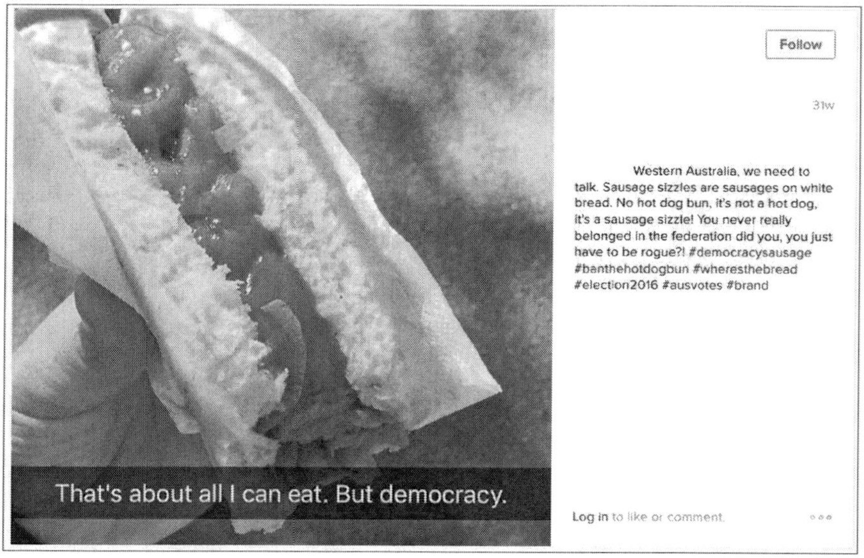

FIGURE 5.2 An Instagram post showing a classic democracy sausage (Example A) and one showing an aberrant version (Example B).

has a continuous presence in social media. *#ausvotes*, on the other hand, tends to emerge and recede around the time of state and federal elections (as evidenced in Figure 5.3), as it relates more specifically to the voting process. For this case study posts using *#auspol* were not collected, due to its more persistent use year-round and more general focus, while posts using the more pertinent hashtag to the federal

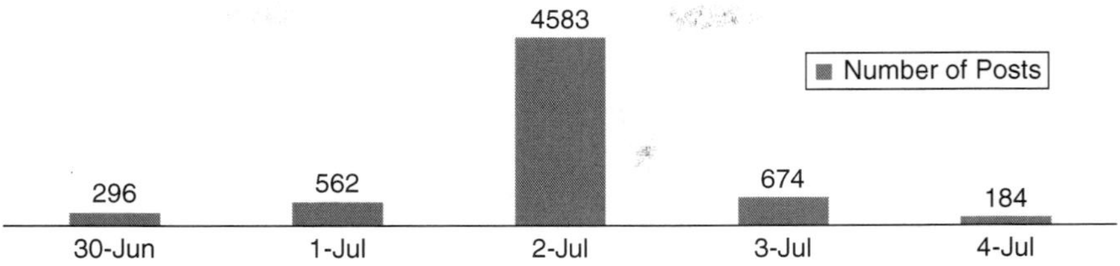

FIGURE 5.3 Number of posts collected using #ausvotes.

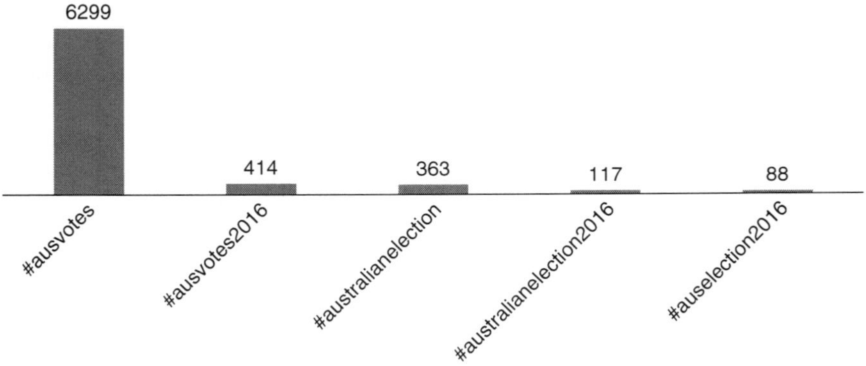

FIGURE 5.4 Total number of Instagram posts per hashtag, June 30 to July 4, 2016.

election *#ausvotes* were monitored and collected, resulting in a more specialised corpus relating specifically to the 2016 federal election. As 2 July drew closer, and from observations of Instagram, a number of ad hoc hashtags emerged (e.g. *#ausvotes2016, #auselection2016*). These were also monitored and collected as a point of comparison, and as Figure 5.4 shows, posts using these hashtags were far less frequent. The use of competing hashtags could well be the result of Instagrammers, who are not yet apprenticed into communities forming around particular events, experimenting with a variety of hashtags, or as Bruns and Burgess (2015: 22) suggest 'including multiple potential hashtags in their message in order to ensure that it is visible to the largest possible audience'. Most posts using *#auselection2016*, for example, also listed the other more well-known hashtags, as shown in the following example caption: '*Watching this election like... #auspol #ausvotes #auselection2016.*'

Posts using *#ausvotes*, including the photograph, caption (verbal text and hashtags) and other linguistic metadata such as location, date, time, username, user bio, and the number of likes, followers and following, were collected using a combination of manual and automated data collection methods. Photographs were collected into folders and assigned unique ID numbers, while linguistic data was saved as a UTF-8 encoded TXT file that can be exported into a number of software programs, including AntConc (Anthony 2014), FireAnt (Anthony & Hardaker 2017), MS Excel spreadsheets and relational databases. Each linguistic entry (post) is also linked to each image via the unique ID number assigned to the image.

Analysing both verbal and visual elements of each Instagram post concurrently involves importing all the data into a software interface such as a relational database, as will be demonstrated later in the chapter. The next section introduces how the data has been scrutinized using these various software programs and then presents the results of the analyses carried out on the data collected.

5.5.3 Using AntConc to interrogate the caption (Phase 1: Mono-modal analysis)

Given the complexity of both the data set itself and the different ways in which it has been interrogated, I made use of a topology (Figure 5.5) for situating the analysis (Bednarek and Caple 2017a: 9–11) at each stage in the process. This should act as a means of guiding the reader through what each approach brings to our understanding of how Australians responded to the election through Instagram.

Phase 1 of the analysis interrogated the captions used on each post using AntConc and was situated in Zone 2 of the topology, since it entailed the mono-modal (intrasemiotic) analysis of the captions (verbal text and hashtags) across all 6,299 posts using the hashtag #ausvotes. In this chapter, I use the term 'caption' to refer to any text that is placed in the space below or to the side of the image, and that is included in the original Instagram post. This 'text' may be made up of meta-data only (lists of hashtags, or @user mentions, used to tag a particular social media user), as shown in example 3 in Table 5.1, and which accounted for 7 per cent of the contributions using #ausvotes. The caption may consist of verbal text only, ranging from nominal groups and fragments, e.g. '*Democracy cake*', '*Stealing votes and stealing hearts*', to clauses and sentences, e.g. '*There's nothing like the smell of corfluting in the morning*', '*Oh, and be nice to ALL of the volunteers, even if you think the party they're volunteering for is lame*'; or it may be a combination of both metadata and verbal text. In some cases, the hashtag may be integrated into the linguistic structure of the verbal

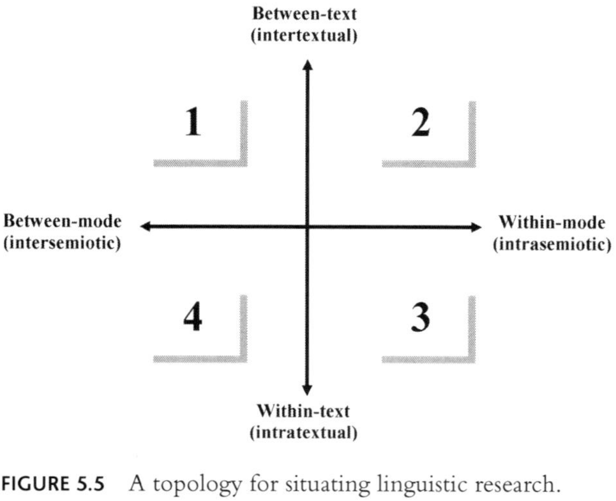

FIGURE 5.5 A topology for situating linguistic research.

TABLE 5.1 Make up of captions in Instagram posts

Caption:	*Number*	*%*	*Example text:*
Verbal text + metadata (hashtags)	5841	93	(1) Great crowd in #Wodonga tonight for #thefeedSBS coverage of #indivotes. #ausvotes (2) Wasted vote some may say but comedy is never wasted. #ausvotes2016 #ausvotes #fuckturnbull #kebab
Metadata only	458	7	(3) #malcomturnbull #malcom #australia #ausvotes #votes #election #fuckyou #government #patriotism #kickthisgovernmentout

text, e.g.'*I didn't get a #democracysausage today, but in lieu of that, I'm holding my #ausvotes parties-to-vote-for scribble paper*', as in-line metadata (Zappavigna 2012: 85; and example 1 in Table 5.1), or listed at the end of the verbal text (as in example 2 in Table 5.1). Such use accounted for 93 per cent of all posts in the #ausvotes corpus.

The use of emoticons in Instagram posts is highly frequent, with *emoji* appearing either first or second in frequency lists across all data sets captured. However, given the space constraints of this chapter it is not possible to account for their use in this case study (but see Vidal et al. 2016 on their use and meaning on Twitter).

A frequency list using AntConc's default settings gave 17,253 word types (from a total of 132,909 tokens) in the #ausvotes corpus.[4] Further, due to the nature of the initial data capture, the captions were entered into AntConc as a single file. Thus it was not possible to assess dispersion/range across each caption.[5] The top 20 most frequent words in the #ausvotes corpus are shown in Table 5.2.

The most frequent lexical words *election, vote* and the hashtag *#auspol* confirm that the topic of the verbal text remained focused on the election and/or the political process, while the lexeme *australia* confirms the location of the election. From the most frequent non-lexical items, I examined *the, a, to,* and *for* using three-word clusters with a minimum frequency of 10 and with the determiners *the* and *a* in the L1 position and with *to* and *for* in both the L1 and R3 positions. Looking at three-word clusters has the advantage of being more frequent than longer clusters, while also providing useful information about how such grammatical words are used. Table 5.3 presents the results of this analysis.

As can be seen in Table 5.3, the majority of three-word clusters involving these most frequent word forms are clearly related to the semantic field of elections and to issues of importance to Australian voters: the right to vote, key policy issues, civic duty and opportunity for change, and very few are varied in their focus. This adds further evidence to the claim that this is a very cohesive corpus and that the topic remains firmly focused on the election, voting, democratic obligation/duty and right, and, of course, the central role of the sausage sizzle.

By expanding our view to the top 100 most frequent words, the continued presence of words associated with the political process such as *democracy, voting, polling, electionday, voted, politics,* and *booth*, further demonstrate that the conversation in

TABLE 5.2 Top 20 word forms in the #ausvotes corpus

Rank	*Word form*	*Frequency*	*Rank*	*Word form*	*Frequency*
1	the	4304	**11**	i	1435
2	emoji	2787	**12**	vote	1400
3	to	2640	**13**	s	1067
4	election	2611	**14**	is	1042
5	a	2155	**15**	on	912
6	and	2088	**16**	you	903
7	auspol	1771	**17**	it	894
8	for	1756	**18**	australia	889
9	in	1707	**19**	this	878
10	of	1562	**20**	my	823

TABLE 5.3 Three-word clusters among most frequent non-lexical words

Word form	*Used in association with the elections*	*With varied uses*
The	the polling booth; the sausage sizzle; the seat of; the federal election; the election results; the right to; the election coverage; the future of*; the ballot paper; the senate ballot; the great barrier*; the house of*; the rest of*; the results of; the australian federal; the people of*; the polling booths; the smell of*	the link in; the next few
To	to vote for; to vote in; to vote today; to vote cards; to the polls; to have a*; to live in*; to vote at; to vote and; to exercise my; to the polling; to see the*	
	t forget to*; the right to; out how to*; is going to*; thank you to*; democratic right to; looking forward to*; a chance to*; i want to*; my right to*; re going to*; too close to*; you want to*	
A	a sausage sizzle; a vote for; a democracy sausage; a hung parliament; a lot of*; a bit of*; a chance to*	a.akamaihd.net
for	for the greens; for the next*; for the sausage; for what matters; for the future*; for election night	
	to vote for; june – pray for*; a vote for; you vote for; m voting for; standing up for	

*Concordance lines were examined to confirm that these three-word clusters also referred to the election.

these Instagram posts does not deviate from the election. Seemingly unusual word forms like *democracysausage* (ranked 24) point to the unique nature of Australian elections (noted above) and the important place that this particular food has in the Australian psyche. In the top 100 most frequent words, we also get first mentions of political parties with *greens* ranked 38 with 421 instances and *labor* ranked 47 with 302 occurrences (*liberal* is ranked 104 with 147 instances). Examining the concordance lines for these word forms confirms that these are references to the major political parties contesting the election. From such results, it might be tempting to claim that the Greens are talked about the most in this corpus. However, closer inspection of the captions shows that such word forms may appear several times in one post, as in the following caption: '*I love the Greens because the Greens love what I love. #love #Greens16 #AusPol #AusVotes #LetsDoThis #Election16 #greensforsturt*,' where *greens* is mentioned four times. Thus, a qualitative dimension needs to be added to the analysis to get at such usage (but see Endnote 5 on data collection changes that have eliminated this problem). Adding in closer examination of the hashtags used in this corpus not only confirms that the topic is clearly focused on the election (Table 5.4), but also that some Instagrammers take a negative stance towards certain political parties (Table 5.5). Taking a stance in a social media post has also been shown to be a strategy for 'ambient affiliation' (Zappavigna 2012: 87) with other social media users, who may share the sentiments being expressed. Thus, the (dis)affiliative strategies Instagrammers use to show allegiance with or distance from political parties also function to create communities with other like-minded Instagrammers.

By changing AntConc's global settings to include # as a User-defined Token Class, a word list of all hashtags used in the #ausvotes corpus can be generated, and ordered according to number of instances. Table 5.4 shows the top 10 hashtags used in the #ausvotes corpus. The Greens are the only major party to feature in the top 10. Again, this would suggest that the Greens are represented the most in the #ausvotes corpus. However, closer inspection of the range of hashtags relating to political parties presents a much more nuanced picture. Table 5.5 lists references to political parties made via hashtags, consisting of five instances or more. These include naming major parties (*#greens* (n=281), *#labor* (n=147), *#liberal* (n=69)), key politicians (*#billshorten* (n=46), *#malcolmturnbull* (n=44)) and electorates where a party has a safe sitting member (*#wentworth* (n=23), *#grayndler* (n=18)). Key slogans used throughout the campaign are also prevalent with *#jobsandgrowth* (n=37) for the Liberal Party, and *#savemedicare* (n=60) and *#betterfuture* (n=42) featuring prominently for Labor. The hashtags also give an indication of voter preferences from the more formal *#voteliberal* (n=7), through the less formal *#golabor* (n=8), to diminutives such as *#albo* (n=5) (referencing Labor's Anthony Albanese) and the

TABLE 5.4 Top 10 most frequently used hashtags in the #ausvotes corpus

Number of instances	*Hashtag*
1720	#auspol
1321	#election
706	#democracysausage
488	#australia
283	#vote
281	#greens
256	#electionday
215	#democracy
173	#federalelection
155	#politics

TABLE 5.5 Hashtags mentioning the major political parties (n=<5)

Party	*Total number of mentions*	*Examples*
Labor	718	#labor, #thisislabor, #alp, #savemedicare, #billshorten, #betterfuture, #votelabor, #medicare, #labour, #grayndler, #gellibrand, #australianlaborparty, #lindaburney, #protectmedicare, #laborandproud, #laborparty, #wills, #golabor, #shorten, #wearelabor, #barton, #albo, #australianlabourparty, #dogsofaustralianlabor, #walabor, #wearewalabor, #whitlam
Greens	487	#greens, #thegreens, #votegreen, #australiangreens, #votegreens, #green, #adam, #batman, #greenout, #gogreens, #jasonball, #jasonforhiggins, #adambandt, #greensaustralia, #richarddinatale
Liberal	394	#liberal, #malcolmturnbull, #jobsandgrowth, #lnp, #wentworth, #teamwarren, #primeminister, #turnbull, #teamentsch, #liberalparty, #higgins, #warringah, #backingbarnaby, #nationals, #coalition, #liberals, #voteliberal, #liberalpartyofaustralia, #malcomturnbull, #votingliberal, #barneyarmy, #chisholm, #juliebishop
Anti-Liberal	174	#puttheliberalslast, #putlibslast, #putthelibslast, #votelnplast, #fizza, #putliberalslast, #tonytimetogo, #putlnplast, #imissmalcolm, #libslast, #puttheclplast, #putthelnplast

playful and intertextually loaded *#barneyarmy* (n=5) (referencing Nationals MP Barnaby Joyce).

What also becomes clear by examining the hashtags more closely is the volume of anti-Liberal sentiment expressed via hashtags (Table 5.5), through which Instagrammers mainly urge voters to put the Liberals last on the ballot paper. No other political party attracted such a large amount of negative evaluation through the use of hashtags. Investigating how Instagrammers demonstrate their (dis)affiliation with various political parties is one way to assess how Australians responded to the election. Analysis of the hashtags shows clear positive preferences for the Greens and Labor while the Liberal Party attracts both lovers and haters.

The extent to which one could argue that Instagram is a good predictor of the election results is open to interpretation. The Liberal/National Coalition, which received the most negative responses on Instagram, did eventually win the election, but having opted for the double dissolution election, the Liberals had been hoping to increase their majority. Instead, the election almost ended in a hung parliament, with neither of the major parties able to form a majority government, until the Liberals eventually inched ahead. Labor gained 14 seats, and on Instagram Labor received the most favourable coverage, while the Greens had a somewhat disappointing election, but very positive coverage on Instagram.

Further qualitative corpus linguistic analysis of the captions using concordances would reveal other affiliative strategies as realised linguistically. However, I am going to examine this through a different method, as this chapter is charged with tackling the multimodal text. Instagram is an image-centric social media platform and as Figure 5.6 demonstrates, political parties are also represented visually in the #ausvotes corpus, and not necessarily verbally. In both examples in Figure 5.6, the verbal text makes no mention of any political party, but the images clearly reference the Greens (in example A) and the Liberal Party (in example B). Visual resources deployed in these images are also clearly evaluative, showing affiliation with the Greens (thumbs up) but distancing from the Liberals (obscene gesture). Further, as a modal ensemble, one can assess the voting preference of (A) through the combination of caption and image, which can be verbally rendered as 'I voted for the Greens'. These examples from the #ausvotes corpus highlight two key blind spots in studies that only consider the verbal component of contemporary written communication: the inability to assess the full range of representational and evaluative strategies deployed across the whole text (realised across a range of semiotic modes); and the inability to assess the ways in which words and images jointly construct meaning as a modal ensemble (as shown in Figure 5.6). In a corpus like #ausvotes, assessing evaluative meaning is central to understanding how Australians responded to the federal election, and this evaluation is constructed multimodally. Thus, we now move onto Phase 2 of the analysis of the #ausvotes corpus, analysing both words and images together.

5.5.4 Using a relational database to interrogate the accumulation of evaluative meaning across words and images (Phase 2: Multimodal analysis)

Since the focus of phase two of the analysis of the #ausvotes corpus shifts from mono-modal to multimodal (intersemiotic) analysis across a number of texts, this analysis is located in Zone 1 of the topology presented in Figure 5.5. Further, because this is a qualitative multimodal analysis and is inherently more time-consuming, it becomes necessary to down sample in order to make the analysis more realistic/achievable. There are a number of ways in which one could down sample from the #ausvotes corpus depending on the research focus. The corpus linguistic analysis has already revealed that Instagrammers not only mention the political parties, but also (dis)affiliate with them, and the researcher could continue to investigate these, focusing on one or more of the major parties, which is the pathway this chapter will pursue (for an explanation of other ways in which a corpus of this nature could be down sampled see Caple in preparation). For now, the focus returns to the question of how Instagrammers relate to political parties contesting the election, and whether the addition of the multisemiotic aspects of the Instagram post tells us more than the language-only corpus linguistic analysis.

The multimodal analysis was conducted using a relational database (MS Access), where image and linguistic data can be co-hosted and analysed in the same interface

EXAMPLE A

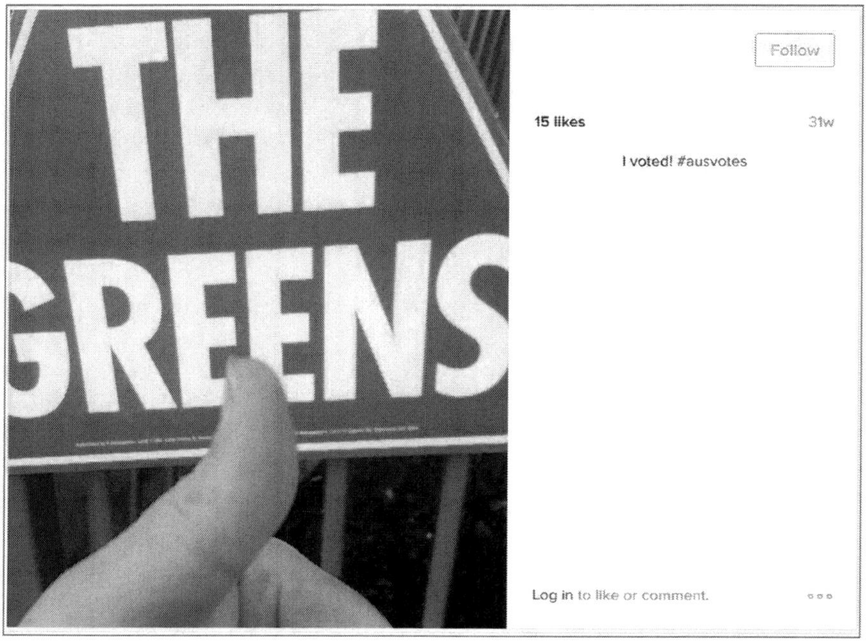

EXAMPLE B

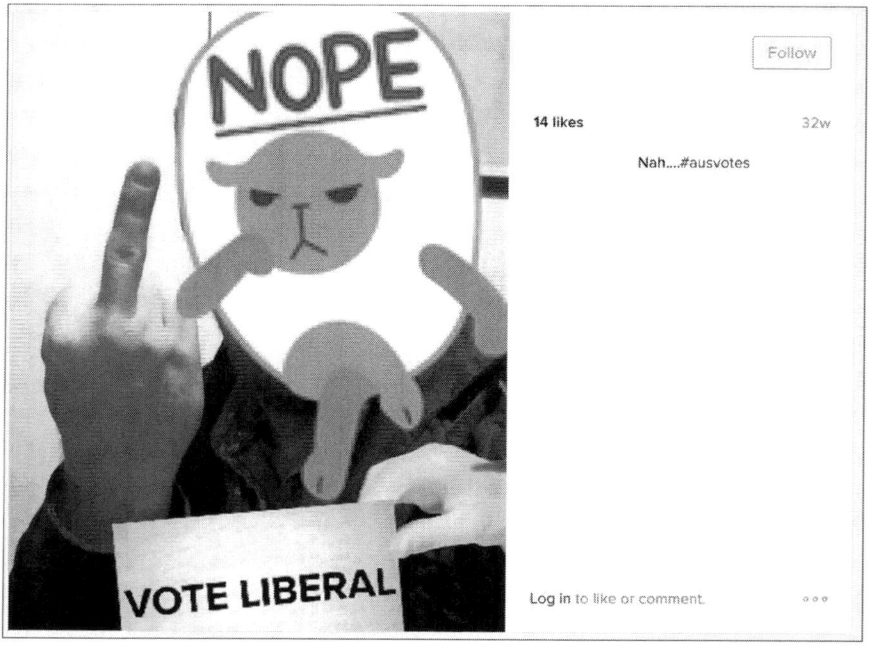

FIGURE 5.6 Examples of political party representations in images.

(Figure 5.7). Any number of queries of the collected analysis can be created, which allows the researcher to also examine text–image relations. In the remainder of this section, I focus only on two of the major political parties, the Liberal/National Coalition and the Greens, as these two parties are highly represented in the linguistic data (but at the same time are of a manageable size for multimodal analysis) and are furthest away from each other ideologically. Thus, one might expect Greens supporters to not only affiliate with the Greens but to distance themselves from the Liberals/Nationals, and vice versa. I also only look at posts made by members of the public (rather than those made by the press, politicians or PR organisations), as a means of further delimiting the size of the data set. The total number of posts analysed multimodally is 982.

First, the pic_caption field was filtered to show all instances of *green**, then all instances of *lib** and *national**. The fields assessing where (dis)affiliative strategies were deployed in the image, verbal text or hashtag and in relation to which party were then populated for each post (Figure 5.7). Once this analysis was completed, all remaining images posted by members of the public were assessed for further (dis)affiliative strategies realised visually.

Visual semiotic resources coded as 'affiliating' with a particular party included positive gestures along with signage (as in Figure 5.6 Example A), items of clothing (e.g. campaign t-shirts, caps or badges, and clothing of a particular colour associated with a particular party – green for the Greens, blue for Liberal/National – worn by image participants and forming the point of focus in the image), colour filters applied to the image (e.g. green filter to show support for the Greens), posters or how-to-vote leaflets for a particular candidate or party, or linguistic text added to the image (as in Figure 5.7).

Visually distancing strategies include those realised through obscene gestures (as in example B in Figure 5.6), especially in relation to the 'vote Liberal' SnapChat filter that the Liberal party created, through negative verbal text in the image, on posters

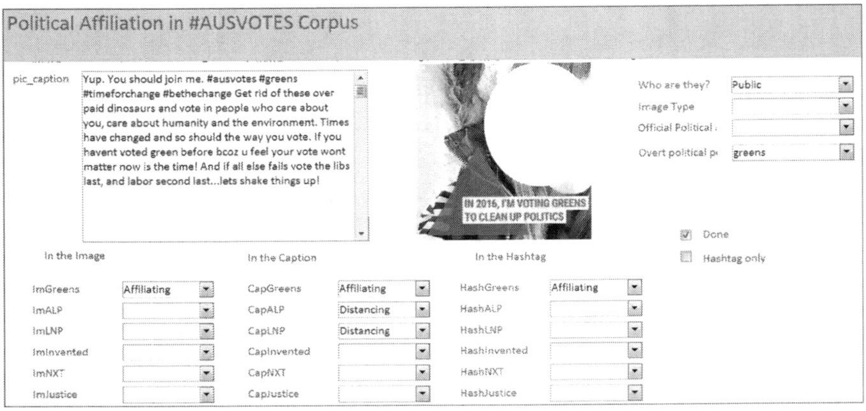

FIGURE 5.7 Relational Database Interface for multimodal analysis of political affiliation in #ausvotes corpus.

(and the defacing thereof) and in relation to the #savemedicare campaign which handed out fake Medicare cards with the words 'PUT THE LIBERALS LAST!', as in example A in Figure 5.8. Close up shots of ballot papers with the party numbered last also indicate visual distancing strategies. The Liberal Party also attracted the most negative memes (example B in Figure 5.8). Memes include formulaic language (and intertextual references) often with typographic devices such as hashtags and image-text combinations, and are deployed for social bonding rather than for sharing information (Lankshear and Knobel 2006: 101). Photographs including the Fizza poster were also coded as distancing from the Liberal Party (example C in Figure 5.8). This poster was created by artist Michael Agzarian from a quote made by former Labor Prime Minster Paul Keating who said of Liberal leader Turnbull (featured in the poster) 'You light him up, there's a bit of a fizz, but then nothing ... nothing' (Hack 2016).

Affiliative strategies in the caption text and hashtags included the use of commands (Vote Green, #vote1green), statements clearly stating how the person voted, e.g. '*I voted Greens*', the inclusion of evaluative language further reinforcing voting preference, e.g. '*I'm proud to vote #ausgreens in this election*', '*Super happy to volunteer for @adambandt today*'.

Verbal distancing strategies include the command form plus negation, as in '*Don't vote LNP*', or '*Don't vote for these green galahs*', the negative evaluation of a party and/or its policies, '*The LNP have had their chance & blown it*,' and putting the evaluation inside the hashtag, as in the many variations on *#putthelibslast* shown in Table 5.5, and which Zappavigna (2012: 93) suggests 'flags the universality of the complaint/feeling, as it suggests that others share the same experience'. The results of this analysis are summarised in Figure 5.9.

The results of the qualitative multimodal analysis shown in Figure 5.9 demonstrate first that Instagrammers are far more likely to show their affiliation with the Greens through images than in words. In both sets of data, affiliative strategies are more likely to be deployed in the images and hashtags, rather than in the verbal text, while, again in both datasets, distancing strategies are more likely to be used in the verbal text than in the image or hashtag. Such results show the varying degrees to which each semiotic mode is deployed by Instagrammers to show both association with and distance from political parties. Thus, examining only one semiotic mode

EXAMPLE A EXAMPLE B EXAMPLE C

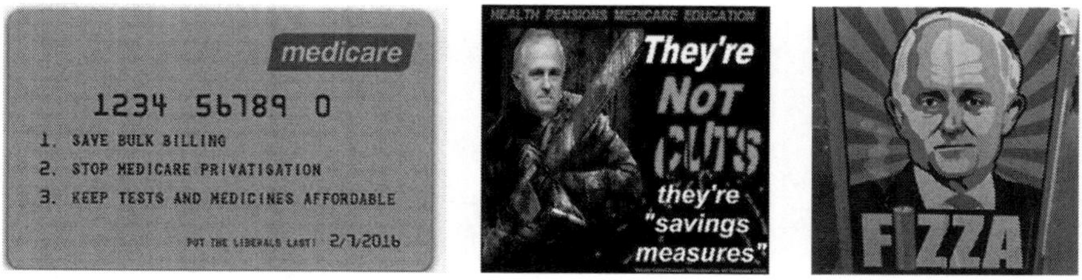

FIGURE 5.8 Fake medicare cards (example A), a negative meme (example B), and the Malcolm Turnbull Fizza poster (example C) all targeting the Liberal Party.

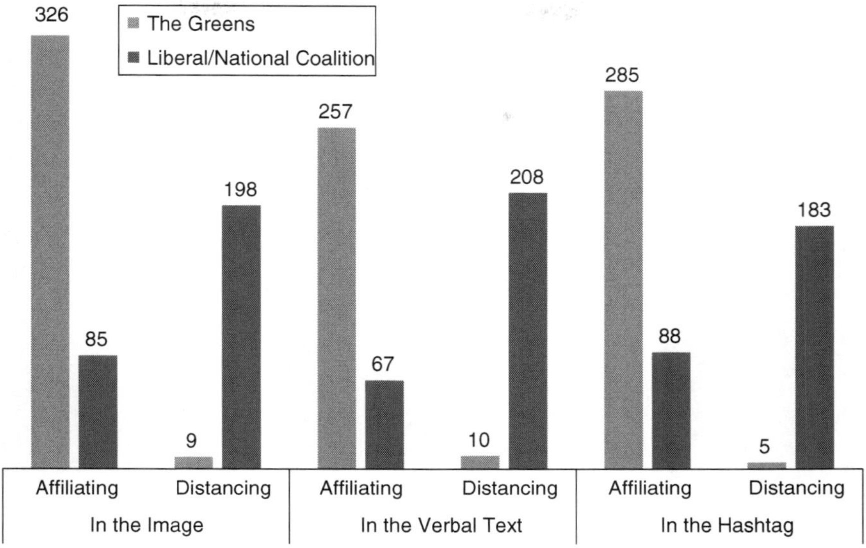

FIGURE 5.9 (Dis)affiliative strategies in Instagram posts made by members of the public.

elides the complexity of construction of meaning across modes, and will at best give only a partial picture of what is actually going on in the modal ensemble. The qualitative analysis also reveals that a small proportion of Instagrammers distance themselves from the Greens, which was not apparent in the large-scale analysis.

Since the multimodal analysis was carried out using a relational database, the depth to which one can query this complexity of construction of meaning across modes is contingent mostly on the space one has in the chapter/article to explore such findings. Focusing only on the Greens and briefly exemplifing the semiotic distribution of affiliative strategies, Figure 5.10 clearly shows that posts that affiliate with the Greens are most likely to do so in the image, verbal text and hashtag together. Thus, as a modal ensemble, these Instagram posts accumulate affiliation with the Greens across semiotic modes. Further, the image, either solely or in combination with the hashtag or the verbal text (in a total of 164 posts or 39 percent), is far more likely to show affiliation with the Greens than the verbal text is by itself (in 98 posts or 23 percent).

5.5.6 Visualising the results of CAMDA

Such qualitative analyses can be extended to include other parties that are mentioned in the #ausvotes corpus and allow the researcher to uncover any combination of affiliative and distancing strategies across words, images and political party. To display such complex findings in a static, written text, however, is very difficult, and a dynamic visualization tool capable of demonstrating relations between multiple variables and across multiple texts might prove a better method to display such complex intersemiotic and intertextual results. One such visualisation

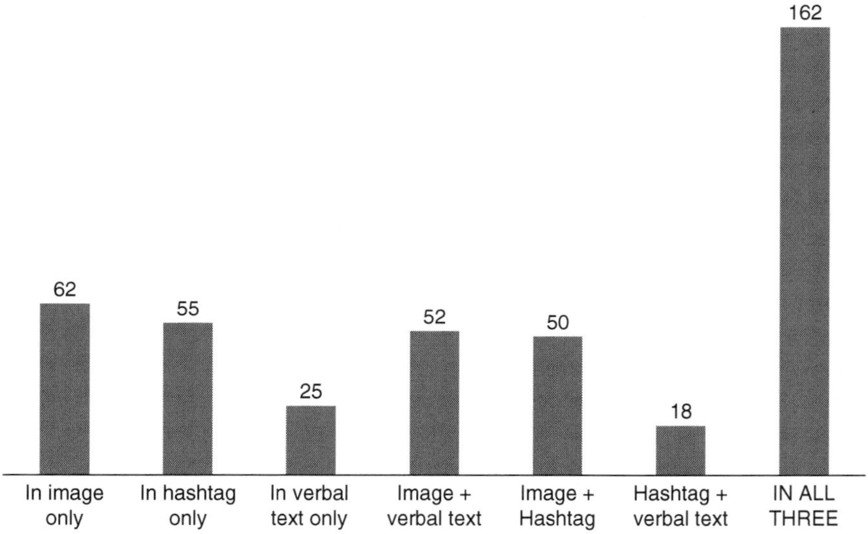

FIGURE 5.10 The semiotic distribution of affiliating strategies with the Greens.

tool is Kaleidographic (Caple & Bednarek 2017), which was developed out of another CAMDA project investigating the construction of news values in different parts of multimodal news discourse (Bednarek & Caple 2017a) and which can be viewed in action at www.newsvaluesanalysis.com/kaleidographic/. Just as a kaleidoscope works on the principle of multiple reflections, so are multiple perspectives possible in representing the relations between data units in the visualization tool Kaleidographic. And just like a kaleidoscope, Kaleidographic allows the user to see patterns recede and emerge in a dynamic way, depending on agency and choice – what elements and variables one chooses to focus on and the speed that one selects to 'play' the Kaleidographic. Further explanation of these aspects of Kaleidographic can be found in Bednarek and Caple (2017b) and at the websites mentioned here.

The Kaleidographic of the complete analysis of the affiliative strategies uncovered in the #ausvotes corpus can be viewed at www.helencaple.com/kaleidographic/, and a screenshot of the tool is provided in Figure 5.11. As Kaleidographic 'plays', one can see patterns in each text of the analysed corpus in turn, hence allowing the user to explore relations across texts, at the same time as exploring relations across modes (words and images), all in relation to the chosen set of variables. The data point shown in Figure 5.11 shows the results of the analysis of post number 606.[6] It reveals how this Instagram post shows allegiance to the Greens in both image and hashtag (the colour of the segment aligns with political party colours, green for the Greens, red for Labor, blue for Liberal and so on), while at the same time distancing itself from the Liberal/National, Labor and One Nation parties through the verbal component of the caption (segment is coloured black to signify distancing). This is one of 2,279 results from the #ausvotes corpus displayed in this Kaleidographic, and to show such complex relations in a static, written form would be impossible;

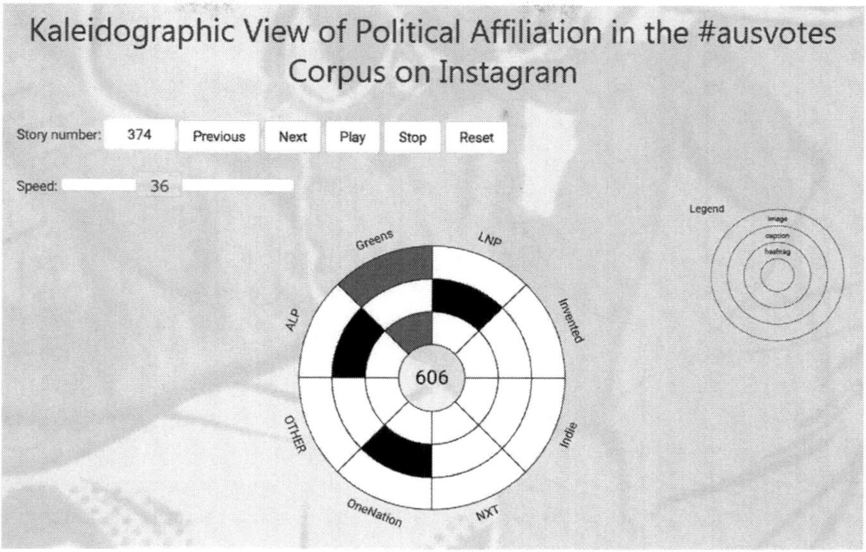

FIGURE 5.11 One screen taken from the Kaleidographic view of political affiliation in the #ausvotes corpus on Instagram.

however, the size of the dataset that one is able to usefully engage with through such a dynamic visualisation tool also needs further consideration. It takes seven minutes 30 seconds for this Kaleidographic to play through all of the results from this analysis on a speed setting of 10. The attention span of the user may be a factor compromising the effectiveness of displaying the results of such complex and very large datasets in this way. It may be more rewarding to focus on fewer variables (e.g. just the major parties contending the election).

Kaleidographic offers considerable flexibility in relation to the type and number of data units available for comparison, depending on the perspective the researcher wishes to focus on. The number of segments and layers can be increased or decreased to suit the data that the researcher wants to compare; and any segment or layer can be deactivated to concentrate the focus. So for example, in relation to the configurations shown in Figure 5.11, the user may wish to only view one political party at a time, and can thus deactivate all other segments, or may wish to only focus on one mode, image, and deactivate all other layers. The speed at which the results are displayed can also be manipulated. Thus, speeding up the transition between results makes it clear that only a few parties receive continual attention.

5.6 Evaluation

This chapter has focused on the multisemiotic blind spots associated with corpus approaches to discourse analysis, and asked whether CAMDA can shine a light on some of these blind spots and more boldly whether it will tell us the whole story. CAMDA has indeed brought a number of blind spots in corpus approaches to discourse analysis into focus, the key one being the potential for non-verbal elements to carry the full burden of meaning making. It also does tell us more of the story as it allows the researcher to begin to unpack some of the complexity in the modal ensemble and to uncover the special qualities that different semiotic modes bring to a text. Depending on how far into that complexity the researcher wishes to delve, a much more nuanced story of how meanings are spread or accumulated across semiotic modes can emerge. CAMDA also opens up the opportunity to tell a range of stories from multiple perspectives, depending on where the researcher's interests lie (see Caple in preparation, and discussion of Kaleidographic above). This is where the topology (Figure 5.5) becomes useful in making it possible to talk about approaches to CAMDA that are *mainly* intersemiotic or *more* intertextual than intratextual.

As noted at the beginning of this chapter, triangulation on multiple levels is necessary when dealing with corpora of multimodal texts. CAMDA is a first step into dealing with the complexity that comes with this, and should offer encouragement to corpus linguistic researchers who wish to dip their toes in the multimodal pond. Just be mindful of the ripples this is likely to cause.

Acknowledgements

I would like to thank the editors for their excellent stewardship of the book. Thanks to Monika Bednarek for her assistance with the corpus linguistic analysis of my election data, and to Laurence Anthony for his technical expertise in creating the visualisation tool, Kaleidographic. To the reviewers, thank you for helping me to see and correct the blind spots in my own writing.

Funding

This project was funded by an Australian Research Council Discovery Early Career Researcher Award, DE160100120.

Notes

1 For qualitative studies of the hashtag see for example Scott 2015 and Heyd and Puschmann (in press).
2 Manovich (2011: 41) uses the term 'visualisation without reduction' to refer to the preservation of the properties of data objects from which we create visualisations directly. Thus, photographs can be arranged into patterns according to non-spatial visual characteristics like hue, brightness, saturation. Such visualisations would be useful for semioticians interested in longitudinal studies examining, for example, how visual design features have changed over time.
3 The 5-day data collection period was determined on the basis of this case study being part of a much larger research project investigating the ways in which citizens and organisations outside of journalism are re-shaping and re-defining photojournalistic practice through their engagement with the digital economy (ARC DECRA Project ID: DE160100120).

4 Using the default settings also meant that the symbol # was initially ignored in creating wordlists. In so doing the duplication of the same word as a separate entity was eliminated. So for example 'I just voted in the #election' and 'I just voted in the election' were counted under the word form 'election'.
5 This has since been amended in the data collection procedure so that captions can be directly imported as individual files into AntConc.
6 In this version of Kaleidographic, the 'story number 374' (at top left) does not correspond with the actual post number '606' in the centre of the visualisation tool. This is because the post numbering follows the numbering system used on the raw data in the database, so that the analysis of this particular post can be quickly retrieved from the database for verification or other purposes.

References

Adolphs, S. & Carter, R. 2013. *Spoken Corpus Linguistics. From Monomodal to Multimodal.* London & New York: Routledge.

Adolphs, S., Knight, D. & Carter, R. 2015. Beyond modal spoken corpora: A dynamic approach to tracking language in context. In P. Baker & T. McEnery (eds.) *Corpora and Discourse Studies: Integrating Discourse and Corpora*. Basingstoke: Palgrave Macmillan. pp. 41–62.

Anthony, L. 2014. *AntConc* (Version 3.4.4) [Computer Software]. Tokyo, Japan: Waseda University. Available online at: http://www.antlab.sci.waseda.ac.jp/

Anthony, L. & Hardaker, C. 2017. *FireAnt* (Version 1.1.3) [Computer Software]. Tokyo, Japan: Waseda University. Available online at: http:// www.laurenceanthony.net/

Australian Electoral Commission, AEC (2017) 2016 federal election: Key facts and figures. Available online at: http://www.aec.gov.au/Elections/Federal_Elections/2016/key-facts.htm (accessed 8 Febuary 2017).

Bednarek, M. 2015. Corpus-assisted multimodal discourse analysis of television and film narratives. In P. Baker & T. McEnery (eds.) *Corpora and Discourse Studies: Integrating Discourse and Corpora*. Basingstoke: Palgrave Macmillan. pp. 63–87.

Bednarek M. & Caple H. 2014. Why do news values matter? Towards a new methodological framework for analyzing news discourse in Critical Discourse Analysis and beyond. *Discourse & Society*, 25(2), 135–158.

Bednarek M. & Caple H. 2017a. *The Discourse of News Values: How News Organizations Create Newsworthiness*. New York: Oxford University Press.

Bednarek, M. & Caple, H. 2017b. Introducing a new topology for (multimodal) discourse analysis. In J.S. Knox (ed.) *Proceedings from the 2017 International Systemic Functional Linguistics Congress*, Wollongong, Australia.

Bogle, A. 2016. #auspol: The Twitter hashtag Australia can't live without. *Mashable*, 20 March 2016. Available online at: http://mashable.com/2016/03/21/twitter-australia-auspol/#7V3cvLzFAEqg (accessed 8 Febuary 2017).

Bruns, A. 2016. #ausvotes: A Final Update from the Social Media Hustings. *Mapping Online Publics*, 1 July 2016. Available online at: http://mappingonlinepublics.net/2016/07/01/ausvotes-a-final-update-from-the-social-media-hustings/ (accessed 15 February 2017).

Bruns, A. & Burgess, J. 2015. Twitter hashtags from ad hoc to calculated publics. In N. Rambukkana (ed.) *Hashtag Publics: The Power and Politics of Discursive Networks*. New York: Peter Lang. pp. 13–28.

Caple H. in preparation. 'Lucy says today she is a Labordoodle': How the Dog-of-Instagram reveal voter preferences.

Caple H. & Bednarek, M. 2017. Kaleidographic [Computer Software]. Created by AntLab Solutions (Laurence Anthony), Tokyo, Japan. Available online at: www.kaleidographic.org/

Egbert, J. & Baker, P. 2016. Research synthesis. In P. Baker & J. Egbert (eds.) *Triangulating Methodological Approaches in Corpus-Linguistic Research*. New York: Routledge. pp. 183–208.

Hack 2016. Malcolm Turnbull FIZZA poster is back after electoral advertising complaints. *ABC Radio Triple J*, 26 May. Available online at: http://www.abc.net.au/triplej/programs/hack/malcolm-turnbull-fizza-poster-is-being-sent-all-over-the-country/7448424 (accessed 15 February 2017).

Hardaker C. & McGlashan M. 2016. 'Real men don't hate women': Twitter rape threats and group identity. *Journal of Pragmatics*, 91, 80–93.

Heyd, T. & Puschmann, C. in press. Hashtagging and functional shift: Adaptation and appropriation of the #. *Journal of Pragmatics* (Online First).

Highfield, T. & Leaver, T. 2014. A Methodology for Mapping Instagram Hashtags. *First Monday*, 20(1). Available online at: http://firstmonday.org/ojs/index.php/fm/article/view/5563/4195

Hjorth L. & Burgess, J. 2014. Intimate banalities: The emotional currency of shared camera phone images during the Queensland flood disaster. In G. Goggin & L. Hjorth (eds.) *The Routledge Companion to Mobile Media)*. London: Routledge. pp. 499–513.

Hochman, N. & Manovich, L. 2013. Zooming into an Instagram city: Reading the local through social media. *First Monday*, 18(7), 1–51. Available online at: http://firstmonday.org/ojs/index.php/fm/article/view/4711/3698#p1

Hutchby I. 2014. Communicative affordances and participation frameworks in mediated interaction. *Journal of Pragmatics*, 72, 86–89.

Knight, D. 2015. e-language: Communication in the digital age. In P. Baker & T. McEnery (eds.) *Corpora and Discourse Studies: Integrating Discourse and Corpora*. Basingstoke: Palgrave Macmillan. pp. 20–40.

Kress, G. 2010. *Multimodality: A Social Semiotic Approach to Contemporary Communication*. London & New York: Routledge.

Lankshear, C. & Knobel, M. 2006. *New literacies: Everyday practices and classroom learning*, 2nd ed. New York: Open University Press.

van Leeuwen, T.J. 2005. *Introducing Social Semiotics*. London/New York: Routledge.

van Leeuwen, T.J. 2011. *The Language of Colour – An Introduction*. London: Routledge.

Manikonda, L., Hu, Y. & Kambhampati, S. 2014. Analyzing User Activities, Demographics, Social Network Structure and User-Generated Content on Instagram. arXiv. Available online at: https://arxiv.org/abs/1410.8099 (accessed 7 March 2017).

Manovich, L. 2016. *Instagram and Contemporary Image*. Available online at: http://manovich.net/index.php/projects/instagram-and-contemporary-image (Parts 1, 2 and 3 accessed 13 September 2016).

Marchi, A. & Taylor, C. 2009. If on a winter's night two researchers … A challenge to assumptions of soundness of interpretation. *Critical Approaches to Discourse Analysis across Disciplines (CADAAD)*, 3(1), 1–20.

Mitchell, W.T.J. 2011. *Cloning Terror: The War of Images, 9/11 to the Present*. Chicago: University of Chicago Press.

O'Halloran, K.L. 2008. Multimodality around the world: Past, present, and future directions for research. *35th International Systemic Functional Congress (ISFC)*, Sydney, 21–25 July 2008.

Page, R. 2014. Saying 'sorry': Corporate apologies posted on Twitter. *Journal of Pragmatics*, 62, 30–45.

Scott, K. 2015. The pragmatics of hashtags: Inference and conversational style on Twitter. *Journal of Pragmatics*, 81, 8–20.

Vidal, L., Gastón A. & Jaeger, S.R. 2016. Use of emoticon and emoji in tweets for food-related emotional expression. *Food Quality and Preference*, 49, 119–128.

Zappavigna, M. 2011. Ambient affiliation: A linguistic perspective on Twitter. *New Media & Society*, 13(5), 788–806.

Zappavigna, M. 2012. *Discourse of Twitter and Social Media*. London: Continuum.

Zappavigna, M. 2014. enjoy your snags Australia … oh and the voting thing too #ausvotes #auspol: Iconisation and affiliation in microblogging during election campaigns. *Global Media Journal: Australian Edition*, 8(2), 1–16.

Zappavigna, M. 2015. Searchable talk: the linguistic functions of hashtags. *Social Semiotics*, 25(3), 274–291.

Zappavigna, M. 2016. Social media photography: Construing subjectivity in Instagram images. *Visual Communication*, 15(3), 271–292.

Zhao, S. & Zappavigna, M. 2015. The recontextualisation of subjective images in three (social) media platforms: A methodological exploration. *Paper Presented at MODE Conference – Multimodality: Methodological Explorations*, London, 15–16 January.

6

USING MULTIPLE DATA SETS

Sylvia Jaworska and Karen Kinloch

6.1 Introduction

The aim of this chapter is to illuminate the exploratory and explanatory power of using multiple data sets, or in other words, data triangulation in a corpus-assisted discourse study (CADS) (Partington; Duguid & Taylor 2013). We would like, in particular, to focus on the benefits of comparisons across contexts, to which data triangulation ultimately lends itself. It was Descartes who famously proclaimed comparison as the only tool of knowledge, asserting that 'it is only by way of comparison that we know the truth precisely'.[1]

For the purposes of this chapter we adopt the critical realist perspective (Harré 2009) of the understanding of knowledge. Therefore, we see knowledge and truth as forms of social practice constituted in and through symbolic means utilised by social agents in accordance with established discursive rules. Seen from this vantage point, knowledge and truth are never static entities waiting to be discovered. They are always partial and changing dependent on social contexts, and thus never universal and impossible to know *precisely*. Nevertheless, echoing Descartes in a more postpositivist vein, we show that comparison of multiple data sets can bring us a little closer to the phenomena we study, allowing richer and more comprehensive understandings, while the corpus analytical methods that we use to interrogate the data can add more evidence-based precision and rigour to the process of data analysis, and guide interpretation.

Triangulation is not a new territory in corpus linguistics; some researchers have adopted forms of triangulation, specifically investigator triangulation (Marchi & Taylor 2009) and method triangulation (Baker & Egbert 2016) demonstrating their benefits as well as limitations for CADS research. Yet, little attention has been paid to multiple data sets and data triangulation. This chapter sets out to address this gap by presenting a hands-on framework for using data triangulation in multi-contextual CADS research.

We begin first by outlining the rationale for using data triangulation and how it can help identify blind spots and enrich CADS research. Subsequently, we move on to the nitty-gritty of the methodological decision-making involved in selecting appropriate data sources and analytical tools, and outline a hands-on and flexible framework for doing CADS with multiple data sets. How this framework can be used in practice is demonstrated in the case study, which focuses on the discursive constructions of postnatal depression in medical, media and lay accounts.

6.2 Rationale for using multiple data sets

Before we begin with articulating the rationales for using multiple data sets, we need to, at least briefly, indicate the general theoretical understanding (set of ontological and epistemological principles) that has driven our research agenda and the use of data triangulation. The choice of method(s) and analytical procedures must be congruent with and follow from the general ontological and epistemological context in which one formulates research questions.

A substantial bulk of research in (critical) discourse analysis is carried out using the post-structuralist (Williams 2014) or constructivist frameworks (Maturana & Varela 1987), which reject empiricism as the basis of inquiry and presume a relativist stance, for example, the constructivists argue that reality is a construction of the human mind. However, we argue, such research would not be congruent with corpus-linguistic tools and methods that are essentially grounded in the empirical tradition. Our ontological and epistemological position derives from the critical realist stance (Sealey 2010), especially as formulated by Harré (2009) in his notion of critical realism. For Harré (2009), the dominant form of practice of social life is that of *conversation* understood as any kind of meaningful performance (or discourse) spoken and written, produced by social actors and normatively guided by discourse conventions that both constrain and enable what one can do or say. Corpus linguistic tools and methods are well suited to study the prime practice of social life – that is, discourse as seen from the vantage point of social realism (Sealey 2010). They provide important evidence for regularities and patterns in language use through analysing what is frequently said. Equally, they can shed light on the less frequent and unusual patterns that may seem contradictory, but, in fact, show the diversity of choices made by individuals (Sealey 2010).

One important aspect emphasised by realists is that there are no universal rules that guide social practices. Rather, these are contextually dependent. The way we produce discourse varies as we move from one social context to another because each context comes with its own set of rules and conventions that enable and constrain what can be said in given circumstances. However, it needs to be stressed that, at the same time, discourses are rarely confined to a particular context and mostly travel across contexts. There might be therefore several commonalities in the ways in which a discursive phenomenon 'behaves' across contexts, but we would not know until we compare this 'behaviour' across contexts (cf. Partington, Duguid & Taylor 2013: 12). This inevitably invites the researcher to collect data produced in different contexts and hence, to use multiple data sets. But what is context?

At least since Malinowski's seminal essay 'On the problem of meaning in primitive languages' (1923), the notion of context and the relevance of taking context into account has become a kind of linguistic truism. Previously context was defined in a narrow sense as a stretch of texts (sentences) that immediately precedes or follows a passage of interest to an analyst (what in corpus linguistic terminology would be called *cotext*). Malinowski insisted on expanding the boundaries of context beyond mere linguistic structures to the wider conditions under which speech is produced. Since then, several attempts have been suggested to conceptualise context, of which the most influential is the model proposed by Halliday based on three dimensions: *tenor*, *field* and *mode* (Halliday 1978). *Tenor* refers to the participants, their roles, goals and relations, and it is sometimes described as a domain. *Field* is understood as a subject matter (topic) and *mode* describes the channel of communication and rhetorical mode (informative, persuasive etc.). Language use is heavily dependent upon such dimensions and will change as each changes. Although the Hallidayan model of context has been critiqued for being rather static and less suitable to study digital contexts (Jones 2004), it can offer a useful heuristic for delineating contexts when compiling multiple data sets. In any case, the researcher needs to consider the key variables of communication in social settings, specifically who speaks to whom, when and for what purpose (function) (Coupland 2016), including the type of texts and the mode (e.g. spoken or written).

As with any other field of linguistic inquiry, corpus linguistic research has taken context into consideration, but has so far been mostly preoccupied with selected contexts or in Hallidayan terms with one tenor or mode. Extensive research has been conducted on differences in language use across speech and writing (e.g. Biber 1998) or texts produced by, for example, learners vs. proficient users, novice vs. expert writers (e.g. Chen & Baker 2010). In CADS, most attention has been paid to topics, themes and discourse of X, but this has been investigated predominantly in print media though arguably there is a diversity of text types within this medium. With the exception of work by Baker and McEnery (2005), Demmen et al. (2015) and cross-linguistic comparisons (e.g. Jaworska & Krishanmurthy 2012; Taylor 2014; Vessey 2016), researchers using some forms of CADS rarely venture outside these contextual boundaries. This has some benefits in that it allows the researcher to engage in depth with the chosen context. However, such an approach is limited in several ways. Firstly, findings represent the studied context only with generalisations or more broader views being impossible to formulate. Secondly, the significance of findings might be unconsciously over- or under-estimated. There might be ample examples of contradictory results in other contexts, but the researcher would not know and risk overestimations. Equally, other contexts may supply further evidence and, thus, strengthen findings obtained from the analysis of one context only. Similar to the blind men from the Indian folktale 'The Blind Men and the Elephant', when using one data set from one context, the researcher might be inclined to believe that the one part or pattern which he or she has found represents the 'whole' thing. Studying how a discursive phenomenon behaves across contexts with multiple data sets can liberate us from the confines of a contextual circumference. It helps the researcher discover differences and commonalties that exists in the ways in which discursive phenomena are constructed and how this depends on the participants, their roles, relations and the domain in which they operate, as well as the constrains and affordances of the medium. In doing so, the researcher is able to arrive at a much more comprehensive understanding of the phenomena under study; results obtained from multiple sets of data collected from different contexts can carefully guard against over- or under-interpretation. At the same time, the researcher is able to see more clearly how each context and the language used within that context differ. And vice versa, having results from multiple contexts, the researcher can see commonalties between the contexts. This can illuminate discursive trajectories that a phenomenon leaves when travelling from one domain to another, showing aspects of discourse that are taken up, and equally aspects that are marginalised or silenced altogether. In this way, using multiple data sets can significantly increase our understanding of recontextualisation and intertextuality – that important discursive processes which simultaneously bind and transform texts, make communication possible and meaningful (Fairclough 1992). These processes are never neutral, but always intertwined with ideological positionings. As Bernstein (2000: 32–33) observes: 'every time a discourse moves, there is a space in which ideology can play. No discourse moves without ideology at play.' Investigating how a discursive phenomenon behaves in multiple contexts using multiple data sets can therefore help the researcher not only explore recontextualisations and intertextuality but also uncover the playgrounds of ideologies and help understand the mechanics of ideological work in and through discourse.

6.3 Doing CADS with multiple data sets

We need to highlight at the outset that our understanding of *data set* is consonant with a corpus and a corpus with a specific context. Therefore, each corpus represents a different but relevant context. This inevitably raises the following questions: 1) which contexts are relevant, 2) how much data is needed from each to make the multiple data sets (corpora) representative and appropriate for CADS research, and 3) which analytical corpus tools best serve a comparative inquiry? We begin by answering the first question guided by the Hallidayan model of context.

As with any piece of research, all should start with a research question. Most CADS studies are interested in a particular discourse type (topic, theme) and their representations. This already delineates research to a specific thematic area. While Halliday's model of context offers a range of possible combinations, in a CADS research, *field* will, in most cases, remain the same, while *tenor* and *mode* can be changed to include different contexts. An ideal scenario would be to collect data from all possible participants who are involved in the production and dissemination of the discourse type in question. But this would be difficult to achieve not only because some discursive domains are huge in scope, but also due to the sometimes very strict rules (e.g. confidentiality) that govern the production and dissemination of texts. Hence, in most cases the researcher needs to make a decision and select the aspects of the domain which are the most *relevant* to his or her research questions and possible to obtain. This is inexorably linked with ethical considerations and in the case of textual data with copyright issues. At any stage of data collection, researchers are urged to check the copyright status and obtain permission from the copyright holder if necessary.

The question of how much data is needed is dependent on issues involved in the corpus building, specifically representativeness and balance. However these are potentially contentious when building a specialist corpus to study a specific topic or genre (Koester 2010). A somewhat pragmatic approach is often needed and preferred. While an ideal scenario would be to include all possible data produced in a given context in order to claim, in a scientific manner, a total accountability, this is in practice rarely possible. With some exceptions – for example, the works of Shakespeare or speeches of a famous politician – most domains are open systems with language data being produced continuously. Most corpora or data sets are therefore subsets (samples) presenting in most cases a partial representation of a discursive phenomenon. Having said that, some contexts might be more exhaustive than others, allowing the researcher to collect a good representation of the phenomenon under study. Given the contextual differences in the production and dissemination of texts, CADS research based on multiple data sets is very likely to be based on corpora of unequal sizes, which might involve the pitfalls of normalised frequencies. To avoid this drawback, the researcher might want to balance the sizes through, for example, random sampling, but this could also mean a huge topical sacrifice in that the researcher could lose some important data. Although having unequal sizes can have implications for statistical data analysis, for CADS research it is probably more important to have data which is relevant, appropriate and exhaustive enough to address research aims. In sum, how much data to include in a comparative CADS research with multiple data sets should be a question of relevance and appropriateness rather than representativeness and balance. Prior engagements with the contexts and participants can assist the researcher in making an informed decision regarding what kind of data and how much can be collected (see Section 6.4).

Once appropriate and relevant data sets have been created, the next question is which analytical tools are suitable to interrogate and compare data sets that are very likely to be of unequal sizes. There are two procedures to bear in mind: the first is to consider tools and metrics that do not depend on the total size of a corpus, thus allowing for meaningful comparisons across data sets of unequal sizes; the second is to use them consistently on all data sets involved.

If we want to compare the usage of a particular concept or term in corpora of different sizes, then normalised or relative frequencies need to be calculated in any case. However, the researcher needs to be aware that normalised frequencies do not give a true account of the total corpus data because language data is not normally distributed. This is why it is considered good practice in corpus-based research to provide both raw and normalised frequencies when comparing a use of a particular item across corpora (McEnery & Hardie 2012).

Keyword analysis is a useful 'way in' to identify salient or distinctive lexical items in multiple data sets and it can be speedily conducted using the commonly employed corpus linguistic software programmes such as WordSmith Tools, AntConc and Sketch Engine (see also Chapter 11). The way in which keywords are computed in Sketch Engine is especially useful for comparing multiple data sets because it does not rely on significance testing, which in turn depends on the sample size (cf. Gabrielatos & Marchi 2012). Whereas WordSmith Tools and AntConc use cross-tabulation and loglikelihood (LL) to compute statistically significant keywords, Sketch Engine provides a keyword score based on a normalised frequency ratio 'word W is N times as frequent in corpus X versus corpus Y' with a simple math parameter added to account for the zero problem in divisions (Kilgarriff 2005). Kilgarriff (2005) argues that the use of significance testing is problematic in keyword retrieval because all it does is disprove the null hypothesis – that language is random, which it is not. Retrieved keywords can be grouped manually into semantic domains to identify dominant topics and themes in data sets (Baker et al. 2013) and compare them across the sets to see which themes are more salient in which data set.

It needs to be noted that manual classification into semantic domains is a subjective and time-consuming process. It cannot just proceed from the lists of keywords because the lists present words as isolated items, 'hiding' meanings that they may have in context. Hence, checking corpus evidence by reading concordance lines is an essential procedure. In order to reduce the level of subjective judgement and ensure a better consistency, it is recommended if feasible, to use interraters (multiple judges) and measures of interrater reliability, for example, Cronbach's Alpha.

Another way of performing a keyword analysis is to compare the data sets against each other. This is often preferred by researchers who work with two corpora as it allows them to tease out differences that exist between two data sets by simultaneously avoiding problems associated with a general reference corpus. While this procedure is useful for highlighting differences in a more precise manner, it will overlook what the data sets have in common, 'hiding' shared discourses (see also Chapter 2). This would limit the perspectives on how discourses travel across contexts making it impossible to explore recontextualisations and intertextuality. Using one reference corpus as a benchmark can therefore be more insightful for research based on multiple data sets in that it allows the researcher to reveal keywords that are both unique and also shared across data sets. Unique keywords highlight the contextual specificity, while shared keywords can be useful pointers to discursive recontextualizations and intertextuality.

To explore aspects of recontextualizations and intertextuality in more depth, studying collocational patterns of relevant unique and shared keywords can be very helpful. The metric for collocation retrieval offered in Sketch Engine – the Log Dice – seems particularly suitable for comparing collocations across corpora. In contrast to other commonly used statistics such as Mutual Information or T-test, Log Dice is a ratio with a maximum value (theoretically 14, but practically 10 or below) and it does not depend on the total size of the corpus (Rychlý 2008). This allows the researcher to have a consistent comparison measure across multiple data sets.

Summarising the above, we propose a framework for doing CADS with multiple data sets and combining both quantitative corpus techniques and qualitative discourse-analytical procedures (see Table 6.1).The framework is partially modelled on Baker et al. (2008) and consists of methodological procedures and practical steps to guide the researcher through the process of data collection and analysis.

TABLE 6.1 Framework for CADS with multiple data sets

1. Settle on research aims and questions and ground them in a relevant theoretical, ontological and epistemological model; bear in mind that it may not be appropriate or necessary to use corpus-based techniques within some models;
2. Consider contexts in which the topic or a type of discourse is produced and disseminated;

2a. if necessary narrow down the contexts to key domains, to make the analysis feasible; relevance to the research questions should guide the selection;

2b. delineate contexts demonstrating their relevance to the research aims; the Hallidayan model of context and consideration of who speaks to whom, when and for what purpose offer a useful heuristic;

3. Identify data sources within the contexts that are most relevant and appropriate to address the research questions; prior engagement with contexts and participants, if possible, can offer relevant pointers;
4. Collect data bearing in mind the access, availability, amount, ethical considerations and copyright issues;
5. Interrogate the data sets using quantitative corpus-based techniques to identify lexico–grammatical and semantic/thematic patterns, and to select texts or potential sites for further qualitative analyses (step 6);

5a. keywords are a useful way in; identify keywords of interest and worth investigating further;

5b. classify the most distinctive keywords into semantic domains to explore dominant themes; the use of interraters and statistical measures of consistency can help to produce a more robust classification;

5c. study collocations of selected keywords bearing in mind the differences in outputs that the commonly used metrics produce; collocations of shared keywords can point to paths of recontextualization and shed light on intertextuality and interdiscursivity; unique keywords highlight the distinctiveness of a given data set;

5d. study frequencies and collocations of selected lexical items (not keywords) that name and reflect the studied discourse;

6. Interrogate subsections of the data sets using (critical) discourse-analytical techniques;

6a. study concordance lines to identify specific usage of an item or a collocation paying attention to devices that were not accounted for by corpus interrogation (for example, pragmatic markers and pragmatic patterns, metaphors);

6b. go into the text to explore additional discourses and strategies;

7. Consider sources outside the data sets (dictionaries, manuals, historical records, statistical/demographic data etc.) to further explore and contextualise the studied discourse/lexical item (this step should be integrated at every stage of research).
8. All steps could be replicated in another linguistic context adding a cross-linguistic and cross-cultural dimension to the original research.

It needs to be noted that not all stages and steps are relevant for every project and the researcher might select those that are most suitable to answer his or her research questions.

6.4 Case Study: discursive constructions of postnatal depressions in medical, media and lay contexts

To demonstrate how the framework can be put in practice, this section presents a case study which explores the discursive constructions of postnatal depression (PND) in medical, media and lay accounts. It does so by outlining the process of data collection, ethical considerations and analytical tools selected for comparisons of multiple data sets.

The case study forms a part of a larger project which investigates public discourses around PND (Jaworska & Kinloch 2016). PND is a type of depression which can occur within one year of childbirth; it is a highly stigmatised condition, which in the UK affects 10–15 per cent of mothers, with suicide due to PND being the leading cause of maternal death (NHS 2016).

6.4.1 Data collection

The first question which needs to be answered is what are the contexts in which discourses of interest to the researcher are likely to be produced and disseminated. PND is a mental health condition and the obvious answer is the medical domain. But the medical domain is a multilayered profession and an industry with many sites and participants who have different status, roles and goals. It includes medical researchers, clinicians and practitioners who all are involved in production and 'consumption' of a variety of texts and operate in various modes sometimes simultaneously. The ideal would be to collect data about PND from all possible participants but this would be difficult to achieve not only because of the enormous scope of the domain, but also due to the strict confidentiality that surrounds dissemination of texts in medical contexts.

Our initial interest was in lay discourses of PND and how they are influenced by wider discourses around the condition disseminated in the UK. For the purpose of our study, Context 1 were conversations about PND produced by lay participants in online discussions on Mumsnet. Mumsnet is the largest online parenting forum in the UK, attracting over 6 million unique visitors per month. The data are examples of spontaneous written conversations and the dominant purpose is information and support. Since the lay person was our prime focus, we decided to select medical contexts and texts that a lay person with PND is likely to encounter. This was based on the authors' insider knowledge and experience of being involved with mothers' groups and personal encounters with women who had PND. Through the engagement with the participants, it became clear that mothers learn about PND primarily through consultations with medical professionals (GPs, health visitors, midwifes) and by reading materials produced by medical professionals for lay people, many of which are distributed online and mothers are often directed to consult these resources. In this way, we were able to select a subdomain from the domain of the medical profession that was directly relevant to our study and offered pointers to texts that were produced for and used by women with PND. Context 2 was, therefore, written texts about PND produced by medical professionals for lay people. Because most of the texts produced in Context 2 were derived from medical context *per se* and included references to medical, academic and clinical literature, we also decided to include medical literature about PND produced by medical professionals for medical professionals. Since media play a significant role in the dissemination of discourses around health and illness, and this significance became apparent when engaging with Context 1, we also decided to include news stories about PND published in the major British national newspapers since 2000. Table 6.2 presents the four contexts that were considered in our study. The appropriateness of each context is ensured by the focus on the topic, the relevance of texts produced in each context and the geographical location (UK).

Once we settled on the contexts from which to obtain data, the next question was how much data to collect. Again, an ideal scenario would be to include all possible language data about PND produced in the four contexts, but this was not possible, because some of the domains (Mumsnet) are open systems with language data being produced continuously. As far as online data is concerned, we first identified threads (an original post to Mumsnet followed by responses) that included the terms postnatal depression or PND and downloaded all the posts from these threads. This generated a corpus (Data Set 1) of 4,778,285 words, which we considered large given its 'specialist' status. Other domains were more closed in nature, leading to smaller data sets. For example, in Context 2, we included guidelines and information brochures produced by the main health service provider in the UK, the National Health Service (NHS), and affiliated medical organisations or charities to which mothers are directed on the websites of the NHS, including the Royal College of Psychiatrists (RCP), National Collaborating Centre for Mental Health (NCCMH), Association for Post Natal Illness (APNI), PANDAS Foundation and

TABLE 6.2 Contexts of PND in the UK

Context	*Context 1*	*Context 2*	*Context 3*	*Context 4*
Topic	PND discourse	PND discourse	PND discourse	PND discourse
Participants	Lay participants with experience of PND	Medical professionals writing for lay audience	Medical professionals writing for medical professionals	News media
Mode	written as spoken	written	written	written
Purpose (function)	informative, support	informative	informative, legislative, clinical	informative, persuasive

private healthcare providers such as BUPA. It quickly became apparent that there was a great deal of similarity and repetition in the texts produced in Context 2, which is not surprising given that healthcare providers need to get across consistent information. The data set collected from Context 2 was therefore considerably smaller than Data Set 1 and included 50,113 words, but it was felt to be exhaustive and representative of Context 2. A similar collection method was used in Context 3, which comprises professional guidelines for healthcare professionals in the field of perinatal mental health. The total size of data collected stands at 187,940 words.

As far as Context 4 is concerned, the procedure was straightforward; we built on previous CADS research and utilised the newspaper database LexisUK to obtain relevant data since 2000. We settled on the year 2000 because some of the important national newspapers with the highest number of readers (e.g. *Daily Mail*, *Sun*) were only added in the late 1990s or 2000. We wanted to make sure that our corpus represented a variety of sources and not only broadsheets. While the choice of the start point might appear arbitrary, it was justified (and constrained) by the availability of data. We used again the terms *postnatal depression* and *PND + depression* to retrieve topical articles with the research terms occurring three times or more in the text. Newspapers differ in terms of coverage (regional vs. national), style (e.g. broadsheet vs. tabloid), and despite supposed neutrality, always have some kind of political leaning. These are important factors that impact dissemination, audiences, style and persuasion, and need to be taken into consideration when collecting and analysing media data. Since we were interested in wider discourses around PND, the decision was made to include UK national newspapers only, and as our project was not concerned with strictly political matters, the political orientation of a newspaper was a lesser concern to us. We made a distinction between broadsheets, tabloids and middle-range tabloids to account for the degree of formality and sensationalism. This led to the creation of a media corpus (Data Set 4), which consisted of 845 articles with 1,585,954 words. Table 6.3 shows the size of each data set.

Throughout the process of data collection, we engaged with ethical matters concerning the data. Medical guidelines were the least problematic as they are in the public domain designed for public consumption. Newspaper articles are protected by copyright laws but newspaper data can be collected for non-commercial research purposes and if single articles are not distributed as a whole, permission is not normally required. [2] Online conversations produced by human subjects, even if anonymously, present more of a grey area and researchers are divided by opinion on how to treat them. Some argue vehemently that informed consent from

TABLE 6.3 Sizes of data sets

Data set	*Corpus name*	*Words*
Context 1 => Data Set 1	MUMSNET	4,778,285
Context 2 => Data Set 2	MEDLAY	50,113
Context 3 => Data Set 3	MEDICAL	187,940
Context 4 => Data Set 4	MEDIA	1,585,954

online participants should be obtained in any case, whereas others insist that by posting anonymously participants automatically give their consent (Roberts 2015). No agreement has been yet reached, although guidelines in this area have been produced by the Association of Internet Researchers (AOIR) and the British Psychological Society,[3] and we consulted these.

Our online data was collected from a discussion forum on Mumsnet called *Talk*. *Talk* is a public forum that can be browsed by members and non-members, but only registered members can post. The terms and conditions of Mumsnet stipulate that *Talk* is a public space and users are made aware that anyone can view their posts. Following procedures adopted in previous research using posts from Mumsnet (e.g. Pedersen 2016), consent was not sought from the participants because the material used was not directly elicited from them and only obtained after it was spontaneously generated. Yet, the terms and conditions of Mumsnet state that all content published on its site including *Talk* are the sole property of Mumsnet and reproduction of any parts without approval is prohibited. Consent was therefore sought from Mumsnet to use *Talk* data and approval was granted. The approval stated that usernames or any other potentially identifying details must be removed to protect posters' anonymity and this procedure was adopted throughout.

6.4.2 Analysis

This section shows how the retrieval of keywords and a subsequent classification of keywords into semantic domains can provide a useful way in to multiple datasets and how the further interrogation of selected keywords using Word Sketch can give insights into how discourses are taken up and potentially contested across contexts. To showcase the rather neglected area of similarities (Taylor 2013) and recontextualisations, we focus on shared keywords only.

Sketch Engine was used to produce and compare keyword lists from our data sets using the BNC as the reference corpus. Subsequently, we selected the 100 most distinctive content keywords in each data set and grouped them manually into semantic categories, a procedure adopted from previous CADS research (Baker et al. 2013).

It is worth clarifying at this point what we gloss as 'semantic domains' are thematic categories developed inductively and reiteratively from studying the keyword data, as distinct from automated classification through tools such as Wmatrix (Rayson 2008). This inductive process means that the coding for some categories is more fine-grained than others, as appropriate to the particular topic. In the case of PND, we first began with identifying general categories, for example, Actors, Medical Actions, Emotions etc., but quickly noticed that there exist subcategories within each general category. For example, the general category Actor included a variety of actors that could be further grouped into subcategories depending on their role in the process. This approach reflects the multiplicity of discourses and practices around the biomedical model of perinatal mental health. In Table 6.4 below we show the set of semantic categories developed and examples of the

TABLE 6.4 Semantic categories

Semantic category	*Examples of keywords*
A ACTOR GENERAL	woman, women
AI Institutions as Actors	NICE, NHS, PANDAS, Hospital
AM Medical Actors (Roles)	Midwife, GP, health visitor
AP Personal Actors (Roles)	mum, mother, baby, husband, child, family
B BODILY EXPERIENCE	birth, breastfeeding, pregnancy, tiredness
E EMOTIONS	feel, feeling
EN Negative emotions	worry, stressed, upset, hate
EP Positive emotions	happy, love, lucky, hopefully
MA MEDICAL ACTION	healthcare, admission
MA_A Alternative therapies	CBT, counselling, therapy
MA_M Medical management	screening, identification, refer
MA_P Pharmacological intervention	antidepressants, medication, drug
ML MEDICAL LABELLING	depression, disorder, psychiatric, postnatal

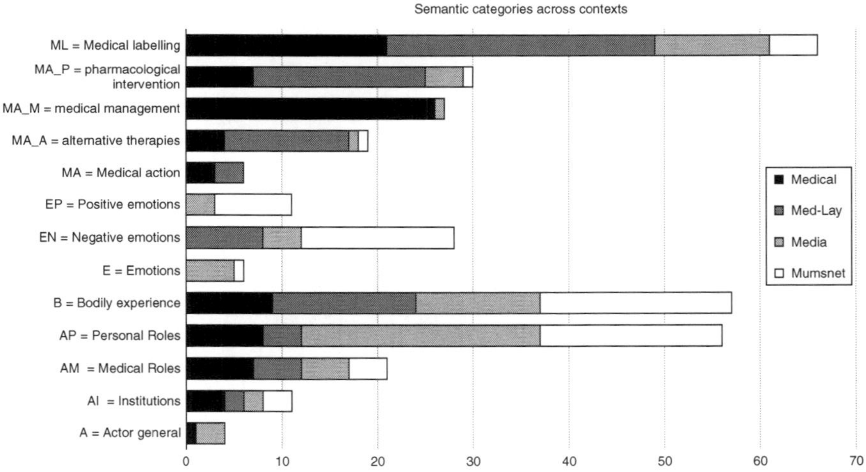

FIGURE 6.1 Semantic categories across contexts.

keywords for each domain, whilst Figure 6.1 illustrates the comparison of their normalised frequency across the four corpora.

The comparison of semantic domains across corpora is one method for eliciting the commonalities and differences on a particular topic, highlighting the specificity of each context. For example, it is not surprising to see that Medical Labelling plays a much more important role in MEDICAL and MEDLAY, while Emotions, particularly Negative emotions, are prevalent in MEDIA and MUMSNET. However, while Figure 6.1 provides a broad-brush view of the topics for closer analysis, we turn to the keywords which are found in all of the corpora. While we acknowledge the usefulness of looking at keywords unique to a particular tenor or mode – for example, in the Mumsnet corpus the use of acronyms such as DD (dear daughter) and FF (formula feeding) is a stimulating topic for stylistic investigation – this is not central to this particular case study.

A calculation of shared terms in the top 100 keywords for each corpus elicited 21 words for investigation of patterns and paths of recontextualisations, including *women*, *NHS*, *GP*, *midwife*, *baby*, *mothers*, *mother*, *babies*, *child*, *birth*, *pregnancy*, *health*, *illness*, *breastfeeding*, *anxiety*, *help*, *depression*, *postnatal*, *mental*, *PND*, *parenting*. In the example analysis, we address one keyword from the Medical Labelling semantic domain, *depression*, and one from the Personal Actors domain, *mother*, in order to illuminate the discursive constructions and recontextualisations of the medical condition itself and the key social actor in these texts. We begin with the keyword *depression* and its Word Sketches across the corpora.

The most frequent collocational pattern of *depression* identified using the Word Sketch function is modifier + depression and the significant collocates are shown in Table 6.5 below. We consider collocations with the Log Dice value of 7 or above, which points to strong associations (Rychlý 2008) and the minimum frequency of 3.

The modifiers of *depression* indicate the extent to which the biomedical model of depression is accepted and recontextualised from medical texts across media and lay accounts of PND. The use of diagnostic modifiers, such as *postnatal*, *antenatal*, and medical gradation markers, such as *severe*, *major*, *mild* are used even in lay accounts, suggesting acceptance of this model, and through this adoption of biomedical explanation potentially destigmatising those experiencing PND. Interestingly, however, the MUMSNET corpus shows use of two modifiers that were not found in the other data sets, that is, *reactive* and *chronic*. The term *reactive* is a scientific term from the domain of chemistry, which is sometimes used in psychiatry to refer to the recurrence of mental illness (Oxford English Dictionary, OED). Similarly, *chronic* is a medical term which is used to describe long-lasting and intensive illness. Both emphasise the temporality of PND as an ongoing or recurring event in the lived experience. This aspect of PND seems unaccounted in MEDICAL and MEDLAY which emphasise depression as a stable entity to be diagnosed and treated (see below). There are other conspicuous differences that may warrant further investigation. For example, the use of *manic* and *terrible* in MEDIA is striking and not matched by other domains, potentially hinting at sensationalist media attitudes towards PND.

The second most frequent collocational pattern is verb with depression as an object and it is to this we turn in the next part of our analysis to unpick how postnatal depression is acted upon (see Table 6.6).

In comparison with the modifiers of *depression*, the collocational patterns in Table 6.6 indicate greater variation across the corpora. Whilst the lexis of biomedical action, for example *diagnose*, *treat*, *prevent*, occurs across all four corpora, the lexis of the experience of PND varies. While more neutral terms such as *have* and *experience* show high significance in all texts, in the media and lay corpora *suffer* is the strongest association, potentially passivizing those who experience PND. Interestingly, the linguistic choices in the media contexts draw on well-documented, war-related

TABLE 6.5 Modifiers of *depression*

MEDICAL		*MEDLAY*		*MEDIA*		*MUMSNET*	
Collocate	*LD*	*Collocate*	*LD*	*Collocate*	*LD*	*Collocate*	*LD*
postnatal	12.82	postnatal	13.53	postnatal	13.74	postnatal	12.16
major	10.46	severe	10.47	severe	10.41	post-natal	11.27
post-natal	10.21	post-natal	9.86	post-natal	10.40	antenatal	10.84
antenatal	10.03	moderate	9.34	antenatal	9.15	severe	10.27
severe	9.99	mild	8.99	clinical	9.06	ante-natal	9.72
perinatal	9.80	antenatal	8.51	manic	8.56	mild	8.68
minor	9.69	postpartum	8.48	maternal	7.61	reactive	8.47
maternal	9.25	clinical	8.19	paternal	7.48	chronic	7.76
moderate	9.22	major	8.16	serious	7.34	serious	7.72
paternal	8.71	maternal	8.16	prenatal	7.18	previous	7.32
mild	8.70	untreated	7.80	mild	7.18	bad	7.30
untreated	8.29	disorder	7.78	terrible	7.15	untreated	7.28
possible	8.17	previous	7.75				
non-remitted	7.32						
blue	7.32						

TABLE 6.6 Verbs with *depression* as an object

MEDICAL		*MEDLAY*		*MEDIA*		*MUMSNET*	
Collocate	*LD*	*Collocate*	*LD*	*Collocate*	*LD*	*Collocate*	*LD*
experience	11.50	have	11.75	suffer	12.46	suffer	10.52
treat	10.72	experience	10.88	develop	10.55	cause	9.70
detect	10.11	treat	10.80	experience	10.15	develop	8.86
diagnose	9.91	prevent	10.40	battle	9.83	treat	8.80
prevent	9.64	develop	10.30	diagnose	9.74	trigger	8.79
associate	9.58	cause	10.25	have	9.72	experience	8.78
compare	9.57	make	9.83	treat	9.25	diagnose	8.24
target	9.42	diagnose	9.79	get	9.20	have	8.06
identify	9.34	be	9.48	cause	9.09	lift	7.85
assume	9.02	include	9.12	trigger	8.93	cure	7.75
get	8.94	understand	9.04	prevent	8.71	underlie	7.21
have	8.75	recognise	9.04	beat	8.05	understand	7.20
develop	8.74			tackle	7.86	prevent	7.12
address	8.67			fight	7.86		
include	8.40			combat	7.65		

metaphors for illness (Semino et al. 2017) as indicated in the prominence of *battle*, *beat*, *fight*, *tackle* and *combat* in MEDIA. While previous research suggests the prominence of war and fight metaphors in the experience of illness, our findings confirm it only to the domain of media suggesting that the use of this type of metaphors might be condition- and context-specific.

Drawing on the idea of an explanatory model for destigmatizing the experience of PND, the patterns *cause/trigger depression* are prevalent in MEDIA and MUMSNET but less so in texts produced by medical organisations. Interestingly, when *depression* is an object of *cause* in MEDLAY, four out of the eight occurrences point to unknown aetiology and four are carefully formulated references to social and bodily factors accompanied by question marks or hedges (see Figure 6.2).

In both MEDIA and MUMSNET the patterns *cause/trigger depression* elicit examples of a desire to explain PND either through external social factors, as in the reactive or chronic depression explanatory model, or hormonal/chemical imbalances. Interestingly, the latter themes occur only in MEDIA and MUMSNET suggesting that women possibly draw on MEDIA discourses to explain PND (see Figure 6.3 and 6.4).

The pressure of the expectations of parenthood versus the imperfect reality and the strain of living up to the public image of the 'ideal' mother are often cited as

if PND is suspected. What *causes* postnatal **depression** ? PND can affect a new mum

postnatal depression? The *cause* of postnatal **depression** isn't completely clear. Some of the

your baby and family. " The *cause* of postnatal **depression** isn't clear, but it's thought to be the

vulnerable to infections. What *causes* postnatal **depression** ? No one really knows for sure;

help if you are like this. What *causes* postnatal **depression** ? The exact cause is not clear.

FIGURE 6.2 Concordance lines of the pattern *cause* and *depression* in MEDLAY.

with antidepressants to no effect. Their **depression** is *caused* by a hormone imbalance that is

resented itself to the naked eye as postnatal **depression** *caused* by postpartum hormonal flux, it

helpline was part of a wider study into **depression** *caused* by pregnancy and the arrival of

these negative emotions *causes* postnatal **depression** . Here's the good news children for

it? Hormone imbalance a role in *causing* **depression** . Feeling overwhelmed of having a baby

serotonin and dopamine. Low levels *cause* **depression** but the boffins say drugs could control

baby when she sank into severe postnatal **depression** *caused* by her husband cheating on her,y

compounds in the brain that may *cause* **depression** . Previous studies have suggested that

, both to understand mechanisms that *cause* **depression** and to find a new treatment for the one

whether changes in brain chemicals *cause* **depression** , or result from it. SUZI'S ILLNESS

FIGURE 6.3 Concordance lines of the pattern *cause* and *depression* in MEDIA.

the chemical vs social argument Some **depression** is *caused* by chemical imbalances - I never

tested for thyroid function as it *causes* **depression** as well as other symptoms (weight gain,

that it was the anxiety that *caused* the **depression**. I'm still suffering badly with anxiety

which let's face it a baby is) can *cause* **depression**, if you add in lack of sleep too it can

where you are. Ironically, a big part of my **depression** was *caused* by my not being able to bf.

issues in my life that have been *causing* my **depression** /general low mood. That's another reason

their babies. I think that postnatal **depression** is *caused* by chemistry of the brain

medication sometimes forever whereas other **depression** is *caused* by something such as grief and

because of stress & depression. The stress & **depression** were *caused* by crap in my life. If I'd

having a baby in our society that *causes* **depression** in many and instead plants the idea that

FIGURE 6.4 Concordance lines of the collocation *cause* and *depression* in MUMSNET.

TABLE 6.7 Modifiers of *mother*

MEDICAL		*MEDLAY*		*MEDIA*		*MUMSNET*	
Collocate	*LD*	*Collocate*	*LD*	*Collocate*	*LD*	*Collocate*	*LD*
new	11.95	new	12.46	new	11.91	new	9.97
in-patient	10.42	depressed	11.58	single	10.47	bad	9.73
depressed	10.42	many	11.17	bad	9.91	single	9.03
specialist	9.94	bad	10.76	depressed	9.73	other	8.93
many	9.30	non-depressed	10.32	good	9.66	good	8.71
expectant	9.15	most	9.91	young	9.56	perfect	8.65
group	8.60	other	9.69	other	9.54	most	8.49
				first-time	9.52	bf	8.46
				many	9.45	own	8.35
				perfect	9.38	many	8.27
						time	8.22
						terrible	8.21
						young	8.16
						ff	8.14

possible causes of PND (e.g. Kantrowitz-Gordon 2013). In order to explore this further, as the second part of this example we look at the representation of the key social actor in question, that is, the keyword *mother*.

The representation of *mother* is integral to any study of the discursive construction of postnatal depression as the condition affects mostly mothers. We focus on the pre-modification of *mother* using Word Sketch to show salient ways in to how mothers are characterised and evaluated across the contexts.

As seen in Table 6.7, the most striking points of the pre-modification of *mother* are the foregrounding of *new* mothers and the evaluative extremes which are present in the MEDIA and MUMSNET datasets. The highlighting of inexperience in the terms *new* and *first-time* in co-occurrence with PND constructs new mothers as a vulnerable group in need of medical attention. This construction occurs in the MEDICAL corpus:

1 All **new mothers** and their partners would benefit from sensitive and supportive care from consistent professionals during the perinatal period. (MEDICAL)

Also, the expectation that some level of depression or mental distress is 'normal' for new mothers is 'rehearsed' in the other domains:

1 Remember that some of these things can also be a normal part of being a **new mother**, such as disturbed sleep or lack of energy. (MEDLAY)
2 The gruelling 'graveyard shift' can reduce even the most level-headed **new mother** to a stressed-out zombie. (MEDIA)
3 Many **new mothers** are misdiagnosed as having PND when really they need to be told that what they're experiencing is pretty normal. (MUMSNET)

This is potentially problematic for women experiencing PND as they may resist help-seeking due to the expectation of the problematic emotional experience of being a 'new mother' and the feeling that as they become more experienced at childcare this will dissipate.

The societal expectations of mothers and related judgemental attitudes towards this group clearly manifest in the wide range of evaluative and polarising lexicon including *perfect*, *good*, *bad*, *terrible*, before we even begin to approach the problematic constructions of *working*, *stay at home*, *single*, *FF* (formula feeding) and *BF* (breastfeeding) which also modify *mother*. The use of this evaluative language is again less frequent in the medical texts (both MEDICAL and MEDLAY) and is used exclusively in the context of reassurance that help-seeking for PND does not equate to being a 'bad' mother and pressure to be a good mother is unhelpful. Indeed, the MEDLAY corpus highlights mother guilt or fear of being a 'bad' mother as a potential symptom of perinatal mental health problems. The MEDIA and MUMSNET corpora also show the construction of *bad mother* is most commonly used in the context of fear and stigmatisation around a diagnosis of PND, and seek to provide reassurance:

1 Many are afraid to tell their health visitors how they feel for fear of having their children taken away, or being seen as **bad mothers**. (MEDIA)
2 You are being the best **mother** you can be and seeking help when you need it. You are not a **bad mother** and guilt will not help either you or your dd. (MUMSNET)

While the non-medical corpora show a self-reflexive awareness of how expectations around mothering can be problematic, it is also clear in the self and other construction of mothers that fear of stigma and possible aversion to seeking help are critical issues. But why, if it is acknowledged in this range of texts that motherhood is difficult, poorly supported and potentially stigmatised, is this problematic construction of 'perfect' mother still perpetuated? The fact that MEDIA and MUMSNET refer to this wide range of evaluative and polarising lexis shows the perpetuation of normative ideologies surrounding motherhood; as soon as a woman gives birth, she is automatically subject to powerful moral judgments that deem her either 'good' or 'bad' and there is very little in between.

6.5 Evaluation

Using multiple data sets allowed us to gain a much more profound understanding of discourses around PND by reducing some of the blind spots that often lurk in discourse analysis based on a single set of data. It allowed us to see the contexts with fresh perspectives and to notice much more clearly similarities and differences among the data sets. Investigating keywords shared across contexts revealed aspects of recontextualisation by showing how specific discourses are appropriated in multiple ways to fulfil distinctive purposes. An example of this is the way in which women with PND recontextualise the voice of biomedicine via a pseudo-scientific explanatory model of chemical imbalances to legitimise the otherwise stigmatised condition (Kantrowitz-Gordon 2013). Further comparisons of keywords enabled us to discover discursive specificities and absences in the contexts we studied, which brought to light a number of more concrete and evidence-based implications of our research. A good example of this is the significance of the temporality in the lived experience of PND so prominent in the lay accounts but clearly absent in the medical understanding of the condition. Similarly, results from the multiple data sets illuminated how discourses around PND are intrinsically interwoven with powerful societal ideologies about motherhood and how these are reproduced in the media and lay accounts and again are absent from medical texts. Given the power of the biomedical model (also demonstrated here), engagement on the part of medical professions with ideologies of 'good' motherhood and specifically the unrealistic expectations impressed on mothers could be a possible way forward to help reduce the stigma surrounding PND.

We hope that the many benefits of using multiple data sets in CADS research are now evident. Having said that, there are some caveats that need to be kept in mind before embarking on this kind of research journey. Firstly, the approach can be time-consuming, especially the task of data collection. Secondly, CADS with multiple data sets can benefit from the knowledge of and exposure to contexts under study and this may not always be possible. Thirdly, we focused here on the synchronic perspectives of a discursive phenomenon leaving out the historical or (modern) diachronic dimensions that could add yet other valuable insights (see Chapter 9). Fourthly, our research was positioned in one geographical and cultural context and the results cannot in any way be generalised beyond it. Replicating the same procedures in a different cultural and linguistic environment might lead to very different results. Despite these limitations, we feel this method has much to add to the study of discursive constructions of social phenomena, recognising and interrogating discursive mobilities and recontextualisations which are retained across contexts.

Notes

1 Original citation: 'Ce n'est que par une comparaison que nous connaissons precisement la verite', Rene Descartes, Regulae ad directionem ingenii, Rule XIV, Oeuvres Philosophiques, 9 vols., ed. Ferdinand Alquie, Paris, Garnier, 1963, vol. 1, p. 168.

2 The British Library offers a useful guide on copyright issues regarding newspaper articles, see http://www.bl.uk/reshelp/findhelprestype/news/copynews/.

3 https://aoir.org/reports/ethics2.pdf and https://beta.bps.org.uk/news-and-policy/ethics-guidelines-internet-mediated-research-2017.

References

Baker, P. 2006. *Using Corpora in Discourse Analysis*. London: Continuum.

Baker, P. & McEnery, T. 2005. A Corpus-Based Approach to Discourses of Refugees and Asylum Seekers in UN and Newspaper Texts. *Journal of Language and Politics,* 4(2), 97–226.

Baker, P. & Egbert, J. (eds.) 2016. *Triangulating Methodological Approaches in Corpus-Linguistic Research*. London: Routledge.

Baker, P., Gabrielatos, C., Khosravinik, M., Krzyzanowski, M., McEnery, T. & Wodak, R. 2008. A useful methodological synergy? Combining critical discourse analysis and corpus linguistics to examine discourses of refugees and asylum seekers in the UK press. *Discourse & Society*, 19(3), 273–306.

Baker, P., Gabrielatos, C. & McEnery, T. 2013. *Discourse Analysis and Media Attitudes.* Cambridge: Cambridge University Press.

Bernstein, B. 2000. *Pedagogy, Symbolic Control, and Identity*. Oxford: Rowman & Littlefield.

Biber, D. 1998. *Variation across Speech and Writing*. Cambridge: Cambridge University Press.

Chen, Y. H. & Baker, P. 2010. Lexical bundles in L1 and L2 academic writing. *Language Learning & Technology*, 14(2), 30–49.

Coupland, N. 2016. Sociolinguistic theory and the practice of sociolinguistics. In N. Coupland (ed.) *Sociolinguistics: Theoretical Debates*. Cambridge: Cambridge University Press. pp. 1–34.

Demmen, J., Semino, E., Demjen, Z., Koller, V., Hardie, A., Rayson, P. & Payne, S. 2015. A computer-assisted study of the use of violence metaphors for cancer and end of life by patients, family carers and health professionals. *International Journal of Corpus Linguistics*, 20(2), 205–231.

Fairclough, N. 1992. *Discourse and Social Change.* Oxford: Polity Press.

Gabrielatos, C. & Marchi, A. 2012. Keyness: Appropriate metrics and practical issues. CADS International Conference 2012. 13–14 September, University of Bologna, Italy. Available online at: http://repository.edgehill.ac.uk/4196/1/Gabrielatos%26Marchi-Keyness-CADS2012.pdf (accessed 28 June 2017).

Halliday, M. A. K. 1978. *Language as a Social Semiotic: The Social Interpretation of Language and Meaning.* London: Edward Arnold.

Harré, R. 2009. Saving critical realism. *Journal for the Theory of Social Behaviour,* 39(2), 129–143.

Jaworska, S. & Krishnamurthy, R. 2012. On the F-word: A corpus-based analysis of the media representation of feminism in British and German press discourse, 1990–2009. *Discourse & Society*, 23(4), 1–31.

Jaworska, S. & Kinloch, K. 2016. On 'bad' mothers and hormonal imbalances: Comparing discursive constructions of postnatal depression in lay, media and medical accounts. BAAL SIG Health and Science Communication: Experiences of illness and death. 28 November, Open University, UK. Available online at: https://www.researchgate.net/publication/317225754_On_'bad'_mothers_and_hormonal_imbalances_Comparing_discursive_constructions_of_postnatal_depression_in_lay_media_and_medical_accounts (accessed 28 June 2017).

Jones, R. 2004. The problem of context in computer-mediated communication. In P. LeVine & R. Scollon (eds.) *Discourse and Technology: Multimodal Discourse Analysis*. Washington, DC: Georgetown University Press. pp. 20–33.

Jones, R. 2013. *Health and Risk Communication*. London & New York: Routledge.

Kantrowitz-Gordon, I. 2013. Internet confessions of postpartum depression. *Issues in Mental Health Nursing*, 34(12), 874–882.

Kilgarriff, A. 2005. Language is never ever ever random. *Corpus Linguistics and Linguistic Theory*, 1(2), 263–276

Kim, J., La Porte, L., Corcoran, M., Magasi, S., Batza, J. & Silver, R.K. 2010. Barriers to mental health treatment among obstetric patients at risk for depression. *American Journal of Obstetrics and Gynecology*, 202(3), 1–5.

Koester, A. 2010. Building small specialised corpora. In A. O'Keeffe & M. McCarthy (eds.) *The Routledge Handbook of Corpus Linguistics.* London: Routledge. pp. 66–79.

McEnery, T. & Hardie, A. 2012. *Corpus Linguistics: Method, Theory And Practice*. Cambridge: Cambridge University Press.

Malinowski, B. 1923. The problem of meaning in primitive languages. In C. K. Ogden & I.A. Richards (eds.) *The Meaning of Meaning. A Study of the Influence of Language upon Thought and of the Science of Symbolism*. Reissue Edition. London: Kegan Paul. pp. 296–336.

Marchi, A. & Taylor, C. 2009. If on a winter's night two researchers … A challenge to assumptions of soundness of interpretation. *Critical Approaches to Discourse Analysis across Disciplines*, 3(1), 1–20.

Maturana, H. R. & Varela, F. J. 1987. *The Tree of Knowledge: The Biological Roots of Human Understanding*. Boston: Shambhala Publications.

National Health Service (NHS). 2016. Postnatal depression. Available online at: http://www.nhs.uk/Conditions/Postnataldepression/Pages/Introduction.aspx (accessed 28 June 2017).

Partington, A., Duguid, A. & Taylor, C. 2013. *Patterns and Meanings in Discourse. Theory and Practice in Corpus-Assisted Discourse Studies (CADS)*. Amsterdam: John Benjamins.

Pedersen, S. 2016. The good, the bad and the 'good enough' mother on the UK parenting forum Mumsnet. *Women's Studies International Forum*, 59, 32–38.

Rayson, P. 2008. From key words to key semantic domains. *International Journal of Corpus Linguistics*, 13(4), 519–549.

Roberts, L. D. 2015. Ethical issues in conducting qualitative research in online communities. *Qualitative Research in Psychology*, 12(3), 314–325.

Rychlý, P. 2008. A lexicographer-friendly association score. In P. Sojka and A. Horák (eds.) *Proceedings of Recent Advances in Slavonic Natural Language Processing*, RASLAN 2008. Brno: Masaryk University. pp. 6–9.

Scott, M. 2010. Problems in investigating keyness, or clearing the undergrowth and marking out trails. In M. Bondi and M. Scott (eds.) *Keyness in Texts*. Amsterdam: John Benjamins. pp. 43–58.

Sealey, A. 2010. Probabilities and surprises: a realist approach to identifying linguistic and social patterns, with reference to an oral history corpus. *Applied Linguistics*, 31(2), 215–235.

Semino, E., Demjén, Z., Demmen, J., Koller, V., Payne, S., Hardie, A. & Rayson, P. 2017. The online use of violence and journey metaphors by patients with cancer, as compared with health professionals: A mixed methods study. *BMJ Supportive & Palliative Care*, 7, 60–66.

Taylor, C. 2013. Searching for similarity using corpus-assisted discourse studies. *Corpora*, 8(1), 81–113.

Taylor, C. 2014. Investigating the representation of migrants in the UK and Italian press: A cross-linguistic corpus-assisted discourse analysis. *International Journal of Corpus Linguistics*, 19(3), 368–400.

Vessey, R. 2016. *Language and Canadian Media: Representations, Ideologies, Policies*. London: Palgrave.

Williams, J. 2014. *Understanding Poststructuralism*. London: Routledge.

7

INTERDISCIPLINARY APPROACHES IN CORPUS LINGUISTICS AND CADS

Clyde Ancarno

7.1 Introduction

In academia, interdisciplinarity has become a watchword for many individuals, groups and institutions internationally. It is so well established that the features of interdisciplinary discourse(s) have themselves become the focus of investigation[1]. Academics worldwide are encouraged to take part in interdisciplinary projects (e.g. my institution has a funding stream dedicated to seed funding projects 'that will deliver on King's multi and inter disciplinary vision for research'[2]); many academic institutions and departments explicitly integrate interdisciplinarity in their research agenda; the media report on the implications of doing interdisciplinary research from a career perspective (e.g. Byrne 2014); and research funding bodies promote their interdisciplinary funding opportunities, e.g. the ESRC mission statement includes a section entitled 'Interdisciplinarity'[3] (*my emphasis*):

> Interdisciplinarity
> As part of our portfolio, we also expect to support new and exciting *research which combines approaches from more than one discipline.* We recognise that many of the most pressing research challenges are interdisciplinary in nature, both within the social sciences and between the social sciences and other areas of research. However, we also remain committed to the support of excellent research within a single discipline.

The list goes on. But underlying this debate on the role of interdisciplinarity in higher education seem to be a range of often unspoken assumptions, understandings (e.g. interdisciplinarity is seen to mean a combination of disciplinary approaches by the ESRC) and appreciations for interdisciplinarity. On the other hand, there also seem to be different kinds of interdisciplinarities. For example, bridging the gap between 'hard' and 'soft' sciences has been salient in this debate, as indicated by widespread commitments to support interdisciplinary projects involving the arts and sciences (e.g. New College of Interdisciplinary Arts and Sciences in Arizona State University).

A complete assessment of the landscape of interdisciplinarity in academia worldwide, in the UK or in linguistics is beyond the scope of this chapter (for such reviews see for example Pan and Katrenko 2015). This chapter focusses on specific interdisciplinary ventures in linguistics, namely those where insights from a particular kind of linguistic research (linguistic research where corpus linguistic methods are used) is integrated with research from disciplines other than linguistics. The core 'discipline' focussed on throughout this chapter is therefore linguistics, not corpus linguistics or corpus-assisted discourse studies (henceforth CADS). Although these are sometimes referred to as disciplines by some, as I explain later, I consider them to be a set of methods and a specific methodological approach in corpus linguistics respectively.

Before exploring such interdisciplinary ventures in linguistics, I will explain the view of interdisciplinarity in this chapter. Despite the extensive literature on interdisciplinarity in academia and beyond, there is little consensus on what interdisciplinarity is (e.g. Moran 2010: 14 refers to the 'slipperiness' of the term). Interdisciplinarity is also consistently considered to be similar to or to overlap with other kinds of integration of disciplines, e.g. cross-, multi-, trans- and pluri- disciplinarity. Stember usefully distinguishes between different kinds of integration of disciplines (1991: 4), representing interdisciplinarity, crossdisciplinarity and other kinds of integration as a continuum focussed on capturing the extent to which the disciplines are integrated with each other. This continuum is ordered as follows: intradisciplinarity, crossdisciplinarity, multidisciplinarity, interdisciplinarity and transdisciplinarity. Intradisciplinary research involves, for example, no integration of disciplines whereas transdisciplinary research leads to a transcending of the intellectual frameworks at work, i.e. the development of new intellectual frameworks. In this chapter, I adopt Stember's (1991: 5) view of interdisciplinarity which focusses on fully integrating the disciplines involved (rather than merely 'combining' them as in crossdisciplinary or multidisciplinary research):

> A genuinely interdisciplinary enterprise is one that requires more or less integration and even modification of the disciplinary contributions (...) In interdisciplinary efforts, participants must have an eye toward the holistic complex of interrelationships and take into account contributions of others in making their own contributions. Interdisciplinary, then, is a complex endeavour that seeks to explicate relationships, values and context using the diversity and unity possible only through collaborative approaches.

Following this definition of interdsiciplinarity, I argue that linguistic work utilising corpus linguistic/CADS methods or methodology while drawing on one or more branches of linguistics (i) is not 'interdisciplinary' (it is likely to be 'multimethod') and that (ii) rather than being referred to as 'disciplines' appropriate terms must be found to refer to the other branches of linguistics utilising corpus linguistic/CADS methods or methodology (e.g. 'branches', 'cognate fields', 'perspectives', 'approaches', 'sub-disciplines'). 'Interdisciplinary applications in corpus linguistics' therefore refer to applications of corpus linguistic methods in non-linguistic fields and collaborations between corpus and other linguists are excluded from the discussion in this chapter because they raise starkly different questions (in comparison with collaborations between corpus linguists and scholars from non-linguistic fields). The increasing use of corpus linguistic methods within and outside linguistics recall their ability to explore any kind of discourse (in some ways CADS is the prototypical example of this ability). Meanwhile this flexibility also shows that in comparison with methods and methodologies used in other branches of linguistics, corpus linguistic/CADS research is therefore more susceptible of interdisciplinary applications than research in these other branches.

In the light of the recent and unexpected burgeoning of interdisciplinary projects in corpus linguistics/CADS, this chapter aims to examine the range and applications of such research. For several reasons, this is challenging. Notwithstanding the issues concerning the sometimes-problematic way(s) in which corpus linguistics is integrated in such interdisciplinary studies (e.g. studies where the corpus basis relies on a limited understanding of what corpus linguistics is/does), it is difficult to know with precision 'how much' interdisciplinary corpus linguistic research is indeed carried out. In my personal experience, I have been startled by the extent to which corpus linguistic methods are used inside of the research centre I belong to in my own institution (let alone outside). There are several reasons for this. When interdisciplinary journals (e.g. *Interdisciplinary Journal for Germanic Linguistics and Semiotic Analysis*, *Soundings*) are not available, interdisciplinary corpus linguistics/CADS research may be published in discipline-specific journals corpus linguists are unlikely to ever read. Other reasons include the fact that interdisciplinary corpus linguistic/CADS research may not be described as such by scholars when they are reporting their research (e.g. Hoover et al. 2014 make no reference to interdisciplinarity) or that it is sometimes difficult to gauge how interdisciplinary a project is. In corpus linguistics, the lack of a clear definition of interdisciplinarity seems to lead to a multilayering of interdisciplinarity with corpus linguistics and some of its constituencies all being labelled as 'interdisciplinary', e.g. (*my emphasis*):

> To help demonstrate that it falls within the scope of CALL [computer-assisted language learning], let us clarify terms. *Corpus linguistics is an interdisciplinary field closely related to or overlapping computational linguistics.* (…) As many research tools in these two fields are identical, the difference between computational and corpus linguistics is not easy to tell, lying basically in approach and research goals. (…) to paraphrase, the goal of corpus linguistics could be defined as the empirical study of language based on electronic corpora, carried out with the help of computer software, with the aim of using its results in a range of fields, such as computational linguistics or language teaching.
>
> *(Szirmai 2002: 92)*

Partington (2007: 267) also refers to CADS as a 'nascent interdisciplinary field' while Marchi et al., 10 years on, highlight the tension between its interdisciplinary potential and the scarcity of actual interdisciplinary CADS research:

> Because of its explorative nature and omnivorous interests, CADS appears to have an intrinsic interdisciplinary vocation, and yet there are very few examples of actual interdisciplinary research to date.
>
> *(Marchi et al. 2017: 174)*

Discussing how right/wrong these statements are (e.g. like me, some of you may take issue with Szimai's (i) suggestion that there is no distinction between language and language use and (ii) conflation of computational and corpus linguistics) is not my intent here. However, these observations usefully underline that, like in many other academic disciplines, there can be a lack of clarity about disciplinary boundaries or for the questions which arise when boundaries are crossed, transcended, blurred, etc. in corpus linguistic work. This lack of clarity of what constitutes interdisciplinary applications in corpus linguistics/CADS is further exemplified by the fact that research using corpus linguistic methods in certain branches of linguistics is referred to as 'interdisciplinary'. Romero-Trillo (2013), for example, refers to the purpose of his edited book 'Yearbook of corpus linguistics and pragmatics' as one which explores 'the interface between these disciplines [corpus linguistics and pragmatics] and offers a platform to scholars who combine both research methodologies to present rigorous and interdisciplinary findings about language in real use'.[4] Comparable positions are found in many other branches of linguistics. As indicated above, I contend that these are not interdisciplinary applications and would therefore be best described as multimethod or multimethodology.

The integration of linguistic research utilising corpus linguistic methods and research in other disciplines is particularly relevant to debates in linguistics concerning the greater impartiality achieved through the quantification of linguistic phenomena in corpus linguistics (this is questioned by Widdowson (2000) and others who argue that corpus enquiries are necessarily partial). Such a focus on the benefits of quantifiable results is not limited to linguistics (e.g. in the UK there is increasing pressure from funders to include more quantification in our academic work). It is therefore highly possible that scholars from other disciplines may be attracted to corpus linguistics because of its assumed quantitatively informed impartial insights into language. This is problematic and I argue that, from the point of view of non-linguists, a better perspective on collaborations with corpus linguists is to envisage the integration of corpus methods as one potentially allowing scientifically more sound insights into texts (both quantitative and qualitative) than if other methods were utilised. Interdisciplinary applications in corpus linguistics/CADS may therefore become more impartial, but not necessarily so. For example, rather than greater impartiality, the main contribution of the work may be to make the analysis more systematic and rigourous. In addition, these debates often presuppose that ad hoc observations or intuition (to name but a few) provide flawed insights into language. In interdisciplinary work involving disciplines relying heavily on these 'subjective' methods (e.g. history and anthropology), and even more so in multimethod interdisciplinary work such as the one presented in the case study (which combines corpus analyses with qualitative analyses informed by ethnography), these claims of greater impartiality seem untenable.

With these thoughts and limitations in mind, I will first focus on the key affordances and challenges presented by interdisciplinary corpus linguistic/CADS research. I will then use a corpus-assisted discourse analytic research project I have been involved in (as part of a larger five-year anthropological project) to illustrate some of the issues brought up in the first part of the chapter. To conclude, I will comment on and evaluate the contributions made by interdisciplinary approaches to corpus linguistic and CADS research. In doing so, I will situate such approaches within the increasingly variegated landscape of corpus linguistics/CADS, where the speed at which new corpus tools are developed and banks of electronically available data are gathered keep expanding the potential of corpus research. The triangulation of disciplines is therefore often one of many factors contributing to the increasing diversification of corpus linguistic/CADS research.

7.2 Interdisciplinary approaches in corpus linguistics and CADS

7.2.1 What is 'interdisciplinary' in corpus linguistics and CADS?

Drawing on the distinctions between four kinds of integration established earlier (see Stember 1991), I discuss below three *a priori* kinds of interdisciplinary approaches in corpus linguistic research (the last approach only corresponds to interdisciplinary work as understood in this chapter). First, there are instances when corpus linguistic research informs or is informed by research carried out in other disciplines. This applies to research where corpus linguists and scholars from other disciplinary fields each contribute their expertise to the study and where the engagement with each other's discipline is limited. A range of disciplines have thus become acquainted with corpus linguistics and vice versa (e.g. health and business studies). However, such research tends to be multidisciplinary rather than interdisciplinary in that the researchers involved work 'alongside' each other rather than 'together'.

Second, there are instances where corpus linguistics informs endeavours by individuals, groups and institutions outside of academia to gain insights into issues or situations they are interested in. An example is the *Beyond the checkbox project* based in the ESRC Centre for Corpus Approaches to Social Science (CASS) which aims to support the National Health Service in bettering their understanding of patient feedback to improve their services (Brookes & Baker 2017). These are not interdisciplinary *per se* and would be more adequately defined using terminology from engaged research literature, e.g. some of these projects may be qualified as community-engaged, participatory, action, co-created.

Third, there is research where corpus linguistics is used in synergy with other disciplines. In Wear's terms (1999: 299) – although his discussions concern collaborations between the social and natural sciences – these are 'truly interdisciplinary research endeavours where each constituent discipline informs the investigation of the others and where hypotheses might even be jointly formed'. A salient feature of such interdisciplinary applications is their integration rather than combination of disciplines (these are far less frequent than multidisciplinary applications). This means that knowledge and outputs are co-created, i.e. the disciplinary insights from all disciplines involved are integrated rather than presented alongside each other/combined. This is where, as I shall explain later, the corpus-assisted anthropological research presented in the case study lies.

This threefold classification of integration of corpus linguistic/CADS methods or methodology with other disciplines underlines the importance of understanding triangulation in discussions of interdisciplinarity (at least five types of triangulation tend to be identified; 'discipline triangulation' is one of them). Underpinning each one of the three different types of integration outlined above is a different type of engagement between corpus linguistics and the disciplines other than linguistics, communities, professional practitioners, etc. involved. In corpus linguistics, triangulation has received attention. This applies to the triangulation of disciplines (Nolte, Ancarno and Jones forthcoming) but also of texts[5], methods and researchers (e.g. Baker & Egbert 2016; Marchi & Taylor 2009), data triangulation (see Chapter 6 in this volume), statistical methods (the extent to which statistical calculations can lead to significantly different results) and software. The main argument of such studies is that triangulation can be useful in exploring areas in corpus linguistic research which can be (and often are) undetected or under-analysed, a view that is supported by the forthcoming case study.

There obviously is not a one-size-fits-all approach to interdisciplinary corpus linguistic/CADS research and those conducting this kind of research clearly need to consider carefully whether or not the other discipline involved is really a discipline. When undertaking what may seem an interdisciplinary corpus linguistic/CADS project, corpus linguists must therefore ask important questions such as:

> How cognate to linguistics are the other disciplines involved?
>
> Do the other scholars hold the same kinds of beliefs as corpus linguists (e.g. about the issue at stake, ontological and epistemological beliefs)?
>
> Does the work undertaken provide a linguistic theory or, like corpus linguistics, a set of methods which can help in developing theories?
>
> *(See Sharoff 2017: 543, who suggests that corpus linguistics provides a set of methods – as opposed to a linguistic theory)*

In addition, and in the light of the many discussions concerning the implications of interdisciplinarity for an academic's career, corpus linguists would seem to be well advised to reflect on their place in the interdisciplinary constituencies emerging from the kind of interdisciplinary work focussed on in this chapter (e.g. what it might mean for their professional identity) and the dangers of being merely at the service of or 'data/number providers' for scholars from non-linguistic fields. Crucially, I hope to have shown that distinguishing between interdisciplinarity and other kinds of integration of disciplines is often challenging (see Section 7.4.2 for a reflection on what corpus linguists/CADS scholars gain from working with other disciplines).

7.2.2 Scope

In Gries' article *Methodological and interdisciplinary stance in corpus linguistics* (2011), there is no mention of the ways in which corpus linguistic tools and methods can be used beyond linguistics. This underscores how recent the use of corpus linguistics by scholars other than linguists is (except for early work in lexicography, e.g. Sinclair's work – see Moon 2007 for a review of his work in lexicography in relation to the Cobuild Project). Two initiatives, however, have played a key role in promoting interdisciplinary applications in corpus linguistics: the community of researchers linked to *Critical Approaches to Discourse Analysis Across Disciplines* (CADAAD)[6] and the scholarly work undertaken in CASS mentioned above (concerned with promoting corpus linguistics in social sciences).

Reviewing interdisciplinary approaches in CADS research raises the issue of deciding whether corpus linguistic research is or is not CADS research (hence my focus on corpus linguistics and CADS simultaneously in this chapter). The understanding of CADS I work from here is that it concerns studies which combine explorations into (i) broad discursive patterns (i.e. corpus analyses underpinned by corpus outputs such as word frequency lists, keyword lists) with (ii) insights into more specific and detailed aspects of discourse(s) (i.e. discourse analyses informed by concordance lines, n-grams, whole texts). Although clarity about where we position our work is of course desirable, it is mainly positioned by others (e.g. when they cite our work in their publications or debate it in online academic forums). These 'others' may therefore not always appreciate (or have little interest in), for example, the distinction established by Baker et al. (2008) between (i) CADS approaches and (ii) approaches combining corpus linguistics and discourse historical approach (DHA):

> Although this article focuses on the research synergy of CL and CDA (and more specifically, on the discourse–historical approach; DHA), it will, perhaps unavoidably, also comment on the more general use of CL techniques in what has been termed corpus-assisted discourse studies (CADS; Partington, 2004, 2006). In examining the combination of methods normally used by CDA and CL, we undertake to show that neither CDA nor CL need be subservient to the other (as the word 'assisted' in CADS implies), but that each contributes equally and distinctly to a methodological synergy.
>
> *(Baker et al. 2008: 274)*

Although this is not the view of the authors, some may consider both approaches to be CADS. They may argue, for example, that to a certain extent corpus-assisted DHA research satisfies the definition of CADS by Partington as a field interested in exploring non-obvious meanings within specific discourses (2010). Besides recalling the need to refrain from attaching too much importance to labels, this may be seen to echo the phenomena of narrow specialisation and diversification in applied linguistics, and the consequent issues with its disciplinary identity referred to by Cook (2015: 427). Cook notably suggests that the variety and differences of the theoretical premises represented in applied linguistics research pose a potential threat to its identity.

Among the disciplines represented in this landscape of research integrating insights from one or more discipline(s) with insights from corpus linguistics/CADS are sociology (e.g. Zinn 2010 – this special issue of the *CADAAD Journal* is mainly about crossdisciplinary work), history (e.g. McEnery & Baker 2017; Byrne 2016; the *History and corpus linguistics network* at the University of Oxford), business and economics (e.g. Jaworska & Nanda 2016), geography (e.g. Donaldson et al. 2016 – work exploring the spatial dimension to corpus analysis by drawing on the field of Geographical Information Systems), education (see the *Quantitative language research: exploring the potential of Corpus Linguistics in Education* project[7]), organisational studies (e.g. Pollach 2012), social science and medicine (e.g. Seale et al. 2006), diplomatic history (e.g. Marchi et al. 2017; Marchi & Marsh 2016), law (see recognition that corpus linguistics may be of use in the courtroom itself: Zimmer 2011; or in addressing issues of legal interpretation: Mouritsen 2011), political sciences (e.g. Mulderrig 2011), literature/stylistics (e.g. Hoover et al. 2014), health studies (Semino et al. 2017) and anthropology (Nolte, Ancarno & Jones forthcoming).

First, some of the work cited in this by no means exhaustive list combines rather than integrates disciplines, which recalls the difficulty in identifying but also distinguishing multidisciplinary, crossdisciplinary, interdisciplinary and transdisciplinary and research. Besides, certain combinations of disciplines have already produced a lot of multidisciplinary work. For example, a lot of corpus linguistic/CADS research explores media texts, with studies on corpora of newspaper articles being particularly numerous (the large-scale Siena, Bologna, Portsmouth (SiBol/Port) corpus linguistic project which was set up in 2005 led to many such publications[8]). This may be linked to the ease of collection of newspaper corpora thanks to availability of electronic databases of newspapers in many languages (e.g. Nexis database). Corpus investigations into literary texts are widespread too (e.g. work in corpus stylistics such as the work of Mahlberg, Smith & Preston 2013; McIntyre 2012; Biber 2011; O'Halloran 2007). In discussions about and reflections on interdisciplinarity, it therefore seems important to realise that this work is very different in kind from 'truly' interdisciplinary work. Second, the variety of disciplines illustrated in this list reveals the diversity of topics inevitably covered by interdisciplinary work in corpus linguistics/CADS. Third, the breadth of interdisciplinary applications it foregrounds underscores that allowing for new explorations into the boundaries and limitations of corpus linguistics/CADS research has changed the latter tremendously (in terms of methods or methodology but also in terms of the nature of questions asked and the research process more broadly). Fourth, despite the challenges of such interdisciplinary applications (this is covered at length in the case study), the list points to the flexibility of corpus linguistics. Fifth, it also implicitly recalls the limitations and benefits of branding academic work (e.g. becoming invisible because the label is 'niche'). For example, one can easily imagine that the interdisciplinary work presented in the case study could be branded as 'corpus linguistic' by some and 'anthropological' by others.

This scoping of interdisciplinary approaches in corpus linguistic/CADS research has therefore demonstrated that truly interdisciplinary research may be less frequent than we may first think. The case study below will help illustrate some of the points evoked in this first part of the chapter, particularly the complexity of interdisciplinary approaches in corpus linguistic/CADS research, the difficulty in separating the triangulation of disciplines from other inherent features of interdisciplinary research, and the time required for interdisciplinary research.

7.3 Case study: combining corpus linguistics and anthropology

The case study concerns a collaboration between a social anthropologist (Insa Nolte), an anthropologically informed literary scholar (Rebecca Jones), and a corpus linguist and discourse analyst (myself) as part of the 'Knowing each other: everyday religious encounters, social identities and tolerance in southwest Nigeria' (henceforth KEO) project. This collaboration occurred after the project data was collected, hence some of the challenges mentioned relate to this. I will first introduce the anthropological project (particularly the survey data we used as a corpus), our corpus-assisted anthropological methodology and the challenges we faced using this methodology. I will then provide a sample of findings (based on the trigram 'do not like') to illustrate the greater complexity of insights we gained into the data (in comparison to more traditional anthropological methods such as ethnographic observations). The strengths and weaknesses of the corpus-assisted anthropological work represented by this data are discussed in Section 7.4 of this chapter.

7.3.1 'Knowing each other: everyday religious encounters, social identities and tolerance in southwest Nigeria'

Aims

Between February 2012 and July 2017, the KEO project was based at the University of Birmingham and Osun State University in Nigeria.[9] Led by Insa Nolte, the project included up to 22 staff in the first two years but thereafter between 12 and 16 staff, mostly based in Nigeria. For most of my collaboration with the KEO project, Insa Nolte and Rebecca Jones were based at the University of Birmingham and there were a further 11 researchers based at Osun State University in Nigeria. The scope of the collaboration did not allow for me to meet the latter colleagues, but in addition to statisticians and literary scholars, most of them were historians and anthropologists.

The project examined how Muslim, Christian and 'traditionalist'[10] Yoruba speakers from southwest Nigeria relate to each other. Although the Yoruba of southwest Nigeria have converted both to Islam and Christianity in significant numbers, Yorubaland has, unlike many other multi-religious societies in Africa or beyond, not experienced sustained religious conflict. At the same time, interpersonal relationships between Yoruba Muslims, Christians and traditionalists are also markedly different from those in most other religiously mixed societies, as members of different religions among the Yoruba interact with each other frequently and on an everyday basis. A key focus of the project was to explore the social mechanisms by which relations between these members of different religions are negotiated, and the project findings continue to inform ongoing research by several of its former members, including Nolte, Jones and myself.

A corpus of elicited data in Nigerian English

Extensive qualitative data (e.g. interviews, archival research, ethnographic observation) and quantitative data (e.g. large-scale ethnographic survey which produced quantitative information about religion in Yorubaland) were produced and collated as part of the project.

The corpus examined for this case study was taken from the large-scale ethnographic survey carried out in 2012–2013. The survey reached 2,819 respondents from different Yoruba-speaking communities, with each person answering 60 open-ended questions (as well as a wealth of questions for quantitative analysis). The open-ended questions asked respondents to discuss their own or family members' experiences of inter-religious relations, and their views on a range of scenarios involving inter-religious encounters. For example, respondents were asked to provide information about their own or family members' experiences of inter-religious encounters and about the reasons why they, their spouse, parents or grandparents had converted to another religion. Other questions prompted respondents to report attempts other people had made to try and convert them, the reasons why they felt people in general convert to other religions, the ways they participated in practices associated with other religions or Yoruba traditions and how they accommodated people of other religions in their own social or family lives.

Respondents' answers were on average one to two sentences long, although some respondents gave longer answers. Respondents filled in the questionnaire in English and Yoruba, i.e. the overall corpus is bilingual (in roughly equal proportions). The results reported here focus on the English sub-corpus (henceforth the KEO English corpus) only, a corpus of approximately 450,000 words. A number of respondents used code-switches to Yoruba or Arabic within their otherwise English-language answers, e.g. when quoting Yoruba-language proverbs.

Since the data was not gathered for the purpose of corpus analysis, much of the literature on corpus design and collection is not immediately relevant (e.g. considerations regarding the range and types of texts to be included in a corpus). This is often true of projects using corpus tools and methods not because of what they can help them say about language, but because they can be useful in gaining new insights into social issues represented through language (this applies to many interdisciplinary projects). It may therefore be argued that our corpus collection consisted mainly in tidying and formatting the data in a way that would allow us to be as flexible as possible when we interrogate it (e.g. being able to devise sub-corpora to answer specific research questions). The KEO project's focus on a region of the world in which not all adults finish school and where levels of literacy vary greatly across the society meant that many of the questionnaires featured a high level of incorrect or idiosyncratic spelling and grammar. In addition, research assistants who helped with the data entry were also sometimes inconsistent. For example, they had their own spelling mistakes/idiosyncrasies (e.g. there were 21 variations on the spelling of 'Christian' e.g. 'Chrisitan', 'Chirtian', 'Christien', 'Chritian', 'Cristian' and 'Xtian'). With the help of a research assistant familiar with Nigerian English, Olufemi Olumide, spelling variations and other issues were standardised in the KEO English corpus. Insofar as the survey was in a spreadsheet format, it was turned into a searchable corpus by means of a script[11] which extracted the text in all cells corresponding to answers to open ended questions in the survey data. Although we were able to keep some of the information originally available in the spreadsheet (see below), we were unable to keep information regarding the questions which had been asked (when necessary we therefore had to go back to the original survey data). No standard markup system (such as the Text Encoding Initiative/TEI) was used but information about the following aspects of the texts/respondents was nevertheless captured:

1 Gender: M/F
2 Current faith: Christian/Muslim/Traditionalists
3 Conversion:

  a Participant has never converted.
  b Participant used to be Christian and has converted to Islam.
  c Participant used to be Muslim and has converted to Christianity.
  d Participant used to be traditional worshipper and converted to Islam.
  e Participant used to be traditional worshipper and converted to Christianity.
  f Participant used to be Christian and converted to traditional worship.
  g Participant used to be Muslim and converted to traditional worship.
  h Participant used to be Christian and a traditional worshiper and converted to Christianity.
  i Participant used to be Muslim and a traditional worshiper and converted to Islam.
  j Participant used to be Christian and Muslim and converted to Islam.
  k Participant used to be Muslim and converted to Islam and traditional religion.

4 Local Government Areas (x16 + 2 pilots = 18 LGAs)
5 Language used during the interview or to fill out the questionnaire: English, Yoruba, both
6 Generation: 18–20, 21–25, 26–30, 31–35, 36–40, 41–45, 46–50, 51–55, 56–60, 61–65, 66–75, 76+

What kind of interdisciplinarity?

As noted previously, the work discussed here is 'truly' interdisciplinary for the outputs and knowledge created as part of it draws on corpus linguistics and discourse analysis (since we adopted a CADS approach) but also anthropology. An initial interest in collaboration emerged from a conversation between Nolte and myself in 2012, as the survey was carried out. With the aim of finding an area where corpus analysis would contribute to the larger questions asked by the project, I acquainted myself with relevant anthropological methods and anthropological research on Yorubaland (particularly the place of religion in this religiously diverse environment) over a two-year period. During this time, Nolte and Jones also learnt about corpus linguistics, its software and the kinds of outputs corpus linguistics studies can produce. We all had to read quite extensively during that time and were in a position to consider approaches and exploratory findings only after this initial time period.

Although some may consider our work resembles work in the interdisciplinary fields of linguistic anthropology (broadly understood as the study of how language influences social life) or linguistic ethnography (work drawing on linguistics and ethnography to address a wide range of questions in various disciplines such as education, anthropology, linguistics, health – see Maybin & Tusting 2011: 515), it seems to differ from more than shares similarities with such work. We note for example that anthropological knowledge about Yoruba society rather than knowledge about the linguistic landscape/languages in Yoruba society was our starting point, hence distinguishing it from linguistic anthropological work which would rely firstly on language. In addition, our work does not use the kinds of linguistic procedures traditionally used in linguistic ethnographic work to describe patterns of communication (Rampton et al. 2004, 2007 special issue of the *Journal of Sociolinguistics* Vol. 11 Issue 5).

7.3.2 Methodology

In linguistic work using corpus linguistic methods, as in work carried out in many other disciplines, there is sometimes a lack of distinction between methods and methodologies.[12] For example, Baker et al. (2008 – the article focusses on presenting a methodological 'synergy' combining corpus linguistics and CDA) seem to use 'methodologies traditionally associated with corpus linguistics (CL)' and 'the combination of methods normally used by CDA and CL' interchangeably (Baker et al. 2008: 273–274). Corpus linguistics is widely understood as a methodology,[13] hence potentially making CADS a specific methodological approach within corpus linguistics. However, following the understanding of methods and methodology underpinning this chapter, I find it more accurate to understand corpus linguistics as a set of methods and CADS as a methodology in linguistics (one utilising methods traditionally associated with corpus linguistics and discourse analysis).

The corpus-assisted anthropological case study is therefore characterised by a triangulation of disciplines, but also of methodologies/methods for our methodological integration draws on corpus linguistic methods and methods of analysis used in anthropology and is informed more broadly by CADS methodology. Our work is therefore both interdisciplinary and multimethod/multimethodology. The methods used for each methodology are potentially vast (e.g. corpus queries formulated to address specific research questions, word/lemma frequency list analysis for CADS; participant observation, oral histories, textual analysis, historical analysis, comparative analysis, large-scale quantitative data collection for anthropology). Three sets of methods were used for the case study presented here: (i) corpus methods (analyses of a list of trigrams and concordances), (ii) methods of analysis traditionally associated with anthropology (particularly information gained through participant observations, interviews, field notes, the original ethnographic survey and reflexivity) and (iii) to a much lesser extent quantitative methods of analysis in anthropology (information provided by respondents in the survey data). The corpus methods, however, are always our first and main point of entry into the data, namely anthropological methods are only used to supplement the corpus analyses.

One of the most significant strengths of CADS methodology is its ability to accommodate the needs of researchers from different (disciplinary) backgrounds. This is evoked by Partington (2016) and other CADS scholars who highlight how corpus outputs may indicate multiple explanations for phenomena. In addition, methods of analysis used in anthropology are well-known for the rich ('thick') descriptions of complex human behaviours it allows. While our corpus methods of analysis give us quantitative insights into our data, our methodology gives us mostly qualitative insights into the survey data we turned into a corpus. Our methods of analysis are clearly distinct from those traditionally used in anthropology (no research to date in anthropology, has, to my knowledge, relied on corpus methods to analyse text-based anthropological data) and is also relatively innovative in the landscape of interdisciplinary CADS research.

7.3.3 Challenges

Before discussing a small sample of findings and why we felt corpus methods gave us insights into the survey data which would not have been possible without using corpus methods, the challenges we faced in adopting the interdisciplinary and multimethod/methodology approach described above are explored.

The interpretation of the data raised many questions. For example, we were aware of the possible influence of pre-existing views on the data (e.g. other publications based on the project include Nolte et al. 2017; Nolte 2017) and the risk of cherry-picking what we thought was interesting in our corpus outputs. A corpus linguistic/CADS approach helped minimise this effect by relying on patterns to decide what is interesting. This did not mean, however, that we excluded more marginal facts (these are mostly acceptable and welcome in anthropological inquiry).

There were also challenges pertaining to the difficulty in understanding what claims we could make based on our findings and the style of our arguments. Nolte and Jones remarked that unlike corpus linguists, anthropologists commonly state claims or reflections concerning their findings at the beginning of a paragraph or discussion, and they set out how these arguments are supported by findings subsequently.

Time was also a significant challenge, particularly the time taken by the tidying and formatting of the data and the two-year period of crossdisciplinary familiarisation I have already referred to.

From an epistemological point of view, the process of integrating corpus and anthropological methods of analyses was a fruitful exercise (e.g. some of the questions we asked of the data were radically different from the ones we would have asked had we not been engaged in this collaborative interdisciplinary work).

Another challenge was the fact that corpus linguistics was integrated in the project after the data was collected. This has meant that we have sometimes been limited in the way we could engage with the data (e.g. we could not include information about the questions asked).

More recently, we have discussed the validity of our methodological approach among scholars in anthropology and linguistics. So far, we have predominantly engaged with corpus linguists/CADS scholars (our methodological innovations have been met with more caution in anthropology and we are yet to fully engage with anthropologists). However, the lack of interest ('caution') of some scholars regarding interdisciplinary scholarly work may also be linked to 'interdisciplinary fatigue' (an argument I have heard on several occasions in research-focussed meetings with fellow colleagues).

Although these challenges were embraced by the three of us and mostly seen as an opportunity to develop as researchers, they nonetheless echo challenges inherent to any interdisciplinary work, namely (i) the challenge of reconciling our different disciplinary traditions, epistemologies, ontologies and ways of doing research and (ii) the time this process can take.

7.3.4 Linguistic and anthropological insights into trigrams

I have chosen to comment on insights we gained into the data from looking at phraseology in the KEO English corpus (trigrams/most frequent strings of three words in a corpus). This is because trigrams allow insights into complex/intricate aspects of the data and raise issues that corpus outputs focussed on single-words do not raise. My comments largely draw on findings having emerged from our first attempt at applying the interdisciplinary methodology outlined above (see Nolte,

Ancarno and Jones forthcoming[14]). The aim of this initial article was exploratory, namely to provide insights into inter-religious relations in Yorubaland and test our methodological approach. The KEO English corpus underpins the analyses. I have chosen trigrams as I think they illustrate particularly well the extent to which corpus linguistics and anthropology were 'integrated' rather than 'combined'. The discussions will highlight that with interdisciplinary work, debates concerning the centrality of interpretation in corpus linguistics (e.g. the outputs are not analysis and do not speak for themselves) are revived. I will now present how we analysed and interpreted trigrams, while making sure to explicate the interdisciplinary process in this instance (see Table 7.1).

The list of lemmatised trigrams (Table 7.1) was calculated using Sketch Engine. As might be expected, Nolte, Jones and I noticed different things in this output. For example, we had lengthy discussions about the meaningfulness of pronouns (they were at first surprised that I should find such linguistic units of any interest). This crossdisciplinary exchange process is of course cumulative in that as we continue to work together we use previous discipline-focussed exchanges to inform the way we engage with new corpus outputs. This informs various stages of our collaboration (e.g. formulation of research question integrating theoretical insights from all disciplines, decision to focus on a particular theme/word etc.).

We looked at concordances and collocates of specific trigrams, e.g. 'do not like' which I focus my attention on in Table 7.2. As previously suggested, these corpus methods of analysis were also supplemented by insights from Nolte and

TABLE 7.1 Top 20 lemmatised trigrams for the KEO English corpus

	Lemmatized trigram	*Raw freq.*
1.	i do not	3038
2.	do not have	1042
3.	i be a	660
4.	it be a	634
5.	do not believe	622
6.	i can not	615
7.	because it be	601
8.	not believe in	576
9.	it be not	559
10.	be a christian	548
11.	the same god	519
12.	because i be	502
13.	i be not	480
14.	because i do	457
15.	do not know	432
16.	it depend on	422
17.	if it be	395
18.	it be against	378
19.	do not like	368
20.	be against my	364

Jones based on their anthropological work in (southwest) Nigeria (e.g. they used their extensive ethnographic knowledge of Yoruba society to add to, corroborate or invalidate insights gained from corpus analyses) and results yielded by other analyses of the project data (e.g. the survey as well as other data). This is how we were able to arrive at the findings I am presenting below.

Based on Table 7.1, our first (and joint) observation was that many of the lemmatised trigrams in our corpus had an interpersonal function (see Carter & McCarthy 2006: 834–837 for a list of all the functions of n-grams) and that these tended to be used by respondents to assert boundaries between themselves and people from different religious backgrounds. However, it also emerged that pronouns were often used to express personal preferences (e.g. *do not believe* [as in 'I do not believe in the rites of our family'], 'it BE against' [as in, 'it is against my religion']).

While focussing on pronouns, the trigram 'do not like' (19th most frequent lemmatised trigram in the corpus, 368 occurrences) stood out with concordances showing how the respondents manage personal preferences, including their dislike of certain religious practices. At this point I should mention that during one of our many discussions Nolte and Jones alerted me to the fact that the expression of personal preference in everyday life is handled differently in Nigeria than in the UK and other Western countries. They explained it would be common for people not to take offence at statements that expressed personal preferences and would be considered offensive in the UK and other Western countries. They explained that conversations in southwest Nigeria are framed by the relative importance of the speakers' statuses, with juniors in the presence of seniors normally only expressing their personal likes or dislikes if invited to do so. However, among peers, or in response to an invitation to share one's views, telling someone who is wearing trousers that you 'don't like trousers' (a true anecdote) would normally be perceived as not or only very mildly face-threatening. Nolte and Jones explained that such a statement would be perceived as an expression of personal preference rather than a normative statement, and that it could be glossed as 'I do not like to wear trousers myself but that does not mean that I would want to limit the rights of others, such as yourself, to wear trousers'. While examining concordances of 'do not like', we gained insights into the interplay between personal preferences and societal norms. As this phrase tended to be used almost exclusively in combination with the first person singular pronoun 'I' (338 out of 368 occurrences of 'do not like'[15]), we used it to explore what the respondents do not like.

To do so, we used the concordances of 'I do not like' to devise a frequency-based list of things or people respondents said they did not like (see Table 7.3). Some answers, such as 'to be famous' and 'to be noticed' refer to respondents' reluctance to take chieftaincy titles. While these do not explicitly relate to religion, Nolte and Jones, drawing on their ethnographic fieldwork, were able to observe that they nonetheless refer to local hierarchies closely associated with traditional practices and authority. Over 90 per cent of the occurrences of this trigram relate closely to religion. They reveal that respondents often describe not liking 'anything' about

TABLE 7.2 Sample of concordance lines for lemmatised trigram 'I DO NOT LIKE'

religions. Belief matters, I don't adopt what I	don't like	as solution. Since their medicine also
God so as to be worthy of his kingdom. I	don't like	asking for advice from such people. for
supported Sagamu day because it's fun. I	don't like	because some people use charm for one another
I don't like them. In the sense that God	doesn't like	being sharing praise with all this small
religion . I can't serve two God. because I	don't like	celebrating family customs. Giving them
involve rituals. I don't have interest. I	don't like	chieftaincy title. My belief do not support
of it. It is the right of my lineage. I	don't like	chieftaincy title. It requires a lot of
that I will not accept their religion. I	don't LIKE	CHIEFTAINCY TITLE. because I knows nothing
Christian. because I do not have faith in it. I	do not like	chieftaincy titles. because it is an honour
because I am next child of my parents. I	do not like	chieftaincy titles. It is my right. because
serve my people. I am a female child. I	do not like	chieftaincy titles. because, I am a born
of the traditions. Respect for elders. I	do not like	customs and traditions. I believe they
because we are living together as family. I	don't like	discrimination. because they too can gain
come in good faith. They are my people. I	didn't like	discrimination in anything I do. Tree ca
my problems. If I trust his divination. I	don't like	divination. I don't have faith in it. I
issues. Personal relationship with God. I	don't like	divination. Most of them are liar. I had
is my way of life. I believe in God . I	don't like	divination because it is un Godly. But
if he is Christian and a truthful one. I	don't like	diviner. Diviners glorifies demons. As
They should not discriminate. God him self	don't like	does who join order Gods with him. Positively
always invite me. don't believe in it. I	don't like	doing so. neighbours share gifts during
and pastor to do that for me. No. I just	do not like	doing such. I don't believe in asking for
because of their usual worship before God.I	don't like	everything in it. We don't belong to the
created by same God . Except Christians. I	don't like	excess celebration. The love I have for

TABLE 7.3 Frequency list of objects of 'do not like' (grouped into categories, e.g. 'chieftaincy titles' and 'chieftaincy title' grouped together as 'chieftaincy titles')

Object of 'do not like'	*Frequency*
It	151
Chieftaincy titles	23
Them	18
Yoruba customs and traditions	12
Anything about them	13
Such/such things	11
The way they worship/do their service	9
Islam/Muslims	8
The religion	6
Their religion	5
Anything	4
Divination or diviners	4
Traditional medicine	4
Any	3
Anything about it	2
Discrimination	2
Doing so/such	2
Getting involved in fetish/traditional	2
Going to hospital	2
His	2
That	2
Their behaviours	2
Their doctrine	2
This	2
To give them money	2
To hold such a post	2
Traditional things	2
All	1
Any more	1
Any of it	1
Any publications	1
Anything contrary to God	1
Anything in	1
Anything in their life	1
Anything in their traditions	1
Anything that goes with rituals	1
Asking for advice	1
Celebrating family customs	1
Everything in it	1
Excess celebration	1
Family customs	1
Going to Nasfat every Sunday	1
Her husband's religion	1
Her religion	1

(continued)

TABLE 7.3 (Continued)

Object of 'do not like'	*Frequency*
Inter-religion marriage	1
King	1
Moving around	1
None of their customs	1
Pay instruction	1
Sharing in celebrations	1
Taking medicine	1
The Catholic doctrines	1
The festival	1
The idea of going to a mosque	1
The rituals they perform during the festivals	1
The service	1
The song	1
The type of cloth they are using	1
The way Muslims do their burial	1
Their way	1
These festivals	1
Things like that	1
To associate with traditionalist	1
To be famous	1
To be noticed	1
To consult them	1
To do their husband's religion	1
To follow their wife	1
To get involved in them	1
To marry another religion	1
To support them	1
To	1
Traditional engagement ceremony	1
Traditionalist Christian friend	1
Traditional friend Muslim	1
Traditionalist religions	1
Using it	1
Visiting Muslims during this period	1
Walking by my foot	1

other religions, especially traditional religion, or express dislike for aspects of religious life that respondents were asked about in the survey (e.g. divination).

Respondents also describe actions they do not like, referring to ways they manage encounters with religious difference while drawing boundaries around personal behaviour (e.g. 'taking medicine', 'sharing in celebrations'). Thirteen respondents used 'their' after 'do not like', to refer to their 'behaviour', 'customs', 'doctrine', 'religion', 'ways', or 'ways of worship'. This indicated a distancing from the actions, preferences or beliefs of others. The phrase 'I do not like' also revealed that while the respondents asserted boundaries and active disavowals of certain practices, they often did so to express *personal* taste, rather than more normative beliefs about the world.

In 18 cases 'I do not like them' also featured. These concerned responses to questions about how respondents interacted with people or events associated with other religions (we had to check this in the original dataset). This phrase was used to justify their lack of interaction with people from different religions. This seemed surprising since behaviour vis-à-vis others was found in other parts of the data to be subjected to shared norms (e.g. behaving normally and co-operating and tolerating one another). The concordances revealed, however, that 'I do not like them' was used by respondents not to condemn aspects of others' behaviour but rather to describe avoiding situations in which shared social norms might force them to accommodate certain religious practices. Thus, our analyses highlighted that while respondents' behaviour seems to be informed by a set of norms, these do not proscribe the expression of personal preference provided they do not impinge on others' choices.

The respondents also expressed disagreement about religious differences (albeit to a lesser degree), e.g. they refer to instances when they felt their religious or personal freedoms had been impinged upon because of others' religious practices. In response to a question about whether they had experienced religious disagreements in their town, two respondents said the following:

1 Churches and mosques disturbing with their loud speakers at night cos of night prayers.
2 During the last Agemo festival where the traditionalists tried to force an alfa to remove his cap in respect of their religion.

Critique of religious others is clearly expressed as a perception that those others impose their religion, rather than as the respondents' desire to restrain others' freedoms. This supports the view that in Yorubaland, it is socially unacceptable to impose one's own religious preferences on others, and echoes the suggestion made above that the trigram 'do not like' tends to indicate personal preference rather than a disapproval of others' behaviour.

In summary, by integrating insights gained from corpus outputs (i.e. the list of lemmatised trigrams for the KEO English corpus; concordances for 'do not like') with those gained from Nolte and Jones's anthropological knowledge of the area and topic under investigation, we were able to uncover the complexity of the ways respondents assert their freedom to like (and dislike) particular religious practices. This applies to traditional practices which are recurrently referred to in the collocations of 'do not like' (e.g. 'I do not like divination'; 'I don't like getting involved in fetish/traditional practices'). However, our analyses also revealed that respondents claimed not to encroach on the freedom of others to assert their own likes and dislikes. In other words, when respondents withdraw from religious activities they do not like, they assert the boundaries between religions, rather than question the validity of other religions. Concerning these findings (and other findings utilising other corpus outputs as a starting point), Nolte and Jones noted for example that although they had been aware that formulations such as 'I do not like' were used by individuals to distance themselves from certain objects or practices without recourse to normative discourse, they had not been aware that the expression was used so frequently to express religious preferences. Moreover, they had not been aware that criticism of others centred less on their pursuit of different religious practices but on the (perceived) imposition of these religious practices on others. They considered the direct and indirect emphasis in the corpus on the importance of respondents and others' freedom to make and respect religious choices an important insight into the coexistence of Yoruba Muslims, Christians and traditionalists. The fact that they had so far been unable to gain the kinds of detailed insights our methodology allowed them to arrive at, indicates that corpus linguistic methods provide additional insights into the data we focussed on. However, they both reported that to date the most significant contribution of our collaborative work to their understanding of the project data was their discovery that the shared/overarching group (Yoruba) identity is closely linked to gender and social difference.

7.4 Discussion and conclusion

7.4.1 The case study

Clearly the way corpus linguistics engages with but also conceptualises language can benefit 'other' disciplines, providing different insights into textual data, making descriptions of language richer and more complete. For example, the analysis of trigrams allowed us to gain nuanced insights into the inter-religious discourse captured by the KEO English corpus which would have not been possible using anthropological methods alone.

But, was it worth it? It is only upon honestly weighing the benefits against the challenges and limitations of interdisciplinary work (see Section 7.3.3) that this question can be answered. Concerning the corpus-assisted anthropological work presented in the case study, the benefits outweighed the drawbacks but this was only true of the Nigerian English data (the Yoruba data is yet to be explored using a similar methodology).

The case study, like many other interdisciplinary projects, involved a triangulation of methods and methodologies. Nevertheless, the relatively neat picture of our methods and methodologies I painted in this chapter was inevitably deceptive to some degree. Understandings and usage of methods and methodologies vary greatly across disciplines (e.g. some historians consider they do not have methods *per se*, ethnography is both described as a methodology and a method in the anthropology literature) and the boundaries between methods and methodologies on the one hand, and methodology and theory on the other, are often uncertain. With interdisciplinary corpus linguistic/CADS research, finding ways for corpus methods to be accepted by the other discipline(s), especially when this/these other discipline(s) (like anthropology) is/are mainly driven by qualitative methods, can also be a challenge. Conversely, this type of triangulation also requires that corpus linguists accept methods other than theirs, which challenges both the future and definition of corpus linguistic/CADS research.

The case study also illustrates how well-trodden debates in corpus linguistics can usefully be reopened. For example, representativeness, corpus size and annotation (all perceived as key issues in corpus design), take new meanings in research where the corpora were not purpose-built.[16] In recent years, corpora have become increasingly more diverse. For example, while the size of corpora has got smaller, with some corpora now sometimes representing very narrow aspects of language use (e.g. because they are thematic or represent a specific genre), technologies have also allowed us to retrieve increasingly diverse ranges of corpora (e.g. tweets, multimodal data) but also much larger corpora (with web-crawled corpora allowing for very large corpora – with trillions of words – to now be compiled, e.g. the English Web 2013 enTenTen13 corpus in Sketch Engine). Corpora therefore include a greater diversity of genres and modalities. The data used in the case study is evidence of these changes in corpus linguistics, e.g. it focusses on elicited data (data which corpus linguistics shunned until recently for its naturalness may be questioned). The triangulation of disciplines, as important as it may be, is therefore one of many ways in which the scope of corpus linguistic research has been broadened and in which theoretical and methodological debates in corpus linguistics have been reinvigorated (e.g. half a day at the 2016 Corpora and Discourse International Conference focussed on methods and engaged with some of these challenges).

Although this chapter has concentrated on collaborative research projects, there is no denying that research where a single researcher might invest time in understanding the other discipline(s) can also be 'truly' interdisciplinary and raise similar questions.

7.4.2 What changes for corpus linguistics?

Like many branches of linguistics, corpus linguistics could until recently have been accused of being narrow and lacking a cross-, multi-, trans- or interdisciplinary basis (see Capone & Mey 2015: 90 for similar claims about pragmatics). I hope to have shown that the research using this method has been able to overcome such criticisms and that corpus linguistics has played a key role in bringing linguistics and language to the attention of other disciplines (something linguistics has traditionally had very limited experience of).

Although this chapter has mostly focussed on what corpus linguistics has to contribute to other disciplines (this can be linked to the fact that the contribution of corpus linguists in interdisciplinary projects is usually framed in these terms) and although it is too early to say with precision what kinds of changes in corpus linguistics/CADS have ensued as a result of interdisciplinary endeavours, at least two changes are already noticeable. First, these endeavours underline that partiality in corpus linguistic/CADS work, far from being an issue, does not preclude compelling insights into texts (e.g. the partiality can be accrued if corpus methods are combined with other methods of analysis). Second, the kind of work discussed here usefully encourages corpus linguists/CADS scholars to reflect on their unit of analysis, the text, but also on the centrality of language in their work, what it is and how it can be analysed. Indeed, in working across disciplinary boundaries, corpus linguists/CADS scholars have to acknowledge that the non-linguists colleagues they work with may have a different understanding of texts and/or very little formal processes for analysing texts (this seems true in anthropology).

Despite the rise in the number of interdisciplinary approaches in corpus linguistic/CADS research, relatively little formal support for such work is identifiable. The lack of literature, tools and resources accessible to scholars from other disciplines interested in using corpus linguistics in their own research is therefore in dire need of addressing. In addition, similar resources from other disciplines for corpus linguists/CADS scholars to learn about them (e.g. literature for non-specialists) is also not readily available.

In our era of 'big data' and its sometimes warped focus on truth, objectivity and accuracy, corpus linguistics and its tools and methods (often seen to reduce bias) have an undeniable appeal to scholars outside of linguistics. Corpus linguistics is clearly impacting on knowledge creation outside linguistics, a trend which, judging by what has happened so far, is likely to continue growing stronger over the coming years. Yet in the light of this exponential diversification of the landscape of corpus linguistic research, determining what constitutes corpus linguistic research will become more challenging. Many questions will need addressing, e.g. questions concerning the ways in which corpus linguistic work produced within the disciplinary boundaries of linguistics is going to co-exist with that produced outside. This obviously raises the issue of fragmentation of the field and maintenance of its conceptual coherence.

Notes

1 E.g. the ESRC-funded project *Investigating interdisciplinary research discourse: the case of Global Environmental Change* (IDRD) led by Paul Thompson and Susan Hunston. This is a collaboration between the Centre for Corpus Research at the University of Birmingham and the scientific publisher Elsevier.
2 https://www.kcl.ac.uk/innovation/research/support/Kings-Funding-Opportunities.aspx [last accessed 30 May 2017].
3 http://www.esrc.ac.uk/funding/guidance-for-applicants/impact-innovation-and-interdisciplinarity/ [last accessed 30 May 2017].
4 http://www.springer.com/series/11559 [last accessed 30 May 2017].
5 This refers to instances when different kinds of texts are used to explore a topic; e.g. in the 'People', 'Products', 'Pests' and 'Pets' project (funded by The Leverhulme Trust, grant number RPG-2013-063), the (nearly) 9 million-word corpus of texts about animals includes 9 different kinds of texts including transcripts of broadcasts, leaflets and labels.
6 http://www.cadaad.net/ [last accessed 30 May 2017].
7 http://www.stir.ac.uk/corpus-linguistics-in-education/ [last accessed 30 May 2017].
8 http://www.lilec.it/clb/?page_id=8 [last accessed 30 May 2017].
9 The project was funded by the European Research Council, through a Starting Researcher Grant (grant number 283466). It ended in July 2017.

10 In Yorubaland, these involve a range of eclectic practices, including but not restricted to the worship of ancestors and many deities (locally known as *òrìṣà*) which are linked to important personalities or natural phenomena (e.g. 'Yemoja' is the Yoruba deity of the sea hills and 'Oshun' that of the river and fresh water).

11 The formatting of the data was largely achieved with the support of Akira Murakami. He wrote an R script that allowed to convert each cell in the spreadsheet containing an answer to an open-ended question to be converted into a text file. All the resulting text files constitute our KEO English corpus. Akira Murakami also wrote two other R scripts, one that converted the data to a format that can be analysed through Sketch Engine and another which allows us to compile ad-hoc subcorpora combining the variables listed above in whichever way we want.

12 I acknowledge debates suggesting that the distinction between methods and methodologies is not always clear and that the boundaries between methodology and theory can also be blurred (I return to this later). For the purpose of this chapter, methodology is broadly understood as the principles which determine how certain methods are used in a piece of research, and methods as the 'tools' used to carry out this research.

13 This position is informed by the extensive debate between those arguing that corpus linguistics is a discipline/theory (the neo-firthian position in general, e.g. Tognini-Bonelli 2001; Teubert 2005: 2; Stubbs 1993: 2; Leech 1992: 106) and others that it is best understood as a methodology (the stance of most corpus linguists in CASS for example). Literature useful in understanding this debate includes McEnery and Hardie (2012), Gries (2010) and Taylor (2008). In addition to being seen as a discipline and methodology, corpus linguistics has also been seen as a method, approach, paradigm, discipline, to name but a few.

14 This concerns Section 7 of this article.

15 There were very few mentions of things 'they' (7 occurrences), 'some' (1), 'she' (6), 'he' (2), 'she/he' (2) 'husband' (6), 'God' (2), 'some' (1) or 'people' (3) do not like.

16 Such issues are echoed in other disciplines too (albeit framed in non-corpus terms). For example, the kind of large-scale survey data collection method used by Insa Nolte in her project is unusual in anthropology but it was used precisely to collect a sample of data representative of Yorubaland as a whole. This data is therefore distinctive as, unlike most research on Yorubaland, it explores social mechanisms observed far beyond urban centres.

References

Baker, P. & Egbert, J. (eds.) 2016. *Triangulating Methodological Approaches in Corpus Linguistic Research* (Vol. 17). London: Routledge.

Baker, P., Gabrielatos, C., Khosravinik, M., Krzyżanowski, M., McEnery, T. & Wodak, R. 2008. A useful methodological synergy? Combining critical discourse analysis and corpus linguistics to examine discourses of refugees and asylum seekers in the UK press. *Discourse & Society*, 19(3), 273–306.

Biber, D., 2011. Corpus linguistics and the study of literature: Back to the future? *Scientific Study of Literature*, 1(1), 15–23.

Brookes, G. & Baker, P. 2017. What does patient feedback reveal about the NHS? A mixed methods study of comments posted to the NHS Choices online service. *BMJ open*, 7(4), e013821.

Byrne, R. 2016. A historian's perspective on context and corpora. Paper presented at the IVACS Conference, Bath.

Byrne, S. 2014. Interdisciplinary research: why it's seen as a risky route, *The Guardian*, 19 February [online]. Available online at: https://www.theguardian.com/higher-education-network/blog/2014/feb/19/interdisciplinary-research-universities-academic-careers (accessed 5 May17).

Capone, A. & Mey, J.L. (eds.) 2015. *Interdisciplinary Studies in Pragmatics, Culture* and *Society* (Vol. 4). Dordrecht: Springer.

Carter, R. & McCarthy, M. 2006. *Cambridge Grammar of English: A Comprehensive Guide; Spoken and Written English Grammar and Usage*. Cambridge: Cambridge University Press.

Cook, G. 2015. Birds out of dinosaurs: The death and life of applied linguistics. *Applied Linguistics*, 36(4), 425–433.

Donaldson, C.E., Gregory, I.N. & Taylor, J.E. 2016. Implementing corpus analysis and GIS to examine historical accounts of the English Lake District. In P. Bol (ed.) *Historical Atlas: Its Concepts and Methodologies.* Seoul: Northeast Asian History Foundation. pp. 152–172.

Gries, S.T. 2010. Corpus linguistics and theoretical linguistics: A love–hate relationship? Not necessarily ... *International Journal of Corpus Linguistics*, 15(3), 327–343.

Gries, S.T. 2011. Methodological and interdisciplinary stance in corpus linguistics. In V. Viana, S. Zyngier & G. Barnbrook (eds.) *Perspectives on Corpus Linguistics*. Amsterdam: John Benjamins. pp. 81–98.

Hoover, D. L., Culpeper, J. & O'Halloran, K. 2014. *Digital Literary Studies: Corpus Approaches to Poetry, Prose, and Drama*. London: Routledge.

Jaworska, A. & Nanda, A. 2016. Doing well by talking good: A topic modelling-assisted discourse study of corporate social responsibility. *Applied Linguistics*, amw014.

Leech, G. N. 1992. Corpora and theories of linguistic performance. In J. Svartvik (ed.) *Directions in Corpus Linguistics. Proceedings of Nobel Symposium 82, Stockholm, 4–8 August*. Berlin/New York: De Gruyter Mouton. pp. 105–126.

L'Hôte, E. 2014. *Identity, Narrative and Metaphor: A Corpus-Based Cognitive Analysis of New Labour Discourse*. Basingstoke: Pallgrave Macmillan.

McEnery, A. & Baker, H. 2017. *Corpus Linguistics and 17th-century Prostitution: Computational Linguistics and History*. Bloomsbury Academic.

McIntyre, D. 2012. Corpora and literature. In C.A. Chapelle (ed.) *The Encyclopedia of Applied Linguistics*. Hoboken, NJ: John Wiley and Sons.

Mahlberg, M., Smith, C. & Preston, S. 2013. Phrases in literary contexts: Patterns and distributions of suspensions in Dickens's novels. *International Journal of Corpus Linguistics*, 18(1), 35–56.

Marchi, A. & Taylor, C. 2009. If on a winter's night two researchers ...: A challenge to assumptions of soundness of interpretation. *Critical Approaches to Discourses Analysis across Disciplines CADAAD Journal*, 3(1), 1–20.

Marchi, A. & Marsh, S. 2016. Churchill, Fulton and the Anglo-American special relationship: Setting the agenda? *Journal of Transatlantic Studies*, 14(4), 365–382.

Marchi, A., Lorenzo-Duz, N. & Marsh, S. 2017. Churchill's inter-subjective special relationship: A corpus-assisted discourse approach. In A.P. Dobson & S. Marsh (eds.) *Churchill and the Anglo-American Special Relationship*. London: Routledge.

Maybin, J. & Tusting, K. 2011. Linguistic ethnography. In J. Simpson (ed.) *Routledge Handbook of Applied Linguistics*. London: Routledge. pp. 515–528.

Moon, R. 2007. Sinclair, lexicography, and the Cobuild Project: The application of theory. *International Journal of Corpus Linguistics*, 12(2), 159–181.

Moran, J., 2010. *Interdisciplinarity*. London & New York: Routledge.

Mouritsen, S.C. 2011. Hard cases and hard data: Assessing corpus linguistics as an empirical path to plain meaning. *Columbia Science and Technology Law Review,* 13(Fall 2011), 156.

Mulderrig, J. 2011. The grammar of governance. *Critical Discourse Studies*, 8(1), 45–68.

Nolte, I. 2017. *'Ede is one Room': Encounters between Muslims, Christians and Traditionalists in a Yoruba Town*. Ondo: Adeyemi College Academic Publishers.

Nolte, I., Ogen, O. & Jones, R. (eds.). 2017. *Beyond Religious Tolerance: Encounters between Muslims, Christians and Traditionalists in an African Town*. Rochester, NY: James Currey Publishers/Boydell and Brewer.

Nolte, I., Ancarno, C. & Jones, R. (in press). Using corpus methods to explore a survey on inter-religious relations in Yorubaland, southwest Nigeria. *Corpora*.

O'Halloran, K., 2007. The subconscious in James Joyce's 'Eveline': A corpus stylistic analysis which chews on the 'Fish hook'. *Language and Literature*, 16(3), 227–244.

Pan, L. & Katrenko, S. 2015. A review of the UK's interdisciplinary research using a citation-based approach. Bristol: HEFCE.

Partington, A. 2004. Corpora and discourse, a most congruous beast. In A. Partington, J. Morley & L. Haarman (eds.) *Corpora and Discourse*. Bern: Peter Lang. pp. 11–20.

Partington, A. 2006. Metaphors, motifs and similes across discourse types: Corpus-Assisted Discourse Studies (CADS) at work. *Trends in Linguistics Studies and Monographs*, 171, 267.

Partington, A. 2007. Metaphors, motifs and similes across discourse types: Corpus-assisted discourse studies (CADS) at work. In A. Stefanowitsch & S.T. Gries (eds.) *Corpus-based Approaches to Metaphor and Metonymy* (Vol. 171). Berlin: Walter de Gruyter. p. 267.

Partington, A. 2010. Modern Diachronic Corpus-Assisted Discourse Studies (MD-CADS) on UK newspapers: An overview of the project. *Corpora*, 5(2), 83–108.

Partington, A. 2016. Corpus-assisted Discourse Studies (CADS). *6th Critical Approaches to Discourse Analysis across Disciplines (CADAAD) Conference*. Catania, Sicily, 5–7 September.

Pollach, I. 2012. Taming textual data: The contribution of corpus linguistics to computer-aided text analysis. *Organizational Research Methods*, 15(2), 263–287.

Rampton, B., Tusting, K., Maybin, J., Barwell, R., Creese, A. & Lytra, V. 2004. UK linguistic ethnography: A discussion paper. *UK Linguistic Ethnography Forum*. Unpublished.

Romero-Trillo, J. (ed). 2013. *Yearbook of Corpus Linguistics and Pragmatics*. Dordrecht: Springer.

Seale, C., Ziebland, S. & Charteris-Black, J. 2006. Gender, cancer experience and internet use: A comparative keyword analysis of interviews and online cancer support groups. *Social Science & Medicine*, 62(10), 2577–2590.

Semino, E., Demjén, Z., Demmen, J., Koller, V., Payne, S., Hardie, A. & Rayson, P. 2017. The online use of violence and journey metaphors by patients with cancer, as compared with health professionals: A mixed methods study. *BMJ Supportive & Palliative Care*, 7(1), 60–66.

Sharoff, S., 2017. Corpus and systemic functional linguistics. In T. Bartlett and G. O'Grady (eds.) *The Routledge Handbook of Systemic Functional Linguistics*. London: Routledge. pp. 533–546.

Stember, M. 1991. Advancing the social sciences through the interdisciplinary enterprise. *The Social Science Journal*, 28(1), 1–14.

Szirmai, M. 2002. Corpus linguistics in Japan: Its status and role in language education. In P. Lewis (ed.) *The Changing Face of CALL (Vol. 2)*. Lisse, Netherlands: CRC Press. pp. 91–108.

Taylor, C., 2008. What is corpus linguistics? What the data says. *ICAME Journal*, 32, 179–200.

Teubert, W. 2005. My version of corpus linguistics. *International Journal of Corpus Linguistics*, 10(1), 1–13.

The Conversation. 2015. Ruth Wodak's profile. *The Conversation* [online]. Available online at: https://theconversation.com/profiles/ruth-wodak-192748 (accessed 20 April 2017).

Tognini-Bonelli, E. 2001. *Corpus Linguistics at Work* (Vol. 6). Amsterdam: John Benjamins.

Wear, D.N. 1999. Challenges to interdisciplinary discourse. *Ecosystems*, 2(4), 299–301. Available online at: https://www.jstor.org/stable/3659022?seq=1#page_scan_tab_contents (accessed 20 January 2017).

Widdowson, H.G. 2000. On the limitations of linguistics applied. *Applied Linguistics*, 21(1), 3–25.

Zimmer, B. 2011. The corpus in the court: "Like lexis on steroids". *The Atlantic*, 4 March [online]. Available online at: https://www.theatlantic.com/national/archive/2011/03/the-corpus-in-the-court-like-lexis-on-steroids/72054/ (accessed 30 May 2017).

Zinn, J.O., 2010. Risk as discourse: Interdisciplinary perspectives. *Critical Approaches to Discourse Analysis across Disciplines*, 4(2), 106–124.

PART C

Research design (avoiding pitfalls/re-examining the foundations)

8

THE ROLE OF THE TEXT IN CORPUS AND DISCOURSE ANALYSIS

Missing the trees for the forest

Jesse Egbert and Erin Schnur

8.1 Introduction

Increasingly, researchers in discourse analysis and critical discourse analysis (CDA) are relying on corpora and corpus linguistic methods in their research. This has led to the establishment of new fields of study, such as corpus-assisted discourse studies (CADS: Partington 2004; 2006) and the integration of corpus linguistic and CDA methodologies (e.g. Baker et al. 2008; Fairclough et al. 2007). There are many advantages of using corpora – large and representative samples of natural texts – and corpus linguistic methods in discourse analysis. The use of large, representative corpus samples increases the generalisability of research findings, and the use of computer-based corpus methodologies can offer increased efficiency, reliability and objectivity.

There are clear benefits to using corpora in discourse analysis, but there are also some important drawbacks. Interestingly, these drawbacks are related to the two advantages mentioned above: size and computer-based methods. The massive size of many contemporary corpora offers a wealth of data, but it can also lead discourse analysts to become out of touch with the texts included in the corpus. The text is the fundamental unit of discourse. As such, patterns in discourse are most meaningful and interpretable when analysed at the level of the text, not the corpus. Corpora are useful because they offer a rich data source composed of many texts. However, the corpus as a unit lacks linguistic validity; corpora are created by linguists whereas texts are created by language users. In order for discourse analysts to learn about language use within a discourse community, their focus must be on the actual texts created by individual members of that discourse community, rather than on a contrived data set.

The second drawback to using corpora in discourse analysis is related to the use of computers. While computer programs offer many benefits, most existing corpus software programs (e.g. concordancers, web-based corpus interfaces) analyse and present linguistic patterns at the level of the corpus, rather than the level of the text. This has created a situation in which many discourse analysts investigate and report discourse patterns in terms of results from an entire corpus rather than individual texts. For example, keyword analysis is frequently used in discourse analysis studies as a method for revealing words that are important, or 'key', in a particular discourse domain. However, many researchers who use keyword analysis entirely ignore textual boundaries and word dispersion across texts (see Section 8.4). Instead, these researchers report words that are statistically more frequent in a target corpus when compared with a reference corpus. This means that a word could be (and often is) identified as a keyword even though it occurs in only a small handful of the many texts in the corpus. Keywords such as these are virtually meaningless because not only do they tell us little to nothing about the corpus as a whole (i.e. they only occurred in a small fraction of the corpus), they also tell us little to nothing about generalisable patterns across texts in a discourse domain. It is important to note that although most current keyword methods disregard text dispersion, it is certainly possible for researchers to account for dispersion across texts as an additional research step (see, e.g. Baker, 2004). We return to this example with a case study in Section 8.4.

Keyword analysis is just one example of many computer-based corpus methodologies that use the corpus, rather than the text, as the unit of observation. In computational linguistics, these methods are often referred to as 'bag of words' approaches, where important discourse characteristics such as word order, grammar, cohesion/coherence and textual boundaries are entirely disregarded and replaced by simple frequency data. 'Bag of word' approaches are problematic for discourse analysts because they can draw attention away from the text, the fundamental discourse unit within which the patterns were produced. While some scholars have stressed the importance of using texts as the basis for analysis in CADS research (see e.g. Stubbs 2007; Partington, Duguid & Taylor 2013), there seems to be a trend in corpus-based discourse analysis away from using the text and towards using the corpus as the unit of analysis.

A comparison to data in the natural sciences may help to illustrate the importance of texts in concrete terms. In this example, we will compare texts to trees. Like texts, each individual tree is naturally occurring, distinct and self-contained. Thus, it makes sense that the tree is a common unit of observation in research on forestry and ecology. We might think of parts of a tree in the same way that we think of parts of a text. Just as discourse analysts explore textual characteristics by analysing words, grammatical constructions and discourse organisation, forestry researchers might attempt to learn about trees by measuring tree core samples or analysing the chlorophyll content of leaves. The analysis of these parts can provide important information, but this data is most meaningful when contextualised and interpreted at the level of the observational unit: texts or trees, as the case may be. Building on this example, in order to better understand general patterns across trees of a certain species, forestry researchers often analyse systematic patterns across trees in a forest in the same way that discourse analysts are increasingly relying on corpora composed of many texts. Forests and corpora are similar in that each is a large sample that comprises many instances of the observational unit of interest. In both cases, the presence of many observations makes it possible to obtain generalisable results. However, the fact that we are analysing patterns in a sample of multiple observations does not necessarily change our observational unit. In both cases, we are still likely to be primarily interested in our original unit, whether it be trees or texts.

There is nothing inherently wrong with analysing discourse at the level of text parts or large samples of texts. The key is to remember that text parts only exist as parts of texts, and corpora only exist because of the texts they are composed of. In other words, just as neither leaves nor forests can exist without trees, textual features and corpora cannot exist without texts. The challenge is that there seems to be a tendency for discourse analysts to lose sight of the text when their focus is on patterns within the text (e.g. words, grammatical structures) and/or across texts (e.g. in corpora). The use of corpora and corpus linguistic methods seems to compound this problem, especially since existing software makes it difficult or impossible to visualise and describe findings from a corpus at the level of the text. The purpose of this chapter is to establish the importance of the text in corpus-based discourse analysis and encourage researchers in this area to focus their research on texts rather than corpora.

The remainder of the chapter is organised as follows. In the next section, we propose a definition for text and discuss some challenges associated with defining and operationalising texts in discourse analysis. Section 8.3 addresses the importance of using the text as the sampling unit and the observational unit in corpus-based research. In Section 8.4, we offer a brief case study that demonstrates the crucial role of texts. Section 8.5 concludes the chapter.

8.2 Defining text

The word 'text' is a term of art in discourse analysis, and as such, we feel it must be clearly defined in this chapter in order to avoid confusion with more general uses of 'text' (e.g. a book or printed work, a computer file, etc.). A survey of previous literature reveals that there is considerable variation in the way discourse analysts define the word 'text'. Below, we provide a brief sample of definitions that have been proposed by researchers.

A text has been defined as:

- 'the verbal record of a communicative act' (Brown & Yule 1983: 9);
- 'any product whether written or spoken' (Fairclough 1992: 4);
- 'an instance of language in use, either spoken or written: a piece of language behaviour which has occurred naturally, without the intervention of the linguist' (Stubbs 1996: 1–2);
- 'a recognizably self-contained unit of "natural language used for communication, whether it is realized in speech or writing"' (Biber & Conrad 2009: 5);

- 'a passage of discourse which is coherent in these two regards: it is coherent with respect to the context of situation, and therefore consistent in register; and it is coherent with respect to itself, and therefore cohesive' (Halliday & Hasan 1976: 23).

These definitions vary considerably with regard to both content and specificity. In defining 'text' here, we have borrowed elements from several definitions above – most notably from Biber and Conrad (2009) and Halliday and Hasan (1976) – in an attempt to provide a clear and concrete conceptual definition of the term. We define a text as a written or spoken unit of language that meets the following three criteria:

1 **Naturally occurring**: Texts must represent genuine instances of language use that, generally, are created without the intervention of a linguist.
2 **Recognisably self-contained**: Texts must be internally coherent in a way that can be attributed to authorial intention – that is, the language is cohesive as a unit. In addition, texts must be recognisable as a unit based on their external or situational characteristics – that is, texts share characteristics in common with other texts in a given register (see e.g. Biber & Conrad 2009: 40).
3 **Functional:** Texts must be functional units of language. Texts do not occur randomly or haphazardly. Rather they can be characterised by communicative functions that are intended by the author/speaker and interpretable by the reader/listener.

Texts, as conceptually defined using this definition, are linguistically valid, and a natural starting point for investigations of discourse. They are instances of real language produced in authentic contexts that represent a recognisable and coherent unit, both internally and externally. In addition, we propose that language users naturally think about language in terms of texts. This is easy to see in writing, where the colloquial use of 'text' generally corresponds with our more technical definition. We talk about reading *a novel*, writing *an email*, or sending *a text message*, all of which are naturally occurring, recognisably self-contained and functional units of language. Even within spoken language, where the colloquial definition of 'text' is seldom applied, we refer to having *a conversation*, listening to *a lecture* and delivering *a wedding toast*. Again, these naturally occurring speech events are recognisably self-contained and functional. Research into the segmentation of spoken language into sub-units supports the claim that language users recognise self-contained and functional texts within transcripts (e.g. Flammia & Zue 1995; Passonneau & Litman 1997).

While this definition of 'text' is conceptually easy to apply to the language events we encounter both in research and in day-to-day life, operationalising 'text' in research presents some challenges. In some research, it may be most appropriate to operationalise 'text' as the entirety of a language event. In some instances, this operationalisation of 'text' is fairly straightforward. For example, when working with some types of written language, such a text would comprise all of the words written by an author in a given document, beginning with the first word and ending with the last. This type of self-contained unit is easy to visualise with text types such as personal correspondence, or academic or news articles. In fact, many types of writing are inherently discrete; they have a clear beginning and end. Discourse analytic studies that are focused on investigating and/or describing the entirety of these language events can simply operationalise 'text' in this way. When working with spoken language, in some instances, the same logic that is often applied to writing can be used; that is, spoken texts can be defined as a language event that begins when speakers come together and concludes when they part.

However, for other discourse types, both written and spoken, it may be challenging to identify the start and end of a language event. This is particularly true for interactive discourse types. For example, researchers examining interactive writing on the internet, such as interactive discussion forums or social media posts, will need to decide whether a text comprises a single post, or a single post and accompanying responses. Similarly, a researcher investigating the language of academic lectures will need to decide when the language event begins and ends – does it begin when the participants enter the room and include pre-lecture chatter between individual participants, or does it begin when the lecturer first addresses the entire group of listeners? In cases such as these, the identification of an entire, self-contained language event can be challenging and require principled decision-making on the part of researchers.

When working with both written and spoken language, operationalising 'text' to include the entirety of a language event is not always useful or appropriate given the particular research questions being investigated. A research article, for example, can be segmented into its parts (introduction, methodology, etc.), and depending upon the researcher's goal, it may be useful to operationally define the 'text' as individual sections of research articles. Similarly, when working with spoken language, the domain of inquiry in a particular study may be focused on units that occur within a larger language event. For example, a researcher may be interested in the conclusion portion of academic lectures, which would require the identification of lecture conclusions within much longer language events (lectures). In such a case, the identification of segments or sections of language, which will serve as 'texts' in answering a specific research question, can be challenging, although certainly there are often recognisably self-contained units of natural language within many longer spoken language events. Colloquially, for example, we often refer to having 'a discussion', 'a talk', or 'a conversation' about a particular topic, which may have occurred within the context of a longer interaction, and yet seem clearly discrete. Similarly, the concept of a lecture conclusion neatly fits the conceptual definition of 'text' – it is naturally occurring, self-contained and functional.

Generally, within written language, researchers who wish to identify texts within larger pieces of writing are aided by orthographic conventions such as section headings (in some registers) or paragraph breaks. Within spoken language, on the other hand, this type of segmentation of an entire spoken language event into useful and self-contained texts may present significantly greater challenges due to the absence of these conventions.

A number of researchers have proposed both theory and method for segmenting pieces of writing or spoken language into useful and appropriate textual units (e.g. Crookes 1990; Polanyi et al. 2004; Van Dijk 1982). Researchers have proposed and tested a variety of methods of segmenting both pieces of writing and transcripts of spoken language into self-contained sections. However, a majority of segmentation research has focused on spoken language, due largely to the difficulties of identifying self-contained units of speech without the aid of orthographic conventions (e.g. sentences, paragraphs, section headings). These methods generally fall into two categories: manual segmentation and automatic segmentation.

Manual segmentation methods rely on human judgement to identify self-contained units within spoken transcripts (e.g. Flammia & Zue 1995; Passonneau & Litman 1997). Automatic text segmentation methods rely on computational algorithms that identify changes in the lexical or grammatical characteristics of documents in order to recognise and segment documents (e.g. Biber, Connor & Upton 2007; Sardinha 2001). Regardless of the methods used, the primary challenge in operationally defining texts for researchers who do not adhere to a simple definition (all words within a piece of written language, or the entirety of an interaction in a spoken transcript) lies in the granularity with which textual units are identified. By granularity, we mean the level of fineness with which a text is segmented. For example, a telephone conversation may cover several topics, each of which may contain sub-topics. This challenge has been discussed at length (see Flammia & Zue 1995; Hearst 1997), and solutions have been proposed for both manual and automatic segmentation. Ultimately, the segmentation of spoken language into operationalised texts must be achieved with careful consideration of what is appropriate and useful given the aims of a particular study.

In this section we have established and explained our conceptual definition for 'text'. It is the responsibility of the researcher to establish an operational definition for 'text' based on the goals and design of a particular study. We have briefly described some of the challenges associated with operationalising 'text' in specific research contexts, particularly those that involve spoken discourse and/or units that are sub-components of larger language events. The likelihood of establishing a useful operational definition for 'text' in any study is increased when researchers are familiar with the discourse domain that is the target for their research. It can also be useful for researchers to engage in pilot research, possibly in the form of a series of attempts that proceed in a cyclical fashion until an acceptable operational definition has been achieved.

8.3 The text in corpus-based discourse analysis

Our objective in this section is to establish the importance of treating the text as (1) the sampling unit in corpus design and construction and (2) the observational unit in quantitative and qualitative corpus-based research.

8.3.1 The text as a sampling unit

One of the first and most important steps in the collection of a sample from a population of interest is establishing an appropriate sampling unit. Collecting a corpus sample is no exception. To many researchers, the text is the logical choice for a sampling unit. For example, Biber (1993) refers to corpora as "text corpora" and bases all of his recommendations for corpus design and construction on the text as a sampling unit (see also Stubbs 2007; Partington, Duguid & Taylor 2013). In contrast, over the years researchers have often disregarded the text when compiling corpora. For example, the entire Brown family of corpora (e.g. Brown, LOB, Frown, FLOB) contains language samples with lengths restricted to roughly 2,000 words. These samples were collected by selecting the beginning of a sentence in a text at random and sampling all of the text up to the end of the first sentence after the 2,000 word mark was reached.[1] This method allowed the corpus compilers to collect a balanced corpus sample. This approach also allowed the corpus compilers to collect a relatively large number of samples while still restricting the size of the corpus to address the limitations in computer memory and processing speed that existed in the 1960s.

The Brown family of corpora have been invaluable data sources for many research purposes. However, the nature of the language samples in these corpora present major limitations for discourse analysts who are interested in questions that can only be answered through analyses of complete, intact texts. Corpora that include only text excerpts raise important concerns about representativeness. Language is rarely spoken, written, read or heard in the form of random, decontextualised text segments. This raises questions about what exactly is represented by a corpus that contains only text snippets. Using the text as the sampling unit allows corpus compilers to ensure that a corpus sample represents the way naturally occurring discourse is actually produced. Moreover, the presence of complete texts makes it possible for researchers to generalise their results to texts which, for most discourse analysts, is the primary goal.

When situated in proper historical context, the use of 2,000-word text excerpts as the sampling unit in the collection of the Brown family of corpora was logical, if not absolutely necessary. However, computer technology has developed to the point where limiting text length is no longer necessary. We believe the benefits of sampling complete texts far outweighs any potential limitations associated with imbalance in text lengths, especially in corpora used for discourse analysis. While the practice of compiling corpora of text fragments is no longer commonplace, it is still quite common for researchers to use these corpora in research. In some cases, researchers may be using these corpora without even being aware of what it is that the texts in these corpora actually represent.

Many of the original challenges of using the text as the sampling unit that were faced by early corpus builders are no longer present. It has become so easy to collect large corpora that multimillion word corpora can be collected through the internet in a matter of a few hours. Many large corpora are collected automatically by computer programs (e.g. COCA, GloWbE, and many Sketch Engine corpora). In fact, it is possible for corpus builders to collect and analyse corpora without ever looking at a single intact text in the sample. This 'hands-off' approach to corpus collection makes it unappealing, if not impossible, to accurately record accurate metadata for each text, which is crucial for many research questions in discourse analysis. Useful metadata can include demographic information about the author/speaker and reader/listener (e.g. sex, age, location), date of publication/production, and other situational characteristics (e.g. production circumstances, relations among participants).

Without an easy way to record and store useful metadata for texts, some corpus compilers see little purpose in collecting, storing or analysing corpora at the text level. As a result, it is becoming increasingly common for corpus compilers to capitalise on data structures such as relational databases in which corpora are often stored and organized at the level of the word, rather than the text. For example, the entire suite of corpora created and maintained at Brigham Young University are organised in this way (Davies 2009). Although there is information in the database that links words to information about their source texts, it is currently not possible for users of these corpora to analyse patterns at the level of the text. Search queries can produce two sets of results: (1) frequency results for the entire corpus and (2) concordance lines (10–15 words on each side of the search hit) that can be expanded to extended concordance lines that include a slightly longer excerpt from the text. These concordance lines, while useful for some linguistic analyses, are often inadequate for discourse analysis because they do not provide sufficient discourse context to allow for detailed analysis and interpretation of discourse patterns.

Up to this point, this section has painted a fairly grim picture of the status of the text in corpus sampling. While there are certain characteristics of many corpora that make them less than ideal for discourse analysis, there are also many existing corpora that (1) contain complete texts, (2) include relevant metadata, and (3) allow access to full texts for analysis (e.g. BNC, ICLE, MICASE). We call on researchers, especially discourse analysts, to focus on creating and using corpora that have these characteristics, whenever possible. Corpora that are designed in this way are more representative of naturally occurring discourse and more amenable to discourse analytic research.

8.3.2 The text as a unit of observation

In the previous section we have attempted to establish the ideal sampling unit in corpus design and construction. In this section we turn to the benefits of using the text as the unit of observation in corpus-based discourse analysis. A unit of observation is the object upon which measurements are taken. According to Biber and Jones (2009), corpus-based studies can be divided into three categories based on their unit of observation.

- Type A studies use one or more linguistic features as the observational unit. Examples of this type of study are variationist studies and research focused on collocation.

- Type B studies use individual texts as the unit of analysis, allowing researchers to investigate patterns in texts and text varieties.
- In Type C studies the unit of analysis as an entire corpus or sub-corpus. Although Type C study designs can be used to answer some of the same research questions as Type B studies, as we have mentioned above, they are fundamentally different because they disregard the text entirely and focus only on general patterns within corpora.

These three study designs align with the three approaches introduced through the tree metaphor in the first section of this chapter. Type A designs are focused on text parts (i.e. branches and leaves), Type C designs are focused on corpora (i.e. forests) and Type B studies are focused on texts (i.e. trees).

There are useful applications for each of the three study designs in corpus linguistics and their corresponding units of observation. However, we propose that the Type B design, with its focus on individual texts, is ideal for discourse analysis research. Focusing on the text as the unit of observation allows discourse analysts to measure features of language within a discourse domain in terms of central tendency (e.g. mean) and dispersion (e.g. standard deviation). When the corpus is the unit of analysis (Type C design) it is possible to measure frequencies or normalised rates of occurrence for features within the corpus. However, researchers often focus their results and conclusions entirely on these frequencies, offering no insight into how language is used in texts. Whereas rates of occurrence in a Type C study reveal the frequency of a feature within a corpus, generally, the mean rates of occurrence across texts in a Type B study reveal the central tendency of a distribution that represents the use of that feature across naturally occurring texts. Furthermore, the presence of multiple texts in a Type B design also allows researchers to quantify the dispersion – or variance – in the use of a feature. For example, the standard deviation, a commonly used measure of dispersion, quantifies how far away from the mean values tend to be. This reveals important information about the degree to which individual authors and speakers vary in their use of language features across texts. Taken together, the measures of central tendency and dispersion allow corpus linguists and discourse analysts to discover patterns of language use that can be directly generalised to individual texts. The central tendency provides information about the characteristics of average or 'typical' texts, and measures of dispersion reveals the degree to which texts vary in their use of these characteristics.

For researchers interested in quantifying discourse patterns, the benefits of treating the text as the unit of observation go far beyond simply descriptive measures such as the mean and standard deviation. With Type B designs, researchers are able to use inferential statistics for the purpose of measuring the 'significance' of their quantitative findings (i.e. how likely it is that results from a corpus occurred by chance alone). Inferential statistics can be used to compare group means (e.g. t-test, ANOVA) and relationships between variables (e.g. correlation, regression). Assuming that the corpus is a representative sample from a well-defined population and that the researcher used appropriate quantitative methods, conclusions based on these inferential statistics can be generalised to the population. In this way, it is possible for discourse analysts to learn about more than just one or a few texts. These methods enable them to draw generalisable conclusions about the larger discourse domain they are interested in. To be more precise, these methods allow discourse analysts to make generalisable conclusions about *the texts* in a discourse domain.

The valuable information offered by the inferential statistics described here can lead researchers to further investigate important linguistic and discourse characteristics using qualitative methods. Because measurements are taken on each text, researchers can identify texts that are 'prototypical', in the sense that they fall close to a group average, or 'deviant', in the sense that they fall far from the average. By focusing their efforts on qualitative explanation and interpreting quantitative patterns of language use in different texts, discourse analysts can account for the full range of variability in the use of a particular feature or set of features. This mixed-methods approach is natural when the unit of observation is the text.

8.4 The text in keyword analysis: a case study

The purpose of this section is to demonstrate the value of using the text as the unit of observation in corpus-based discourse analysis through a case study based on keyword analysis. Keyword analysis is one of the most commonly used methods in corpus-assisted discourse analysis. However, it is common for discourse analysts who use keyword analysis to disregard the texts that they are making claims about.

While there are many different methods that could be used to identify keywords, the standard practice is to measure 'corpus frequency' keyness. This method identifies words that are statistically more frequent in a target corpus than in a reference corpus. This method is also a prime example of the perils of missing the trees for the forest. In corpus frequency keyword analysis, the unit of observation is the corpus, and texts are entirely disregarded in the analysis. As a result, the list of words that is produced does not represent general patterns across texts, but only the corpus as a whole. This means that a word can be, and often is, awarded a high keyness value even though it only occurs in a single text or just a few texts in the corpus. Words such as these do not represent general discourse patterns across texts. In fact, these words are often among those with the most skewed frequency distributions in the whole corpus.

Egbert and Biber (forthcoming) introduce a new method for keyword analysis – *text dispersion keyness* – that takes a radically different approach to measuring keyness. Text dispersion keyness disregards corpus frequency entirely and focuses instead on identifying words that are used (at least once) in significantly more texts in the target corpus than in the reference corpus. By focusing on the number of texts within the corpus that contain a given word (or n-gram), rather than the number of occurrences of that word in the corpus as a whole, this approach identifies words that typify the texts in a given domain, rather than words that occur frequently in that domain with no consideration of dispersion across texts within the sample. This allows researchers to make meaningful generalizations about the nature of texts within the discourse domain of interest. In this study, the researchers use quantitative and qualitative methods to compare the lists produced by the traditional corpus frequency keyness method with those from the new text dispersion keyness method in terms of their:

1 relative frequency;
2 relative dispersion;
3 content-distinctiveness;
4 content-generalisability.

While relative frequency and dispersion are useful metrics for evaluating keyness methods, we propose that the two most important criteria for evaluating keywords are content-distinctiveness and content-generalisability. The modifier 'content' is used here because both of these criteria measure the extent to which keywords offer insight into the actual content-'aboutness' of those texts. Hence, they give preference to content words over grammatical or function words. Content-distinctiveness refers to the strength of the association between a keyword and the content of the discourse in the target corpus. In other words, the significance of distinctive keywords to a particular discourse domain can be interpreted with relative ease because they are relevant to that domain. Content-distinctiveness is also related to accountability: because distinctive keywords are interpretable and relevant, researchers are more likely to account for them instead of excluding them from the analysis. We define content-generalisability as the degree to which a keyword represents the content of the discourse used across the texts in the target corpus. Content-generalisability is important because it determines the extent to which a keyword is representative of and meaningful for the entire target corpus.

Egbert and Biber's (forthcoming) study focuses on a corpus of travel blogs as the target corpus and a general web corpus as the reference corpus. Each text in those corpora includes all of the language from a webpage. The results of this study focus on comparisons of the top 100 keywords identified using the two methods described above: corpus frequency keyness and text dispersion keyness. Egbert and Biber determine that 100 keywords is enough to evaluate and compare the keyword methods, while still allowing them to conduct in-depth qualitative investigations. The results reveal that text dispersion keyness produces higher quality keyword lists according to each of the four criteria listed above. In terms of relative frequency, the words identified by the corpus frequency method were 1.36 times more frequent in travel blogs than in the reference corpus. In contrast, the words identified by the text dispersion method were 5.75 times more frequent in the target corpus. The relative dispersion results were similar. The corpus frequency keywords occurred, on average, in 1.74 times more travel blog texts when compared with the reference corpus. In contrast, the text dispersion keywords were 4.29 times more widely dispersed in the target corpus than in the reference corpus.

Egbert and Biber (forthcoming) also compared the lists produced by corpus frequency keyness and text dispersion keyness for their content-distinctiveness and content-generalisability. Non-distinctive words were defined as function words and high frequency verbs. The list of high frequency verbs used in this study include all forms of (1) three primary verbs (*be*, *have*, *do*) and (2) the top 10 most frequent lexical verbs in English (*say*, *get*, *go*, *know*, *think*, *see*, *make*, *come*, *take*, *want*) (see Biber et al. 1999: 110). Non-generalisable words were defined as abbreviations and proper nouns. However, the authors acknowledge that it is certainly not always true that abbreviations and proper nouns are non-generalisable and function words and high frequency verbs are non-distinctive. Whereas 22 of the top 100 corpus frequency keywords were classified as non-distinctive, only one of the top 100 text dispersion keywords fell into that category. Nine of the top 100 corpus frequency keywords were classified as non-generalisable. None of the text dispersion keywords fell into this category.

Table 8.1 displays the top 100 keywords identified by these two methods. The first column contains words that occurred only on the corpus frequency list. The third column contains words that occurred only on the text dispersion list. The middle column contains words that overlapped between the two lists. The words with questionable content-distinctiveness are italicised and the words with questionable content-generalisability are bolded. A careful investigation of the keyword lists in this table offers strong support for text dispersion keyness. Nearly all of the words identified using this method (Table 8.1: columns 2 and 3) were relatively frequent and dispersed, and were distinctive and generalisable to the texts in travel blogs. On the other hand, the keyword list identified using corpus frequency keyness (Table 8.1: columns 1 and 2) contains many words that have low relative frequency and dispersion, and are questionable in their content-distinctiveness and content-generalisability.

The results of this case study reinforce the claims we have made throughout this chapter about the importance of analysing discourse at the level of the text. Although the two keyword lists were created based on the same two corpora and the same statistical technique (log-likelihood), the text dispersion keyness method resulted in a much higher quality list. This is because the unit of observation in text dispersion is each text, rather than the entire corpus, which increases the chances that the words in the list will be distinctive and generalisable to the texts in the target corpus. One of the added benefits of text dispersion keyness is that the top-ranking words in the list can be interpreted as key for *the texts* in the target domain – rather than for the corpus as a whole – which is the information that most discourse analysts actually want to know.

Most discourse analysts are likely to agree that the text should be the primary focus, but there has been a recent trend away from text-based discourse analysis, particularly in CADS. In order to test this claim we carried out a brief survey of 10 recent corpus-based discourse studies that (1) use keyword analysis and (2) make

TABLE 8.1 Comparison between lists of top 100 corpus frequency keywords (CF) and top 100 text dispersion keywords (TD)

CF only		*Both*		*TD only*	
We	place	trip	water	ride	cliffs
contiki	*col*	beach	boat	sights	trails
de	metres	travel	trail	restaurant	located
he	**had**	tour	night	photos	hike
that	*asia*	city	scenery	travellers	delicious
our	castle	road	visited	booked	visitors
krakow	**along**	bus	mountains	journey	ferry
his	rain	park	sea	village	sunset
lake	**a**	visit	travelling	shops	flights
hrp	tent	day	south	weather	sun
madrid	*thailand*	hotel	steep	explore	nearby
was	ridge	island	beaches	hills	hour
refuge	**has**	walk	flight	streets	hostels
route	**la**	town	museum	stunning	biking
i	valley	river	hiking	guide	north
be	morning	**around**	adventure	sunny	afternoon
or	**back**	tours	walked	rocks	visiting
path	climb	tourists	attractions	enjoyed	swimming
up	campsite	walking	islands	photo	lovely
not	canyon	mountain	amazing	trees	gardens
will	**said**	tourist	beer	scenic	exploring
thai	*paphos*	hostel	airport	spectacular	villages
		arrived	destination		
		locals	lunch		
		headed	dinner		
		beautiful	famous		
		places	holiday		
		hotels	restaurants		

claims about texts. We found that nine out of the 10 articles used the corpus frequency keyness method described above, effectively disregarding the texts they set out to describe.

8.5 Conclusion

In this chapter we have attempted to (re-)establish the text as the fundamental unit of discourse in discourse analysis based on corpus research. We provided a working conceptual definition for text in discourse analysis and discussed practical challenges associated with developing an operational definition for text in practice. We have also argued that regardless of the methods used to analyse discourse, analysis of discourse patterns will be most fruitful and meaningful when the text is regarded as the the sampling unit in corpus design and organisation, and the unit of observation in research design and methods, both quantitative and qualitative. The case study in

Section 8.4 provided empirical evidence to support these claims and illustrates the importance of accounting for texts in CADS.

The introduction of corpora and corpus linguistic methods is an exciting development in discourse analysis. However, discourse analysts must be wise in their use of corpus data and methods to ensure that the text retains its rightful status as the fundamental discourse unit. To revisit the metaphor introduced earlier, we hope that through this chapter we have sent a simple, yet important message to discourse analysts who use corpora and corpus linguistic methods: Don't miss the trees for the forest by missing the texts for the corpus.

Note

1 http://clu.uni.no/icame/brown/bcm.html.

References

Baker, P. 2004. Querying keywords: Questions in difference, frequency, and sense in keyword analysis. *Journal of English Linguistics*, 32(4), 346–359.

Baker, P., Gabrielatos, C., Khosravinik, M., Krzyżanowski, M., McEnery, T. & Wodak, R. 2008. A useful methodological synergy? Combining critical discourse analysis and corpus linguistics to examine discourses of refugees and asylum seekers in the UK press. *Discourse & Society*, 19(3), 273–306.

Biber, D. 1993. Representativeness in corpus design. *Literary and Linguistic Computing*, 8(4), 243–257.

Biber, D. & Conrad, S. 2009. *Register, Genre, & Style.* Cambridge: Cambridge University Press.

Biber, D. & Jones, J.K. 2009. Quantitative methods in corpus linguistics. In Anke Lüdeling & Merja Kytö (eds.) *Corpus Linguistics: An International Handbook.* Berlin: Walter de Gruyter. pp. 1286–1304.

Biber, D., Johansson, S., Leech, G., Conrad, S. & Finegan, E. 1999. *Longman Grammar of Spoken and Written English.* Harlow: Longman.

Biber, D., Connor, U. & Upton, T. A. 2007. *Discourse on the Move: Using Corpus Analysis to Describe Discourse Structure.* Amsterdam: John Benjamins.

Brown, G. & Yule, G. 1983. *Discourse Analysis.* Cambridge: Cambridge University Press.

Crookes, G. 1990. The utterance, and other basic units for second language discourse analysis. *Applied linguistics*, 11(2), 183–199.

Davies, M. 2009. The 385+ million word Corpus of Contemporary American English (1990–2008+): Design, architecture, and linguistic insights. *International Journal of Corpus Linguistics*, 14, 159–90.

Egbert, J. & Biber, D. (forthcoming). Incorporating text dispersion into keyword analysis.

Fairclough, N. 1992. *Discourse and Social Change.* Cambridge: Polity.

Fairclough, N., Cortese, G. & Ardizzone, P. (eds.) 2007. Discourse and Contemporary Social Change. Bern: Peter Lang.

Flammia, G. & Zue, V. 1995. Empirical evaluation of human performance and agreement in parsing discourse constituents in spoken dialogue. In the Proceedings of EUROSPEECH, Madrid, Spain.

Halliday, M. A. K. & Hasan, R. 1976. *Cohesion in English.* London: Longman.

Hearst, M. 1997. TextTiling: Segmenting text into multi-paragraph subtopic passages. *Computational Linguistics*, 23(1), 33–64.

Partington, A. 2004. Corpora and discourse, a most congruous beast. In A. Partington, J. Morley & L. Haarman (eds.) *Corpora and Discourse*. Bern: Peter Lang. pp. 11–20.

Partington, A. 2006. Metaphors, motifs and similes across discourse types: Corpus-assisted Discourse Studies (CADS) at work. In A. Stefanowitsch & S. Gries (eds.) *Corpus-Based Approaches to Metaphor and Metonymy*. Berlin: Mouton de Gruyter. pp. 267–304.

Partington, A., Duguid, A. & Taylor, C. 2013. *Patterns and Meanings in Discourse: Theory and Practice in Corpus-Assisted Discourse Studies (CADS)* (Vol. 55). Amsterdam: John Benjamins.

Passonneau, R. & Litman, D. 1997. Discourse segmentation by human and automated means. *Computational Linguistics*, 23(1), 103–139.

Polanyi, L., Culy, C., Van Den Berg, M., Thione, G. L. & Ahn, D. 2004. A rule based approach to discourse parsing. *Proceedings of SIGDIAL*, 4(1), 108–117.

Sardinha, T. B. 2001. Lexical segments in text. In M. Scott & G. Thompson (eds.) *Patterns of Text: In honor of Michael Hoey*. Amsterdam: John Benjamins. pp. 213–237.

Stubbs, M. 1996. *Text and corpus analysis: Computer-assisted studies of language and culture*. Oxford: Blackwell.

Stubbs, M. 2007. On texts, corpora and models of language. In M. Hoey, M. Mahlberg, M. Stubbs & W. Teubert (eds). *Text, Discourse and Corpora: Theory and Analysis*. New York: Continuum. pp. 127–161.

Van Dijk, T. A. 1982. Episodes as units of discourse analysis. In D. Tannen (ed.) *Analyzing discourse: Text and talk*. Washington, DC: Georgetown University Press. pp. 177–195.

9

DIVIDING UP THE DATA

Epistemological, methodological and practical impact of diachronic segmentation

Anna Marchi

9.1 Introduction

Diachronic analysis is intrinsically comparative, in fact 'a prerequisite for diachrony is that at least two different time points are compared' (Jucker & Taavitsanien 2014: 5). The way we divide up the data, i.e. what we choose to compare, determines what we see. However obvious this may seem, there is remarkably little discussion (a notable exception being Gabrielatos et al. 2012) about the effects of time segmentation in diachronic discourse analysis using corpora, or Modern Diachronic-Corpus Assisted Discourse Studies (Partington ed. 2010).

Gries and Hilpert (2008: 61) lament that 'in both synchronic and diachronic linguistics, there often seems to be an underlying (or at least unquestioned) assumption that there is one, single, reasonable way of dividing up the corpus into different parts'. And they continue 'the assumption of a single gold standard in structuring any corpora is false [...] the homogeneity of a corpus can only be defined with respect, specifically, to both a particular level of granularity and a particular linguistic phenomenon' (ibid.). They then focus on establishing a sophisticated empirical method to identify diachronic sub-corpora on the basis of cluster variability.

This chapter is not especially concerned with particular statistical approaches to compiling and segmenting diachronic corpora, but with the very issue of reflection (or lack of it, as suggested by Gries and Hilpert) on the implications of discretional choices in defining units of analysis, in this case units of time. I use here the term 'discretional' to emphasise that as in all matters of analytic choices (which imply alternatives to those choices) here lies a potential pitfall, i.e. an aspect that necessarily affects the results and may skew them. However, being 'discretional', that is making distinctions, is at the very core of any analysis. Both corpora and the units we apply to analyse them are designed, and this non-randomness is the whole point of a good corpus and of good research. A much quoted line by Sinclair (1991: 13) puts it very simply: '[T]he results are only as good as the corpus.' Just as 'the corpus data we select to explore a research question must be well matched to that research question' (McEnery & Hardie 2012: 2), so must the discrete portions of a corpus (or corpora) we use for diachronic analysis.

> Men can do nothing without the make-believe of a beginning. Even science, the strict measurer, is obliged to start with a make-believe unit, and must fix on a point in the stars' unceasing journey when his sidereal clock shall pretend that time is at Nought.
>
> *(George Eliot, incipit of Daniel Deronda, 1996: 3)*

Appropriate 'make-believe' units are our analytic artefacts, our tools. In this chapter I wish to discuss and encourage reflection on the epistemological impact of these tools.

9.2 Modern diachronic discourse analysis using corpora

The area of interest of this discussion may go under a variety of labels and definitions – *modern-diachronic corpus-assisted discourse analysis*, or *corpus-based analysis of modern language*, or *discourse-oriented diachronic analysis of modern corpora* – depending on where we want to place the accent of our research. I will hence adopt the acronym MD-CADS, coined by Partington and Duguid (2008), as a tool, not a school: simply as a lean umbrella term to encompass the work of a large and varied family of scholars who use corpora to study changing and/or enduring 'ways that language is used in the construction of discourses' (Baker 2006: 1) across or among different moments of contemporary time. The present-day or current element is relevant because modern-diachronic linguistics, which typically covers a time frame of a few decades, has different characteristics and concerns from historical diachronic linguistics. Because of the short time-span involved in modern diachronic studies, Mair (1997) proposes the term *brachychrony* instead of diachrony. Yet the prefix *brachy* (from the Greek brakhus: short and used as a prefix, for instance, in medicine to indicate shorter than normal) implies that the time span considered is 'too' short to allow for diachronic comparisons, that is for comparisons of phenomena through time or between times, whereas for a MD-CADS researcher the time(s) under investigation is just appropriate to the research question. Furthermore, the label brachychrony also overshadows the concept of comparison intrinsic to diachrony, which is precisely to do with the study evolution (or stability) and transition (or absence of it) in time.

As Partington (2010: 84) notes, modern 'diachronic corpus linguistics is, of course, nothing new', and a great deal of important work has been done (for example Mair et al. 2002, Leech & Smith 2006 or Leech et al. 2009) on the 'synchronic but parallel "standard" corpora, Brown, Frown, LOB and FLOB' (Renouf 2007: 36), particularly regarding variation of lexico–grammatical features between the early 1960s and early 1990s. To complement these resources, researchers at Lancaster

University built a version for the early 1930s (BLOB or Before-LOB corpus) and Baker (2009) recently added another Brown-type comparable corpus (the BE06 corpus and the AmE06) for the early 2000s. What is particularly interesting in Baker's diachronic work on the extended Brown-family corpora is that he goes beyond grammatical features and is interested in the discursive level. He looks at lexical change and considers the socio-cultural significance of the shift of linguistic patterns: in Baker (2011) he looks at keywords and lockwords[1] (discussed also by Taylor in Chapter 2 of this volume) examining frequent lexical words (such as the lockwords *time* and *money* of the article's title) as well as functional ones across the four corpora; in another study (Baker 2010a) he compares the use of gendered-marked terms across the four corpora and associates changing linguistics choices with transformations of the representation of women and with a trend towards a more gender-neutral language.

Renouf describes Modern Diachronic Corpus linguistics as 'an area ripe for growth' (Renouf 2002: 41) and offers a list of ways to use diachronic corpora, hinting that the area is still largely under-researched; this is particularly true for discourse-oriented diachronic work. Browsing over 450 titles included in Gabrielatos's extremely comprehensive (and constantly growing[2]) bibliography of Corpus Approaches to Discourse Studies, I could find only 25 publications over the past 10 years which could be classified as MD-CADS. Restricting the spotlight to work even more specifically dealing with corpora and discourse, just about 16 per cent of the articles published in *Corpora* journal between its foundation (2006) and 2016 deals with diachronic research and this includes the special issue on MD-CADS edited by Partington, which accounts for half of the total.

The relative scarcity of diachronic studies is not unique to corpus-based research: Stanyer and Mihelj (2016) reviewed diachronic work in communication and media studies based on the articles published in three major media journals over a 15-year period and found it amounted to just 1 per cent of the total output of the journals. Of particular relevance to the aims of the present chapter, Stanyer and Mihelj also noted a lack of reflection on the methodological implications of dealing with temporal variables and, similarly to the aforementioned Gries and Hilpert, state that:

> periodisation is often used as seemingly neutral instrument for organising historical materials and narrating change. Yet the division of a time line into periods inevitably carries with it assumptions about the nature of change, and even about the casual relationships driving change.
>
> *(Stanyer & Mihelj 2016: 273)*

Their article, albeit provocative in intent, remains unfortunately vague, still the typology they devise to distinguish different kinds of diachronic analysis is useful. They identify three kinds of diachronic research:

1 trend mapping – tracking the development of a chosen phenomenon over time;
2 temporal comparison – comparing two moments in time;

3 turning points – defining *a priori* critical junctures and comparing before and after.

While trend-mapping studies are the most frequent type in Stanyer and Mihelj's review, applying these categories to the 25 diachronic studies in Gabrielatos's bibliography we find a balance between tracking over continuous data (12 publications) and comparing between two or more distinct moments (13 publications). There was however no study strictly speaking fitting the turning-point definition. This is easily (and we may add reassuringly) explained by the empirical nature of corpus-based research: turning points are indeed identified in a number of MD-CADS-type studies, but these tend to emerge bottom-up from the analysis or at least from testing hypotheses on the data, rather than being part of the research design.

Half of the trend-mapping titles surveyed in the bibliography are related to either the *RASIM* or the *Islam* studies conducted at Lancaster University (reviewed in detail below). Nine out of the 13 temporal comparison ones are related to the *SiBol* project and the thereof named Siena and Bologna universities group. It seems fair to deduce that *RASIM/Islam* and *SiBol* have a progenitor status for modern diachronic discourse analysis using corpora.

The *RASIM* (Refugees Asylum Seekers Immigrants and Migrants) project saw the collaboration of a group of scholars from Lancaster University, combining theoretical backgrounds and methods traditionally associated with corpus linguistics and critical discourse studies (Baker et al. 2008). They built a 140-million-word corpus, spanning a nine-year period, which included a large selection of British broadsheet and tabloid articles dealing with refugees, asylum seekers, immigrants and migrants, and they pursued a variety of threads of analysis, including an investigation of diachronic change or stability of representations, looking, for example, at 'consistent collocates', i.e. collocates that remain stable over time. Gabrielatos and Baker (2008) spell out in their *RASIM* work the now much employed distinction between 'consistent' and 'seasonal' collocates (Gabrielatos & Baker 2008: 12), thus reinforcing the diachronic interest of a long-standing idea: that semantic prosody is the node's property of being associated with a 'semantically *consistent* set of collocates' (Bublitz 1996: 9; italics mine), or, as Bill Louw first put it, 'the *consistent* aura of meaning with which a form is imbued by its collocates' (Louw 1993: 57; italics mine).

A similar corpus and a similar approach to that used for *RASIM* was adopted by Baker, Gabrielatos and McEnery to study the representation of Muslims and Islam in the British press between 1999 and 2010 (Baker 2010b; Baker et al. 2012). The diachronic work in this project is, according to the authors themselves, more sophisticated than the 'limited and statistically naïve' (Gabrielatos et al. 2012: 158) approach used for *RASIM*, and it is, in my view, a methodological model for thorough and aware design for the analysis of continuous chronological datasets. The authors analyse the correlation between frequency peaks in the output of newspaper articles and trigger events which may have caused the surge of reporting, aiming at 'objectively identifying' (Gabrielatos et al. 2012:157) relevant contextual elements, in order to optimise the segmentation of the data set. '[C]rucial for the utility of a diachronic corpus study – they explain – is the number of time-points at which frequencies have been measured' and the proportion of the sampling points on the temporal length of the corpus, i.e. the granularity of the analysis. The spikes and troughs which were identified bottom-up thanks to this meticulous quantitative comparison at 144 sampling points over a span of 12 years informed the subsequent linguistic analysis of change over time. The diachronic study (Baker et al. 2012) tackles multiple levels: from identification of unique and shared keywords among the discrete calendar years, through the tracking of the evolution in the proportion of tokens in key semantic areas, to the closer examination of changing collocates. The sole limitation of this remarkably accurate and reflective piece of work is that 'for the sake of simplicity' (Baker et al. 2012: 94) it does not ultimately exploit the full potential and rigour detailed in the seminal paper by Gabrielatos et al. (2012).

If the *RASIM* and *Islam* projects are the main reference for diachronic work of trend-mapping (as well as data-driven turning-point identification), the work done on the *SiBol* corpora accounts for a fundamental block of corpus-assisted discourse studies on temporal comparisons. The name *SiBol* is a portmanteau of the universities of Siena and Bologna, which were the original affiliations of the founders of the project. The *SiBol* corpora are large newspaper corpora of a parallel structure and content collected at different moments: the complete output of three British broadsheets (*Guardian*, *Times* and *Telegraph*) in 1993 (100 million words), 2005 (150 million words) and 2010 (140 million words).[3] The aim of *SiBol*, according to the group's website, is 'to track changes in modern language usage but also social, cultural and political changes over modern times, as reflected in language'.[4] While the *RASIM* and *Islam* datasets were collected for a specific project and research questions, the *SiBol* corpora were compiled to be re-used for a variety of purposes. *SiBol* was really built as a resource for unknown questions: the researchers who used it started from something which emerged from the keywords comparisons, but then each analyst was primed by their own interests to pursue very different questions. *SiBol* data have been, for example, employed to study changing representations of the EU (Marchi & Taylor 2009), morality (Marchi 2010), science (Taylor 2010), anti-Semitism (Partington 2012), as well as to investigate general linguistic change in newspaper discourse (Duguid 2010) or to address broad methodological issues (Taylor 2013). Reusability and availability (*SiBol* can be accessed on the *Sketchengine* platform) potentially[5] make of corpora such as *SiBol* research tools (rather than data sets), in a way that RQ-customised corpora could never be.[6] Yet any corpus has limitations, or at the very least a palpable impact on the analysis, due to the assumptions built into its design. For example, for the *SiBol* corpora, which collect the entire yearly output of the newspapers, compilers made the assumption that a calendar year was an appropriate unit of analysis and that a 12-year gap (i.e. the time distance between the two first corpora, on which the majority of the analysis to date is based) was a significant distance, or at least a useful, multipurpose one. The issue of an appropriate distance is solved when we use corpora covering the entire output of sources over a continuous stretch of time, a notable example being the impressive tools provided by Mark Davies's BYU historical corpora.[7] A corpus that covers an unbroken stretch of time may also use years as units for data collection, but it allows for finer-grained divisions that can be derived bottom-up, for example on the basis of peaks and troughs in the frequency of specific items/phenomena (as in Gabrielatos et al. 2012). An analysis based on complete continuous data sets is nevertheless also subject to influence of pre-assumptions and arbitrariness; particularly because tracking studies are still comparative and, as stated at the outset, different units of comparison produce different findings.

The rest of this chapter is devoted precisely to reflecting on this influence, the following section will discuss time units and segmentation in general, while Section 9.4 will illustrate potential pitfalls by means of a case study.

9.3 Segmentation and units

Ample space was devoted to the review of the *SiBol* and *RASIM/Islam* projects because they are prototypical examples of two types of MD-CADS: studies comparing two (or more) 'points' in time and studies tracking the development of a phenomenon over a continuous stretch of time. In the case of *SiBol*, preliminary decisions concerning the unity of a calendar year as a 'point' and the appropriateness of variously commensurable distances between 1993, 2005, 2010 and 2013, determine the course and the reach of the analysis. The asymmetrical distance among intervals is justified by the assumption that newspapers change ever more rapidly, but it is unrelated to the individual phenomena/events that may be compared. To evaluate the RQ-specific appropriateness we need an *a posteriori* reflection of the impact of corpus-design. The issue of *post-hoc* evaluation could be avoided by collecting an uninterrupted stretch of data designed ad hoc to answer a specific RQ, in the *RASIM/Islam* fashion. Besides the limited re-usability, however, with this type of design we lose relevant information about weight of the topic under investigation with respect to the whole output within a unit of time. We know, in fact, that the size of newspapers has changed considerably over the years (e.g. a year of the *Guardian* in 1993 corresponds to 55,514 articles and about 30 million words, in 2005 it is 85,929 articles and nearly 49 million words). This implies that were we to identify peaks and troughs of a theme at sample points relative to the volume of the whole output at the corresponding sample point, we may get a different distribution compared to that shown by the absolute frequencies and therefore this may ultimately determine a change in the temporal boundaries constituting different units.

The ideal solution, in terms of corpus compilation, appears to be collecting the complete output of a source of data for a continuous stretch of time. However, a minimization *a priori* impact of corpus-design still does not efface the impact of the decisions we make about the temporal variable.

We can consider three ways to determine the level of aggregation of consecutive time periods in order to identify time units:

1 Text-lifecycle segmentation: based on the periodicity characterising the text type (e.g. a daily edition for a newspaper).

2 Top-down segmentation: based on standardised spans (typically a calendar year), or on contextual historical knowledge (e.g. a timeline of events), which is used to inform the segmentation (see for example Bartley & Hidalgo-Tenorio 2016).
3 Bottom-up segmentation: based on internal variability, i.e. using distributional information to identify milestones in time, which can in turn be used to divide the corpus in subsets of data to compare against one another (Gries 2011).

I would like to argue that no one of these solutions is intrinsically optimal, but that the value of appropriateness always depends on the research questions.

The small-scale case study that follows is based on a 1.3-million-word corpus comprising the entire White House Press Briefings between December 2010 and November 2011. At the origin of the temporal delimitation of the corpus is a 'make believe beginning': the start of the so-called Jasmine revolution in Tunisia (17 December 2010), and an arbitrary end: the UN report on Syrian security forces' 'crimes against humanity' (Human Rights Council 2011: 1), published on 23 November 2011. Two diachronic RQs were addressed:

1 How much space was devoted to the so-called Arab Spring in the WHPB with respect to other topics at different points in time?
2 Did the representation of the places and people involved evolve over the time period and how?

In order to ask these questions the corpus could be divided in a variety of ways (i.e. comparable units), for example:

- 4 seasons (winter, spring, summer, fall)
- 12 months
- 51 weeks
- 171 briefing days
- 214 individual briefings (each one a sequence of questions and responses).

As will emerge from the next section, there is no universally optimal segmentation; appropriateness depends both on specific contextual elements (i.e. extralinguistic knowledge about the topic/event) and on purpose.

9.4 Case study: the Arab seasons

9.4.1 A general note of warning

In line with the methodological nature of this chapter, little space will be devoted to reporting the actual findings about representations of the so-called Arab Spring, therefore readers are warned that they will probably be none the wiser in that respect, while the case study will focus on the process: on the handling of the data and of the diachronic variable.

The initial work on this case study was conducted in 2012 (Marchi 2012) and is here reprised using a cleaner version of the same data set. In any research using contemporary data the time of observation seems to be an essential element to acknowledge and consider, all the more so in the case of corpus-based studies with an interest in discourse, which typically deals with 'areas of pressing concern', as stated on Lancaster's Corpus Approaches to Social Sciences (CASS) website.[8] The interest in current affairs may (as happens in CDA) or may not be associated to political engagement, but it inevitably means that the point of observation is likely to be (temporally) immersed in the observed situation, which, in turn, often is a developing one (e.g. immigration, climate change, etc.), rather than a finite event. A corpus compiled in 2012 to investigate the representation of countries involved in the uprising, is necessarily different from a corpus compiled to investigate the same question five years later, and so – we may add – is the perspective of the analysts as a result of their different temporal positioning. In 2012, for example, the conflict in Syria had only just begun: the insurgency started in 2011 grew into a civil war which is still going on at the time of writing and has since seen, and keeps seeing, the military intervention of foreign countries, such as Russia, Turkey and most recently the United States (April 2017). The very questions we ask are time dependent, as is the contextual knowledge available to the analyst.

9.4.2 Content analysis: space over time

The first question addressed is one of distribution: how much space was devoted to the so-called Arab Spring in the WHPB with respect to other topics at different points in time?

CADS studies often start with some sort of quantification (or quantification comes into play in the early stages of the analysis), in this case estimating the proportion of briefings where the three countries under scrutiny (Egypt, Libya and Syria) are discussed: 62 per cent of the briefings mention at least one of the countries at least once.

A preliminary rough idea of distribution helps predict what could be a useful unit of comparison, as it tells us when something was being discussed. Mere distribution however does not give us an idea of the relevance of the topics, of their comparative dominance or subordination in the discussion. A useful way to determine the relevance of a topic with respect to other topics at different points in time is keyword analysis.

9.4.3 Keyword analysis: aboutness through time

Keywords, as we know, are words 'whose frequency is unusually high in comparison with some norm' (Scott 1996:53), the norm being the frequency of those words in a reference corpus. Keyword analysis does not make visible what is characteristic

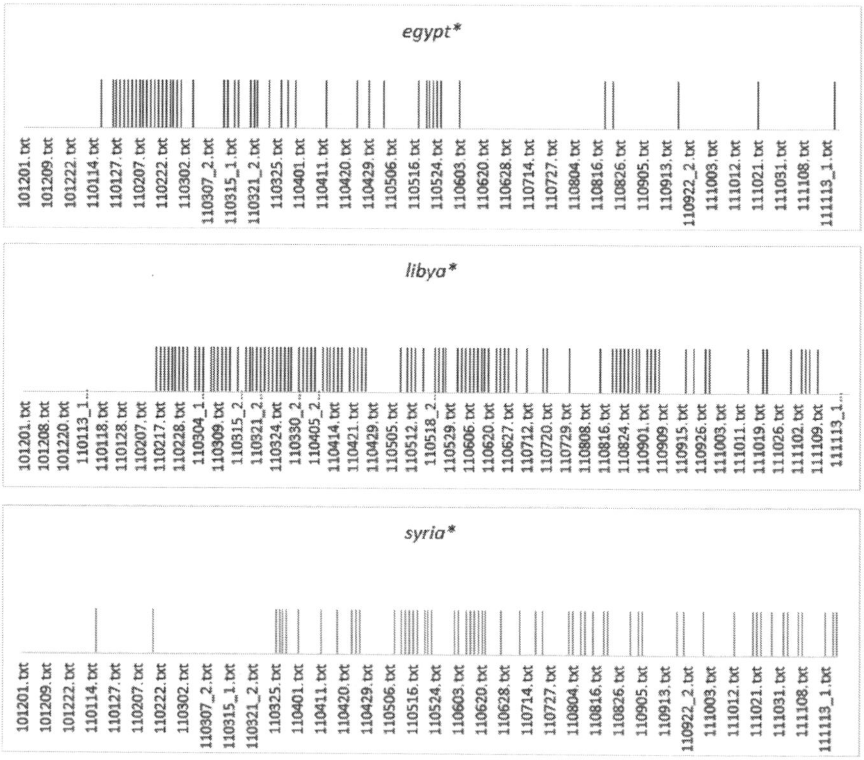

FIGURE 9.1 Diachronic plots of the briefings mentioning *egypt** *libya** and *syria**.

of a set of data, but what is characteristically different between that set and another set; in our case between a moment in time and another. Naturally if we segment the data in different ways (i.e. temporal subsets) we will most likely get different keywords.

Keywords are calculated here adopting Gabrielatos and Marchi's (2012) method, which expresses, as Gabrielatos (chapter 11, this volume) explains in detail, the effect size of a statistically significant difference. I applied the arbitrary (and common) cut-off point of the top 100 keywords by percentage difference and reordered them by log-likelihood. I experimented with a variety of comparisons on the WHPB corpus using different time units (e.g. months or seasons), different combinations of comparisons (e.g. month one vs. month two, month one vs. all following, month one vs. everything else) in both temporal directions and using symmetric as well as asymmetric units. The word clouds below offer an at-a-glance illustration of different comparisons. Again, naturally rather different pictures emerge from the various comparisons. I opted for very informal word cloud displays here because, as explained earlier, the aim is not presenting findings, but illustrating the repercussions of research design and methods. Keyword analysis is often used in CADS as a source of insight pointing towards potentially interesting items for closer observation and offers a relatively objective parameter of salience (see Baker 2006), provided that by 'objective' we mean impartial rather than factual. Figures 9.2 and 9.4 simply show that choosing a different span for the unit of comparison (seasons as opposed to months) may lead to different first impressions and may, consequently, inform the next step of the analysis in a different way, or at least present options of further investigation with different accents. Again, as stated at the outset, this is fairly obvious, but it is also very rarely reflected upon and we do not frequently see systematic experimentation with different time units, or acknowledgement that this has been a concern. From Figure 9.4, comparing February against the January and December briefings, what emerges quite clearly is that with reference to the so-called Arab Spring, the February briefings ought to be in the Spring set rather than in the Winter one, were we to opt for a less granular segmentation, as the output is strikingly similar to what we get in Figure 9.3. In Figure 9.5 we can observe that what distinguishes the month of February from the following months is the massive prominence of Egypt in the briefings.

Once we have decided on a time unit, there are a variety of options for comparison: we can compare what has become a 'point in time' in our corpus to the previous point in time and to the following, we can compare it to everything that precedes it and everything that follows, we can compare non-contiguous periods, or we can compare it against the rest of points in time included in the data set. The choice is all but obvious and all but neutral: it depends on the questions we are asking, it depends on the corpus (the nature of the data), it depends on the context (the nature of the event/topic we are examining) and it also depends on an implicit theory of time itself. For example, our expectations about progression or recurrence, about linearity or fragmentation, acceleration or deceleration, and so on, affect (and are inscribed in) the way we decide to look at the data. As the physicist Sean Carroll sums up, '[c]oncepts like "time" are not handed to us unambiguously by the outside world but are invented by human beings trying to make sense of the universe' (Carroll 2010: 19).

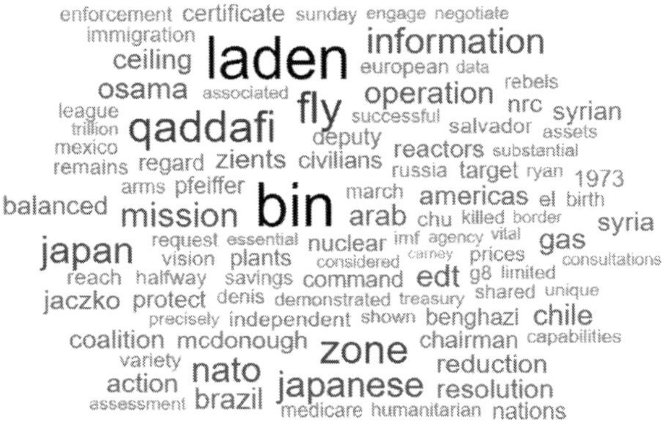

FIGURE 9.2 Word cloud of keywords comparing Spring subset vs preceding unit (Winter subset).

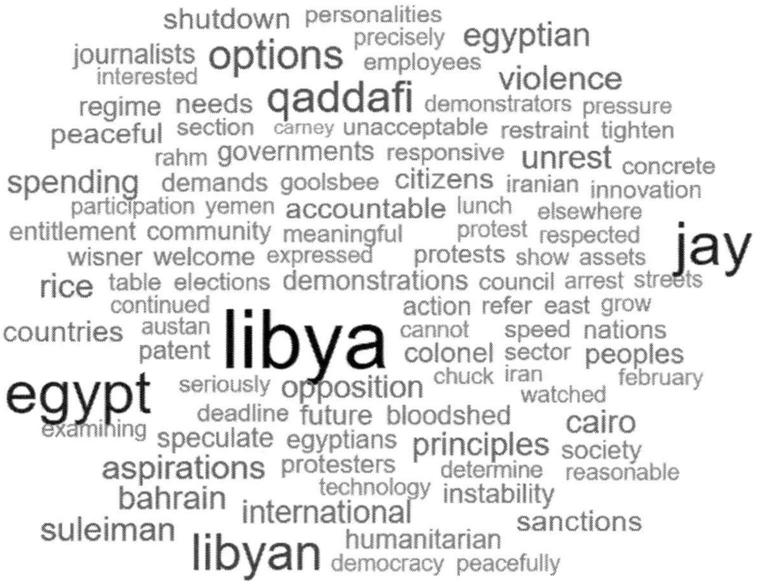

FIGURE 9.3 Word cloud of keywords comparing Spring subset vs following units (Summer and Autumn subsets).

FIGURE 9.4 Word cloud of keywords comparing February subset vs preceding months (December and January).

FIGURE 9.5 Word cloud of keywords comparing February subset vs Spring.

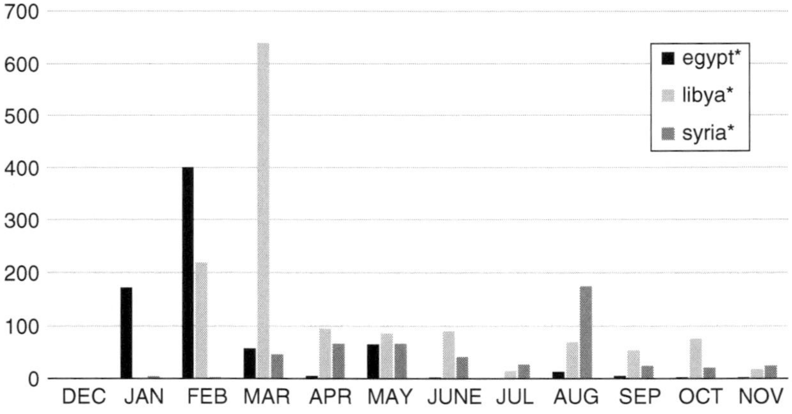

FIGURE 9.6 Mentions of *egypt**, *libya** and *syria** in the WHPB corpus, by month.

9.4.4 Analysing/comparing different things within the same corpus

The key countries involved in the so-called Arab Spring discussed in the briefings are Egypt, Libya and Syria. Events in these three countries had a very different pace.

The uprising in Egypt has a very short cycle, the mass protest begins on 25 of January 2011 and on 11 of February President Hosni Mubarak steps down. Figure 9.7

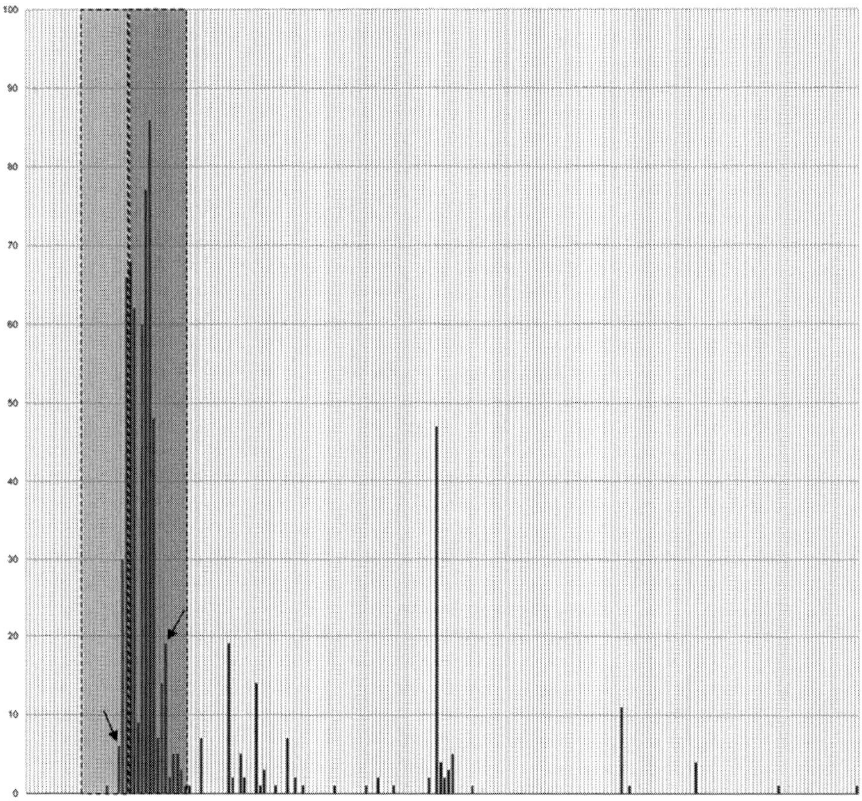

FIGURE 9.7 Mentions of *egypt**, *libya** and *syria** in the WHPB corpus, by briefing and area overlap for the months of January and February.

shows the overlap between the distribution of mentions of *egypt** in the individual briefings and the area covered by January and February, the arrows signal 25 January and 11 February respectively. This implies that it would be of little use to investigate diachronically the case of Egypt using months as unit of analysis.

I will use naming strategies as a brief illustration of how different time divisions provide entirely different results for the analyst to interpret. Figure 9.8 shows the way Mubarak is referred to in the briefings dividing them by month; Figure 9.9 breaks down the occurrences by week, offering an illustration of the decline in the use of the title *President* that reflects the context and the timeline of the events taking place in Egypt.

This example provides a rather blatant demonstration of how contextual knowledge is essential to identifying a useful and most importantly appropriate segmentation. It also gives an indication, more in general, of how change and stability are the effect of different segmentations: depending on the specific case, aggregating data may emphasise or flatten the visibility of variation or the perception of similarity. This is very relevant to longitudinal studies looking at consistent collocates over extended periods of time. The case study used in this chapter is too small and too specific to

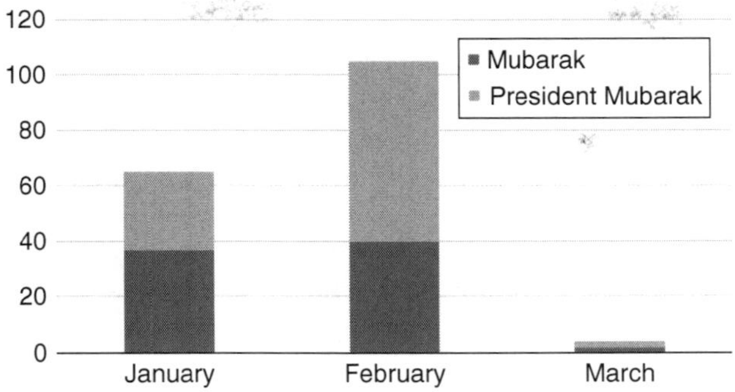

FIGURE 9.8 Proportion of mentions of *Mubarak* preceded by *President* over total mentions, using months as time unit.

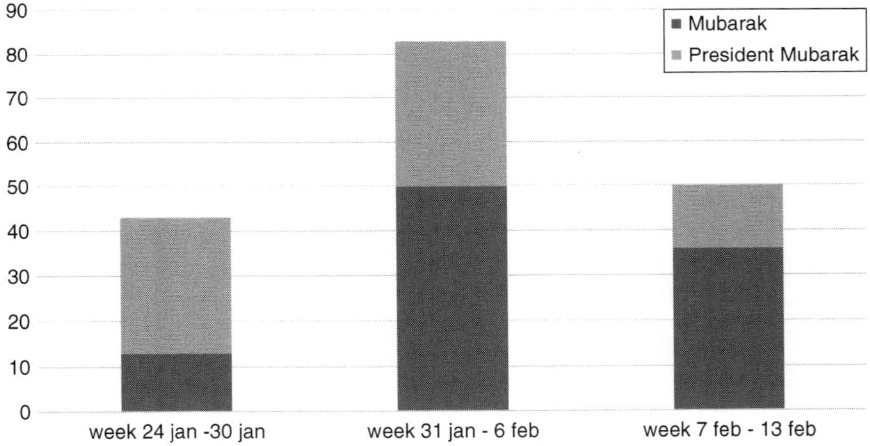

FIGURE 9.9 Proportion of mentions of *Mubarak* preceded by *President* over total mentions, using weeks as time unit.

usefully demonstrate work on c-collocates, for which a large-scale study would be more suitable. For example, at the Festival of Methods hosted during Corpora and Discourse International Conference 2016, Taylor and Marchi presented an analysis of stable representations of *Irish* and *Ireland* in UK parliamentary debates between 1900 and 2000 and they showed that consistent collocates vary depending on the level of aggregation (decades vs. paired decades) as well as on direction of the comparison (older towards more recent vs. more recent towards older).

9.4.5 The pace of change

Even though any work on c-collocates is beyond the possibilities of this case study, collocates can here be used to illustrate the usefulness of adopting a shared unit of time when comparing different items within a corpus.

In February the most frequent collocate of *libya** in the briefings is *government*, from March onwards the top collocate is *people*, in March the collocate *government* disappears, while a series of new (with respect to February) subsequently enduring collocates emerges: *situation*, *civilians*, *opposition* and *regime*. As described elsewhere by Partington and Marchi (2015: 228): '[t]he evaluatively neutral *Libyan government* has rapidly been replaced in briefings discourse with the negative *Qaddafi regime* to create diplomatic distance between the White House and the Libyan administration.'

The word *government* is the top collocate of *syria** until June when it is supplanted in ranking by *people*, and when the term *regime* enters the list, the collocate *government*, however, does not disappear from the list. In August the references to *regime* largely outnumber those to *government* (Figure 9.11), but the decline of the label *government* has a rather slow pace.

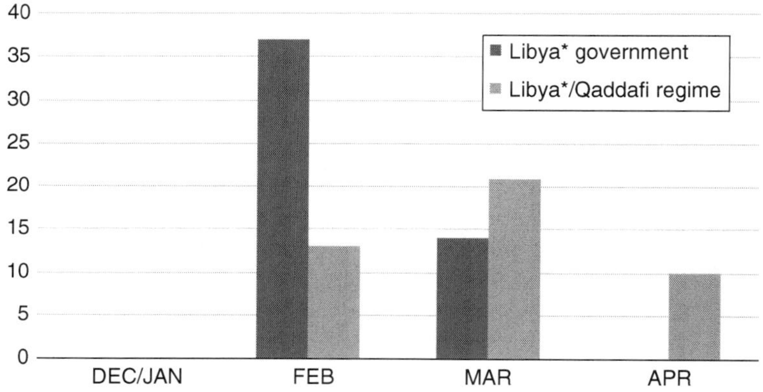

FIGURE 9.10 Naming of the Libyan administration in the WHPB during the first months of 2011.

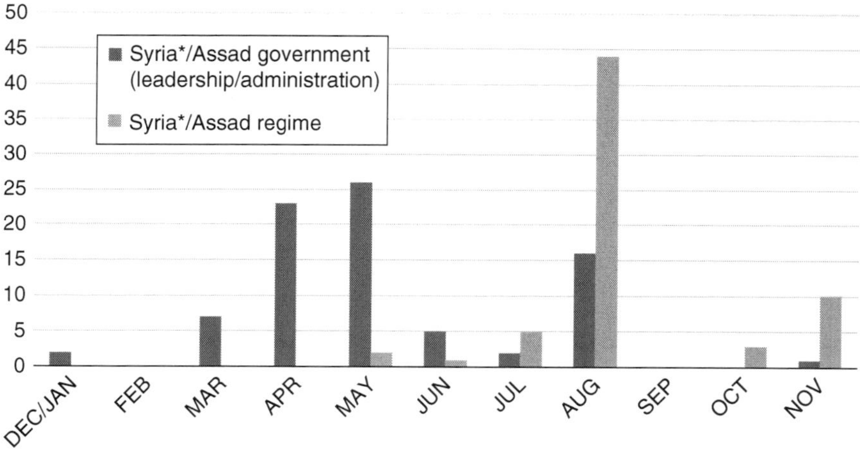

FIGURE 9.11 Naming of the Syrian administration throughout the corpus.

The change in naming participants in the case of Libya corresponds, as we know, to the military intervention which began in March. The greater reluctance of the White House to switch to *regime* in the case of Syria corresponds to a relative absence of discussion about Syria altogether in the briefings until August. Taking into consideration the extratextual context, this absence (see Duguid & Partington in Chapter 3 of this volume) is rather interesting because it certainly did not find a matching uneventfulness in the real world: the civilian death toll in Syria between April and July was dramatic.

Making a concession to the temptation to look outside the corpus to more recent data, it may be interesting to note that even though in 2012 in the White House Press Briefings 33 per cent of references to *Assad* co-occur with *regime*, we still find he is occasionally referred to as *President Assad* (32 occurrences).

Partington and Marchi (2015) explain the different lexical choices and pace of change in lexical choices and thus the different evaluative reactions to the various uprisings, using the podium's own words (Partington & Marchi 2015: 231):

> MR CARNEY: Well Dan, as I have said, **each country** that has been affected by this unrest is **different. Each country** in the region is **different**. **Each country** has **different** traditions, political systems and relationships with the United States [...] (24/02/2011)

9.4.6 *Analysing across corpora: the usefulness of calendar units and looking at the timeline*

Adopting uniform time units becomes if not necessary, then particularly useful when comparing data sets with very different characteristics of size, number of texts, text lifecycles, periodicity and so on. I will attempt a brief illustration of this issue by comparing the WHPB corpus with a corpus of CNN output compiled

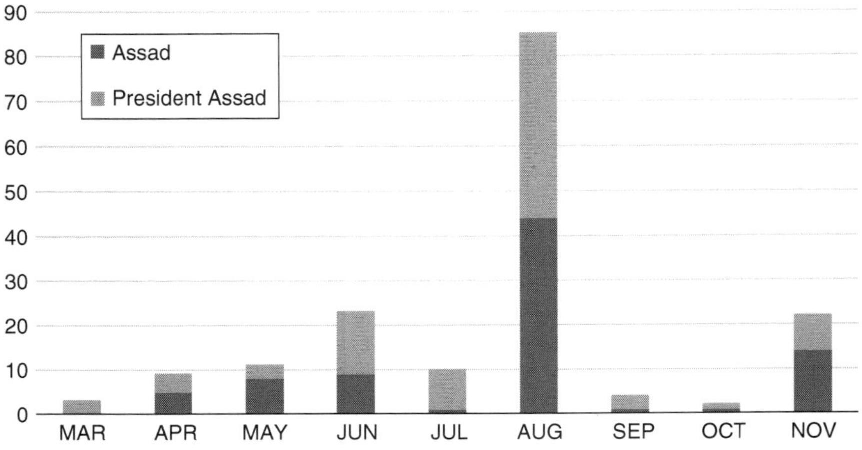

FIGURE 9.12 Proportion of mentions of *Assad* preceded by *President* over total mentions.

TABLE 9.1 Corpus composition of the WHPB corpus and the CNN corpus

	CNN corpus	*WHPB corpus*
Size	63 million words	1.3 million words
Texts	7,261 transcripts	214 briefings
Periodicity	365 news days	171 briefing days
Coverage	12 months	12 months

over the same time period (Table 9.1). Adopting (top-down) month units we can easily align the results.

CNN is one of the news outlets (mostly broadcast) with a front row seat in the James S. Brady Press Briefing Room and thus is both audience and interlocutor of what goes on in the briefings. I pursue here a very simple question: Is there any correspondence (both in terms of chronology and in terms of meanings) in the use of the phrase *arab spring* in the WHPB and in the CNN corpus?

In the CNN data the phrase *arab spring* is used 859 times, with a relative frequency 0.013 ptw, in the Briefings it appears only 36 times, though in relative terms it is twice as frequent as in the CNN corpus (with a normalised frequency of 0.026 ptw). *Spring* is the second most frequent collocate of *arab* (after *league*) in the briefings and it is the favoured lexical choice in referring to the unrest in the Middle East (there is one reference to the *arab uprising* and two to the *arab awakening*). In the CNN corpus *spring* (distribution of *arab spring* shown later in Figure 9.3) is the third most frequent collocate of *arab* (after *league* and *world*) and here too it is the preferred descriptor with 62 references to *arab protests*, 49 to *arab* UPRISING, 29 to *arab awakening*, 23 to *arab* REVOLUTION, nine to *arab revolt* and four to *arab upheaval*.

The term makes its first appearance in the CNN data in January, but it refers to the original Arab Spring of 2004 and 2005: a period of unrest in a series of Arab countries in the wake of the elections in Iraq (so-called purple revolution), protests in Lebanon (so-called cedar revolution) and the Palestinian presidential elections. The first recorded reference to an Arab Spring dates back to 2003:

> The war, which is vastly unpopular in the Arab world, is far more likely to improve the fortunes of the Islamists, he says, and provoke governments to tighten their grip, than to ventilate the region with an Arab spring.
>
> *(George Packer, 'Dreaming of democracy'. The New York Times Magazine, 02/03/2003)*

In February, we find a second occurrence in the CNN data, uttered by a correspondent referring to *this arab spring*:

> the name of course has long been synonymous with chaos in the region, but this **Arab spring**, let's call it, continuing to bloom across the Middle East.
>
> *(CNN 28/02/2011)*

TABLE 9.2 Distribution of *arab spring* in the WHPB and in the CNN corpus in 2011

Month	*CNN hits*	*CNN (ptw)*	*WHPB (hits)*	*WHPB (ptw)*
JAN	1	0.0002	0	0
FEB	1	0.00026	0	0
MAR	24	0.00445	0	0
APR	22	0.00456	1	0.09
MAY	191	0.03745	3	0.36
JUN	74	0.01524	6	1.72
JUL	32	0.00627	0	0
AUG	40	0.00747	0	0
SEP	99	0.01997	7	1.51
OCT	203	0.04039	1	0.17
NOV	58	0.01203	3	0.33

The term never drops out of the CNN data, with peaks in May and then in October. In the WHPB it is first mentioned at the end of March. The total absence of earlier references is rather surprising if we consider the dominance of discussion about Egypt in February and the fact that the term *arab spring* had already spread (even though its use was not frequent) in the media. A rapid look at the output of global media outlets on the Nexis database reveals that the first reference to this *arab spring* appeared in January 2011 in *Foreign Policy*, in January we find mentions in the *Jerusalem Post* and in the *Christian Science Monitor* and in February it is mentioned in most major English language papers.

Going back to the CNN corpus, *arab spring* appears 39 times in the cluster *so-called arab spring*, echoing the *let's call it* of the first mention, and which is the most frequent cluster for the phrase *arab spring*, though it potentially leaves us with 820 cases where the *arab spring* is not 'so-called' at all, but is just called that. A closer examination of concordance lines reveals that about 9 per cent of the occurrences have a 'so-called' status, as illustrated by the examples in Table 9.3.

If we look at occurrences chronologically rather than by volume we discover that there is a strong peak of 'so-called' references to the *arab spring* during the first months of 2011. Figure 9.13 shows the percentage of so-called occurrences over the total occurrences by month, I excluded February because there was only one occurrence which was also a so-called (thus a 100 per cent) and it compromised the readability of the figure.

In March, 33 per cent of CNN mentions are what have been labelled here so-called mentions; see examples in Table 9.3.

In the briefings none of the occurrences of *arab spring* is a so-called mention, when the podium (27 times) or the journalists (nine times) refer to the *arab spring* it is always in very real terms, for example: *the Arab Spring that we have been witnessing*; *the Arab Spring that we've seen*; *the Arab Spring that's caused a surge in oil prices.*

So looking at the broader context and timeline we learn the term *arab spring* is a coinage of the Western media, originally referring to the change that some

TABLE 9.3 Examples of 'so-called occurrences' of *arab spring* in the CNN corpus

Example	*speaker*
but this **Arab spring, let's call it**	(CNN correspondent)
what many described as a historic **'Arab Spring'**	(CNN host)
it's being called the Arab spring	(CNN contributor)
we think of it as an Arab spring	(CNN host)
We are calling it Arab spring	(CNN host)
we locked on **the term 'Arab Spring'** to describe the remarkable upheaval	(CNN host)
I don't like **the phrase 'Arab Spring'**	(expert)
why is a popular protest **called the Arab Spring**? We are going to tell you why [...] So where does **the term 'Arab Spring'** even come from?	(CNN host)
if you look at Syria and Libya, it's hard to use **the term Arab Spring** there	(expert)
stirred **what we call the 'Arab Spring'**	(CNN host)
set in motion **what we call the 'Arab Spring'**	(CNN host)
what we have called the Arab Spring	(CNN host)
in what we now call the Arab Spring	(CNN host)
in what is called now the Arab spring	(President Abbas)
what's called the Arab Spring	(Ehud Barak)
what **became known as the Arab Spring**	(CNN host)

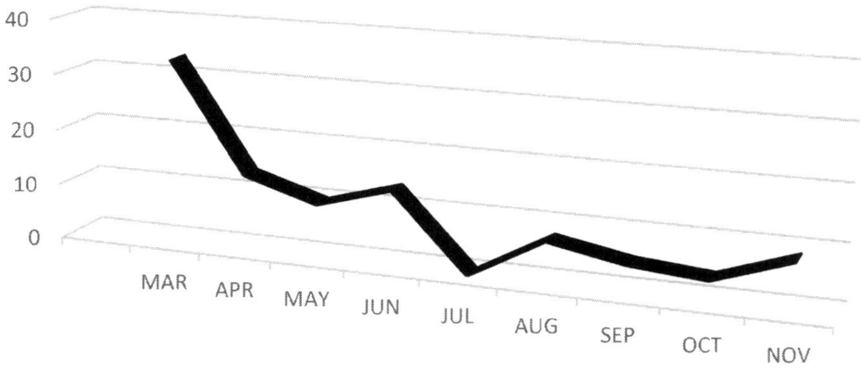

FIGURE 9.13 Percentage of so-called mentions of *arab spring* in the CNN corpus on a timeline.

supposed would spring from the aftermath of the war in Iraq, the media resuscitate the label to define the events of 2011 (the CNN calls it *the year of the arab*). The origin of the term is obliterated in the CNN corpus, but there is initially quite a lot of metadiscussion about the name; in the briefings the term is picked up once it has been popularised and there is no trace of linguistic discussion, it is always used to describe a set of events.

9.5 Conclusion

The aim of this chapter was to raise some questions about the handling of the diachronic variable in the productive area of MD-CADS. If there was an intent to indicate best practices, the best practice it really wanted to promote is that of reflexivity. As admitted from the very beginning, stating that different choices of time units produce different results is rather obvious, and yet we see that these choices generally go unquestioned, or at least they often remain undiscussed.

What I hope to have shown is that there is no ultimately 'right' unit and that defining the appropriate level of aggregation, and the parameter on which to establish it, depends on establishing 'appropriate for what purpose'? In the case study, different kinds of units were used: bottom-up derived divisions (both data-driven and context-informed), comparable calendar (top-down) units, and text-lifecycle units, in the case of distribution across individual briefings. We may need not one optimal segmentation, but several useful ones.

The case study I chose here has several limitations in terms of what could be done diachronically, but in the trade-off between showing a wide range of techniques and discussing a wide range of problems I favoured the latter. There are excellent diachronic studies out there (such as the work discussed in Section 9.2) and in this volume too (see Taylor's work on c-collocates in Chapter 2 of this volume) that the reader can turn to for good techniques, but there is very little reflection on the variety of issues to consider in MD-CADS, as well as on their specificity. I purposely chose a small corpus with a short overall span and recent data to stress the fact that anything can be studied diachronically. Furthermore, MD-CADS interest in current affairs augments the possibility that we will have to handle a short span and focus on events that may have a very short shelf life, if considered in a broader historical perspective. The issue of 'perspective' is not secondary either: the fact that oftentimes researchers interested in using corpora to analyse discourse are interested in 'areas of pressing concern' (as discussed at the beginning of this chapter), entails a closeness between the time observed and the time of observation, with its own epistemological perils.

In short, not only is there a need to be aware of the variety of possible choices and of their methodological implications, but there is also a need to be aware that any choice we make as analysts has theoretical baggage. On a broader philosophical level, defining time units implies a theory of time, on a smaller, and yet not so distant, practical level, defining time units is imbued with considerations about the text and the context. By context I mean both the contextual elements characterising the topic under investigation (e.g. the extra-linguistic knowledge available about an event) and the positioning of the analysts themselves.

This is no ultimate admission of inescapable relativism. Methodologically speaking I strongly argue for flexible tools, multiple purpose-based time units, identified both using data-driven information from the corpus and knowledge based on the context, precisely to counter the possibility that our results are entirely relative to default assumptions.

As the Doctor would say: 'People assume that time is a strict progression of cause to effect. But actually from a non-linear, non-subjective viewpoint it's more like a big ball of wibbly-wobbly … timey-wimey … stuff' (Doctor Who, 207). In order to make sense of this 'stuff' we do not just need to consider when the whats are but also what the whens are.

Notes

1 A *lockword* is defined as 'a word which may change in its meaning or context of usage when we compare a set of diachronic corpora together, yet appears to be relatively static in terms of frequency' (Baker 2011: 66).
2 The bibliography is available at: http://www.gabrielatos.com/CLDA-Biblio.htm. My review is based on entries added by the end of September 2016, at the time of writing the number is already up by nearly 200 entries.
3 A further corpus was added for year 2013, but the collection of sources was expanded to 12 newspapers.
4 http://www.lilec.it/clb/.
5 As a matter of fact, to this date, I am not aware of any research based on the *SiBol* corpora, other than the *SiBol* group's.
6 The two sole potential re-uses of a search-term based corpus could be either replication/ parareplication of results, or the longitudinal extension (forwards and/or backwards) of the corpus (using the same query).
7 Freely available through web interface at: http://corpus.byu.edu/.
8 http://cass.lancs.ac.uk/.

References

Baker, P. 2006. *Using Corpora in Discourse Analysis*. London: Continuum.

Baker, P. 2009. The B06 Corpus of British English and recent language change. *International Journal of Corpus Linguistics*, 14(3), 312–337.

Baker, P. 2010a. Will Ms ever be as frequent as Mr? A corpus-based comparison of gendered terms across four diachronic corpora of British English. *Gender and Language*, 4(1), 125–129.

Baker, P. 2010b. Representations of Islam in British broadsheet and tabloid newspapers 1999–2005. *Language and Politics*, 9(2), 310–338.

Baker, P. 2011. Times may change but we'll always have money: A corpus driven examination of vocabulary change in four diachronic corpora. *Journal of English Linguistics*, 39, 65–88.

Baker, P., Gabrielatos, C., Khosravinik, M., Krzyzanowski, M., McEnery, T. & Wodak, R. 2008. A useful methodological synergy? Combining critical discourse analysis and corpus linguistics to examine discourses of refugees and asylum seekers in the UK press. *Discourse & Society*, 19(3), 273–305.

Baker, P., Gabrielatos, C. & McEnery, T. 2012. *Discourse Analysis and Media Attitudes: The British Press on Islam*. Cambridge: Cambridge University Press.

Bartley, L. & Hidalgo-Tenorio, E. 2016. 'To be Irish, gay and on the outside': A critical discourse analysis of the Other after the Celtic Tiger period. *Journal of Language and Sexuality*, 5(1), 1–36.

Bublitz, W. 1996. Semantic rosody and cohesive company: 'Somewhat predictable'. *Leuvense Bijdragen*, 85, 1–32.

Carroll, S. 2010. *From Eternity to Here. The Quest for the Ultimate Theory of Time*. London: Penguin.

Dr Who. 2007. Directed by Hettie MacDonald [TV series]. Episode *Blink*. BBC.

Duguid, A. 2010. Newspapers discourse informalisation: A diachronic comparison from keywords. *Corpora*, 5(2), 109–138.

Eliot, G. 1996. *Daniel Deronda*. Ware, Hertfordshire: Wordsworth Editions Limited.

Gabrielatos, C. & Baker, P. 2008. Fleeing, sneaking, flooding: A corpus analysis of discursive constructions of refugees and asylum seekers in the UK Press, 1996–2005. *Journal of English Linguistics*, 36(1), 5–38.

Gabrielatos, C. & Marchi, A. 2012. 'Keyness: Appropriate metrics and practical issues'. Talk given at CADS International Conference, 13–14 September 2012. Slides available online at http://repository.edgehill.ac.uk/4196/.

Gabrielatos, C., McEnery, T., Diggle, P. J. & Baker, P. 2012. The peaks and troughs of corpus-based contextual analysis. *International Journal of Corpus Linguistics*, 17(2), 151–175.

Gries, S.Th. 2011. Quantitative and exploratory corpus approaches to registers and text types. Plenary given at Corpus Linguistics 2011, University of Birmingham, 20–22 July 2011.

Gries, S. Th. & Hilpert, M. 2008. The identification of stages in diachronic data: Variability-based neighbour clustering. *Corpora*, 3(1), 59-81.

Human Rights Council 2011. Report of the independent international commission of inquiry on the Syrian Arab Republic, A/HRC/S-17/2/Add.1. Available online at: http://www.ohchr.org/Documents/Countries/SY/A.HRC.S-17.2.Add.1_en.pdf

Jucker, A. H. & Taavitsanien, I. 2014. Diachronic corpus pragmatics: Intersections and interactions. In I. Taavitsanien, A. H. Jucker & J. Toumien (eds.) *Diachronic Corpus Pragmatics*. Amsterdam: John Benjamins. pp. 3–28.

Leech, G. & Smith, N. 2006. Recent grammatical change in written English 1961–1992: Some preliminary findings of a comparison between American with British English. In A. Renouf & A. Kehoe (eds.) *The Changing Face of Corpus Linguistics*. Amsterdam/Atlanta, GA: Rodopi. pp.186–204.

Leech, G., Hundt, M., Mair, C. & Smith, N. 2009. *Change in Contemporary English: A Grammatical Study*. Cambridge: Cambridge University Press.

Louw, B. 1993. Irony in the text or insincerity in the writer? – The diagnostic potential of semantic prosodies. In M. Baker, G. Francis & E. Tognini-Bonelli (eds.) *Text and Technology: In Honour of John Sinclair*. Amsterdam and Philadelphia: John Benjamins. pp. 157–176.

McEnery, T. & Hardie, A. 2012. *Corpus Linguistics*. Cambridge: Cambridge University Press.

Mair, C. 1997. Parallel corpora: A real-time approach to the study of language change in progress. In M. Ljung (ed.) *Corpus-Based Studies in English*. Amsterdam/Atlanta GA: Rodopi. pp.195–209.

Mair, C., Hundt, M., Leech, G. & Smith, N. 2002. Short term diachronic shifts in part-of-speech frequencies: a comparison of the tagged LOB and F-LOB corpora. *International Journal of Corpus Linguistics*, 7(2), 245–264.

Marchi, A. 2010. 'The moral in the story': A diachronic investigation of lexicalised morality in the UK press. *Corpora*, 5(2), 161–190.

Marchi, A. 2012. Times, they are a-changeable: Different MD-CADS perspectives on tracking the 'Arab Spring'. Talk given at CADS International Conference, 13–14 September 2012.

Marchi, A. & Taylor, C. 2009. Establishing the EU: The representation of Europe in the press in 1993 and 2005. In A. H. Jucker (ed.) *Corpora Pragmatics and Discourse*. Amsterdam: Rodopi. pp. 203–226.

Partington, A. 2010. *Corpora Special Issue. Modern Diachronic Corpus-Assisted Studies*. Edinburgh: Edinburgh University Press.

Partington, A. 2012. The changing discourses on antisemitism in the UK press from 1993 to 2009: A modern-diachronic corpus-assisted discourse study, *Journal of Language and Politics*, 11(1), 51–76.

Partington, A. & Duguild, A. 2008. Modern Diachronic Corpus-Assisted Discourse Studies (MD-CADS). In M. Bertuccelli-Papi, A. Bertacca & S. Bruti (eds.) *Threads in the Complex Fabric of Language: Linguistics and Literary Studies in Honour of Lavinia Merlini*. Pisa: Felici Editori. pp. 269–277.

Partington, A. & Marchi, A. 2015. Using corpora in discourse analysis. In D. Biber & R. Reppen (eds.) *The Cambridge Handbook of English Corpus Linguistics*. Cambridge: Cambridge University Press. pp. 216–234.

Renouf, A. 2002. The time dimension in modern corpus linguistics. In B. Kettemann & G. Marko (eds.) *Teaching and Learning by Doing Corpus Analysis. Papers form the Fourth International Conference on Teaching and Learning Corpora, Gratz, 19/24 July* 2000. Amsterdam/Atlanta, GA: Rodopi. pp. 27–41.

Renouf, A. 2007. Corpus development 25 years on: From super-corpus to cybercorpus. In R. Facchinetti (ed.) *Corpus Linguistics 25 Years On*. Amsterdam/Atlanta, GA: Rodopi. pp. 27–50.

Scott, M. 1996. *WordSmith Tools Manual*. Oxford: Oxford University Press.

Sinclair, J. M. 1991. *Corpus, Concordance, Collocations*. Oxford: Oxford University Press.

Stanyer J. & Mihelj, S. 2016. Taking time seriously? Theorizing and researching change in communication and media studies. *Journal of Communication*, 66(2), 266–279.

Taylor, C. 2010. Science in the news: A diachronic perspective. *Corpora*, 5(2), 221–250.

Taylor, C. 2013. Searching for similarity using corpus-assisted discourse studies. *Corpora*, 8(1), 81–114.

10

VISUALISATION IN CORPUS-BASED DISCOURSE STUDIES

Laurence Anthony

10.1 Introduction

One of the primary goals of discourse analysis is providing us with an understanding of how written and spoken language influences and is influenced by social identities and relationships between people (Paltridge 2012: 2). In short, it is the study of language in use. Clearly, the interactions and connections between people and language are complex, so it is not surprising that discourse analysts dedicate huge amounts of time to the close reading of texts and the construction of detailed models that explain this complexity. Discourse analysts often exemplify these models using extended text extracts and quotations. It is also common to see researchers using diagrams and infographics to show discourse structure models, turn taking procedures and other features of discourse. However, discourse analysts are much less likely to use bar charts, line charts, scatter plots and other visualisation techniques that are commonly used in quantitative data analysis. As an example, out of the 23 figures included in Paltridge's (2012) introduction to discourse analysis, not one can be considered to be a quantitative data visualisation. Of course, this is not surprising considering the qualitative nature of the subject matter.

Corpus linguists also spend a great deal of their time interpreting language data in a qualitative way (Baker 2006). However, in contrast to discourse analysts, they are more likely to use quantitative data as the starting point for a study. Such data may be word and multi-word unit frequencies, ranked measures of word association strengths and ranked measures of keyness. Corpus linguists also face great challenges in describing and interpreting this quantitative data due to its sheer size and complexity. Word frequency tables, for example, might contain thousands or even millions of rows, and word association strengths may need to be calculated for words that associate with tens, hundreds or even thousands of other words. It might be expected, therefore, that corpus linguists would place a strong emphasis on data visualisation. However, as shown later in this chapter, the role of data visualisation in corpus studies is surprisingly limited. While some corpus linguists use a mixture of traditional and more complex data visualisations to help describe and explain their data, many use no data visualisations at all or opt to use a minimal set of simple data visualisation techniques that can hide or sometimes even misrepresent the complexity of the underlying data.

This chapter looks in depth at the topic of visualisation in corpus-based discourse studies. First, I will define what a data visualisation is. Then, I will explain some of the pitfalls associated with traditional ways to present language data and discuss how the output of corpus software tools has to some degree prevented researchers from using more revealing data visualisation approaches. Next, I will introduce some influential papers on the topic of data visualisation that can help researchers to become more aware of its importance and guide them in their selection and use of different visualisation methods. Then, I will exemplify the ideas introduced in the chapter through a case study of data visualisations that are commonly used in corpus-based discourse studies, revealing their weaknesses and showing how they can be improved. I will finish with a short conclusion.

10.2 Defining visualisation

To understand the pitfalls in the visualisation of language data, it is first necessary to understand what a visualisation is and is not. In other words, we need a definition. Kosara (2007) describes a visualisation as having three defining properties:

1 It is based on non-visual data.
2 It produces an image.
3 The result is readable and recognisable.

The first criterion of this definition rules out most photographs, videos, paintings and illustrations from being considered as visualisations. However, the first criterion does allow for language data (in the form of sounds or words) to serve as the data source. On the other hand, the second criterion rules out text extracts, quotations and tables from being considered as visualisations. Simply putting a quotation inside a box and calling this a 'figure' would also not constitute a visualisation as the language would still be the primary element in the figure. Kosara (2007) describes the third criterion as the most important: a visualisation must provide a way for the observer to learn something new about the data. This is a complex topic that Kosara dedicates much of his 2007 paper to discussing. However, in the scope of this chapter, it is perhaps sufficient to consider that a visualisation should be designed with the intent to communicate data in a way that allows it to be interpreted meaningfully by an observer. The third criterion also leads to the concept of 'visual efficiency', which is a measure of how quickly, accurately and effortlessly the data in a visualisation is communicated to the observer (see, for example, Garlandini & Fabrikant 2009).

Although Kosara's (2007) criteria allow us to categorise many presentations of data, they do not allow us to separate what most people understand to be data visualisations from diagrams and infographics. Diagrams are graphical designs or drawings that explain an arrangement, a set of relations or an operation, such as a drawing showing the main parts of a computer. Infographics, on the other hand, have a broader purpose of not only explaining but also representing arrangements, relations or operations often in a visually striking and often persuasive manner, such as a poster showing how wastewater can be reused. Importantly, both diagrams and infographics are created manually, perhaps with the assistance of a computer-aided design (CAD) tool, such as AutoCAD (AutoDesk 2017), and image processing software, such as Photoshop (Adobe 2017). This means that if the underlying data changes, it is usually no easy matter to recreate the diagram or infographic. In contrast, data visualisations are usually automatically generated based on real or simulated data. If that data changes over time or as a result of some process, the data visualisation can be easily recreated. From this discussion, we arrive at a final definition of a data visualisation as follows:

> A data visualisation is an automatically generated visual representation of real or simulated non-visual data that communicates information about that underlying data in a readable and recognisable way.

Of course, no definition is completely clear cut. One of the most popular ways to present corpus data to students in a Data-Driven Learning (DDL) environment (see, for example, Anthony 2016) is using a Key-Word-In-Context (KWIC) concordance display, as shown in Figure 10.1. KWIC concordance displays date back to the thirteenth century and the handwritten bible concordances of monks such as Antony of Padua and Hugo de Santo Caro (Kitto 1882). Modern KWIC concordance displays are automatically generated by concordance tools and are primarily used to reveal commonly occurring word or grammar patterns in a corpus. In this way, they have many of the defining features of a data visualisation. However, it is not clear if they can be described as a **visual representation** as the only

N	Concordance
1	Britain has been foolish enough to turn itself into a honeypot too attractive to ignore. The incompetence
2	have not even got into Britain would turn Calais into a honeypot for bogus asylum seekers." And UKIP
3	controls will remain feeble and our welfare system a honeypot for migrants. Only last weekend it emerged
4	to Government laxity and EU rules, it has become a honeypot tempting people to take advantage of the
5	impact on our own country of our society becoming a honeypot for terrorists and murderers, simply
6	many flock to Calais, desperate to reach the welfare honeypot across the Channel. Other European
7	No wonder children's societies have described it as a honeypot for those with bad intentions towards

Figure 4. Concordance lines for *honeypot*

FIGURE 10.1 Example of a Key-Word-In-Context (KWIC) display of language data appearing in the *International Journal of Corpus Linguistics*. Reproduced with permission: Taylor (2014).

non-verbal feature they employ is the use of colour to highlight specific words in each line, such as the search term. In essence, they are a table of sorted language data.

A recent practice in corpus linguistics is to present language data in the form of a word cloud. Figure 10.2a shows a word cloud that was used on the cover of the handbook of Vocab@Tokyo 2016 conference (Waring et al. 2016). In this example, the underlying data is clearly non-visual (i.e. words) and is generated automatically, so it satisfies two of the conditions in the definition above. However, the word cloud itself is primarily language-based even though the words are contained within a mask of the Tokyo skyline. Therefore, it is again questionable if the word cloud can be considered to be a **visual representation**. Also, even though the words in the word cloud are sized relative to their frequencies of occurrence in the handbook abstracts, it is likely that this frequency-based information on word importance is not communicated to the audience. Rather, they are likely to view the word cloud as an artistic impression of the Tokyo skyline expressed in word 'shapes'.

In contrast, Figure 10.2b shows a word cloud of the same data as that in Figure 10.2a but with the information on word importance communicated in a more readable and recognisable way. Even in this case, though, it is still not clear whether a plot of scaled words distributed in a two-dimensional narrow space can be considered to be a **visual representation**. However, it is clear that the word cloud exhibits a high visual efficiency. In a very limited space, it is able to present the most unusually frequent 100 words that appear in the conference handbook, thus capturing some of the main themes of the conference in a clear and accurate way. What we can conclude from these examples is that word clouds lie on a cline from true visualisations at one end of the scale to purely artistic images at the other end of the scale, where they make little or no attempt to communicate meaning in the underlying data.

10.3 Pitfalls in the traditional presentation of language data

Discourse studies have traditionally not used data visualisation to represent the underlying complex relations between people and language. Instead, the tendency has been to rely on text-based explanations supported by source text extracts, quotations, and perhaps a diagram or infographic. The danger with relying heavily on text extracts and quotations is that the researcher can be accused of 'cherry picking'. Readers may question how well the chosen extracts and quotations accurately represent the target data as a whole. Also, no limited set of extracts and/or quotations is likely to capture the full complexity of the relationships that exist in the data. Diagrams and infographics can help explain this complexity, but the manual way in which they have to be created limits their utility. Compounding the problem is the fact that most discourse analysts will have had little training in graphic design, making it challenging for them to create diagrams or infographics that represent and explain complex phenomenon. As a result, the diagrams and infographics used by discourse analysts will usually be quite simple and run the risk of overly minimising or greatly exaggerating a particular aspect of a discourse phenomenon.

FIGURE 10.2 Word cloud variations. Fig. 10.2a shows the word cloud used for the cover of the Vocab@Tokyo 2016 Conference handbook. The underlying data comprises all extended abstracts submitted. Fig. 10.2b shows a word cloud created from the top 100 keywords generated from the same underlying data (Keyness measure: Log likelihood; $p < 0.05$ + Bonferroni correction; Ranking measure (effect size): Odds ratio).

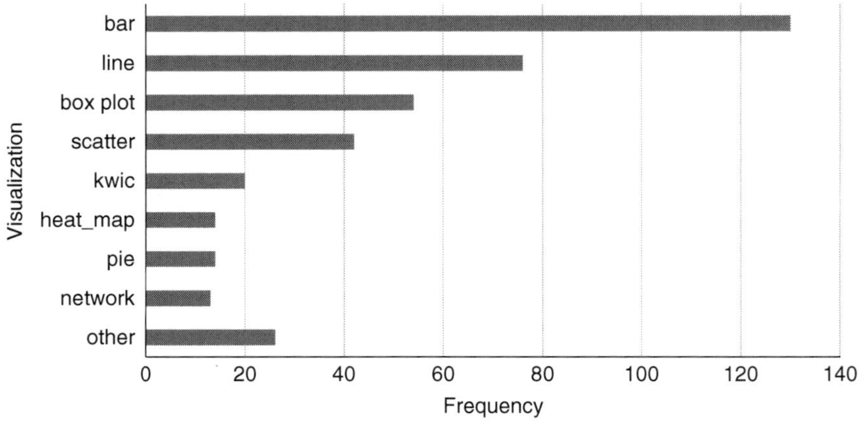

FIGURE 10.3 Frequency of usage of data visualisations in the *International Journal of Corpus Linguistics*. Only data visualisations that are explicitly marked under a heading 'figure' are counted. When two or more data visualisations appear under a single 'figure' heading, the visualisations are counted separately.

Corpus linguists also commonly use lengthy text-based explanations to describe the complex relationships that they find in corpora, and support these explanations with source text extracts displayed in a similar way to those in traditional discourse studies. As a result, they can also risk being labelled as 'cherry pickers'. To allay such fears, they sometimes (although perhaps less frequently than expected) choose to display multiple text extracts in the form of a KWIC concordance display (see Figure 10.1). However, even here, some corpus linguists adopt a practice of deleting 'unwanted' or 'noisy' concordance lines from the KWIC results. This may be willingly done, but it can also be forced on the author as a result of space constraints made by journal/book editors. Worse, this practice of deleting concordance lines is often conducted in a non-transparent and/or non-systematic way, which prevents observers of the data from being able to accurately evaluate and interpret the data.

Due to the quantitative nature of many corpus studies, it is not surprising to find corpus linguists also using tabular data and a range of data visualisation methods to present the results of their research. Figure 10.3 shows a count of all data visualisations used in the *International Journal of Corpus Linguistics* between 2012 and 2016 that are explicitly labelled under a heading of 'figure'. Note that the results include KWIC concordance displays, and a variety of less commonly used visualisations – such as audio signal graphs, word clouds, dendograms and radar charts – are included in an 'other' category. These results highlight the fact that when corpus linguists choose to visualise their data, they primarily adopt one of four methods: bar charts, line charts, scatter plots and box plots. Examples of each of these major types are presented in Figure 10.4.

A closer analysis of the visualisations presented in Figure 10.3 reveal that frequency data across text types and grammatical categories is almost always shown either as a horizontal or vertical bar chart. Changes in frequency data across time,

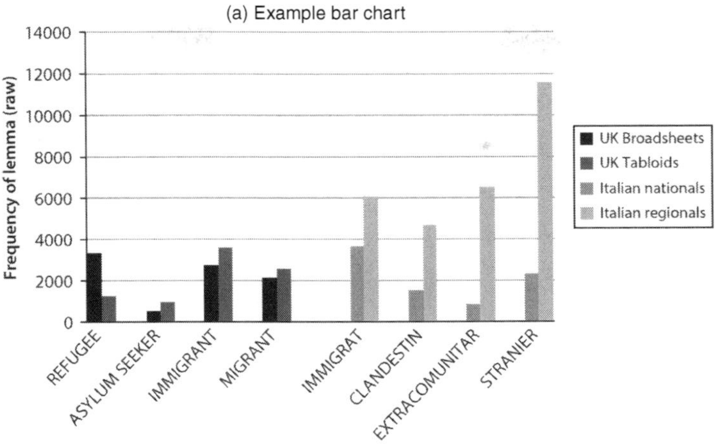

Frequency of RASIM/ICES terms in the sub-corpora

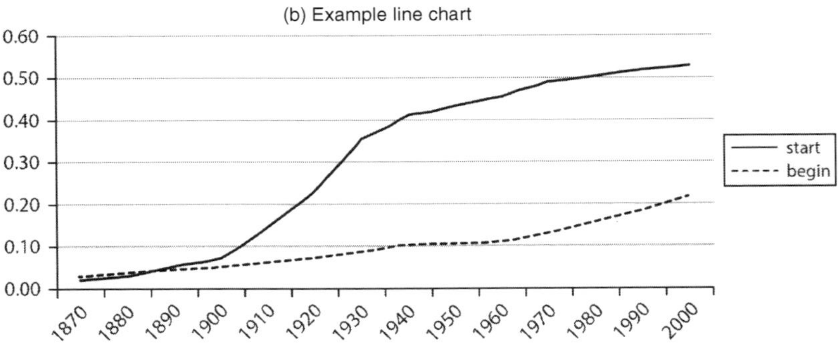

Percentage of clauses with [V-ing] (vs. [to V])

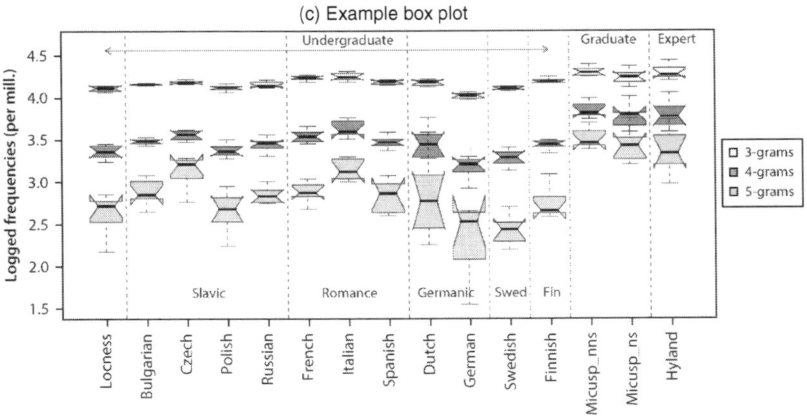

Type frequency of 3-, 4-, and 5- grams using 3+ frequency threshold (Frequency-grams)

FIGURE 10.4 Examples of four main categories of visualisation appearing in the *International Journal of Corpus Linguistics*. Reproduced with permission: 4a) Taylor (2014); 4b) Davies (2014); 4c) O'Donnell et al. (2013); 4d) Gray & Biber (2013). *(Continues on next page)*

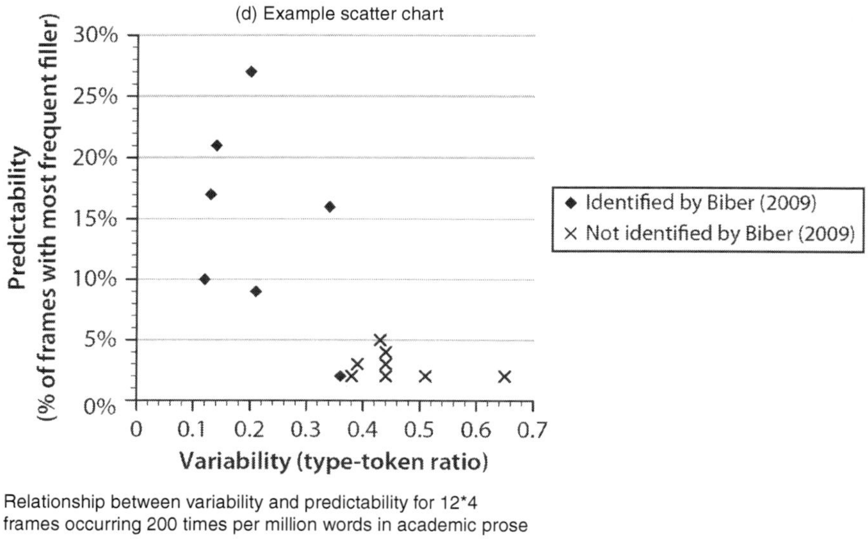

FIGURE 10.4 (Continued)

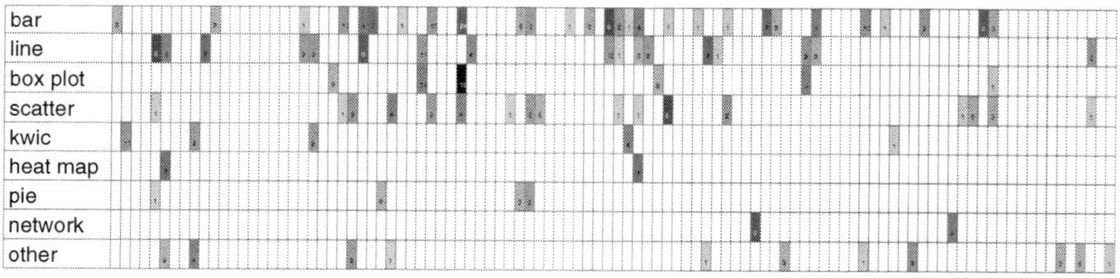

FIGURE 10.5 Example of a heat map showing the frequency of occurrence of data visualisation types in the *International Journal of Corpus Linguistics*. Each cell represents a single article. Increasing shade intensities indicate higher frequencies of usage of a data visualisation type.

on the other hand, are usually depicted using line charts. While neither of these methods is innately problematic, it is important to remember that they are both limited when it comes to showing the central tendency and the degree to which data is dispersed within a particular type, category or time frame. As an example, consider Figure 10.3 itself. This shows the frequency of occurrence of different visualisation types as a bar chart. What the figure does not show is when and where particular visualisation methods are used. For example, it is possible that bar charts were the dominant visualisation at the start of the examination period but have been replaced in recent years by more information-rich box plots. Similarly, it is possible that certain visualisation types are used frequently but only by a small group of researchers, whereas others are used less frequently but by a wider group. Figure 10.3 reveals nothing about the variation in use of data visualisations within a particular category. Of course, there are ways that this variation can be presented. One way is to use a box plot, such as that shown in Fig. 10.4c. An alternative is to use a heat map, as shown in Figure 10.5, where each cell represents a single article and increasing intensities of cell shades reflect higher frequencies of usage of a data visualisation type. Here, the results show that there is indeed great variation in the choices researchers make. Many researchers choose not to use visualisations at all. Others use certain visualisation very frequently, and others again show a preference for using a wide number of different visualisation types. What the figure does not suggest is that there has been any particular shift in the preference for particular visualisation types.

As another example of the way that visualisation can lead to misunderstandings, consider the two time-series charts shown in Figure 10.6. They both represent changes in the total number of visualisations used in the *International Journal of Corpus Linguistics* between 2012 and 2016. In Fig. 10.6a, it appears that the use of visualisations rose in 2013, fell in 2014 and 2015, and rose again in 2016. However,

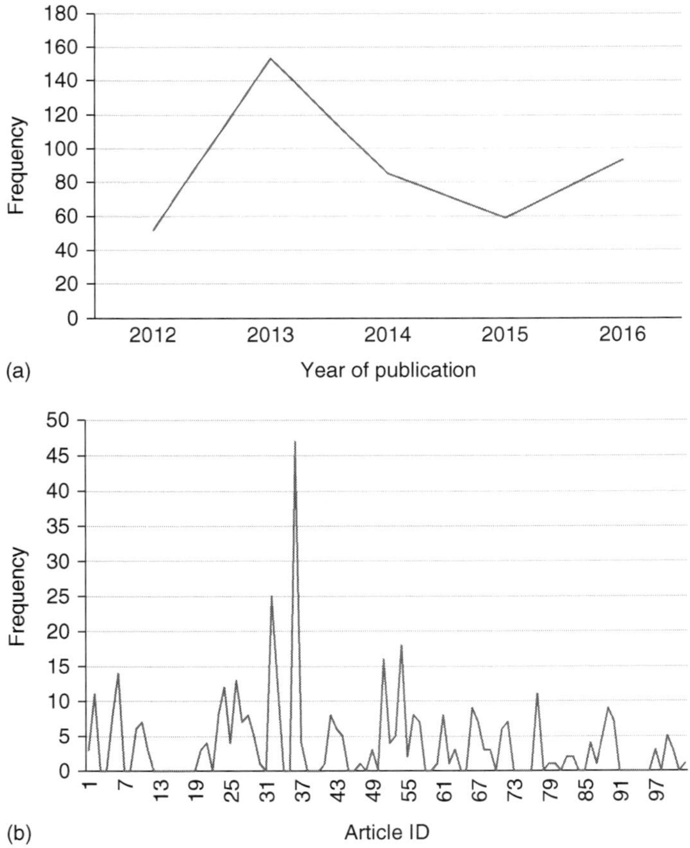

FIGURE 10.6 Time series charts showing frequency of occurrence of data visualisation types in the *International Journal of Corpus Linguistics* between 2012 and 2016. Fig. 10.6a shows the frequency values grouped per year of publication. Fig. 10.6b shows the frequency values on a per-article basis.

Fig. 10.6b shows a quite different trend when each article published between 2012 and 2016 is considered separately. In Fig. 10.6b, it is clear that the rise and fall in use of visualisation can be attributed mostly to two outlier articles that appeared in 2013 that included an unusually high number of visualisations. These two articles can also be seen in Figure 10.5 as having an unusually high 'heat' intensity.

One of the challenges in creating visually efficient and information-rich data visualisations is that they require specialised skills. In the *International Journal of Corpus Linguistics*, some of the more complex visualisations appear in Gries' (2013) study (see Figure 10.7). These are crafted with great skill using the R programming language, which in renowned for its powerful data visualisation packages. The advantage of using a programming language to generate data visualisations is that each aspect of the visualisation can be carefully controlled, from the scaling of the axes, to the transparency and sizing of the points, lines and other visual components. Programming languages also offer a wide variety of visualisation packages aimed at users of different skill levels. So, the task of creating a visualisation may not be as daunting as it first appears. On the other hand, care should always be taken to not inadvertently select an inappropriate type of visualisation or produce a visualisation with obvious errors such as missing or incorrectly labelled data due to a lack of familiarity with the programming language or the inclusion of bugs in the code. A further danger of building a custom data visualisation with a programming language is that it may not be immediately readable or recognisable to the target audience. This is a particularly important consideration to make when preparing visualisations for an audience of discourse analysts, who are likely to have been only exposed to the limited set of visualisations in standard 'office' tools.

An alternative approach to programming is to use one of a growing number of specialised data visualisation software packages. Many companies now develop commercial visualisation tools, with Tableau being one of the industry standards (https://www.tableau.com/). Freeware packages are less common, but one very

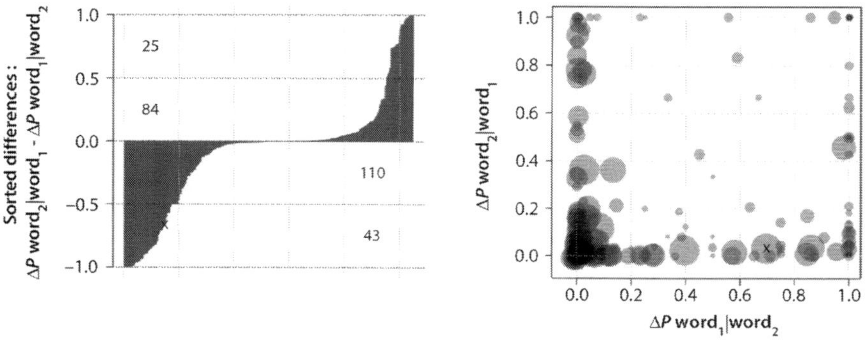

FIGURE 10.7 Custom data visualisations produced using the R programming language appearing in the *International Journal of Corpus Linguistics*. Reproduced with permission: Gries (2013).

powerful tool is Datawrapper (https://www.datawrapper.de/). Compared with direct programming, both commercial and freeware tools are more limited in the types of visualisation that can be produced, and they offer less control over the details of the visualisation. However, they are able to produce far more advanced visualisations than those offered in 'office' tools like Microsoft Excel and Libre Calc. They also offer some degree of 'intelligent' control, automatically selecting default visualisation types, axis scales and settings that supposedly best represent the underlying data. This makes it more difficult to misrepresent the data, but in practice, these automatic functions can inhibit a researcher from displaying the data in a desired way.

One of the reasons why corpus linguists do not opt to use more advanced visualisation techniques perhaps lies in the fact that they are not offered in many popular corpus analysis tools. *AntConc* (Anthony 2017) and *WordSmith Tools* (Scott 2016), for example, generate KWIC concordance displays, tabular displays and specialised one-dimensional scatter plots that appear as 'bar codes' showing the position of words in a text. However, they do not offer ways to produce heat maps, bubble charts or other more advanced visualisations. Instead, they rely on the user exporting raw frequency and word association data, and using programming scripts or a visualisation software package to translate that data into a visual representation. If general purpose corpus tools offered more advanced visualisation methods 'out-of-the-box', it can be anticipated that they would be adopted more widely by the community as a whole. We see an example of this phenomenon in the case of the 'bar code' dispersion plots of *AntConc* and *WordSmith Tools* (discussed later in the chapter). These are complex visualisations that are almost impossible to create within standard 'office' tools such as Microsoft Excel. Yet, they are still used widely by corpus linguists. Another notable exception is provided by the online interface to the corpus.byu.edu family of corpora created by Mark Davies (http://corpus.byu.edu), which automatically generates time-series histograms and heat maps to visualise the results of searches. Figure 10.8, for example, shows a heat map created through the interface that appeared in the *International Journal of Corpus Linguistics* (Davies 2014).

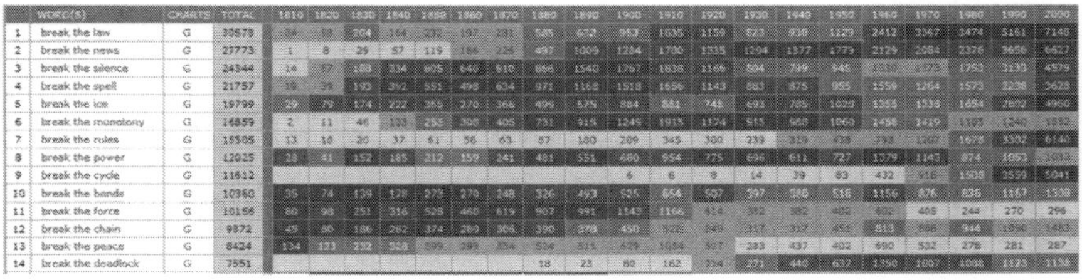

	WORD(S)	CHARTS	TOTAL	1810	1820	1830	1840	1850	1860	1870	1880	1890	1900	1910	1920	1930	1940	1950	1960	1970	1980	1990	2000
1	break the law	G	30578	34	38	204	164	232	197	231	585	632	957	1035	1159	623	938	1129	2412	3367	3474	5161	7148
2	break the news	G	27773	1	8	25	57	119	156	225	497	1009	1284	1700	1335	1294	1377	1779	2129	2084	2376	3656	6627
3	break the silence	G	24344	14	57	183	334	605	640	610	866	1540	1767	1838	1166	504	799	948	1330	1373	1753	2133	4579
4	break the spell	G	21757	18	39	193	392	551	496	634	971	1168	1518	1656	1143	883	875	955	1559	1264	1573	2238	3628
5	break the ice	G	19799	29	79	174	222	353	270	366	494	575	884	881	748	693	785	1029	1355	1338	1654	2802	4900
6	break the monotony	G	16859	2	11	46	103	255	306	405	731	915	1249	1915	1174	515	960	1060	1438	1419	1197	1240	1352
7	break the rules	G	15505	13	18	20	37	61	56	63	87	180	209	345	300	239	319	438	793	1207	1678	3332	6140
8	break the power	G	12025	23	41	152	185	212	159	241	481	551	480	954	775	696	611	727	1379	1143	874	1853	[illegible]
9	break the cycle	G	11612										6	6	9	14	39	83	432	916	1508	2559	5041
10	break the bonds	G	10360	35	74	138	178	273	276	248	326	493	535	664	557	397	586	516	1156	876	836	1167	1308
11	break the force	G	10156	80	98	251	316	528	460	619	907	991	1143	1166	614	392	382	402	802	405	244	270	296
12	break the chain	G	9372	45	80	186	262	374	293	305	390	378	450	522	849	317	317	451	813	696	944	1056	1483
13	break the peace	G	8424	134	123	232	528	299	299	354	534	511	679	1054	357	283	437	402	690	532	276	281	287
14	break the deadlock	G	7551								18	23	80	162	334	271	440	637	1350	1007	1092	1123	1138

Figure 16. "*break* + *the* + NOUN", by decade

FIGURE 10.8 Heat map visualisations produced through the corpus.byu.edu interface appearing in the *International Journal of Corpus Linguistics*. Reproduced with permission: Davies (2014).

10.4 Research on the principles of effective visualisation

A huge growth in the availability of large data sets (commonly known as 'big data') has led to an increased interest in ways to process, analyse and visualise data. Research in this newly forming field of data science offers many insights that can assist researchers in corpus studies on discourse to more effectively visualise their results. Theoretical discussions of data visualisation can be found in books such as those of Evergreen (2016), Fayyad et al. (2002), Few (2012), Knaflic (2015) and Tufte (2001) among many others. There are also various journals that specialise in this area, such as the *IEEE Transactions on Visualization and Computer Graphics*, the *Springer Journal of Visualization* and the SAGE journal of *Information Visualization*, which date back to mid-1990s and early 2000s. As an example, a useful introduction to the topic of visualisation in data mining can be found in Keim (2002). Journals that focus on computer science and data engineering will also include many relevant articles on the subject of data visualisation. One such journal is the *IEEE Transactions on Knowledge and Data Engineering*, which published an interesting article on interactive visualisations of large data sets in 2016 (Godrey et al. 2016). The topic of data visualisation also appears in articles published in the *IEEE Transactions on Professional Communication*.

More practical guides to data visualisation can be found in a multitude of online articles, blog posts and slideshows dedicated to the topic. Robert Kosara of Tableau Software, for example, has written numerous single author and collaborative works on the topic of data visualisation, which make for essential reading. His paper of 2007 defining the term 'data visualization' was cited in Section 10.2 of this chapter (Kosara 2007). Another interesting article is his co-authored review of storytelling in data visualisation (Kosara & Mackinlay 2013). Tory and Moller (2004) have posted online a taxonomy for categorising different visualisations, and Hagley (2017) blogs on the differences between infographics and data visualisations. One useful set of online slides is the set provided by Teate (2015) for her course on cognitive systems engineering which discusses many important principles of effective data visualisation.

In addition to online articles and slides, there are numerous online resources on the topic of data visualisation. Many of these offer interactive experiences that not only inform researchers about which visualisations are effective for a particular purpose but also dynamically show those visualisations in action or provide links to resources for creating them. One particularly impressive website is the *The Data Visualisation Catalogue* (http://www.datavizcatalogue.com/) created by the graphic designer Severino Ribecca. In its current state, the site provides extremely clear and detailed descriptions as well as examples and creation tools for 60 different data visualisation methods. Christian Tominski and Wolfang Aigner provide an accompanying website to their 2011 book (Aigner et al. 2011) called *The TimeViz Browser* (http://survey.timeviz.net/). This site presents a survey of 115 time-oriented data visualisation methods, with associated examples supporting literature references. An internet search for 'best data visualisations' will return numerous links to websites that showcase some of the most recent, novel and visually striking examples of data visualisation.

10.5 Language data visualisation: a case study

Corpus tools are generally limited in the types of visual representation of language data that they offer. As discussed earlier in this chapter, *AntConc* and *WordSmith Tools*, for example, can present language data as Key-Word-In-Context (KWIC) concordance displays, 'bar code' plots of dispersion, and tables of words, keywords, clusters, n-grams and collocates. Although these representations are useful, in many cases, variations on these methods can often prove to be more effective. In addition, recent developments in web and desktop computer graphics have allowed language data to be presented in completely new and sometimes strikingly revealing ways. In this section, I will present a case study showing how standard corpus-tool representations of language data can be modified or replaced with alternative data visualisation methods. I will also introduce several software tools that allow researchers to create these visualisations without the need for programming skills. Note, of course, that all the visualisations introduced here and other even more advanced visualisations can be created directly using a modern programming language.

10.5.1 Visualisation methods for KWIC concordance data

KWIC concordance displays are designed to highlight frequently occurring language patterns in a corpus. They achieve this by showing search hits and a fixed number of surrounding context words or characters in a tabular form with the first word in each hit pattern centred in the table (see Figure 10.1). Although KWIC concordance displays are perhaps the most well-known corpus presentation method, they suffer from a number of weaknesses when it comes to visual efficiency. These are:

1. The arbitrary cut off of the surrounding context leads to language fragments that show incomplete target patterns, ungrammatical elements and/or words that are not fully formed.
2. The surrounding context itself is necessarily limited making interpretation of the presented patterns difficult.
3. The sequential presentation of all hits often leads to a huge number of rows that cannot be observed on a single screen (or printed page). As a result, additional processing (e.g. scrolling) is required before all patterns can be observed.
4. The rows are likely to contain 'noisy' patterns (e.g. very low frequency, non-standard examples) that are presented in an unmarked way, making it difficult to distinguish between relevant and non-relevant information.
5. The initial ordering of rows is usually dependent on the position of hits in the corpus files and the ordering of the corpus file in the corpus as a whole. This

ordering usually inhibits any recognition of the target language patterns. As a result, additional processing (e.g. sorting) is required before any patterns can be observed.

6 The standard way to process the display in order to reveal language patterns is by sorting the rows alphabetically based on words appearing in specific positions (e.g. sorting by the first word to the right of the centre word in each row). This method leads to an ordering that is skewed heavily by the choice of the word position. Worse, it leads to an ordering that is primarily determined by the alphabetical ordering of words in the language patterns. As researchers are normally interested in the frequency of occurrence of the revealed language patterns (not their alphabetical ordering), further processing (e.g. counting the alphabetically ordered patterns) is usually required even after the sorting is completed.

The first limitation of KWIC concordance displays can be partially addressed by better software design. It is a simple matter to code a concordancer to display complete words in each row. Also, if the corpus has sentences marked, these can be easily processed by the tool leading to the display of grammatically correct elements and complete language patterns. However, if sentences are not marked in some way, which is the case with many untagged corpora, the KWIC tools need to include a parser, which will slow the processing, lead to errors due to parsing inaccuracies and limit the tools to languages that the parser could handle.

The second and third limitations are already partially handled by most KWIC tools. To enable more of the context surrounding language patterns to be viewed by the user, most tools offer settings that can change the context window size or offer ways for a user to view individual rows in the larger context of the original text. KWIC tools also offer ways to limit the number of rows displayed on a single screen through a process of 'thinning' the result by showing only every 'Nth' row (e.g. setting N to 5 would shows rows 1, 6, 11, 16, …), or by showing a fixed number of rows (e.g. 10, 100, 1000). It should be remembered, however, that thinning and sampling processes will usually dramatically reduce the total number of patterns that are shown. This is because the frequency of occurrence of many language patterns is Zipfian in nature with a small number of language patterns having a very high frequency but most others having a low frequency (Ha et al. 2002). As a result, thinning or sampling of KWIC lines is likely to reduce the relative frequency of rare items to below one, which will eliminate many of them from the display.

The fourth limitation is usually either ignored by a corpus linguist, resulting in noisy KWIC concordance results, or an attempt is made to delete the noise by removing rows. If the noise is simply ignored, an accurate interpretation of the KWIC display becomes dependent on the reader recognising the noise, which is no easy task especially for those with little experience of this type of visualisation. On the other hand, as described earlier in this chapter, when an attempt is made to delete the noise, the deletion process is often non-transparent or carried out in a non-systematic way, again leading to difficulties when it comes to interpreting the final results.

The fifth and sixth limitations are clearly the most severe in that they highlight the fact that KWIC concordance displays **on their own** are largely ineffective at showing language patterns. By design, the displays require many additional steps on the part of the user before the underlying language patterns in the data can be identified and evaluated in terms of importance. In some sense, KWIC concordance displays are quite crude visual representations of language data, being no more than glorified tables of text fragments that happen to include the search word. Alphabetical sorting goes some way to assisting the user in extracting meaningful patterns, but even here, the implementation of sorting in corpus tools can vary dramatically. *AntConc* and *WordSmith Tools*, for example, sort all the results for the target corpus, which makes sense if all language patterns need to be identified. The interface to the Corpus of Contemporary American English (COCA) corpus, on the other hand, only sorts the results given on the current results page. This means that the tool relies on the current page showing an accurate sample of all relevant patterns in the corpus as a whole, which is not always the case.

Figure 10.9 highlights some of the visualisation problems inherent in KWIC concordance displays. Figure 10.9a shows a 'classic' KWIC concordance display of the first 10 rows of search results for the word *paper* in a small sample of 26 academic research paper introductions in the *Journal of Pattern Recognition* produced

overlaps between neighboring text lines. In this	paper	, we present a new algorithm based on
combination scheme is non-trivial. In this	paper	, we propose an effective bottom-up method
of other languages. The rest of this	paper	is organized as follows. In Section 2, we
rate overlapping or touching components. In this	paper	, we propose a combination method of compleme
or character segmentation. The rest of the	paper	organized as follows: In Section 2, the prop
ommon residual in handwritten documents. In this	paper	, we present a segmentation methodology of ha
against the state-of-the-art. The	paper	is organized as follows: Section 2 is dedica
-class SVM classifier. The structure of this	paper	is as follows. Section 2 reviews related wor
symbol identity and spatial relationship. In this	paper	, we formulate the handwritten ME recognition
handwritten ME recognition. The rest of the	paper	is organized as follows. Section 2 presents

a) Classic KWIC concordance display (un-sorted)

. In the last section, we conclude the	paper	.
ition competition took place at IWFHR 2006. This	paper	focuses on the recognition of Indian and
16], similar to Rubine's algorithms. The current	paper	focuses on the latter approach: the design
to open new worlds to scholarship. This	paper	introduces a handwriting recognizer with a f
patterns will be associated to classes? This	paper	is addressing the first of these questions
-class SVM classifier. The structure of this	paper	is as follows. Section 2 reviews related wor
and meaningful information. The structure of the	paper	is as follows: in Sections 2 and 3, multi-
-of-the-art MQDF-based approach. The	paper	is concluded in Section 5.
case of very old documents, as the	paper	is most often very deformed. The ICA
The research described in this	paper	is motivated by the development of pen

b) Classic KWIC concordance display sorted by the 1st, 2nd, and 3rd words to the right of the search word

FIGURE 10.9 Variations of KWIC concordance displays.

using *AntConc*. The total number of results is 43. It is clear that the word *paper* occurs in the pattern '… this paper, we present/propose …' It is also clear that the word *paper* occurs in the pattern '… this paper is organized as follows …' However, without scrolling down to see other results in the display it is not clear if these patterns are relatively frequent or simply non-standard expressions. Figure 10.9b shows the search results alphabetically ordered by the first, second and third words to the right of the search word. These results suggest that neither pattern is important. Instead, patterns such as '… paper focuses on', and '… This/this/the paper is …' are more salient. However, again, without scrolling down to see other results in the display it is not clear if these pattern are the most frequent.

One way to greatly improve a KWIC concordance display is by visualising the language pattern frequency data in a more transparent way. This leads to the concept of 'KWIC patterns' (Anthony 2013). Figure 10.10 shows two data visualisations of 'KWIC patterns' based on the same results shown in Figure 10.9. In Figure 10.10a, the results are not displayed alphabetically, but by the frequency of occurrence of 'KWIC patterns' formed from the words appearing in the first, second and third positions right of the search word. Again, only the first 10 rows are shown. In this figure, it is clear that one of the 'KWIC patterns' hinted at in Figure 10.9a,

Key-Word-In-Context (KWIC) Patterns

of other languages. The rest of this	paper	is organized as follows. In Section 2, we
against the state-of-the-art. The	paper	is organized as follows: Section 2 is dedica
handwritten ME recognition. The rest of the	paper	is organized as follows. Section 2 presents
the proposed framework. The remainder of the	paper	is organized as follows. Section 2 provides
generative models with the following form: The	paper	is organized as follows. First, we discuss
of IL settings. The remainder of this	paper	is organized as follows. In Section 2 we
Chinese handwriting recognizer. The rest of the	paper	is organized as follows. In Section 2, we
writer T. Table 1. The remainder of this	paper	is organized as follows: Section 2 provides
degraded character recognition. The rest of the	paper	is organized as follows: In Section 2 we
overlaps between neighboring text lines. In this	paper	, we present a new algorithm based on

a) Display of 'KWIC patterns' formed from the 1st, 2nd, and 3rd words to the right of the search word

Key-Word-In-Context (KWIC)Patterns			Freq.
of other languages. The rest of this	paper	is organized as follows. In Section 2, we	9
overlaps between neighboring text lines. In this	paper	, we present a new algorithm based on	3
rate overlapping or touching components. In this	paper	, we propose a combination method of compleme	3
ition competition took place at IWFHR 2006. This	paper	focuses on the recognition of Indian and	2
-class SVM classifier. The structure of this	paper	is as follows. Section 2 reviews related wor	2
motivation of the work presented in this	paper	is to combine these existing systems (see	2
ecognition technology. Keeping this in mind, this	paper	proposes a framework for an automatic segmen	2
to open new worlds to scholarship. This	paper	introduces a handwriting recognizer with a f	1
patterns will be associated to classes? This	paper	is addressing the first of these questions	1
-of-the-art MQDF-based approach. The	paper	is concluded in Section 5.	1

b) Summary display of 'KWIC patterns 'formed from the 1st, 2nd, and 3rd words to the right of the search

FIGURE 10.10 'KWIC pattern' concordance displays.

'... paper is organized as,' is indeed an important pattern in the results. In fact, it is the most frequent pattern in the data. Going one step further, Figure 10.10b shows the first 10 rows from a summary of the different 'KWIC patterns' where the frequency of occurrence of each pattern is explicitly given next to an exemplar. Here, the relative importance of the patterns hinted at in Figure 10.9a is now much clearer. This display also introduces the possibility of using an 'easified' exemplar for each pattern, based on a measure of the complexity of words appearing in each result of the pattern set, or other factors such as sentence length. For a discussion of exemplar detection using weighted features, see Kilgarriff (2008).

10.5.2 Visualisation methods for 'bar-code' dispersion plot data

The 'bar-code' dispersion plots that feature in corpus tools such as *AntConc* and *WordSmith Tools* are information-rich and visually efficient. *AntConc*, for example, not only shows the position and frequency of search hits in every file in a corpus, it also allows the user to zoom in on a particular area of the plot and click on any line in the plot to immediately see the larger context of the hit. *WordSmith Tools* present the 'bar-code' dispersion plots together with a numerical value of the degree of dispersion, which can be used to order the plots. However, the displays from these tools can also be easily misunderstood if the user is not aware of the impact that the default settings have on the way the plots are produced. In both *AntConc* and *WordSmith Tools*, the default settings result is the size of individual files in a corpus being represented by a normalised length in the plot. This is usually the most effective way to visualising the degree to which a search item is dispersed through the corpus, but it can also exaggerate the frequency of items in very long tests and similarly under-represent the frequency of items in short texts. Figure 10.11 highlights the problem for the case of 'this' plotted for three sub-categories of the Brown Corpus (Francis & Kučera 1964) using *AntConc*. In Figure 10.11a, the dispersion plots suggest that the word 'this' is not only dispersed more evenly in the A and J sub-categories than in the M sub-category, but also far more frequently. However, attention needs to be paid to the corpus-size of the M sub-category, which is much smaller than the other two. Figure 10.11b shows the plots with relative-lengths. Here, the differences in length are clear, but the differences in degree of dispersion are now less obvious.

10.5.3 Visualisation methods for cluster, n-gram, and collocate frequency and strength data

Clusters have been defined in the literature in various ways, but in this chapter they refer to contiguous word patterns that include a search term. So, in the sentence 'The cat sat on the mat', the two-word clusters that include the search term 'sat' would be 'cat sat' and 'sat on'. N-grams are a more generalised form of clusters that represent all clusters of a fixed length. Thus, for N = 2, the n-grams for 'The cat sat on the mat' would be 'The cat', 'cat sat', 'sat on', 'on the' and 'the mat'.

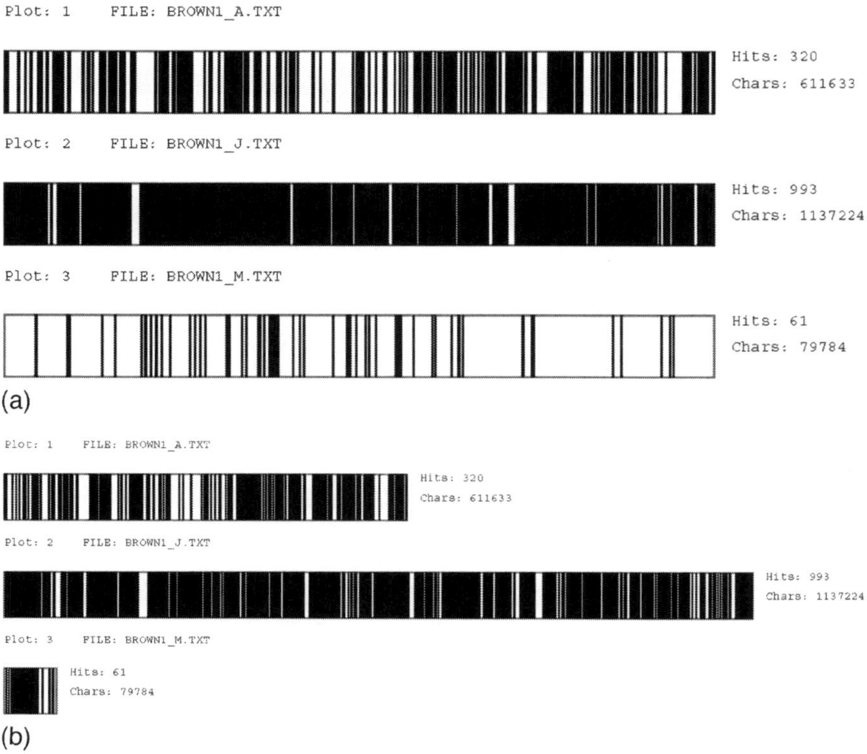

FIGURE 10.11 'Bar-graph' dispersion plots for the word 'this' in three sub-categories of the Brown Corpus (A: Reportage; J: Science; M: Science fiction).

In contrast, collocates are non-contiguous word-word pairs (or possibly word-phrase/phrase-phrase pairs) that show some kind of strength of affinity to each other. The maximum distance between the pairs and the measure of collocation strength are usually fixed by the user, with the most common maximum distance being four or five words, and the most common measure of collocation strength being Mutual Information (MI). However, many other values and measures have been used in the literature. For an in-depth review of collocation measures, see Evert (2008).

Traditionally, corpus analysis tools have presented cluster and n-gram frequencies, as well as collocate frequencies and strengths in a plain tabular form. One way to visualise the data would be to present the frequencies and strengths as bar charts. However, this is seldom done as it would add little to the information already contained in the table while also dramatically increasing the amount of space needed. However, in the case of clusters and collocate pairs, it can be useful to visualise the dispersion of these items through individual corpus texts in the same way that the dispersion of individual words is visualised. Figure 10.12 shows normalised file-length and relative file-length dispersion plots for the 'he'-'said' collocate pair in the same three sub-categories of the Brown corpus discussed earlier. Clearly, the usage of this collocate pair is skewed towards 'reportage' language, which is to be expected.

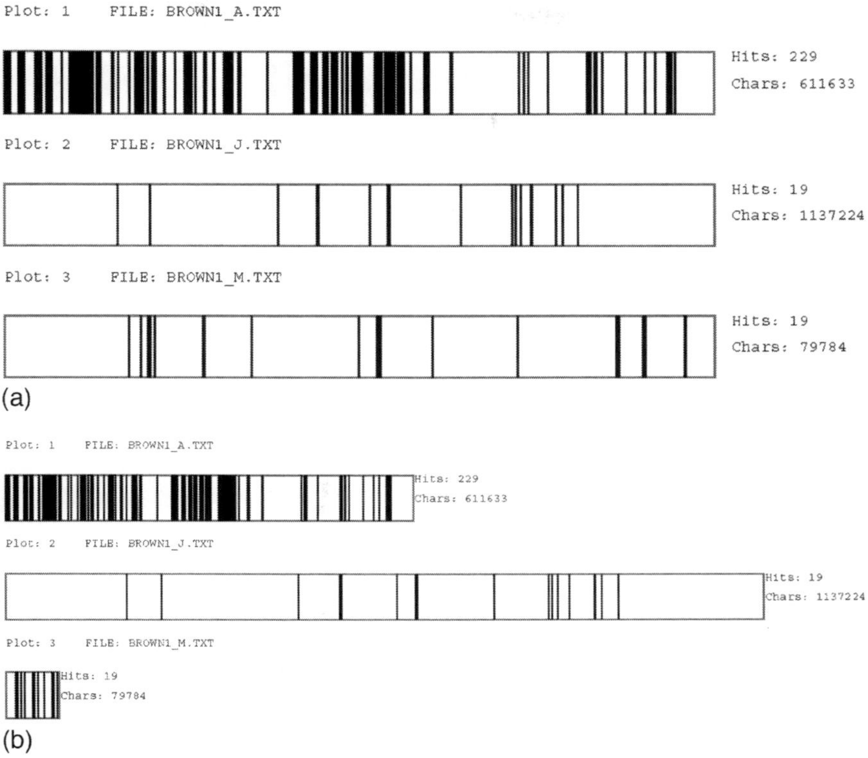

FIGURE 10.12 'Bar-graph' dispersion plots for the 'he'-'said' collocate pair in three sub-categories of the Brown Corpus (A: Reportage; J: Science; M: Science fiction). MI>6.34.

One visualisation of collocate information that has grown in popularity in recent years is a network (or graph) mapping, which shows how multiple node items relate to each other. An early standalone tool for producing collocation networks is *Cone*, which was developed by Gullick (2010) as part of his work at Lancaster University. The *Cone* tool runs as a Java-based multiplatform application, but can only process corpus data once it has been converted into a specialised format. However, after this inconvenient first step, the program is relatively easy to use. Figure 10.13a shows a *Cone* visualisation of collocates of various words in the script for the movie *Star Wars: A New Hope* (Lucas 1976) produced with default settings. In 2015, a similar collocate graph tool was created by another team at Lancaster University called *GraphColl* (Brezina et al. 2015), which was later developed further and included into a tool called *LancsBox*. *GraphColl* can process raw corpus texts making it much easier to get started with the tool. It also includes options to allow a wide number of statistical measures to be used to calculate the collocation strength and shows the directionality of the collocation depending on the statistic used. On the downside, the default settings of *GraphColl* can result in very complex graphs that are rendered in a highly unstable fashion. In these cases, a 'freeze' frame option is offered, but tweaks

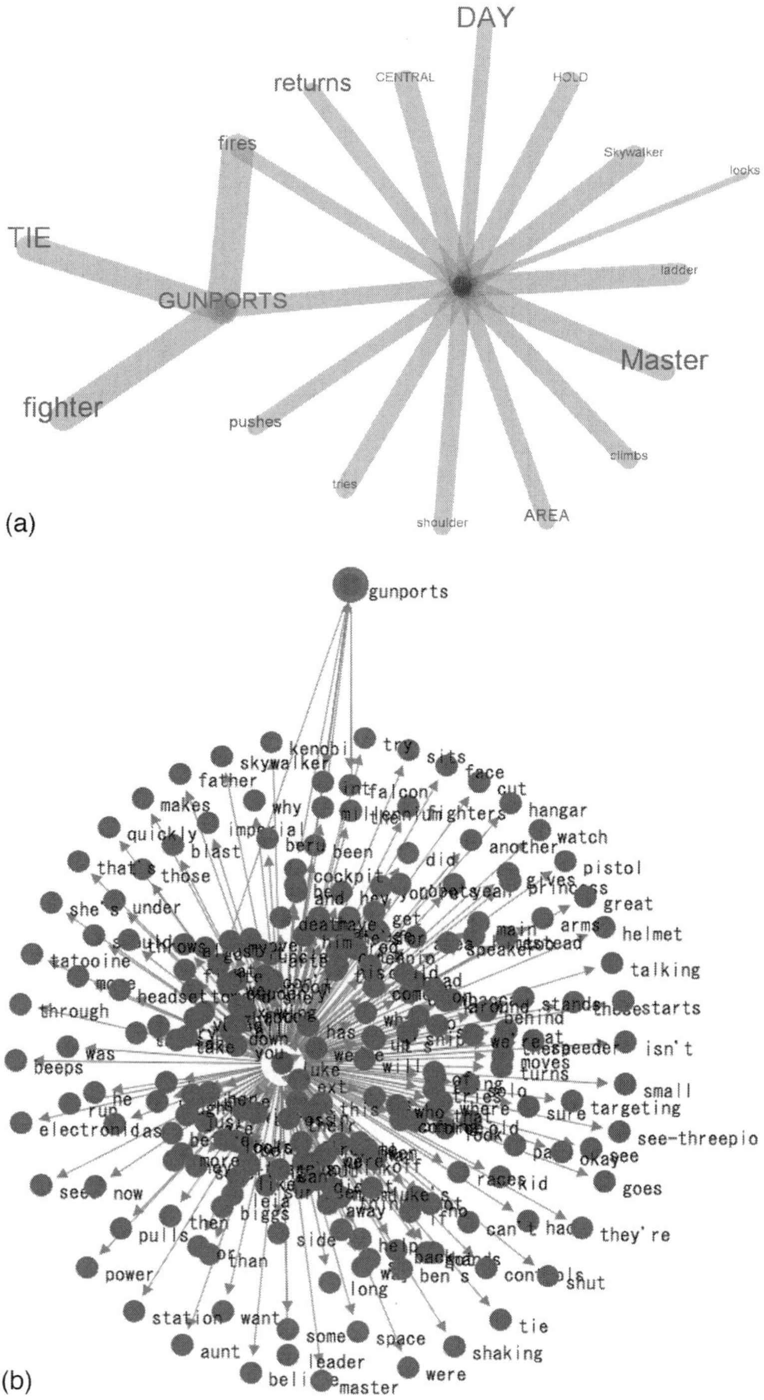

FIGURE 10.13 Network (graph) visualisations of word–word collocation pairs in the script for *Star Wars: A New Hope* (Lucas, 1976).

and adjustments to the settings are likely to produce more meaningful results. Figure 10.13b shows a *GraphColl* visualisation of the same data as that in Figure 10.13a produced with default settings and using the 'freeze' option to capture the snapshot.

10.5.4 Methods to visualise the relationships between language and society

Discourse analysts aim to provide us with insights on how language influences and is influenced by social identities and relationships between people. All the visualisations discussed so far in this chapter can be usefully applied for this purpose. However, in recent years, powerful geo-positional, time-based, and network-based visualisation tools combined with an increasing amount of language data that contains information about the time, place and participants in social interactions have given rise to new and interesting ways to visualise language in use.

All the diachronic corpora available at corpora.byu.edu contain information about the year in which the data was generated. Through the online interface, the results of word- and phrase-based searches can be shown in the form of time-series histograms or heat maps, revealing some interesting trends about language use in society. As an example, Figure 10.14 shows time-series histograms for the search term 'banking crisis' in the TIME Magazine Corpus and the Corpus of Historical American English (COHA) offered on the site. In both histograms, there is a clear spike in usage during the 1930s, which is consistent with the financial crisis that occurred at the time. However, the results diverge considerably in the years after the 1980s, with a fall in usage suggested by the TIME Magazine Corpus and a rise in usage suggested by COHA. As with all visualisation, care needs to be taken when interpreting results of this kind. First, it should be noted that the frequencies of

1920s	0	7.6	0.00	
1930s	12	12.7	0.95	
1940s	0	15.5	0.00	
1950s	0	16.8	0.00	
1960s	0	16.1	0.00	
1970s	0	13.6	0.00	
1980s	6	11.4	0.53	
1990s	5	9.7	0.51	
2000s	3	6.4	0.47	

1920	0	25.7	0.00	
1930	15	24.6	0.61	
1940	1	24.3	0.04	
1950	0	24.5	0.00	
1960	0	24.0	0.00	
1970	1	23.8	0.04	
1980	1	25.3	0.04	
1990	4	27.9	0.14	
2000	8	29.6	0.27	

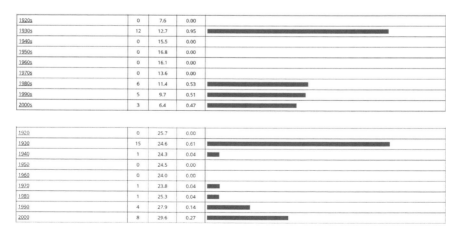

FIGURE 10.14 Time-series histograms of the frequency of usage of 'banking crisis' in two corpora.byu.edu corpora from the 1920s to the 2000s. From left to right, the column values represent the year, the frequency, the sub-corpus size (in millions of words), and the relative frequency (per million words).

occurrence are extremely low in both corpora so these differences may be merely the result of noise. Also, data in the two corpora are collected within different time spans, with the TIME Magazine Corpus collection ending in 2006 and the COHA collection process ending in 2009, which will affect the frequencies of occurrence in the bottom columns of the figure.

Grieve et al. (2014) have made impressive use of Twitter social media data to plot the growth in usage of new words in the English language not only across time but also space. All tweets sent out on the Twitter platform are automatically tagged with a huge amount of meta data, including the user's name and ID, their country of registration on the system and the exact time when the tweet was sent. In addition, users can opt to have their current geo-position automatically assigned to each tweet. As a result, once this data is obtained from the Twitter servers (usually through the official Application Programming Interface (API) or a commercial data collection service) it can then be used for novel corpus-based discourse studies. Figure 10.15 shows an example from Grieve et al.'s study that utilises a huge amount of Twitter data from the US to visualise the growth and spread of the word 'yassss' (a new alternative to 'yes') in US society.

Collecting, analysing and visualising social media data in the same way as Grieve et al. (2014) is no easy task. Simply collecting and storing the 'big data' generated by social media sites requires an understanding of platform authentication and verification procedures, knowledge of the various data search and extraction protocols offered by the platform, and experience in database storage and retrieval methods. Then, the researcher needs to implement custom data analysis and visualisation tools, or gain experience with some of the proprietary tools mentioned earlier in the chapter. These steps create a huge barrier to researchers hoping to use social media to analyse social discourse, but who lack a strong computational background or the resources to hire a software engineer or data scientist to help them.

In response to these challenges, various teams have created all-in-one packages to assist in social media data collection, analysis and visualisation. Online tools such as 'sentiment viz' (Healey & Ramaswamy 2017) offer simple ways to view the sentiment of a subset of public tweets that match a search term using various visualisation methods, including tag clouds and heat maps. Anthony and Hardaker (2016) have released a more general desktop social media data collection, analysis and visualisation tool called *FireAnt*. The current version of this tool can automatically collect Twitter data and store it in a form suitable for analysis with *FireAnt* or for export into a traditional standalone corpus analysis tool, such as *AntConc* or *WordSmith Tools*. *FireAnt* can also filter and process social media data and other types of hierarchical or tabular data to easily create time series plots, geolocation maps and network graphs. In addition, the raw data for these visualisations can be exported to more advanced statistical analysis tools or imported directly into advanced data visualisation tools that offer more refined control over the colours, sizes, and positions of elements in the visualisations. *FireAnt* is certainly limited when compared to powerful programming languages like R. It is also less transparent in terms of the visualisation settings and threshold parameters it uses. Nevertheless, it can be a

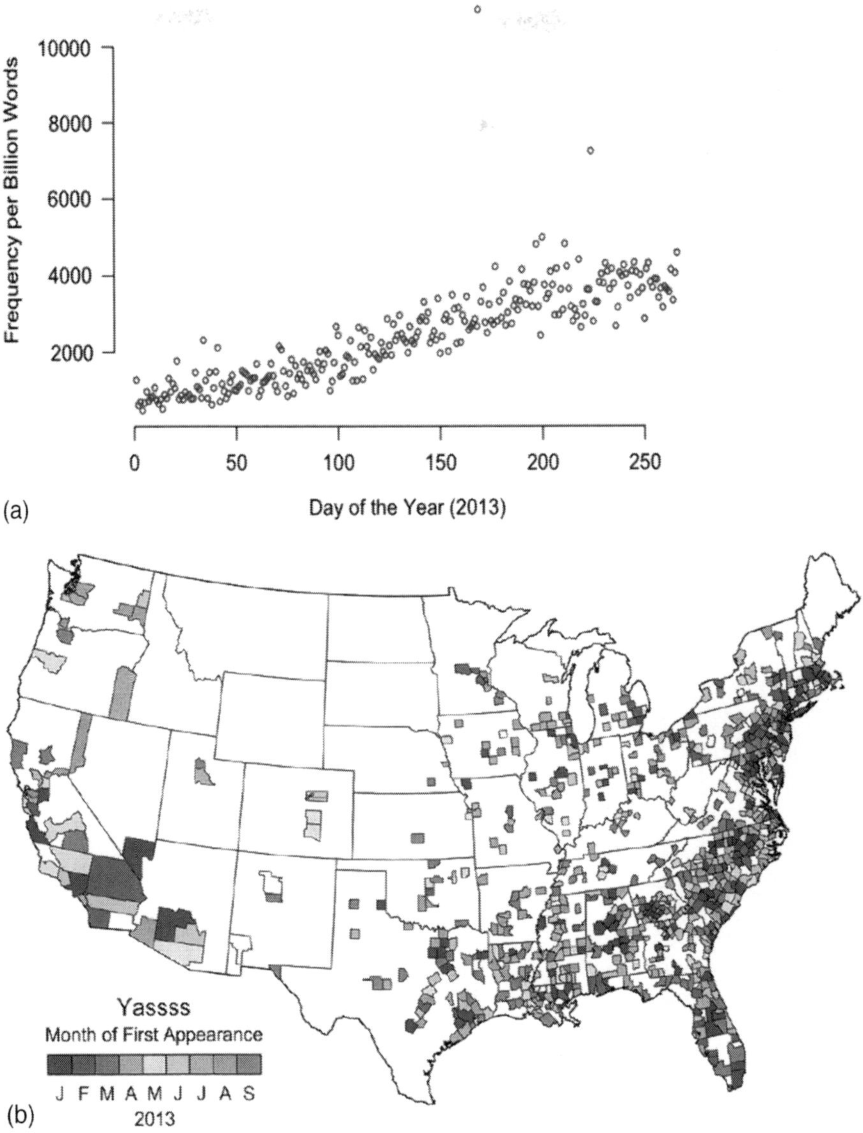

FIGURE 10.15 Growth in usage of the word 'Yassss' in the US as a) time-series scatter plot and b) geo-positional/time-based heat map. Reproduced with permission: Grieve et al. (2014).

useful tool in preliminary corpus-based studies of discourse, requiring a far lower bar of technical knowledge at the outset. Figure 10.16 shows two network maps produced by *FireAnt* that visualise Twitter activity occurring on May 18, 2016 that relate to the two main candidates in the 2016 US Presidential Election campaign, Hilary Clinton (a) and Donald Trump (b). Each circle in the figures represents a

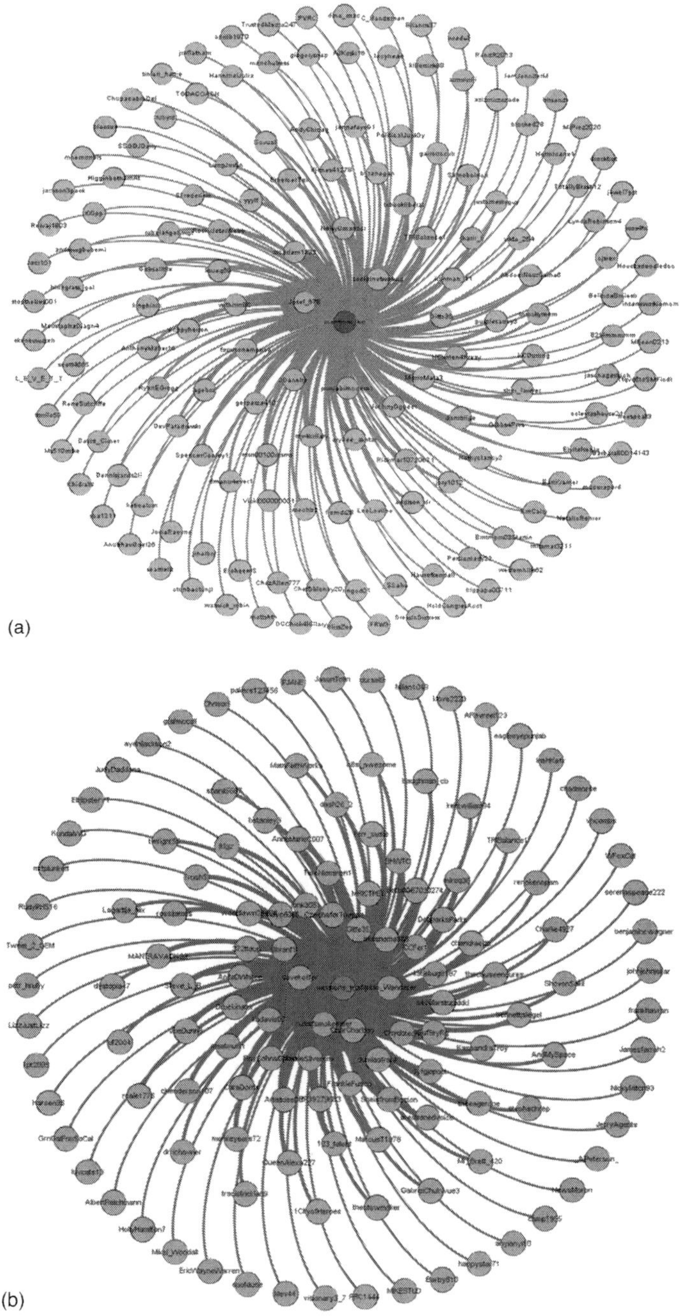

FIGURE 10.16 Network maps of Twitter activity related to the two main candidates in the 2016 US Presidential Election. Data collection and analysis were carried out using *FireAnt* (Anthony & Hardaker 2016). Network map rendered using Gephi 0.9.1 (Bastian et al. 2009) with the 'Force Atlas Layout' and default settings, with repulsion set at 10000.

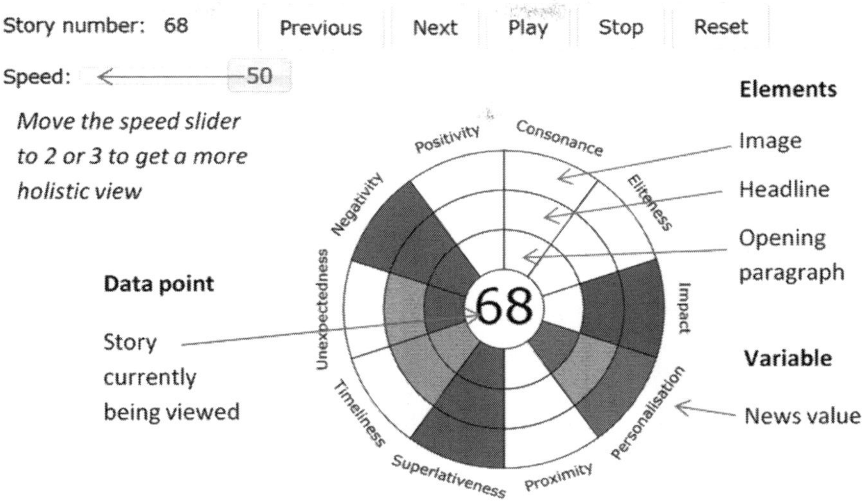

FIGURE 10.17 'Kaleidographic' visualisation of news values. Reproduced with permission. (Caple & Bednarek 2017).

single Twitter account user. The more the user tweets about the candidate, the closer their circle appears to the central node in the figure. The results from this snapshot of Twitter activity suggest that the group discussing Trump is slightly smaller (fewer circles) but more active (closer to the centre) than that of Clinton.

One aspect of the relationship between language and society that must not be forgotten is that language is rarely communicated in isolation. Usually, it is combined with some other mode of communication, such as non-verbal facial expressions and body movements in the case of spoken communication, and diagrams, infographics, photographs and data visualisations in the case of written communication. These multimodal interactions can be analysed in various ways, for example, through a triangulation of research methods as discussed in the collection of works edited by Baker and Egbert (2016). It is also possible to use specially designed tools that work with multimodal data, such as the *Digital Replay System* (Knight & Tennent 2008). On the other hand, presenting a self-contained visualisation of multimodal has proved extremely challenging. To address this problem, Caple and Bednarek (2017) have recently introduced a novel method that they call a 'Kaleidographic' and applied this to the visualisation of news values as expressed in the headlines, images and opening paragraphs of newspaper articles. The 'Kaleidographic' is an interactive visualisation with 'previous', 'next', and 'play' buttons that allow the user to scan through different combinations of news values, which are presented as segments in a circular image producing a view that is reminiscent of a radar chart. It also includes a speed control that can be used to speed up the player to get a more holistic view or slow down the player for a more detailed analysis. Figure 10.17 shows a snap-shot of the tool displaying the news values expressed in news article 68 in their author's data set. Here, the image, headline and opening paragraph all express a value of 'negativity', but only the headline and image express a value of 'impact'.

10.6 Conclusions

In this chapter, I hope to have highlighted the importance of visualisation in corpus-based discourse studies. Understanding the complex interactions and connections between people and language is a challenging prospect for any researcher. In corpus-based studies, this challenge is greatly increased due to the large number of texts that become the target of the analysis. As a result, visualising the data is a crucial step in making sense of what is happening. Many visualisation methods exist, but this chapter has shown that researchers analysing discourse have tended to rely on only a small subset of these when reporting the results of their work. Also, all visualisation methods have strengths and weaknesses, so it is important to understand what these strengths and weaknesses are before choosing a visualisation that is appropriate for the data and results at hand.

Many researchers using corpus-based approaches to discourse analysis have relied on KWIC concordance displays. In this chapter, I have been particularly critical of this method as it suffers from numerous weaknesses that impede on the analysis of data and the interpretation of result. I have also proposed various ways in which the standard KWIC concordance display can be improved. I hope that developers of popular corpus analysis tools will take up the challenge to implement some of these changes so that more researchers, teachers and learners who interact with KWIC concordance displays can take advantage of them.

Finally, I hope that more researchers will take up the challenge of using time-series, geo-position, network-map, and multimodal visualisations in the analysis of rapidly changing online and offline social network interactions and other forms of human communication.

References

Aigner, W., Miksch, S., Schumann, H. & Tominski, C. 2011. *Visualization of Time-Oriented Data*. London: Springer Science & Business Media.

Anthony, L. 2013. Easifying KWIC concordance lines: The case for vocabulary/range-level sorting. Presentation given at the *American Association for Corpus Linguistics (AACL 2013)*, 18–20 January 2013, San Diego State University, San Diego, US.

Anthony, L. 2016. Introducing corpora and corpus tools into the technical writing classroom through Data-Driven Learning (DDL). In J. Flowerdew and T. Costley (eds.) *Discipline Specific Writing*. London: Routledge. pp. 162–180.

Anthony, L. 2017. AntConc (Version 3.5.0) [Computer Software]. Tokyo, Japan: Waseda University. Available online at: http://www.laurenceanthony.net/software/

Anthony, L. & Hardaker, C. 2016. *FireAnt* (Version 1.0) [Computer Software]. Tokyo, Japan: Waseda University. Available online at: http://www.laurenceanthony.net/software/

Baker, P. 2006. *Using Corpora in Discourse Analysis*. London: Continuum.

Baker P. & Egbert J. (eds.) 2016. *Triangulating Methodological Approaches in Corpus-Linguistic Research*. New York: Routledge.

Bastian M., Heymann, S. & Jacomy, M. 2009. Gephi: An open source software for exploring and manipulating networks. *International AAAI Conference on Weblogs and Social Media.*

Brezina, V., McEnery, T. & Wattam, S. 2015. Collocations in context: A new perspective on collocation networks. *International Journal of Corpus Linguistics*, 20(2), 139–173.

Caple H. & Bednarek, M. 2017. Kaleidographic [Computer Software]. Created by AntLab Solutions (Laurence Anthony), Tokyo, Japan. Available online at: http://www.newsvaluesanalysis.com/kaleidographic/

Davies, M. 2014. Making Google Books n-grams useful for a wide range of research on language change. *International Journal of Corpus Linguistics*, 19(3), 401–416.

Evergreen, S. D. 2016. *Effective Data Visualization: The Right Chart for the Right Data.* London: SAGE Publications.

Evert, S. 2008. Corpora and collocations. In A. Lüdeling & M. Kytö (eds.) *Corpus Linguistics. An International Handbook.* Berlin: Mouton de Gruyter. pp. 1212–1248.

Fayyad, U. M., Wierse, A. & Grinstein, G. G. (ed.) 2002. *Information Visualization in Data Mining and Knowledge Discovery.* San Francisco, CA: Morgan Kaufmann.

Few, S. 2012. *Show Me the Numbers: Designing Tables and Graphs to Enlighten.* Bulingame, CA: Analytics Press.

Francis, W. N. & Kučera, H. 1964. *The Brown Corpus.* Available online at: http://icame.uib.no/brown/bcm.html

Garlandini, S. & Fabrikant, S. I. 2009. Evaluating the effectiveness and efficiency of visual variables for geographic information visualization. In *International Conference on Spatial Information Theory.* Heidelberg: Springer. pp. 195–211.

Godfrey, P., Gryz, J. & Lasek, P. 2016. Interactive visualization of large data sets. *IEEE Transactions on Knowledge and Data Engineering*, 28(8), 2142–2157.

Gray, B., & Biber, D. 2013. Lexical frames in academic prose and conversation. *International Journal of Corpus Linguistics*, 18(1), 109–136.

Gries, S.Th. 2013. 50-something years of work on collocations. *International Journal of Corpus Linguistics*, 18(1), 137–166.

Grieve, J. Guo, D., Kasakoff, A. & Nini, A. 2014. Big-data Dialectology: Analyzing Lexical Spread in a Multi-billion Word Corpus of American English. Presentation given at *AACL 2014*, Flagstaff, Arizona, 28 September 2014.

Gullick, D. 2010. *Cone* [Computer software]. Available online at: https://github.com/UCREL/collocation-network-explorer

Ha, L. Q., Sicilia-Garcia, E. I., Ming, J. & Smith, F. J. 2002, August. Extension of Zipf's law to words and phrases. In *Proceedings of the 19th International Conference on Computational Linguistics – Volume 1.* Association for Computational Linguistics. pp. 1–6.

Hagley, J. 2017. What's the difference between an Infographic and a Data Visualisation? [Blog post]. Available online at: http://www.jackhagley.com/What-s-the-difference-between-an-Infographic-and-a-Data-Visualisation

Healey C. & Ramaswamy, S. 2017. sentiment *viz* [online application]. Available online at: https://www.csc2.ncsu.edu/faculty/healey/tweet_viz/tweet_app/

Keim, D. A. 2002. Information visualization and visual data mining. *IEEE Transactions on Visualization and Computer Graphics*, 8(1), 1–8.

Kilgarriff, A., Husák, M., McAdam, K., Rundell, M. & Rychlý, P. 2008, July. GDEX: Automatically finding good dictionary examples in a corpus. In *Proceedings of EURALEX*, Barcelona, Spain. Available online at: https://kilgarriff.co.uk/Publications/2008-KilgEtAl-euralex-gdex.doc

Kitto, J. (ed.) 1882. *The Cyclopædia of Biblical Literature (Vol. 1).* New York: William H. Moore and Co.

Knaflic, C. N. 2015. *Storytelling with Data: A Data Visualization Guide for Business Professionals*. Hoboken, NJ: John Wiley & Sons.

Knight, D. & Tennent, P. 2008. Introducing DRS: A tool for the future of Corpus Linguistic research and analysis. Poster presentation with demo, delivered at the *6th Language Resources and Evaluation Conference (LREC)*, Palais des Congrés Mansour Eddahbi, Marrakech, Morocco. Available online at: http://repository.dlsi.ua.es/242/1/pdf/13_paper.pdf

Kosara, R. 2007, July. Visualization criticism—the missing link between information visualization and art. In *Information Visualization*, 2007. IV'07. Proceedings of the *11th International Conference*. pp. 631–636.

Kosara, R. & Mackinlay, J. 2013. Storytelling: The next step for visualization. *Computer*, 46(5), 44–50.

Lucas, G. 1976. *Star Wars* [screenplay]. Available online at: http://www.imsdb.com/scripts/Star-Wars-A-New-Hope.html

O'Donnell, M. B., Römer, U. & Ellis, N. C. 2013. The development of formulaic sequences in first and second language writing. *International Journal of Corpus Linguistics*, 18(1), 83–108.

Paltridge, B. 2012. *Discourse Analysis*. London: Continuum.

Scott, M. 2016. *WordSmith Tools* (Version 7) [Computer Software]. Stroud, UK: Lexical Analysis Software. Available online at: http://lexically.net/wordsmith/.

Taylor, C. 2014. Investigating the representation of migrants in the UK and Italian press: A cross-linguistic corpus-assisted discourse analysis. *International Journal of Corpus Linguistics*, 19(3), 368–400.

Teate, R. M. P. 2015. Principles of data visualization for exploratory data analysis [Slide show]. Available online at: http://www.becomingadatascientist.com/wp-content/uploads/2015/05/Principles-of-Data-Visualization-for-Exploratory-Data-Analysis-ppt.pdf

Tory, M. & Moller, T. 2004, October. Rethinking visualization: A high-level taxonomy. In Information Visualization, 2004. INFOVIS 2004 (pp. 151–158). Available online at: http://eprints.cs.univie.ac.at/5019/1/2004_-_rethinking_visualization.pdf

Tufte, E. R. 2001. *The Visual Display of Quantitative Information*. Cheshire, CT: Graphics Press.

Waring, R., Anthony, L., Browne, C., Ishii, T. & Kramer B. 2016. *Vocab@Tokyo 2016 Handbook*. Available online at: http://vli-journal.org/vocabattokyo/vocabattokyo_handbook_2016.pdf

11

KEYNESS ANALYSIS

Nature, metrics and techniques

Costas Gabrielatos

11.1 Introduction

This chapter discusses methodological issues relating to keyness analysis, and addresses a number of this volume's interconnected themes. It raises awareness of relevant methodological choices and their implications, and addresses related misconceptions and resulting practices, particularly regarding the selection of linguistic units, appropriate metrics, and thresholds of frequency, effect-size and statistical significance. It also discusses the pervasive *partiality* (Marchi & Taylor, this volume) in keyness analysis, as the vast majority of keyness studies focus on difference, at the expense of similarity. Finally, it discusses the tension between objectivity and subjectivity in relation to methodological choices, and problematises the frequent conflation of quantitative analysis and objectivity. In order to better understand and evaluate the current state of keyness research, however, we need to contextualise current views and practices. Therefore, the chapter will start with a critical overview of the brief history of keyness analysis.

The notion of *keyness*, as it is understood in corpus linguistics,[1] was introduced in the mid-to-late 1990s, and the procedure of keyness analysis was first incorporated in Wordsmith Tools (Scott 1996). Scott (1997) introduced the term 'key word', defined as 'a word which occurs with unusual frequency in a given text [...] by comparison with a reference corpus of some kind' (ibid.: 236), that is, initially, his focus was the examination of textual features (Scott, personal communication). Scott (1997) aimed at establishing words in a corpus, which, when grouped together in 'culturally significant ways', would 'provide a representation of socially important concepts' (ibid.: 233). It seems, then, that from its very introduction keyness analysis was used to examine issues that are at the heart of current corpus approaches to discourse studies. The notion of keyness is closely related to the notion of *aboutness*, that is, the understanding of the main concepts, topics or attitudes discussed in a text or corpus (Phillips 1989: 7–10, 26, 53–54).[2] Phillips (1989: 7) argues that 'aboutness stems from the reader's appreciation of the large-scale organisation of text'. The notion of aboutness informs work on keyness (e.g. Scott 2001: 110) and may have influenced its development, in that a keyness analysis is a way to establish aboutness (Scott 1998: 71).[3] However, in Phillips (1989), aboutness was not established on the basis of frequency differences between (sub-)corpora, but on the examination of collocation patterns within a (sub-)corpus. Despite this difference, the two techniques share a core characteristic: the automated analysis does not usually take into account the meaning of the linguistic forms in focus (but see Rayson 2008); rather, considerations of meaning are introduced in the interpretation of results (Phillips 1989: 21).

During the same period (mid-to-late 1990s), the notions of keyness and aboutness (although not described using these terms) were also extensively investigated by Kilgarriff (1996a, 1996b, 1997) within the framework of research on corpus similarity. Kilgarriff (1997: 233) posited that 'any difference in the linguistic character of two corpora will leave its trace in differences between their word frequency lists', and that, in such an approach, 'the individual meanings of texts are taken out of focus, to be replaced by the character of the whole' (ibid: 232). The former statement can be seen as a justification for carrying out a keyness analysis, whereas the latter statement can be seen as describing the aboutness of a corpus. Of course, a keyness analysis on word-forms in two raw corpora (as is usually the case in corpus-based discourse studies) is 'a fairly blunt instrument' (Gabrielatos & Baker 2008: 28), as it does not cater for a host of linguistic features, most notably homography, polysemy, part of speech, multi-word units and syntactic relations. However, even in this case, the results can be expected to be useful, as, for example, the different senses of a word-form can be expected to have different sets of collocates, at least some of which can be expected to be key. This can be shown through Kilgarriff's (1997) example of the word-form *bank*. Let us assume that the corpora compared have similar frequencies of this word form as a noun, but different frequencies of its two senses (related to money and rivers). Even if the word-form itself is not key, the difference in content is expected to be revealed 'because the one corpus will use *money, account* and *Barclays* more, the other, *river* and *grassy*' (Kilgarriff 1997: 233).

At this point, we need to take into account that corpus linguistics research had been carrying out frequency comparisons between corpora long before the notion of keyness was introduced. For example, Aarts (1971/2004) used a sub-corpus from the Survey of English Usage to compare the frequency of different types of noun phrase (e.g. containing a pronoun or noun) in different syntactic positions (e.g. subject or object). Closer to the nature of keyness analysis as it is currently understood in corpus linguistics, Krogvig and Johansson (1985) compared the frequencies of the modal verbs *will, would, shall* and *should* in two general corpora of American and British English (Brown and LOB, respectively). In a study that can be seen as the first to use a corpus-based approach to discourse studies, and the first such study to employ keyness analysis (although without using this term), Leech and Fallon (1992: 31) compared the frequencies of all the word-forms in the Brown and LOB corpora to study 'social, institutional, linguistic, and other factors which distinguish one culture from another'.

The last two studies above also exemplify two broad approaches to frequency comparisons, which will be termed *focused* and *exploratory*, respectively (see also Gries 2010a: 285; Partington 2009: 286). In Krogvig and Johansson (1985), the comparison focused on the frequency of particular language items in the two corpora, whereas in Leech and Fallon (1992), the frequencies of all words in the two corpora were compared. Focused frequency comparisons are carried out when the researchers have already decided on the linguistic item(s) to be examined, and have already formulated hypotheses or research questions, which the results of the pairwise frequency comparisons are expected to help address. In a focused approach, there is no limit to the selection of the unit of analysis, as such studies usually examine random samples of manageable sizes, which can be manually annotated for particular lexical groups, grammatical constructions, lexicogrammatical patterns or semantic/pragmatic meanings. In this way, a study can establish whether, for example, a particular modal sense or grammatical construction is much more frequent in one of the two compared corpora. Exploratory frequency comparisons are not motivated by particular hypotheses, and any research questions that motivate them are expected to be quite general (e.g. What topics are mentioned more frequently in the two corpora?). Rather, in an exploratory approach, frequency comparisons are used as 'a way in to texts'; as a technique for identifying linguistic items (usually words) that can indicate aboutness or style, and 'repay further study' (Archer 2009: 4–5) or generate hypotheses (Gries 2010a: 285). Exploratory studies use automated techniques for both the frequency comparisons and the corpus tagging/annotation (if required). Once the unit of analysis is selected (e.g. word-forms, n-grams), the frequencies of all such units are compared (see also Section 11.2). It would seem, then, that keyness analysis, particularly as it is usually used in corpus-based discourse studies, is an exploratory approach. However, exploratory and focused approaches are not entirely discrete, but can be combined, as shown in the two examples below.

- Example 1: The research starts with an exploratory approach, by deriving a list of key items ranked according to the value of the keyness metric used in the study. At this point, the researcher may switch to a targeted approach and select particular types of items for concordance analysis according to explicit criteria, such as their normalised or raw frequency, part of speech, core sense or relation to a particular topic.
- Example 2: The research starts with a targeted approach, by specifying items to be included in, or excluded from, the analysis (as in the second stage in example 1 above). Members of the resulting key item list are then selected according to explicit criteria.

In light of the above, a keyness analysis is essentially a comparison of frequencies. As it is currently practised, it usually aims to identify large differences between the frequency of word-forms in two corpora (usually referred to as the *study* and *reference* corpus) – although there is increasing interest in using keyness analysis to establish *similarity* (Taylor 2013, this volume), which can be seen as the lack of frequency difference, or *absence* (Partington 2014; Partington & Duguid, this volume), which can be seen as an extreme case of frequency difference (see also Sections 11.3.2, 11.4.1 and 11.5). Unfortunately, the influence of practices in other quantitative disciplines, and contradicting definitions of keyness, have led to the adoption of inappropriate metrics, which, in turn, have led to a number of misconceptions relating to a) the nature of keyness and keyness analysis, b) the kinds of linguistic units that can be the focus of a keyness analysis, c) the metrics that are appropriate for measuring keyness, and d) the attributes of the corpora to be compared.

Of course, a study employing keyness analysis does not stop at the identification of key items; rather, this is only the first stage, as a manual analysis is required to establish the use of the items in context (e.g. Baker 2006; Baker et al. 2008, 2013; Duguid 2010; Partington et al. 2013). However, the accurate and principled identification of key items is crucial, as their selection will greatly influence the conclusions of such a study. That is, even when the manual analysis is thorough and context-informed, if the selection of key items is flawed, so are the results and conclusions. As the identification of key items, and the selection of those to be included in the manual analysis, is multifaceted and, currently, influenced by a number of misconceptions, it merits a detailed examination here, while, due to space limitations, discussion of the stage of manual analysis must fall beyond the scope of this chapter. The remainder of this chapter will first discuss the nature of *keyness* and *keyness analysis*, the definitions of which will then inform the discussion of the possible linguistic units that can be the focus of a keyness analysis and the selection of appropriate metrics for establishing keyness. This section will also offer a brief historical overview of the notion of keyness and, more generally, the use of frequency comparisons in corpus linguistics. The chapter will then move on to consider principled techniques for selecting the key items to be included in the manual analysis, and issues relating to the selection of the corpora to be compared, and will conclude with an example case study.

11.2 Definitions and related issues

This section will focus on the definition of the terms *keyness*, *keyness analysis* and *key item*, and will distinguish between the nature of keyness and the ways that keyness is measured. The definitions will be discussed extensively, as their nature informs the discussion of all other aspects, in particular, the selection of appropriate metrics for keyness, and of the corpora to be compared.

It needs to be clarified that using 'keyword' as a default term to refer to the linguistic unit of focus in a keyness analysis is both restricted and restricting. Frequency comparisons can involve a host of other types of linguistic units, particularly if the corpus or sample has been lemmatised, or annotated for grammatical, syntactic or semantic categories. For example, exploratory keyness studies have been carried out on lemmas (Utka 2004), n-grams (Andersen 2016), multi-word units

(Gerbig 2010), part of speech tags (Culpeper 2009), lexicogrammatical patterns (Miki 2011), and semantic fields (Rayson 2008). Focused studies carrying out manual annotation of random samples can focus on any type of linguistic unit (form or meaning) or level (e.g. semantic, pragmatic, discoursal). Therefore, it would be appropriate to use the term *keyword* only when the frequency of word-forms is compared, and, in general, to adopt the inclusive term *key item* proposed by Wilson (2013: 3). What also emerges from the discussion so far is that the type of keyness analysis typically employed in corpus-based discourse studies, that is, one involving the automated comparison of the frequency of word-forms in two raw corpora, is only one option among many, and it would be restrictive to treat it as the default approach.

Definitions of the terms *keyness* or *keyword* have tended to conflate their nature with the proposed metric for measuring keyness. Very early on, keywords were defined as 'words whose frequency is unusually high in comparison with some norm' (Scott 1996: 53). It is straightforward to derive from this definition that a keyword is identified by way of a frequency comparison. It should clearly follow, then, that an appropriate metric for keyness would reflect the size of the frequency difference, and that the larger the difference, the more 'key' a word would be. However, elaborations on the definition tied the nature of keywords to a different type of metric. For example, Scott (1998: 71) adds that: a word is said to be 'key' if [...] its frequency in the text when compared with its frequency in a reference corpus is such that the statistical probability as computed by an appropriate procedure is smaller than or equal to a *p* value specified by the user. In other words, the proposed metric for keyness was not the size of a frequency difference itself, but its statistical significance, or, simply put, the extent to which we can trust an observed frequency difference, irrespective of its size (see Sections 11.2.2. and 11.2.3 for details). In adopting a statistical significance score as the indication of keyness, WordSmith Tools conformed to contemporary widespread practice in disciplines employing quantitative analyses (Ellis 2010: viii; Ziliak & McCloskey 2008: xv–xviii, 1–2). In fact, it is not unlikely that the wording of the definition of keywords was influenced by (or reflected) the choice of the particular statistical significance metric in Wordsmith Tools, log likelihood (G^2, also frequently indicated as LL). Dunning (1993) developed the log-likelihood test in order to accurately identify the statistical significance of rare events, and the focus on rare events seems to be reflected in the wording of early definitions: 'unusually high [frequency]' (Scott 1996: 53), 'unusual frequency' (Scott 1997: 236).

However, this is not to say that, at the time (i.e. the mid-1990s), there was consensus among corpus linguists regarding the use of G^2 (or any other test of statistical significance) as a metric for frequency differences. Kilgarriff's work on corpus similarity, based on frequency comparisons, focused on critically examining different types of metrics (e.g. Kilgarriff 1996a, 1996b, 1997; Kilgarriff & Rose 1998) – a clear indication that, at the time, the issue of selecting/devising an appropriate metric for frequency comparisons was anything but settled within corpus linguistics. This is also suggested by the variety of metrics used in corpus studies before 1996. For example, Aarts (1971/2004) used the Chi-Squared test (X^2), which returns the statistical significance of a frequency difference, whereas Krogvig and Johansson (1985) used the difference coefficient (Hofland & Johansson 1982), a metric that reflects the size of a frequency difference, whereas Leech and Fallon (1992) combined the difference coefficient with the Chi-Squared (X^2) value – that is, they took into account both the size and statistical significance of frequency differences (see 11.3 for a detailed discussion of metrics). Soon after 1996, however, due to the availability of an affordable corpus tool (WordSmith) that enabled corpus linguists to easily carry out automated frequency comparisons, and given that corpus linguistics researchers tend to rely on, and trust, corpus tools (Gries 2010b: 124–125), the G^2 score (or the associated *p*-value)[4] was adopted as the metric for keyness by almost all corpus-based studies. Evidence for this comes from Pojanapunya and Watson Todd (2016: 3–10), who reviewed 30 studies employing keyness analysis published between 2002 and 2013. Out of the 20 studies that specified a metric of keyness, all used a statistical significance metric (13 used G^2, seven used X^2). It can also be expected that those studies that did not specify a keyness metric also used a statistical significance metric, as, when the above studies were carried out, it was the default/only keyness metric available in almost all corpus tools (Gries 2015: 55). It is also interesting to note that, at the time when corpus linguistics was about to adopt a statistical significance metric to measure frequency differences, researchers in other fields (e.g. STEM, psychology) were vocally challenging its use as the main/only metric in their studies (e.g. Thompson 1998). This is an important consideration in view of the very recent, and rather sudden, shift in corpus linguistics towards the use of effect-size metrics for keyness, and the inclusion of a large number of statistical metrics in corpus tools, not all of which measure effect-size or are appropriate for all types of keyness analysis. The next section will discuss the issue of metrics and look at the metrics currently offered in corpus tools.

11.3 Identifying key items: appropriate metrics

A core distinction made in any current introductory book on statistics is between *effect-size* and *statistical significance*. The effect-size 'indicates the magnitude of an observed finding' (Rosenfeld & Penrod 2011: 342), that is, it shows 'whether the difference or relationship we have found is strong or weak' (Mujis 2010: 70; see also Ellis 2010: 3–5). Statistical significance indicates 'the high probability that the difference between two means or other findings based on a random sample is not the result of sampling error but reflects the characteristics of the population from which the sample was drawn' (Sirking 2006: 306). Simply put, statistical significance does not reveal the size of a frequency difference, but, indirectly, the level of confidence we can have that the difference we have observed (however large or small) is dependable (e.g. Andrew, Pederson & McEvoy 2011: 60; Sirking 2006: 304).

Statistical significance tests examine the *null hypothesis* (H_0); in the case of frequency comparisons, the null hypothesis would be that there is no real frequency difference, irrespective of the size of the observed difference. The values returned by significance tests correspond to particular *p*-values. Wilson (2013: 4) explains that:

the *p*-value tells us the probability of obtaining an equal or more extreme result, given the null hypothesis [...] If the *p*-value is very small, then one conventionally infers that either (a) a very rare event has occurred or (b) the null hypothesis is unlikely to be true. By this, Wilson means that it is unlikely that there is no frequency difference. The relationship between *p*-values and the level of statistical significance they indicate is an inverse one: the lower the *p*-value, the higher the statistical significance. Instead, the relationship between the value returned by the statistical significance test and the statistical significance level it indicates is direct: the higher the value returned, the higher the significance level. Wilson (2013: 4) also stresses that the *p*-value should not be understood 'as being the actual probability that an observed difference in proportional frequencies between two texts or corpora has occurred by chance' (see also Ellis 2010: 17). For example, if $p=0.01$, this should *not* be interpreted as meaning that the frequency difference we have observed has a 1 per cent probability of having occurred by chance, or, conversely, that we can be 99 per cent confident that the observed frequency difference is real. Rather, it should be interpreted as meaning that there is a 1 per cent chance that we would get the same or a larger frequency difference when, in reality, no such difference exists.

In view of the above, statistical significance is not an appropriate metric for keyness; rather, keyness needs to be established via an effect-size metric (see also Gabrielatos & Marchi 2011; Gries 2010a: 284–285; Kilgarriff 2001). Consequently, effect-size and statistical significance metrics are not alternative measures of keyness, even though the size of a frequency difference is indirectly taken into account in statistical significance tests. Simply put, the two metrics measure different aspects of a frequency difference. Kilgarriff (2005: 264) observed that there are 'papers in the empirical linguistics literature where researchers [...] used the confidence with which H_0 could be rejected as a measure of salience, whereas in fact they were merely testing whether they had enough data to reject H_0 with confidence'. In fact, there are clear indications that this is the practice in almost all keyness studies (Pojanapunya & Watson Todd 2016: 3–10). In addition to being an inappropriate method for measuring frequency differences, statistical significance tests exhibit a number of other limitations, which are discussed below.

11.3.1 Comparing effect-size and statistical significance

Focused studies involving the manual examination of frequency differences of particular sets of words (Gabrielatos 2007; Gabrielatos & McEnery 2005) have revealed large discrepancies in the ranking between, on the one hand, values of frequency difference and, on the other, values of statistical significance. Using an exploratory approach, Gabrielatos and Marchi (2011) carried out frequency comparisons between specialised corpora of different sizes, and compared the ranking of scores derived from an effect-size metric (the per cent difference between the two normalised frequencies, %DIFF)[5] and a statistical significance one (log likelihood, LL), with a cut-off *p*-value of 0.01 ($G^2=6.63$). They used two large corpora, *SiBol 1993*

(96 million words) and *SiBol 2005* (156 million words), each comprising all articles published in British broadsheets in 1993 and 2005 respectively, and two small corpora, comprising different sections from the *Guardian* in 2005: the media section (1 million words) and the home news section (6 million words). Gabrielatos and Marchi (2012) added three further comparisons, using a small specialised corpus (Hutton Enquiry, 1 million words) and two general corpora, one small (FLOB, 1 million words) and one large (BNC, 100 million words). If the two types of metric were alternatives, then they should have returned the same rankings of keywords – for example, the fiftieth keyword according to effect-size should also be the fiftieth keyword according to statistical significance. In other words, the two rankings would fully correlate. Also, even if the two rankings did not fully correlate, the extent to which they did would provide useful indications regarding their similarity in identifying keyness. The correlations of the ranking returned by the effect-size and statistical significance metrics were measured using Spearman's Rank Correlation (r_s), a metric used when values 'are measured on a ranked scale' (Ellis 2010: 11): a value of '1' indicates full positive correlation (i.e. the two metrics produce identical rankings); a value of '0' indicates no correlation; a value of '-1' indicates full inverse correlation (i.e. the two metrics produce exactly opposite rankings) (ibid.). The analysis of the rankings by effect-size and statistical significance revealed extremely weak correlations in all the keyness comparisons, with r_s scores ranging from 0.010 to 0.122 (i.e. all close to no correlation). For example, in the comparison between the Hutton Enquiry and the BNC, the word *pound* ranked at position 12 according to LL, but at position 10744 according to %DIFF. That is, it would appear to be a strong candidate for analysis if statistical significance were used as a metric, but not on the basis of the actual frequency difference shown by the effect-size metric. On the contrary, the rankings according to %DIFF and another effect-size metric (*Ratio*, Kilgarriff 2001)[6] were identical for all keywords.

Gabrielatos and Marchi (2012) also considered the possibility that the extremely low correlations between rankings might mask very small ranking differences among the top-N keywords. For example, a word might rank in position 10 according to one metric and position 20 according to the other – which would mean that both words would be selected for analysis even if a small subset were chosen. To investigate that, they compared the overlap in the top 100 keywords returned by both metrics in all comparisons (see 11.4). Again, there was very little overlap (Table 11.1).

These results clearly indicate that the statistical significance score does not accurately reflect the size of a frequency difference. Gabrielatos and Marchi (2011, 2012) concluded that statistical significance values are an unreliable and misleading measure of keyness, as selecting key items on the basis of statistical significance is very likely to exclude true key items from the analysis and/or result in treating low-level key items as high-level ones. More precisely, they noted the following cases:

- A very large frequency difference may have very low statistical significance.
- A very small frequency difference (even one so small that it could be deemed to show similarity rather than difference) may have very high statistical significance.

TABLE 11.1 Overlap in top-100 keywords returned by the two metrics

Compared corpora	*Shared in top 100*
SiBol 1993 vs. SiBol 2005	3
Guardian 2005: Media vs. Home	0
Hutton vs. BNC	2
Hutton vs. FLOB	8
FLOB vs. BNC	22

- Two very similar frequency differences may have very different levels of statistical significance.
- Two very different frequency differences may have very similar levels of statistical significance.

These observations can also be explained in the light of another aspect of statistical significance metrics. Statistical significance scores are sensitive to the size of the sample: the larger the sample, the higher the statistical significance of all effect-sizes, however small they may be (Ellis 2010: 5; Rosenfeld & Penrod 2011: 84). Owen and Jones (1977: 359, cited in Kilgarriff 1997: 237) point out that 'if we increase the sample [...] we would ultimately reach the point where all null hypotheses would be rejected'. In a keyness analysis, this sensitivity is related not only to the size of the corpora compared, but also to the corpus frequencies of an item. That is, given a frequency difference, the higher the raw frequencies of an item in the two corpora and/or the larger the two corpora, the higher the statistical significance value will be. The corollary of this sensitivity to frequency is that statistical significance scores are not comparable across different keyness analyses. An item may show the same effect-size in two different comparisons, but, because of different corpus frequencies and/or corpus sizes, the same effect-size may have different levels of statistical significance in each comparison. It also follows that statistical significance metrics cannot be used to pinpoint frequency similarities between corpora, whereas effect-size metrics can. Finally, the sensitivity of statistical significance values to the size of one or both of the compared corpora entails that the larger the corpora compared, the higher the number of frequency differences that will be statistically significant. This characteristic has led to two related misconceptions: a) that there is an ideal range of corpus sizes, which returns an optimum number of key items, and b) that the reference corpus must be larger than the study corpus (e.g. Berber-Sardinha 2000). Of course, the smaller the corpora, the smaller the number of frequency differences that can be expected to cross the threshold of statistical significance. However, the objective of a keyness analysis is not to maximise, or minimise, the number of key items, but to derive as true a picture as possible of the differences and similarities of item frequencies between two corpora. Corpus size is not as important as the representativeness and principled selection of the corpora compared, as well as the examination of keyness in appropriate sub-corpora to establish the dispersion of key items (e.g. Paquot & Bestgen 2009).

Kilgarriff (1996b, 2005) argues against the use of null-hypothesis testing in corpus linguistics for two reasons. The first is that 'language is never random, so the null hypothesis is never true' (Kilgarriff 2005: 273). The second reason is related to the sensitivity of statistical significance values to corpus sizes:

> [H]ypothesis testing has been used to reach conclusions, where the difficulty in reaching the conclusion is caused by sparsity of data. But language data, in this age of information glut, is available in vast quantities. A better strategy will generally be to use more data. Then the difference between the motivated and the arbitrary will be evident without the use of compromised hypothesis testing.
>
> *(Kilgarriff 2005: 273)*

This should not however be taken to imply that statistical significance metrics are useless in keyness analysis – quite the contrary, provided that we understand the nature and extent of the contribution of statistical significance to establishing keyness. In fact, Kilgarriff's (2005: 273) second argument can be seen to point towards the utility of using statistical significance testing when the corpora are small (e.g. when data collection is difficult/costly, or the focus of the corpus is restricted). Also, Kilgarriff (2001: 239) states that G^2 'gives an accurate measure of how surprising an event is even where it has occurred only once' and that 'early indications are that, at least for low and medium frequency words [...] it corresponds reasonably well to human judgements of distinctiveness'. In light of the above, statistical significance testing seems particularly useful in cases of small corpora and/or items with low raw frequency – when even large frequency differences may be unreliable. In such cases, statistical significance scores can indicate whether an observed large frequency difference is also dependable enough to merit incorporating the item in the subsequent manual analysis (Gabrielatos & Marchi 2011, Gries 2010b: 130).

11.3.2 Effect-size metrics

This section will examine the effect-size metrics currently available in the most widely used corpus tools: AntConc (Anthony 2017),[7] CQPweb (Hardie 2012), Sketch Engine (Kilgarriff et al. 2014), WordSmith Tools 7 (Scott 2016) and Wmatrix 3 (Rayson 2003, 2009). To these we add the Excel document developed by Paul Rayson, which allows for both manual entry of raw frequencies and corpus sizes (useful for targeted keyness studies), as well as the copy-pasting of frequency lists derived in other corpus tools (useful for exploratory studies).[8] At this point, we need to recognise that the term *effect-size* may be a misnomer as far as keyness analysis is concerned. The choice of the term *effect* seems to have been motivated by the use of such metrics in studies that aimed to measure some kind of cause-effect relationship (e.g. the effect of a medical treatment or a teaching technique), or a correlation/association between two variables (e.g. between the use of a particular linguistic item and sociolinguistic factors, such as age and gender) (Everitt 2002: 20).[9]

However, in a keyness analysis, as used in corpus-based discourse studies, no effect is measured; that is, the frequency of an item in one corpus is not expected to influence the frequency of, or interact with, the same item in another corpus. Therefore, measures of association (e.g. Dice Coefficient)[10] do not seem appropriate for a keyness analysis, unless, of course, what is compared is not the frequencies of items, but their ranking according to frequency in each corpus (e.g. Forsyth & Lam 2009). Also, some effect-size metrics focus on the difference of means in the compared data sets (e.g. Cohen's *d*, Phi Coefficient). Again, this is irrelevant in a keyness analysis, as what is compared is not means of groups of frequencies, but two distinct frequencies.[11] Finally, some metrics that are presented as measuring effect-size in some corpus tools either measure statistical significance (e.g. Bayes Factor), or are 'hybrid' metrics (Hoffmann et al. 2008: 151; see also Ellis 2010: 10; Everitt 2002: 285–286; Kilgarriff 1996a: 35), as their formulas contain the value of a statistical significance metric (e.g. Cramer's V, Phi Coefficient, t-test). In this light, such metrics are not appropriate for keyness analysis (but see Section 11.4.2).

This section will conclude with a discussion of five appropriate effect-size metrics used in one or more of the corpus tools mentioned earlier. Their calculation takes into account one or more of the following: the size of the corpora compared (C1, C2), the raw frequencies of an item in the two corpora (RFC1, RFC2) or the normalised frequencies of the item (NFC1, NFC2). The discussion focuses on their calculation, the interpretation of values and any particular characteristics or limitations.

Ratio (Kilgarriff 2009)

$$\text{Ratio} = \frac{\text{NFC1}}{\text{NFC2}}$$

This is the simplest of the effect-size metrics, only involving the normalised frequencies of an item in the compared corpora. A value of '1' indicates that the item has equal normalised frequency in the two corpora, with higher/lower values indicating higher/lower NF in C1. For example, a value of '4' indicates that the item is four times more frequent in C1 than C2. It must be noted that the values are directional; i.e. they depend on which corpus is used as the study corpus. To use the example above, if C1 is the study corpus, then the value is '4', whereas, if C2 is the study corpus, then the value is '0.25'. Researchers using this metric thus need to understand that the two scores (4 and 0.25) indicate the *same* size of difference, examined from two different perspectives.

Odds Ratio (OR) (Everitt 2002: 271; Pojanapunya & Watson Todd 2016: 15)

$$\text{OR} = \frac{\text{RFC1}/(\text{C1} - \text{RFC1})}{\text{RFC2}/(\text{C2} - \text{RFC2})}$$

This metric takes into account raw frequencies, along with the sizes of the compared corpora. As in the case of Ratio, its values are directional.

Log Ratio (Hardie 2014)

$$\text{Log Ratio} = \log \frac{\text{NFC1}}{\text{NFC2}}$$

This metric is the binary logarithm of the ratio of normalised frequencies. Equal normalised frequencies are indicated by a value of '0', whereas an increase of one indicates a doubling of the frequency difference. For example, a value of '2' indicates that NFC1 is four times NFC2. An advantage of Log Ratio is that, although it is a directional metric, this does not manifest itself in different values (as with the other directional metrics), but in the same value being positive or negative. For example, if RFC1 is four times RFC2, the Log Ratio value will be '2' if C1 is the study corpus, and '-2' if C2 is the study corpus.

%DIFF (Gabrielatos & Marchi 2011)

$$\%\text{DIFF} = \frac{(\text{NFC1} - \text{NFC2}) * 100}{\text{NFC2}}$$

This metric takes into account the normalised frequencies of an item in the two corpora. Equal normalised frequencies are indicated by a value of '0'. Positive values show higher frequency and negative values indicate lower frequency. A value of '100' indicates twice the frequency, and every increase of '100' adds one to the difference – for example a value of '500' indicates six times higher frequency. It is again a directional metric: if RFC1 is four times RFC2, the value is '300' when C1 is the study corpus, but '-75' when C2 is the study corpus. In the latter case, the interpretation is that the item has 75 per cent lower frequency in C2 compared to C1, or, in different terms, that the frequency of the item in C2 is one-quarter of its frequency in C1. A limitation of this metric is that while its score has no upper limit, there is a lower one: negative scores stop at '-100'.

Difference Coefficient (Hofland & Johansson 1982)

$$\text{Diff Coefficient} = \frac{\text{NFC1} - \text{NFC2}}{\text{NFC1} + \text{NFC2}}$$

As with %DIFF, this metric takes account of normalised frequencies. Scores range from '1' to '-1', and are interpreted as follows: '1' indicates that the item only exists in C1 (i.e. it has zero frequency in C2); '0' indicates that the item has the same normalised frequency in the two corpora; '-1' indicates that the item only exists in C2 (i.e. it has zero frequency in C1). Although the metric is directional, its values do not create problems of comparison, due to the plus/minus sign. However, the interpretation of values is less straightforward. For example, if (as in the example above) NFC1 is four times NFC2, the value is '0.6'.

These brief discussions underline that when values of directional effect-size metrics are reported, it must be made clear which corpus was treated as the study corpus (i.e. which corpus was first in the comparison). What is important is that all the above metrics return the same ranking of key items. Therefore, the selection of one rather than another hinges on their availability in corpus tools, and the extent to which researchers find their values easy to interpret.

11.3.3 Dealing with zero frequencies in the reference corpus

A limitation of all but one (Difference Coefficient) of the above metrics is that, when an item has zero frequency in C2, the calculation cannot be performed, due to division by zero. A number of techniques to deal with this limitation have been proposed (Brysbaert & Diependaele 2013). One technique is to remove items with zero frequency from the comparison. However, excluding such instances may well remove very useful differences and, more importantly, prohibit the examination of absence. If we think it interesting that a corpus has more occurrences of an item compared with another corpus, then it is even more interesting that a corpus has no occurrences when another corpus has some. This is because the absence of an item can be seen as characteristic not only of the corpus with non-zero occurrences, but also the corpus with zero occurrences. The importance of zero (and very low) frequencies in a corpus increases with a) the size of the corpus lacking the item and b) the frequency of the item in the other corpus. Simply put, the difference between nothing and something is potentially salient, and the larger the frequency/corpus, the more salient the absence. The second technique, usually termed 'add 1' (Kilgarriff 2009: 2), is to add a small number (no more than '1') to the frequency of every item in each corpus. However, this technique has two flaws. First, it increases the size of the corpora by the number of types in each (or a fraction, if a number smaller than '1' is added). Second, and more importantly, it increases frequencies unevenly: the smaller the frequency of an item, the higher the proportional increase in frequency resulting from the addition of a fixed number. For example, if we add '1' to three items with frequencies of '100', '10', and '1', then the frequency of these items increases by 1 per cent, 10 per cent, and 100 per cent, respectively. The resulting increase in corpus sizes, and the non-proportionate increase in the frequencies of individual items, is likely to skew the results. The third technique is to replace zero frequencies with an infinitesimally small number (0.000000000000000001 – one quadrillionth), which, for practical purposes, is an adequate proxy for zero (Gabrielatos & Marchi 2011; Scott 1996). This technique results in extremely high values when effect-size metrics without upper limits are used (e.g. %DIFF, Log Ratio), which could be seen as a drawback for some types of analysis (Brysbaert & Diependaele 2013: 428). However, for keyness analysis, this is a strength, as it flags up instances of absence.

The next section will discuss the decisions that must be taken after the effect-size and statistical significance scores have been calculated.

11.4 Selecting key items for analysis

Unless the corpora compared are very similar, it is unlikely that a study employing an exploratory keyness approach can carry out a manual analysis of all key items. For example, all the keyness studies reviewed in Pojanapunya and Watson Todd (2016: 3–10) focused on a subset of key items. It follows then that the technique used to select key items for manual analysis is of paramount importance, as it will greatly influence the results of a study. Pojanapunya and Watson Todd's review provides clear indications of the main techniques preferred (2016: 3–10):

1 More than half (16) of the studies selected the top N words (between 10 and 1000, with the average being about 100).
2 About one in four (seven) specified a statistical significance threshold, usually a very high one (with *p*-values ranging from 0.05 to 0.00000000000001).
3 A small number of studies (two) combined a corpus frequency threshold with a statistical significance threshold.
4 One in six (five) selected keywords that were deemed to be related to particular topics.

Of course, as the studies above used statistical significance as a measure of keyness, the top-N items were those with the highest statistical significance (and not necessarily with the highest frequency differences). Similarly, the studies that set a very high threshold of corpus frequency also derived items with the highest statistical significance (since statistical significance scores increase as corpus frequency increases). Therefore, there is little difference between approaches (a)–(c), which were employed in the vast majority (25/30) of the studies examined.

As argued in Section 11.2, the level of keyness of an item needs to be established via the combination of two complementary metrics. The effect-size score will enable the items returned from an automated frequency comparison to be ranked according to the size of the frequency difference. The statistical significance score will provide information regarding the level of confidence we can have that the observed frequency difference is dependable – or, to look at this issue from a different perspective, whether the item is frequent enough and/or the corpora are large enough for the observed differences to be dependable. However, very little work has been carried out to establish thresholds for effect-size values in keyness analyses. The inclusion of an item in the list returned by an automated frequency comparison does not necessarily entail that the item is key, and in this light, it seems wise to initially view the items returned by the keyness function of a corpus tool as *candidate key items* (CKIs).[12] This section will first discuss the issue of threshold values for item frequency and statistical significance, and then propose a technique based on effect-size values for selecting key items in exploratory keyness studies.

11.4.1 Frequency thresholds

As was shown in Pojanapunya and Watson Todd (2016: 3–10), the majority of keyness studies tend to set frequency thresholds, removing low-frequency items from the comparison either directly, or indirectly by setting high statistical significance thresholds. However, this may have unintended consequences. For example, if C1 contains some items with a very low frequency while C2 contains these items with a (relatively) higher frequency, then these items can be expected to register high effect-size values. Applying a low-frequency threshold may remove potentially important items, which may index very pronounced differences (e.g. of topics, attitudes). In the same vein, removing items with zero frequency in one of the compared corpora will prevent the examination of absence (Partington 2014; Partington & Duguid, this volume). Equally problematic is setting high-frequency thresholds to filter out function words, as these can point towards particular attitudinal differences between the compared corpora (e.g. Duguid 2008; McEnery 2006). In his work on swearing, McEnery (2006: 147) found that syntactic coordinators, in particular the word *and*, demonstrated 'the important function of linking objects of offence to form networks of offence'. McEnery (2006: 148) concluded that 'it is a brave, or rather foolish, analyst who assumes that, in any given data set, the words are so unlikely to be key that they can be safely ignored from the very start'. Therefore, it seems wise to avoid setting frequency thresholds, but to generate lists of CKIs which include all items (i.e. all types in both corpora). Researchers can then make principled decisions as to which items to examine, taking into account both the effect-size and statistical significance of CKIs (see Sections 11.4.2, 11.4.3 and 11.5 below), as well as the particular foci of the study. However, if frequency thresholds are to be set, then they should be specified in terms of normalised frequencies (e.g. per million words; pmw), not raw frequencies. This is because in corpora of uneven sizes, the same raw frequency may correspond to very uneven normalised frequencies: a raw frequency of five in a corpus of 10 million words translates into a normalised frequency of 0.5 pmw, whereas in a corpus of 100,000 words it translates into 50 pmw.

11.4.2 Statistical significance thresholds

Before examining the utility of using statistical significance thresholds, we must consider that such thresholds are arbitrary (Hoffmann et al. 2008: 88) and vary between disciplines. For example, in most of the social sciences the usual threshold is p=0.05 (Wilson 2013: 8), whereas in corpus linguistics the threshold is usually p=0.01 at the most. However, as keyness analyses (particularly of large corpora) tend to return too many CKIs for researchers to examine manually, the usual practice (as indicated in Pojanapunya & Watson Todd 2016) is to set a much lower p-value (e.g. 0.000000001), partly in order to reduce the CKIs, and partly because of the misconception of the p-value as a measure of keyness – that is, setting a very low p-value threshold is supposed to return the items with the highest keyness. In light of the discussion so far, we need to examine two interrelated issues: a) the *p*-value that can be seen as low enough for the corresponding frequency difference to be deemed dependable, and b) the wisdom of setting extremely low *p*-value thresholds to reduce the number of CKIs returned by the automated frequency comparison.

It was clarified in Section 11.2, that the *p*-value does not directly indicate the probability that an observed frequency difference is due to chance. However, this is not to say that this probability cannot be calculated; rather, a different statistical measure is needed. Wilson (2013) proposes using the *Bayesian Information Criterion* (BIC), an approximation of Bayes Factor (Raftery 1999: 411), the value of which provides an estimate of 'the amount of evidence against the null hypothesis' (H_0) (Wilson 2013: 5). For the purposes of keyness analysis, BIC is calculated using a) the log-likelihood (LL) value of the frequency difference and b) the combined size of the compared corpora (N), as follows: BIC ≈ LL – log(N) (Wilson 2013: 6).[13] The resulting value is interpreted as indicating the amount of evidence against H_0, as shown in Table 11.2 below (Raftery 1999: 420; Wilson 2013: 6).

An example frequency comparison carried out by Wilson (2013: 6–8) between two small corpora (approximately 10,000 and 150,000 words) yielded the correspondence between *p*-values and BIC values shown in Table 11.3.[14] As Wilson (2013: 8) points out, the BIC values in Table 11.3 suggest that the usual threshold of p=0.01 (G^2=6.63) provides considerably less than positive evidence. These values also put in perspective the threshold of p=0.0001 (G^2=15.13) proposed by Rayson, Beridge and Francis (2004), which seems to provide evidence which is at least positive, given Wilson's results.

However, as BIC takes into account the sizes of the compared corpora, 'there will not always be a direct correspondence' between G^2 and BIC values (Wilson 2013: 7), and given the sensitivity of G^2 values to corpus sizes, it would seem advisable to set statistical significance thresholds in terms of BIC values instead of *p*-values (Wilson 2013: 8). Currently, however, BIC is not included in all corpus tools, and until it is included in other corpus tools, two approaches are possible.

TABLE 11.2 BIC values and their interpretation

BIC	*Degree of evidence against H_0*
<0	No evidence – favours H_0
0-2	Not worth more than a bare mention
2-6	Positive evidence against H_0
6-10	Strong evidence against H_0
>10	Very strong evidence against H_0

TABLE 11.3 Correspondence between *p*-values and degrees of evidence

BIC	*Degree of evidence against H_0*	*p-value*	G^2
2-6	Positive evidence against H_0	0.00018	13.98
6-10	Strong evidence against H_0	0.000014	18.81
>10	Very strong evidence against H_0	0.0000024	22.22

One is to treat the correspondences in Table 11.3 as general guidelines for selecting a *p*-value threshold. A more reliable approach is to a) set the corpus tool threshold to the highest acceptable *p*-value in corpus linguistics (i.e. p=0.01), b) copy-paste the tool's output to Rayson's Excel sheet, and c) filter out CKIs with BIC values below '2' (see Section 11.5 for examples).

In the light of the above, would it be reasonable to argue that the lower the *p*-value the better? The short answer is, no: this will privilege items with very high corpus frequency, which may not show very high frequency differences (effect-sizes), and may well filter out key items with very high effect-sizes simply because these items do not have very high corpus frequencies. Another limitation is that if large effect-sizes are filtered out, the researcher will not even be aware of their existence. As a result, this practice is likely to remove useful key items, and reduce the scope for identifying groups of CKIs, which could help the analysis to more accurately identify patterns of use, and corresponding semantic preferences and discourse prosodies (see Baker 2004; Leech & Fallon 1992: 31). More precisely, given the *p*-value indicating the threshold for very strong evidence in Wilson's (2013) study (Table 11.3), it would seem that a *p*-value threshold below 0.0000001 (i.e. a G^2 score of above 28.38)[15] would be inadvisable, as it could remove very large effect-sizes from consideration, particularly if the items do not have extremely high corpus frequencies, or the corpora are not particularly large. Hoffmann et al. (2008: 88) suggest an alternative approach: 'instead of using pre-defined thresholds, you [...] can simply decide whether you are willing to take the risk indicated by the *p*-value.' This approach allows researchers to have a clear view of CKIs and decide on the items to be included in the manual analysis after examining the range of effect-size values, and the corresponding range of statistical significance levels, or, better still, levels of evidence against H_0 (via BIC scores). Such an approach is particularly useful when small corpora are compared (i.e. when even very high frequency differences can be expected to have low statistical significance). In such cases, the researcher can accept lower significance values than those in Table 11.3, and mitigate the corresponding discussion accordingly.

It must be clarified that such an approach is suitable only when differences are sought. If the study aims to identify similarities, then statistical significance thresholds should not be used, as they remove items with similar frequencies (which have low statistical significance scores); that is, they remove the very items that the study seeks to identify. Since corpus tools always have default statistical significance thresholds, it follows that before carrying out a keyness analysis aiming to identify similarities, the maximum *p*-value must be set at '1': that is, the output of the frequency comparison must contain the effect-size and statistical significance values of all the types in the corpora compared (see Section 11.4.3).

11.4.3 Effect-size thresholds

As the range of effect-size values may vary according to the level of difference or similarity between the two corpora, effect-size thresholds can be expected to be comparison-specific (Gabrielatos & Marchi 2011). Even with a high threshold of statistical significance, frequency comparisons are expected to return a wide range of effect-sizes, some of which will be too small, at least compared to items higher up the list, and may even be small enough to effectively signal similarity. For example, a difference of 100 per cent is comparatively very high if the majority of differences are below 50 per cent, but comparatively very low if the majority is above 100 per cent. In this light, the practice of selecting the top-N CKIs has two important limitations. First, it does not consider the proportion of key items that the top-N represent; for example, the top 100 represent 50 per cent of key items if the total is 200, but only 10 per cent if the total is 1,000. Second, it does not consider whether there are items below rank position 100 which have only marginally lower scores than the 100th item; for example, it does not make sense to include the 100th item with a difference of 100 per cent, but exclude the 101st item with a difference of 99.5 per cent. Therefore, neither selecting the top-N CKIs nor setting a universal threshold would seem advisable.

The approach proposed here is adapted from Gabrielatos (2009, 2010: 52–54, 205–221) and Gries (2010a: 285–288): CKIs are clustered according to their respective effect-size scores. The clustering method suggested is *hierarchical cluster analysis*: a family of statistical techniques used in assigning objects (in this case, CKIs) to groups according to their degree of similarity/dissimilarity in relation to one or more variables (in this case, the effect-size score) (Everitt 1993: 1, 6–7; Gan et al. 2007: 3–5, Romesburg 1984: 2). More precisely, the *agglomerative* method is suggested, which initially treats each CKI as a separate cluster, and then combines CKIs into clusters according to the (dis)similarity of their effect-size scores (Everitt, 1993: 55–57; Gan et al. 2007: 9). The degree of (dis)similarity is measured using the *Euclidian distance*, which computes the square root of the sum of the squares of the pairwise differences in the effect-size scores (Gan et al. 2007: 326). The distance between clusters, or between already established clusters and CKIs not yet assigned to a cluster, is calculated using *average group linkage*: the average of the distances between all the scores in each cluster (Sneath & Sokal 1973: 222). This determines the allocation of CKIs to clusters, as well as the conflation of existing clusters into more inclusive ones, a method which has been shown to consistently produce clear and useful classifications (Adamson & Bawden 1981: 208).

In order to accommodate the usual restriction in the number of CKIs that can be examined manually, the number of clusters can be predetermined. The number of predetermined clusters will vary according to a) the number of CKIs and b) the number of key items that can be examined manually in the particular study (MEKIs). As a rule of thumb, the number of clusters should be the number of CKIs divided by the number of MEKIs (number of clusters = CKIs/MEKIs). For example, if a keyness analysis returns 1,000 CKIs, but only about 50 can be examined manually, then 20 clusters should be specified. Of course, as will be seen in Section 11.5, CKIs are not necessarily grouped neatly in clusters of equal sizes. However, this calculation allows researchers to start from the cluster with the highest effect-size scores (if the focus is differences) or the lowest ones (if the focus is similarity), and, if the cluster does not contain enough CKIs, to then move to the adjacent lower/

higher cluster. Another option is to determine the same number of clusters for both CKI lists: whatever the number of clusters, this approach results in a continuum of clustered CKIs ranked from the highest to the lowest frequency difference (i.e. from difference to similarity). What needs to be stressed is that, as CKIs are clustered according to the proximity of their effect-sizes, once one item in a cluster has been selected for manual analysis, all other items in the cluster must also be selected.

So far, the discussion has been predominantly concerned with issues relating to establishing frequency differences, which is understandable given the definition of *keyness* and the focus of almost all keyness studies. However, in order to avoid the *partiality* discussed in Marchi and Taylor (this volume), it would be useful to expand the notion of keyness, and distinguish between two types: *keyness-D*, relating to difference (and its extreme case, absence), and *keyness-S,* relating to similarity. That is, items may be key (i.e. potentially useful) because their large frequency differences (*key-D items*) or their similar/identical frequencies (*key-S items*) in two (sub-)corpora potentially index differences or similarities (respectively) in content or attitudes. The distinction is also related to methodological issues: keyness-D needs to be established via the combination of effect-size and statistical significance, whereas keyness-S is established via effect-size only. The next section brings together the various aspects discussed so far, and exemplifies the suggested procedures through a case study.

11.5 Selecting key items: a case study

11.5.1 Aims, data and methodology

This section presents a case study of keyness analysis which examines both differences and similarities, and demonstrates different alternatives for the principled selection of CKIs for further manual analysis. As clarified in 11.1 above, the case study does not aim to carry out a manual analysis of CKIs: it is instead used as a springboard for discussion of the methodological options and issues discussed so far.

The corpora to be compared are the 2017 UK election manifestos of the Conservative (CM2017; 29,954 words) and Labour (LM2017; 23,691 words) parties. The largest frequency differences are expected to index aspects of content characterising each manifesto (as compared to the other), whereas the smallest differences are expected to index similarities. In other words, each corpus alternated acting as the study and reference corpus. It will be shown that, even with such small corpora and fairly strict thresholds of statistical significance, the automated analysis returned a good number of CKIs that can be usefully included in the manual analysis. The texts were downloaded from Paul Rayson's Wmatrix webpage[16] (Rayson, 2003, 2009). They had been converted to plain text from the original PDFs and automatically cleaned by Rayson, but further manual cleaning was deemed necessary in order to (fully) remove page numbers, chapter/section numbers, headers and footers, and characters indicating bullet points *(•)* and quotation marks *(&bquo;, &equo;)*.[17]

Two corpus tools were combined: WordSmith 7 (Scott 2016) and Paul Rayson's Excel document. WordSmith 7 was used to derive frequency lists and lists of CKIs, from which only the raw frequencies of CKIs were retained and copy-pasted to the Excel document. All other calculations were carried out using the Excel document, as it offers more effect-size metrics and, more importantly, both G^2 and BIC scores. For simplicity, the focus of the analysis was word-forms, although possessives were treated as separate items. In order to avoid removing items from consideration, the following settings were selected:

- The minimum word frequency was set to '1'.
- The maximum *p*-value was set to '1'; that is, initially, statistical significance was ignored.

This allowed the calculation of an effect-size score for all types in the corpora, and the identification of similarities as well as differences, resulting in 2,316 CKIs in CM2017 and 2,657 CKIs in LM2017. Effect-size was measured by %DIFF, with zeros replaced by 0.000000000000000001; statistical significance was established via BIC (which takes G^2 into account). The cluster analysis was carried out using SPSS 22 (for settings, see Section 11.4.3).[18] Procedures of KI selection differed according to whether the focus was keyness-D (difference) or keyness-S (similarity).

11.5.2 Keyness-D: identifying differences

Keyness-D: alternative 1

This approach filters out all differences with BIC<2, that is, only differences that show at least positive evidence against H_0 are retained. In the particular comparisons, a BIC value of '2' corresponded to G^2 scores of about '13' ($p<0.001$), which is similar to the G^2 score (13.98) corresponding to BIC=2 in Wilson (2013: 8).[19] Due to the small size of the corpora, this leaves a very manageable number of KIs for both comparisons: 31 for CM2017 (Table 11.4) and 34 for LM2017 (Table 11.5). Frequencies are normalised per thousand words (ptw);[20] CKIs are ranked according to effect-size.[21]

A first observation is that, in both comparisons, some CKIs have zero frequencies in the other corpus (five in CM2017, 14 in LM2017), with all differences being statistically significant (BIC≥2) despite the small item frequencies and corpus sizes. This supports the inclusion of zero-frequency items in keyness comparisons, as their exclusion would prevent pinpointing potentially useful absences. For example, *universities* and *United Kingdom* do not appear at all in LM2017, whereas *equality* and *LGBT* are not mentioned at all in CM2017. Another interesting observation is that *Labour* and *Conservative* are CKIs in LM2017, but not in CM2017.

Keyness-D: alternative 2

This second approach is appropriate for keyness comparisons returning a large number of CKIs, or, irrespective of the number of CKIs, for studies preferring to

TABLE 11.4 Differences: CKIs in CM2017 (BIC≥2). RF = raw frequency, NF = normalised frequency (per thousand words)

CKIs in CM2017	*RF CM2017*	*RF LM2017*	*NF (ptw) CM2017*	*NF (ptw) LM2017*	*%DIFF*	*G2*	*BIC*
UNITED	63	0	2.10	0	2.10E+17	73.42	62.53
KINGDOM	45	0	1.50	0	1.50E+17	52.45	41.56
UNIVERSITIES	16	0	0.53	0	5.34E+16	18.65	7.76
SHALL	15	0	0.50	0	5.01E+16	17.48	6.59
SHALE	12	0	0.40	0	4.01E+16	13.99	3.10
STABLE	20	1	0.67	0.04	1481.83	16.90	6.01
DATA	33	2	1.10	0.08	1205.01	26.40	15.51
BELIEVE	37	3	1.24	0.13	875.46	26.71	15.82
GENERATIONS	20	2	0.67	0.08	690.91	13.17	2.28
GO	20	2	0.67	0.08	690.91	13.17	2.28
ONLINE	26	3	0.87	0.13	585.46	15.92	5.02
IF	57	7	1.90	0.30	544.03	33.69	22.80
INSTITUTIONS	24	3	0.80	0.13	532.73	14.04	3.15
LEADERSHIP	24	3	0.80	0.13	532.73	14.04	3.15
TECHNICAL	24	3	0.80	0.13	532.73	14.04	3.15
OPPORTUNITY	24	3	0.80	0.13	532.73	14.04	3.15
TECHNOLOGY	30	4	1.00	0.17	493.18	16.87	5.98
DIGITAL	59	9	1.97	0.38	418.49	30.32	19.43
GREAT	39	6	1.30	0.25	414.09	19.92	9.03
STRONG	51	9	1.70	0.38	348.18	23.42	12.53
BETTER	45	9	1.50	0.38	295.46	18.50	7.61
WANT	40	8	1.34	0.34	295.46	16.44	5.55
HELP	79	17	2.64	0.72	267.54	30.21	19.32
UNION	47	11	1.57	0.46	237.94	16.41	5.52
WORLD	106	27	3.54	1.14	210.51	33.46	22.57
DO	66	17	2.20	0.72	207.06	20.54	9.65
CONTINUE	82	22	2.74	0.93	194.79	24.20	13.31
BEST	48	13	1.60	0.55	192.03	13.99	3.10
SO	102	40	3.41	1.69	101.68	15.41	4.52
CAN	99	40	3.31	1.69	95.75	13.92	3.03
WE	949	419	31.68	17.69	79.14	105.26	94.37

base selection decisions on a fine-grained grouping of CKIs rather than on a simple ranking. It is also suggested for studies that prefer to start with a larger pool of CKIs, from which to select or remove particular types of items. For example, a study aiming to identify key social actors or processes (van Leeuwen 1996) may focus only on nouns or verbs. In the present case study, if a threshold of $p \leq 0.01$ ($G^2 \geq 6.63$) is selected, about three times the number of CKIs is returned (92 for CM2017 and 107 for LM2017) compared to Alternative 1 above. Let us assume that a fine-grained grouping of these CKIs is required, with potentially about 10 CKIs per group. Using the simple formula presented in Section 11.5.1, these CKIs will need to be grouped in 10 clusters (see Tables 11.6 and 11.7 – numbers before CKIs indicate their ranking position). Clusters should be interpreted (other filtering criteria

TABLE 11.5 Differences: CKIs in LM2017 (BIC≥2)

CKIs in LM2017	*RF LM2017*	*RF CM2017*	*NF (ptw) LM2017*	*NF (ptw) CM2017*	*%DIFF*	*G2*	*BIC*
LABOUR'S	21	0	0.89	0	8.86E+16	*34.33*	*23.44*
EQUALITY	19	0	0.80	0	8.02E+16	*31.06*	*20.17*
UNIONS	15	0	0.63	0	6.33E+16	*24.52*	*13.63*
LGBT	12	0	0.51	0	5.07E+16	*19.62*	*8.72*
REINSTATE	11	0	0.46	0	4.64E+16	*17.98*	*7.09*
SCRAP	10	0	0.42	0	4.22E+16	*16.35*	*5.46*
PRIVATISATION	9	0	0.38	0	3.80E+16	*14.71*	*3.82*
BANKS	9	0	0.38	0	3.80E+16	*14.71*	*3.82*
RENTERS	8	0	0.34	0	3.38E+16	*13.08*	*2.19*
WOMEN'S	8	0	0.34	0	3.38E+16	*13.08*	*2.19*
FAILURE	8	0	0.34	0	3.38E+16	*13.08*	*2.19*
ENFORCE	8	0	0.34	0	3.38E+16	*13.08*	*2.19*
EXTENDING	8	0	0.34	0	3.38E+16	*13.08*	*2.19*
CENTRES	8	0	0.34	0	3.38E+16	*13.08*	*2.19*
LABOUR	319	3	13.47	0.10	13344.38	*490.90*	*480.01*
CUTS	24	2	1.01	0.07	1417.23	*27.46*	*16.57*
OFFICERS	12	1	0.51	0.03	1417.23	*13.73*	*2.84*
OWNERSHIP	20	2	0.84	0.07	1164.36	*21.62*	*10.73*
CRISIS	19	2	0.80	0.07	1101.14	*20.18*	*9.29*
GUARANTEE	18	3	0.76	0.10	658.62	*15.69*	*4.80*
REGIONAL	17	3	0.72	0.10	616.47	*14.38*	*3.49*
ARRANGEMENTS	16	3	0.68	0.10	574.33	*13.08*	*2.19*
VITAL	16	3	0.68	0.10	574.33	*13.08*	*2.19*
STAFF	22	5	0.93	0.17	456.32	*15.91*	*5.02*
RIGHTS	66	16	2.79	0.53	421.55	*45.59*	*34.70*
WOULD	22	6	0.93	0.20	363.60	*13.86*	*2.97*
WORKERS	62	17	2.62	0.57	361.12	*38.88*	*27.99*
STANDARDS	40	12	1.69	0.40	321.45	*23.19*	*12.30*
UNDER	35	12	1.48	0.40	268.77	*17.79*	*6.90*
BACK	34	12	1.44	0.40	258.24	*16.76*	*5.87*
CONSERVATIVES	50	19	2.11	0.63	232.73	*22.66*	*11.77*
JOBS	34	14	1.44	0.47	207.06	*13.94*	*3.05*
ALL	100	56	4.22	1.87	125.78	*25.04*	*14.15*
ON	215	168	9.08	5.61	61.81	*22.06*	*11.17*

notwithstanding) as follows: a) CKIs in higher clusters are more key than CKIs in lower clusters, b) all CKIs sharing a cluster should be treated as equally key. The first observation is that the CKIs do not combine neatly into clusters of equal numbers (i.e. 10 clusters of 10 items each); this is because the clustering takes into account the distance between the effect-size scores of consecutive CKIs. The results also highlight the limitations of the 'top-N' technique: if, for example, we decided to manually analyse the top-20 key items, we would select *exceptional* and *things* from cluster 9 (Table 11.6), but we would arbitrarily exclude the remaining nine items of that cluster. The second observation is that the two expanded sets of CKIs obtained

TABLE 11.6 Differences: CKIs in CM2017 (G2≤0.01) grouped in 10 clusters

Cluster	*Difference: CKIs in CM2017*
1	**1:UNITED**
2	**2:KINGDOM**
3	**3:UNIVERSITIES**
4	**4:SHALL**
5	**5:SHALE**
6	6:YOUNGER; 7:AHEAD; 8:YOUR
7	9:EASIER; 10:MERITOCRACY
8	11:DESIGN; 12:MIGHT; 13:ELDERLY; 14:COMPETITIVE; 15:DEEP; 16:ACTIVE; 17:ATTRACT; 18:PUPILS
9	19:EXCEPTIONAL; 20:THINGS; 21:LEADERS; 22:WRONG; 23:GLOBE; 24:EDINBURGH; 25:REGULATORS; 26:EXPLORE; 27:COMBAT; 28:WORRY; 29:GOVERN
10	**30:STABLE**; **31:DATA**; 32:PROSPEROUS; 33:DIFFICULT; 34:FRAMEWORK; **35:BELIEVE**; 36:MUCH; **37:GENERATIONS**; **38:GO**; 39:INFORMATION; **40:ONLINE**; **41:IF**; **42:INSTITUTIONS**; **43:LEADERSHIP**; **44:TECHNICAL**; **45:OPPORTUNITY**; **46:TECHNOLOGY**; 47:OLD; 48:SIGNIFICANT; 49:POOR; **50:DIGITAL**; **51:GREAT**; 52:REMAIN; 53:WORLD'S; **54:STRONG**; 55:PARTNERSHIP; 56:THERESA; **57:BETTER**; **58:WANT**; 59:MARKETS; 60:STRONGER; **61:HELP**; 62:INTERESTS; 63:PROSPERITY; 64:NATION; **65:UNION**; 66:GREATER; 67:NOW; **68:WORLD**; **69:DO**; 70:TOGETHER; 71:LEAVE; 72:SCHOOL; **73:CONTINUE**; **74:BEST**; 75:EUROPEAN; 76:RIGHT; 77:SHOULD; 78:ABOUT; 79:USE; 80:AROUND; 81:TAKE; 82:BRITISH; **83:SO**; 84:THOSE; **85:CAN**; 86:MAKE; **87:WE**; 88:THIS; 89:IT; 90:BRITAIN; 91:PEOPLE; 92:IN

after lowering the statistical significance threshold contain all of the CKIs obtained with the higher threshold used in Alternative 1. However, the most important observation is that the lower statistical significance threshold does not simply result in the addition of CKIs below those derived with the stricter one, but changes the ranking, as is shown in Tables 11.6 and 11.7 (additional CKIs indicated in bold). This is because the lower threshold adds some items with larger frequency differences than some of the items returned by the stricter threshold (Gabrielatos 2017).

11.5.3 Keyness-S: identifying similarities

Assuming that about a hundred CKIs for each corpus could be manually examined, the whole set of CKIs (2,315 in CM2017 and 2,656 in LM2017) was grouped into 232 and 266 clusters respectively, using the simple formula presented in 11.4.3 above (2,315/100 and 2,656/100, respectively). Clusters are ranked in ascending order of %DIFF scores – i.e. cluster '1' contains CKIs with the lowest %DIFF score (Tables 11.8 and 11.9). The smaller the frequency difference, the more a CKI can be deemed to index similarity (i.e. topics/issues mentioned in equal frequency in the two manifestos). A first observation is that there is very little overlap between the

TABLE 11.7 Differences: CKIs in LM2017 grouped in 10 clusters

Clusters	*Difference: CKIs LM2017*
1	**1:LABOUR'S**
2	**2:EQUALITY**
3	**3:UNIONS**
4	**4:LGBT**
5	**5:REINSTATE**
6	**6:SCRAP**
7	**7:PRIVATISATION**; **8:BANKS**
8	**9:RENTERS**; **10:WOMEN'S**; **11:FAILURE**; **12:ENFORCE**; **13:EXTENDING**; **14:CENTRES**; 15:NEGOTIATING; 16:PROBATION; 17:ADULT
9	18:PROCUREMENT; 19:INSECURE; 20:WAGES; 21:HIV; 22:TOURISM; 23:PRIORITISE; 24:REINTRODUCE; 25:PROFIT; 26:YOUTH; 27:TRANSITION; 28:REVERSE; 29:RESOLUTION; 30:NEGLECT; 31:ABOLISH; 32:PROFITS; 33:MATERNITY; 34:OPERATIVE; 35:UNLIKE; 36:LIBRARIES; 37:RECOGNITION; 38:LATE; 39:CONTROLS; 40:HANDS; 41:BALANCE; 42:MUSIC; 43:DELIVERS; 44:JUDICIAL; 45:OPTIONS; 46:FARES
10	**47:LABOUR**; **48:CUTS**; **49:OFFICERS**; 50:UN; 51:FAILED; **52:OWNERSHIP**; 53:EQUAL; 54:ECONOMIES; **55:CRISIS**; 56:WAR; 57:FORMS; 58:PEACE; 59:ALLOWANCE; 60:TARGETS; 61:FEES; **62:GUARANTEE**; **63:REGIONAL**; 64:LEGISLATION; 65:TRADING; **66:ARRANGEMENTS**; **67:VITAL**; **68:STAFF**; 69:LED; 70:RANGE; 71:PLANS; **72:RIGHTS**; 73:HOURS; 74:TOWARDS; **75:WOULD**; 76:FULLY; 77:OWNED; **78:WORKERS**; 79:DISABILITIES; **80:STANDARDS**; 81:DISCRIMINATION; 82:FOOD; **83:UNDER; 84:BACK**; 85:CLIMATE; 86:CONSULT; 87:CUT; **88:CONSERVATIVES**; 89:PRIVATE; **90:JOBS**; 91:ENVIRONMENTAL; 92:TRANSPORT; 93:INVEST; 94:WOMEN; 95:EMPLOYMENT; 96:SECTOR; 97:HOMES; 98:END; 99:MANY; **100:ALL**; 101:FUNDING; 102:PROTECT; 103:REVIEW; 104:BEEN; 105:COMMUNITIES; 106:INTO; **107:ON**

CKIs in Tables 11.8 and 11.9. This is because each set contains CKIs with the smallest frequency differences from the perspective of each corpus. Therefore, a study focusing on similarity would need to combine the two lists. Looking at CM2017 (Table 11.8), 92 CKIs show the smallest %DIFF scores, and are grouped in 74 clusters – a very fine-grained classification, as quite a large number of clusters was specified (if this was deemed unsatisfactory, a smaller number could have been specified). The %DIFF scores of the CKIs range from −.040 per cent to 15.59 per cent in Table 11.8, and from 0.68 per cent to 18.53 per cent in Table 11.9. BIC scores are between −6.19 and −10.89 in Table 11.8, and between −7.79 and −10.89 in Table 11.9 – all indicating that H_0 (i.e. no difference) is strongly supported. If more CKIs can be examined, then CKIs in subsequent clusters can be added. If fewer items are needed, items in lower clusters can be removed, or, alternatively, a lower effect-size threshold can be set (e.g. %DIFF=5 per cent).

TABLE 11.8 Similarities: CKIs with lowest %DIFF in CM2017

Cluster	*Similarity: CKIs CM2017*
1	1:COMPANIES
2	2:BUILD
3	3:HOUSING
4	4:FOR
5	5:AND
6	6:BRITAIN'S
7	7:TAKING
8	8:FAIRER
9	9:RECORD
10	10:NORTHERN
11	11:FROM
12	12:SUPPORT
13	13:WORKING
14	14:DEAL
15	15:TERM
16	16:BEFORE
17	17:TACKLE
18	18:PARENTS
19	19:SHARE
20	20:POLICIES
21	21:DISABILITY
22	22:RETAIN
23	23:AGREEMENT
24	24:GOVERNMENTS
25	25:GENDER
26	26:REFORMING
27	27:LAUNCH
28	28:PROMISE
29	29:REQUIRED
30	30:MEETING
31	31:RESPOND
32	32:MEMBERSHIP
33	33:FISCAL
34	34:PAYMENTS
35	35:FORM
36	36:IMPLEMENTATION
37	37:KIND
38	38:FOUND
39	39:INFLATION
40	40:TARIFF
41	41:CASES
42	42:STREET
43	43:VOTE
44	44:THING
45	45:TOP
46	46:USERS

(*Continued*)

TABLE 11.8 (Continued)

Cluster	*Similarity: CKIs CM2017*
47	47:THIRD
48	48:VETERANS
49	49:STARTING
50	50:DOUBLE
51	51:SEA
52	52:SCALE
53	53:DISABLED
54	54:COUNTER
55	55:SPECIFIC; 56:DECENT; 57:LAW; 58:INCREASE
56	59:OUR
57	60:SUSTAINABLE
58	61:GIVE
59	62:BETWEEN; 63:ADDRESS
60	64:TO
61	65:NEEDS
62	66:THE
63	67:FUTURE
64	68:CHANGES; 69:RESPONSIBILITY
65	70:CREATE
66	71:POWERS; 72:MAKING
67	73:BUSINESSES
68	74:COMMITMENT; 75:DEBT; 76:CENTRE; 77:CORPORATE; 78:LOOK
69	79:ENGLAND
70	80:HAVE
71	81:FUND; 82:KEY; 83:PLANNING; 84:STUDENTS; 85:RECEIVE
72	86:PERSONAL; 87:MARKET
73	88:DOMESTIC; 89:PROVIDING; 90:COUNCILS; 91:WHOLE
74	92:ACTION

11.6 Conclusion

Keyness analysis can be used to identify difference (keyness-D), and its extreme case, absence, as well as similarity (keyness-S), the absence of difference. Both types of keyness must be established via an effect-size metric, but keyness-D needs to be supplemented by a statistical significance metric. However, not all available effect-size metrics are appropriate for keyness analysis, particularly as this technique is used in discourse studies. And while statistical significance is a useful additional metric, its utility is limited to indicating the level of reliability of a given frequency difference: high statistical significance does not necessarily imply keyness-D, nor does low statistical significance necessarily imply keyness-S. As *p*-values are sensitive to item frequency and corpus sizes, the same *p*-value may have different importance in different comparisons. A more useful way of establishing the level of confidence in a frequency difference is via the BIC score, which also allows

TABLE 11.9 Similarities: CKIs with lowest %DIFF in LM2017

Cluster	*Similarity: CKIs LM2017*
1	1:WHICH
2	2:WITHIN
3	3:GIVING
4	4:CURRENT
5	5:HOLD
6	6:BANKING
7	7:BROADBAND
8	8:COVERAGE
9	9:DUE
10	10:PAYING
11	11:DIVERSE
12	12:GOVERNANCE
13	13:ROYAL
14	14:DIRECTLY
15	15:SECOND
16	16:EMPLOYED
17	17:SPEND
18	18:RECENT
19	19:NON
20	20:FUEL
21	21:TURN
22	22:HEALTHY
23	23:CAPACITY
24	24:AVERAGE
25	25:PRICES
26	26:CRIME
27	27:SYSTEM
28	28:OF
29	29:RURAL
30	30:SUCH
31	31:LEGISLATE
32	32:IRELAND
33	33:PENSIONERS
34	34:IMMEDIATE
35	35:COMPANY
36	36:DEVOLUTION
37	37:TIMES
38	38:PRINCIPLE
39	39:MEDICAL
40	40:UK
41	41:LOCAL
42	42:YEARS
43	43:POLICE
44	44:US
45	45:ECONOMY

(*Continued*)

TABLE 11.9 (Continued)

Cluster	*Similarity: CKIs LM2017*
46	46:NHS
47	47:GAP
48	48:DEVOLVED
49	49:ARE
50	50:GOVERNMENT
51	51:WILL
52	52:TOO
53	53:LIVING
54	54:PROGRAMME
55	55:CONSIDER
56	56:RUN
57	57:CURRICULUM
58	58:REPEAL
59	59:INTEREST
60	60:APPROPRIATE
61	61:TEN
62	62:WEALTH
63	63:TAKEN
64	64:FOCUS
65	65:A
66	66:ENERGY
67	67:WHEN
68	68:ACT
69	69:PROTECTIONS
70	70:PROPERLY
71	71:PREVENT
72	72:OFFICE
73	73:LEVELS
74	74:AT
75	75:HAS
76	76:STATE
77	77:CURRENTLY
78	78:UK'S
79	79:HIGH
80	80:DEVELOPMENT
81	81:TWO
82	82:LONDON
83	83:FOUR
84	84:FREE
85	85:FIRST
86	86:OUT
87	87:AN
88	88:HEALTH
89	89:OR
90	90:LEAST
91	91:PROMOTE

(*Continued*)

TABLE 11.9 (Continued)

Cluster	*Similarity: CKIs LM2017*
92	92:FACE
93	93:ENVIRONMENT
94	94:ESTABLISH
95	95:BOTH
96	96:FULL
97	97:EXISTING
98	98:ONE
99	99:ROLE
100	100:WITH

for comparisons of statistical significance between studies. It is, therefore, recommended that all corpus tools allow for the combination of effect-size and statistical significance metrics, and include BIC among the statistical significance metrics they make available.

It has also been shown that the reference corpus does not need to be larger than the study corpus. If the corpora are too small for an observed frequency difference to be dependable, this will be reflected in the BIC score. If the comparison does not yield enough dependable frequency differences, then the researchers must either accept that their study requires larger corpora, or select a lower statistical significance threshold. However, in the latter case, they would be running the risk of including unreliable differences in the discussion. Nor does the reference corpus need to be a general one – as was shown in the case study. In fact, the terms *study corpus* and *reference corpus* can be misleading: there is nothing intrinsic in a corpus that renders it a good selection for a 'study' or 'reference' role. The distinction is just one of focus, and the two compared corpora can alternate in the 'study' and 'reference' roles. Any two corpora can be compared, as long as their characteristics (e.g. nature, content, time-period) help address the particular research questions or hypotheses.

Finally, keyness is not a straightforward attribute. However objectively effect-size and statistical significance are calculated, the identification of an item as *key* depends on a multitude of subjective decisions regarding a) thresholds of frequency, effect-size and statistical significance, b) the nature of the linguistic units that are the focus of analysis and c) the attributes of the compared corpora. Simply put, a quantitative analysis does not necessarily entail objectivity. It is, therefore, crucial that these decisions are both principled and explicitly stated, so that the quantitative analysis can be replicated. More precisely, studies need to report and justify any thresholds, the inclusion/exclusion of particular types of CKIs, and the proportion of CKIs selected for analysis. Above all, it is imperative that researchers using keyness analysis (or any other type of automated analysis) are aware of the nature and limitations of the technique and associated metrics, and the settings of the corpus tool they use.

Acknowledgements

Work on this chapter was partly funded by the Edge Hill University Research Investment Fund. I am grateful to Andrew Wilson for clarifications on statistical significance and BIC, and to Guy Aston, Matteo Di Cristofaro, Anna Marchi and Charlotte Taylor for their comments and suggestions.

Notes

1 See Stubbs (2010) for a discussion of different conceptions of the term *keyword* and, indirectly, the notion of keyness.
2 However, a keyness analysis can also be used to establish (differences in) style (Scott 1998: 71).
3 For other statistical approaches to establishing topics, see Gabrielatos, et al. (2012); Jaworska and Nanda (2016); Riddell (2014).
4 As readers may be familiar with different statistical significance tests (which may return different values for the same significance level), and as the values of every null-hypothesis significance test correspond to a *p*-value, the discussion of statistical significance will refer to *p*-values; however, the corresponding scores of the most commonly used significance test, log likelihood (*G2*), will also be indicated. For reviews of different statistical significance tests, see Gries (2006, 2010a, 2010b, 2015); Hoffmann et al. (2008: 149-158); Kilgarriff (1996a, 1996b, 1997, 2005); Kilgarriff and Rose (1998), Paquot and Bestgen (2009); Rayson et al. (2004).
5 See Section 12.3.2 for details on this metric.
6 See Section 12.3.2 for details.
7 Please note that this relates to a version under development (AntConc 3.5.0); previous versions only offer a statistical significance metric.
8 http://ucrel.lancs.ac.uk/people/paul/SigEff.xlsx (latest version, 4 July 2016). Rayson also maintains a webpage offering a statistical significance calculator, as well as information on a large number of metrics: http://ucrel.lancs.ac.uk/llwizard.html.
9 For more examples, and a detailed outline, see Ellis (2010: 4, 7-15).
10 See Rychlý (2008) for a discussion on Dice and LogDice.
11 Of course, such metrics are appropriate for other types of frequency comparisons: for example, in research on learner language, it is often required to compare means of the frequency of particular items or types of errors in the output of learners grouped according to their proficiency levels (e.g. Gablasova et al. 2017).
12 The term is influenced by the use of 'candidate collocates' in Sketch Engine (Kilgarriff et al. 2014).
13 The symbol '≈' indicates that the value is approximate.
14 Please note that *p*-values are rounded up.
15 This *p*-value is derived by rounding down the value of p=0.0000024 in Table 11.3.
16 http://ucrel.lancs.ac.uk/wmatrix/ukmanifestos2017.
17 The corpus sizes reported here differ slightly from those reported in Wmatrix (28,799 for CM and 23,217 for LM; http://ucrel.lancs.ac.uk/wmatrix/ukmanifestos2017), because of a) the additional cleaning carried out here and b) the fact that the corpora loaded in Wmatrix have been processed to identify MWUs as a single item.
18 Note that, in SPSS, 'average group linkage' is referred to as 'between-groups linkage'.
19 In CM2017, BIC=2.28 corresponded to *G2*=13.17; in LM2017, BIC=2.19 corresponded to *G2*=13.08.
20 The usual normalisation per million words is not appropriate, as it does not make sense to normalise to a corpus size larger than the ones examined.
21 In the %DIFF column of all tables in this section, very large numbers follow the notation used in Excel: the number before 'E+' is multiplied by '1' followed by as many zeros are specified after 'E+'. For example, 2.10E+17 indicates '2.1 x 100,000,000,000,000,000', i.e. the number 210,000,000,000,000,000.

References

Aarts, F. G. A. M. 1971. On the distribution of noun-phrase types in English clause structure. *Lingua*, 26, 281–93. Reprinted in G. Sampson & D. McCarthy (eds.) 2004. *Corpus Linguistics: Readings in a Widening Discipline*. London: Continuum. pp. 35–57.

Adamson, G.W. & Bawden, D. 1981. Comparison of hierarchical cluster analysis techniques for automatic classification of chemical structures. *Journal of Chemical Information and Computer Sciences*, 21, 204–209.

Andersen, G. 2016. Using the corpus-driven method to chart discourse-pragmatic change. In H. Pichler (ed.) *Discourse-Pragmatic Variation and Change in English: New Methods and Insights*. Cambridge: Cambridge University Press. pp. 21–40.

Andrew, D. P. S., Pederson, P. M. & McEvoy, C. D. 2011. *Research Methods and Design in Sport Management*. Champaign IL: Human Kinetics.

Anthony, L. 2017. AntConc Version 3.5.0 [Computer Software]. Tokyo, Japan: Waseda University. Available online at: http://www.laurenceanthony.net/software/antconc/releases/AntConc350

Archer, D. 2009. Does frequency really matter? In Archer, D. (ed.) *What's in a Word List?* Farnham/Burlington: Ashgate. pp. 1–16.

Baker, P. 2004. Querying keywords: Questions of difference, frequency and sense in keywords analysis. *Journal of English Linguistics*, 32(4), 346–359.

Baker, P. 2006. *Using Corpora in Discourse Analysis*. London: Continuum.

Baker, P., Gabrielatos C., Khosravinik, M., Krzyzanowski, M., McEnery, T. & Wodak, R. 2008. A useful methodological synergy? Combining critical discourse analysis and corpus linguistics to examine discourses of refugees and asylum seekers in the UK press. *Discourse & Society*, 19(3), 273–305.

Baker, P., Gabrielatos, C. & McEnery A. 2013. *Discourse Analysis and Media Attitudes: The Representation of Islam in the British Press*. Cambridge: Cambridge University Press.

Berber-Sardinha, T. 2000. Comparing corpora with WordSmith tools: How large must the reference corpus be? *Proceedings of the Workshop on Comparing Corpora Vol. 9*, Hong Kong 7 October 2000, 7–13.

Brysbaert, M. & Diependaele, K. 2013. Dealing with zero word frequencies: A review of the existing rules of thumb and a suggestion for an evidence-based choice. *Behavioural Research Methods*, 45, 422–430.

Culpeper, J. 2009. Keyness: Words, parts-of-speech and semantic categories in the character-talk of Shakespeare's *Romeo and Juliet*. *International Journal of Corpus Linguistics*, 14(1), 29–59.

Duguid, A. 2008. Men at work: How those at Number 10 construct their working identity. In G. Garzone & S. Sarangi (eds.) *Discourse, Ideology and Specialized Communication*. Bern: Peter Lang. pp. 453–484.

Duguid, A. 2010. Newspaper discourse informalisation: A diachronic comparison from keywords. *Corpora*, 5(2), 109–138.

Dunning, T. 1993. Accurate methods for the statistics of surprise and coincidence. *Computational Linguistics*, 19(1), 61–74.

Ellis, P. D. 2010. *The Essential Guide to Effect Sizes: Statistical Power, Meta-Analysis, and the Interpretation of Research Results*. Cambridge: Cambridge University Press.

Everitt, B. S. 1993. *Cluster Analysis* (3rd ed.) London: Edward Arnold.

Everitt, B. S. 2002. *The Cambridge Dictionary of Statistics* (2nd ed.) Cambridge: Cambridge University Press.

Forsyth, R. & Lam, P. 2009. Keyness as correlation: Notes on extending the notion of keyness from categorical to ordinal association. In M. Mahlberg, V. González-Díaz & C. Smith (eds.) *Proceedings of the Corpus Linguistics Conference: Corpus Linguistics* 2009. Liverpool: University of Liverpool.

Gablasova, D., Brezina, V. & McEnery, T. 2017. Exploring learner language through corpora: Comparing and interpreting corpus frequency information. *Language Learning*, DOI:10.1111/lang.12226.

Gabrielatos, C. 2007. *If*-conditionals as modal colligations: A corpus-based investigation. In M. Davies, P. Rayson, S. Hunston & P. Danielsson, P. (eds.) *Proceedings of the Corpus Linguistics Conference: Corpus Linguistics* 2007. Birmingham: University of Birmingham.

Gabrielatos, C. 2009. Corpus-based methodology and critical discourse studies: Context, content, computation. Siena English Language and Linguistics Seminars (SELLS), 11 September 2009. Available online at: http://eprints.lancs.ac.uk/28460

Gabrielatos, C. 2010. A corpus-based examination of English *if*-conditionals through the lens of modality: Nature and types. PhD Thesis. Lancaster University.

Gabrielatos, C. 2014. Corpus approaches to discourse studies: The basics. Discourse and Communication Studies Research Team, Örebro University, 12 September 2014. Available online at: https://www.academia.edu/8406977

Gabrielatos, C. 2017. Clusters of keyness: A principled approach to selecting key items. Corpus Linguistics in the South 15, University of Cambridge, 28 October 2017.

Gabrielatos, C. & McEnery, T. 2005. Epistemic modality in MA dissertations. In P.A. Fuertes Olivera (ed.) *Lengua y sociedad: Investigaciones recientes en lingüística aplicada. Lingüística y Filología no. 61*. Valladolid: Universidad de Valladolid. pp. 311–331.

Gabrielatos, C. & Baker, P. 2008. Fleeing, sneaking, flooding: A corpus analysis of discursive constructions of refugees and asylum seekers in the UK Press 1996–2005. *Journal of English Linguistics*, 36(1), 5–38.

Gabrielatos, C. & Marchi, A. 2011. Keyness: Matching metrics to definitions. *Corpus Linguistics in the South* 1, University of Portsmouth, 5 November 2011. Available online at: http://eprints.lancs.ac.uk/51449

Gabrielatos, C. & Marchi, A. 2012. Keywords: Appropriate metrics and practical issues. *CADS International Conference*, Bologna, Italy, 13–15 September 2012. Available online at: https://repository.edgehill.ac.uk/4196

Gan, G., Ma, C. & Wu, J. 2007. *Data Clustering: Theory, Algorithms and Applications*. Philadelphia: ASA-SIAM.

Gerbig, A. 2010. Key words and key phrases in a corpus of travel writing. In M. Bondi & M. Scott (eds.) *Keyness in Texts*. Amsterdam: John Benjamins, pp. 147–168.

Gries, S.Th. 2006. Exploring variability within and between corpora: Some methodological considerations. *Corpora*, 1(2), 109–151.

Gries, S.Th. 2010a. Useful statistics for corpus linguistics. In A. Sánchez & M. Almela (eds.) *A Mosaic of Corpus Linguistics: Selected Approaches*. Frankfurt am Main: Peter Lang. pp. 269–291.

Gries, S.Th. 2010b. Methodological skills in corpus linguistics: A polemic and some pointers towards quantitative methods. In T. Harris & M. Moreno Jaén (eds.) *Corpus Linguistics in Language Teaching*. Frankfurt am Main: Peter Lang. pp. 121–146.

Gries, S.Th. 2015. Quantitative designs and statistical techniques. In D. Biber & R. Reppen (eds.) *The Cambridge Handbook of English Corpus Linguistics*. Cambridge: Cambridge University Press. pp. 50–71.

Hardie, A. 2012. CQPweb – Combining power, flexibility and usability in a corpus analysis tool. *International Journal of Corpus Linguistics*, 17(3), 380–409.

Hardie, A. 2014. Log ratio – An informal introduction. Post on the website of the ESRC Centre for Corpus Approaches to Social Science CASS. Available online at: http://cass.lancs.ac.uk/?p=1133

Hoffmann, S., Evert, S., Smith, N., Lee, D. & Berglund-Prytz, Y. 2008. *Corpus Linguistics with BNCweb – A Practical Guide*. Frankfurt: Peter Lang.

Hofland, K. & Johansson, S. 1982. *Word Frequencies in British and American English*. Bergen: Norwegian Computing Centre for the Humanities/London: Longman.

Jaworska, S. & Nanda, A. 2016. Doing well by talking good? A topic modelling-assisted discourse study of corporate social responsibility. *Applied Linguistics*. Available online at: https://doi.org/10.1093/applin/amw014

Kilgarriff, A. 1996a. Which words are particularly characteristic of a text? A survey of statistical approaches. In L. J. Evett & T. G. Rose (eds.) *Language Engineering for Document Analysis and Recognition (LEDAR)*. AISB96 Workshop proceedings, Brighton, England. Faculty of Engineering and Computing, Nottingham Trent University, UK, pp. 33–40.

Kilgarriff, A. 1996b. Comparing word frequencies across corpora: Why chi-square doesn't work, and an improved LOB-Brown comparison. *ALLC-ACH Conference*, June 1996, Bergen, Norway, pp. 169–172.

Kilgarriff, A. 1997. Using word frequency lists to measure corpus homogeneity and similarity between corpora. *Proceedings 5th ACL Workshop on Very Large Corpora*. Beijing and Hong Kong, pp. 231–245.

Kilgarriff, A. 2001. Comparing corpora. *International Journal of Corpus Linguistics*, 6(1), 97–133.

Kilgarriff, A. 2005. Language is never ever ever random. *Corpus Linguistics and Linguistic Theory*, 1(2), 263–276.

Kilgarriff, A. 2009. Simple maths for keywords. In M. Mahlberg, V. González-Díaz & C. Smith (eds.) *Proceedings of the Corpus Linguistics Conference, CL2009*. Liverpool: University of Liverpool. Available online at: http://ucrel.lancs.ac.uk/publications/CL2009/171_FullPaper.doc

Kilgarriff, A. & Rose, T. 1998. Measures for corpus similarity and homogeneity. In *Proceedings of the 3rd Conference on Empirical Methods in Natural Language Processing*, Granada, Spain, pp. 46–52.

Kilgarriff, A., Baisa, V., Bušta, J., Jakubíček, M., Kovář, V., Michelfeit, J., Rychlý, P. & Suchomel, V. 2014. The Sketch Engine: Ten years on. *Lexicography*, 1(1), 7–36.

Krogvig, I. & Johansson, S. 1985. *Shall, will, should*, and *would* in British and American English. *ICAME News*, 5, 32–56.

Leech, G. & Fallon, R. 1992. Computer corpora – What do they tell us about culture? *ICAME Journal*, 16, 29–50.

van Leeuwen, T. 1996. The representation of social actors. In C. R. Caldas-Coulthard & M. Coulthard (eds.) *Texts and Practices: Readings in Critical Discourse Analysis*. London: Routledge. pp. 32–71.

McEnery, A. M. 2006. *Swearing in English: Bad Language, Purity and Power from 1586 to the Present*. London: Routledge.

Miki, N. 2011. Key colligation analysis: Discovering stylistic differences in significant lexico-grammatical units. *Proceedings of the Corpus Linguistics 2011 Conference*, ICC Birmingham, 20–22 July 2011, pp. 1–23. Available online at: http://www.birmingham.ac.uk/documents/college-artslaw/corpus/conference-archives/2011/Paper-208.pdf

Mujis, D. 2010. *Doing Quantitative Research in Education with SPSS* (2nd ed.) London: Sage.

Paquot, M. & Bestgen, Y. 2009. Distinctive words in academic writing: a comparison of three statistical tests for keyword extraction. In A. Jucker, D. Schreier & M. Hundt (eds.) *Corpora: Pragmatics and Discourse. Papers from the 29th International Conference on English Language Research on Computerized Corpora ICAME 29*. Amsterdam: Rodopi, pp. 247–269.

Partington, A. 2009. Evaluating evaluation and some concluding thoughts on CADS. In J. Morley & P. Bayley (eds.) *Corpus-Assisted Discourse Studies on the Iraq Conflict: Wording the War*. London: Routledge. pp. 261–303.

Partington, A. 2014. Mind the gaps: The role of corpus linguistics in researching absences. *International Journal of Corpus Linguistics*, 19(1), 118–146.

Partington, A., Duguid, A. & Taylor, C. 2013. *Patterns and Meanings in Discourse: Theory and Practice in Corpus-Assisted Discourse Studies*. Amsterdam: John Benjamins.

Phillips, M. 1989. *Lexical Structure of Text.* Discourse Analysis Monograph no. 12. English Language Research, University of Birmingham.

Pojanapunya, P. & Watson Todd, R. 2016. Log-likelihood and odds ratio: Keyness statistics for different purposes of keyword analysis. *Corpus Linguistics and Linguistic Theory*, DOI:10.1515/cllt-2015-0030.

Raftery, A. E. 1999. Bayes Factors and BIC: Comment on 'A critique of the Bayesian information criterion for model selection'. *Sociological Methods & Research*, 27(3), 411–427.

Rayson, P. 2003. Matrix: A statistical method and software tool for linguistic analysis through corpus comparison. PhD thesis, Lancaster University.

Rayson, P. 2008. From key words to key semantic domains. *International Journal of Corpus Linguistics*, 13(4), 519–549.

Rayson, P. 2009. Wmatrix: A web-based corpus processing environment, Computing Department, Lancaster University. Available online at: http://ucrel.lancs.ac.uk/wmatrix

Rayson P., Berridge D. & Francis B. 2004. Extending the Cochran rule for the comparison of word frequencies between corpora. In G. Purnelle, C. Fairon & A. Dister (eds.) *Le poids des mots: Proceedings of the 7th International Conference on Statistical Analysis of Textual Data JADT 2004., Vol. 2.* Louvain-la-Neuve, Belgium: Presses universitaires de Louvain. pp. 926–936.

Riddell, A. 2014. How to read 22,198 journal articles: studying the history of German Studies with topic models. In Erlin, M. & Tatlock, L. (eds.) *Distant Readings: Topologies of German Culture in the Long Nineteenth Century*. New York: Camden House. pp. 91–114.

Romesburg, H. C. 1984. *Cluster Analysis for Researchers*. Belmont, CA: Wadsworth.

Rosenfeld, B. & Penrod, S. D. 2011. *Research Methods in Forensic Psychology*. New York: Wiley.

Rychlý, P. 2008. A lexicographer-friendly association score. In P. Sojka & A. Horák (eds.) *Proceedings of Recent Advances in Slavonic Natural Language Processing, RASLAN 2008*, Masaryk University, Brno 2008. pp. 6–9.

Scott, M. 1996. *WordSmith Tools Manual*. Oxford: Oxford University Press.

Scott, M. 1997. PC analysis of key words – and key key words. *System*, 25(2), 233–245.

Scott, M. 1998. *WordSmith Tools manual, Version 3.0.* Oxford: Oxford University Press.

Scott, M. 2001. Mapping key words to *problem* and *solution*. In M. Scott & G. Thompson (eds.) *Patterns of Text: in Honour of Michael Hoey*. Amsterdam: John Benjamins. pp. 109–128.

Scott, M. 2016. *WordSmith Tools version* 7. Stroud: Lexical Analysis Software.

Sirking, R.M. 2006. *Statistics for social sciences* (3rd ed.) London: Sage.

Sneath, P.H.A & Sokal, R.R. 1973. *Numerical taxonomy.* San Francisco, CA: Freeman.

Stubbs, M. 2010. Three concepts of keywords. In M. Bondi & M. Scott (eds.) *Keyness in Texts: Corpus Linguistic Investigations*. Amsterdam: John Benjamins. pp. 21–42.

Taylor, C. 2013. Searching for similarity using corpus-assisted discourse studies. *Corpora*, 8(1), 81–113.

Thompson, B. 1998. Statistical significance and effect size reporting: Portrait of a possible future. *Research in the Schools*, 5(2), 33–38.

Utka, A. 2004. Analysis of George Orwell's novel 1984 by statistical methods of corpus linguistics. *Sankirta: A Yearly Internet Journal of Lithuanian Corpus Linguistics*. Available online at: http://donelaitis.vdu.lt/publikacijos/adrtmain.htm

Wilson, A. 2013. Embracing Bayes factors for key item analysis in corpus linguistics. In M. Bieswanger & A. Koll-Stobbe (eds.) *New Approaches to the Study of Linguistic Variability. Language Competence and Language Awareness in Europe*, Vol. 4. Frankfurt: Peter Lang. pp. 3–11.

Ziliak, S.T. & McCloskey, D.N. 2008. *The Cult of Statistical Significance: How the Standard Error Costs Us Jobs, Justice, and Lives*. Ann Arbor, MI: University of Michigan Press.

12

STATISTICAL CHOICES IN CORPUS-BASED DISCOURSE ANALYSIS

Vaclav Brezina

12.1 Introduction

This chapter focuses on the use of statistical techniques in corpus-based discourse analysis. Making informed statistical choices is an essential skill for a researcher, ensuring *reliability* (i.e. how consistently and systematically the study analyses data) and *validity* of a quantitative study (i.e. how closely the study reflects linguistic and social reality). Although the use of statistical procedures might give an impression of impartiality and mathematical rigour of the studies using these procedures, the mere inclusion of numbers, *p*-values and even complex statistical models does not automatically guarantee that the results are meaningful. The risk is obvious: while statistics can help reveal important patterns in the data, it can also, if used inappropriately, hide bias, partiality and analytical sloppiness. For example, while we might be rightly suspicious about an analytical statement based on anecdotal evidence and hearsay, we might not exercise the same critical judgement if the analysis claims statistical significance derived from a large data set; however, the data set can be biased, the statistical test used can be inappropriate and the practical effect observed in the data can be minimal. For discourse analysis to live up to the requirements of a mature scientific discipline, statistical literacy thus should be at the forefront of our efforts.

In this chapter, I outline the connection between statistics and discourse analysis (Section 12.2) before proposing a simple three-step procedure for more rigorous discourse analysis (Section 12.3); this procedure is designed to guide researchers through the analytical process and focus their attention on important features of the scientific protocol. Because coding and categorisation of examples is an important part of discourse analysis, the chapter (Section 12.4) also pays attention to statistical techniques of calculating inter-rater agreement, which make the categorisation process more reliable. The concept of meaning relations (associations and cross-associations) in discourse is then outlined (Section 12.5) and the technique of collocation and collocation networks is introduced. Finally (Section 12.6), inferential statistical techniques such as statistical tests (t-test, Mann-Whitney U test, ANOVA and Kruskal-Wallis test) and confidence intervals are explained and their application in the analysis of discourse is demonstrated.

12.2 Background: statistics meets discourse analysis

Statistical analysis of discourse involves an inherent paradox. While discourse is often fluid, ambiguous and fuzzy, statistics expects rigour, precision and clearly defined categories. So how do we reconcile this tension in statistical analysis of discourse? First, we need to have a good understanding of the nature of the 'beast'. Different definitions of discourse are available (see Baker 2006: 3-5; Partington et al. 2013: 10ff). For the purposes of this chapter, I adopt Blommaert's (2005: 3) broad definition of discourse as 'all forms of meaningful semiotic human activity seen in connection with social, cultural, and historical patterns and developments of use'. From this perspective, discourse is a complex socio-cultural phenomenon which includes different ways of communicating meaning. An appropriate statistical analysis of discourse therefore needs to be oriented towards *meanings* of words, sentences, paragraphs, texts etc. rather than mere formal properties of discourse.

Let us briefly consider the purpose of statistical analysis. To start with a standard definition, '[s]tatistics is the science of collecting and interpreting data' (Diggle & Chetwynd 2011: vii). Statistics therefore can help us throughout the whole analytical process from the research design to final report writing. Statistics is a scientific discipline, which means that it presupposes that questions in our field of interest, which in this case is discourse, are answered empirically by collecting data and evaluating the evidence. In statistics, the evidence is quantified to allow precise evaluation and comparison. For example, we may observe that academic writing when compared with other genres/registers is marked by frequent occurrence of verbs in the passive voice, which focuses the attention of the reader on events and processes discussed in the text rather than on the actors (researchers, investigators etc.). When we ask the question of how large exactly this difference is, we enter the realm of statistical analysis. The answer can be provided in the form of a table, a graph or a result of a statistical test. Table 12.1 shows a comparison of four genres/registers in a one-million-word corpus of written British English, listing the mean frequencies and standard deviations (*SD*) of the passive construction. The mean

TABLE 12.1 Passives in BE06

Genres/registers	*Mean relative frequency of passives per 1,000 (SD)*
Press	11.53 (4.75)
General prose (non-fiction)	10.70 (4.34)
Learned (academic)	16.89 (6.24)
Fiction	5.83 (2.66)

(*M*) is a value representing the arithmetic average – all numbers added together and divided by the number of cases; standard deviation provides information about the variation in the data – in this case, *SD* describes the extent to which frequencies of passives vary across different texts within each genre/register category (discussed further in Section 12.2).

To explore the trends in the data in greater depth, Figure 12.1 displays the information from Table 12.1 in a form of a boxplot. The boxplot shows the distribution of the linguistic feature (in this case passive constructions) in individual texts (marked by circles in the graph) within the genre/register groups. The box itself delineates the middle 50 per cent of the values in the distribution, while the 'whiskers' extending from the box show the minimum and the maximum values with the exception of outliers (—○—), i.e. very distant values from the rest of the group. The long thick horizontal line (——) shows the middle value (median) and the short horizontal line (▬) represents the mean. This form of a boxplot is an informationally rich presentation of data distribution and the group tendency. Finally, based on a statistical test such as the ANOVA (see Section 12.5) we can conclude that there is a statistically significant difference between the genre/register groups in the use of the passives: $F(3, 496) = 103.4$; $p < .001$. All these forms of statistical analysis (tables, graphs and statistical tests) are explored further in this chapter.

Before moving to the discussion of specific statistical procedures, let us note one obvious risk that statistical analysis of discourse involves. Quantitative analysis of language may lead to reductionism, reducing semiotically rich data to surface forms easily analysable by automatic algorithms. This is especially apparent in some of the 'big data' approaches to language, which have recently emerged with the availability of large data sets ('big data'), which due to their sheer size cannot be explored manually. Prime examples of this tendency of reductionism are two methodological approaches used in quantitative discourse analysis: culturomics and topic modelling.

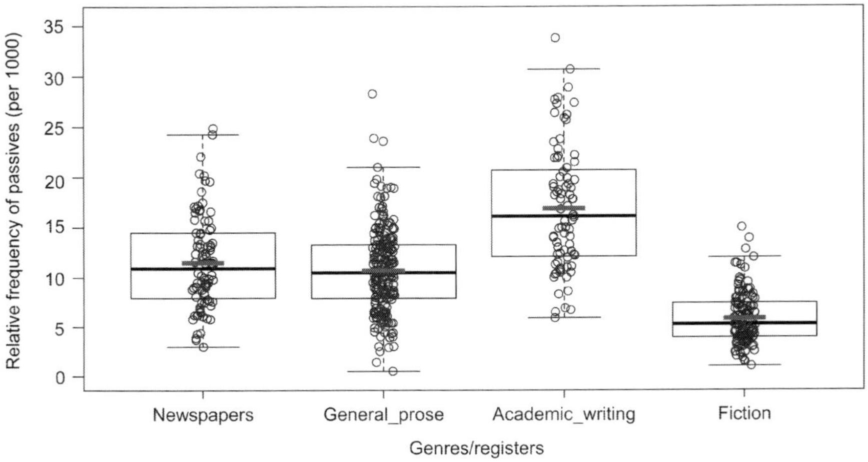

FIGURE 12.1 Passives in BE06.

Culturomics is a new discipline that bases the analyses on large corpora such as the corpus of Google n-grams (Michel et al. 2011). However, as the critics have pointed out (e.g. Pechenick et al. 2015; McEnery & Baker 2017: Section 1.3) culturomics primarily looks at the development of linguistic forms over time thus reducing the linguistic analysis to mere form counting. For example, it is very easy to produce a graph of an apparent linguistic/social change in the use of the word *immigrants* (see Figure 12.2). We can see that over the period of 1800–2000 the form *immigrants* becomes increasingly more frequent in the discourse represented in the Google n-gram corpus. However, it is much more problematic to interpret this evidence in the absence of the actual examples of use (concordance lines) and in the absence of the information about the changing representativeness of the corpus, that is, information about what type of documents (books) are included in each period. This type of analysis is also not sensitive to the existence and change of competing naming strategies (e.g. *migrants, settlers, pilgrims* etc.) that would refer to the group of people we currently label as *immigrants;* so in the diachronic perspective, although we are comparing the same form, we might not be comparing the same meaning.

Similarly, topic modelling (e.g. Jacobi et al. 2016) provides a technique that automatically (statistically) identifies groups of related words ('topics') in the data based on the co-occurrence of words in texts. The output of the analysis is a set of 'topics', which are intended to 'objectively' summarise the corpus. However, this is done at the expense of discarding structural information about text and discourse that includes the syntactic and discourse position and ordering of words in texts thus violating a basic principle of language: in discourse, words are not merely thrown together but are carefully ordered to create meaningful connections that in turn lead to a particular development of the text/discourse. The value of the technique for genuine discourse analysis is thus very limited because the 'topics' are either too general or too incoherent to be useful.

Statistical analysis of discourse involves multiple choices at various levels. As demonstrated above, at the most general level of the 'philosophy' of analysis we need to choose an approach that best corresponds with the theoretical (linguistic) understanding of text and discourse (meaningful semiotic activity). In this chapter, I argue that the role of statistical analysis of discourse is to provide a lens through

FIGURE 12.2 Development of the form 'immigrants' 1800-2000.

which the analyst can interpret, evaluate and contextualise the patterns observed in the data. This lens needs to be flexible enough to enable us to zoom out and see the larger picture as well as to zoom in on specific cases. This means that the statistical procedure does not replace the analyst but is used to focus their attention to important phenomena in discourse such as typical examples of language use, repeated associations and points of semantic change. In addition, when dealing with the analysis of discourse, the scope of the relevant linguistic features needs also to be carefully considered. While at a lower level of language analysis such as grammar we can control the linguistic frame and the forms that express the relevant (grammatical) meaning, discourse analysis encompasses a much broader range of phenomena and involves a higher level of abstraction. For example, when dealing with a grammatical question of the linguistic choice between the simple past tense in English and the present perfect in cases such as 'Did you eat?' and 'Have you eaten?' we can search for these two grammatical structures and identify contexts in which they compete. This is far from trivial, but we are dealing with a lower level of abstraction than in discourse analysis. On the other hand, if we are interested in a discourse feature such as different narrative strategies of past events we need to consider an interplay of different linguistic means including the choice of verbs and their tenses, expressions of speaker's stance, temporal expressions, connectors etc. and how these all contribute to the complex socio-linguistic act of narration. This chapter reviews statistical choices that need to be made at various levels addressing four questions in quantitative discourse analysis:

- Where to start?
- How to categorise data?
- How to capture meaning relations?
- How to compare different discourses?

Finally, one practical note needs to be made. While this chapter focuses on the discussion of the statistical choices in discourse analysis from the conceptual perspective, all statistical procedures introduced in this chapter can be easily calculated using *Lancaster Stats Tools online* (Brezina 2018). These are freely available at http://corpora.lancs.ac.uk/stats.

12.3 Where to start? Research design and planning

Each analysis starts with the research design. This stage involves a number of important choices that have an implication for the validity of the findings. We have to decide on the focus of the research, the data that will be used to answer the research question(s) as well as on the appropriate statistical techniques. Because discourse analysis is often an exploratory approach, this is not a linear process but can be repeated multiple times to reach the required level of detail (granularity) of the analysis. Three key components of this process are: i) construct definition, ii) statistical operationalisation and iii) empirical analysis.

12.3.1 Construct definition

The construct definition involves a clear theoretically grounded specification of what the research wants to investigate. For example, if we want to investigate attitudes in newspaper discourse towards a group of people such as immigrants we need to clearly define what we mean by attitudes – what sort of entity attitudes are. We thus have to decide, with the help of the literature, whether attitudes are psychological entities which are reflected in the discourse or whether we define attitudes as something that is created (constructed) directly in the discourse (e.g. Baker at al. 2013; Oskamp & Schultz 2005; Fowler 1991). The definition of the construct has direct implications for 'measuring' the construct in specific linguistic terms, that is for the identification of linguistic features (e.g. evaluative adjectives, stance adverbs etc.) that will be searched in the data. Based on our construct definition we formulate a hypothesis or a research question that guides the research.

12.3.2 Statistical operationalisation

The next step, statistical operationalisation, brings in a decision about the data and statistical techniques to be used to test the hypothesis or answer the research question. First, let's consider the data. The data needs to be carefully examined in terms of its quality and quantity. When using large amounts of discourse data – language corpora – we need to critically evaluate the choice of the corpus and its appropriateness for our study. The corpus needs to directly represent the type of discourse or discourses that we are interested in. In our newspaper discourse example, we have to decide what sort of newspapers should be included in the corpus, carefully considering the timespan, region, newspaper type (broadsheet vs. tabloid), medium

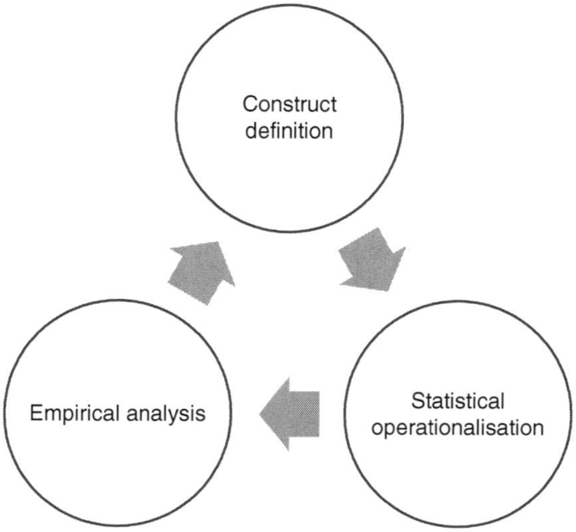

FIGURE 12.3 Research design: key steps.

(online vs. printed) etc. In terms of the quantity, we need to collect enough data for our quantitative analysis to be robust. There is actually no one size of a corpus that could be recommended for quantitative discourse analysis. Much depends on the granularity of the research in terms of the number of variables involved and frequency of linguistic features investigated. For example, in the case of investigating newspaper attitudes towards immigrants we first need to make sure that there are enough examples of the terms *immigrant/immigrants* being used in the corpus for categorising them (see Section 12.3), identifying the associations (collocations) of these terms (see Section 12.4) or comparing different types of newspapers (e.g. broadsheets and tabloids) and their discourses (see Section 12.5). The more detailed categories, the more nuanced collocations and the wider range of types of discourses we intend to investigate, the larger the corpus needs to be. In very practical terms, if our corpus includes 100 examples of the terms *immigrant/immigrants* coming from a variety of sources (texts), we will be able to observe how these terms are used, which words they collocate with and whether there is a broad pattern of these terms occurring in a particular type of texts. If, on the other hand, we are interested in more detailed differences we might need 1,000 or 10,000 examples. Overall, in discourse analysis, corpora used in the studies can be as small as several thousand running words, others as large as several billion running words.

The second aspect of statistical operationalisation involves the choice of statistical techniques. Different statistical procedures can be used depending on the research question and the 'shape' of the data. For example, a traditional approach to discourse data (e.g. Rayson et al. 1997; Abid et al. 2017) would involve general comparisons of large corpora (representing different types of language/discourse) using the chi-squared test or the log-likelihood test; these relatively simple tests are used to compare categorical variables (variables such as gender with two categories 'male' and 'female') by contrasting observed frequencies in the data with frequencies expected by change alone. In this research design, i.e. 'whole corpus' design (cf. Brezina 2018), corpora are analysed as whole units (cases). The problem with this approach is the lack of attention to variation inside corpora: different speakers/texts using linguistic features differently (Brezina & Meyerhoff 2014; Lijffijt 2016, Egbert & Schnur, this volume). In addition, one of the crucial assumptions of the chi-squared test and the log likelihood test – independence of observations – is violated in this 'whole corpus' approach (Kilgarriff 2005). The test assumes that each instance of a linguistic variable (e.g. an evaluative adjective) was produced independently of the other instances of the variable. However, in discourse where individual words are connected with one another to express complex meaning this assumption does not hold. The test would be appropriate, for instance, for analysing answers to a survey. The answers provided by the respondents, unlike uses of language in corpora, are independent. In discourse analysis, instead of using the whole corpus research design, we can trace the frequencies of variables in individual texts/speakers (individual speaker/text research design). This research design (discussed in Section 12.5) is much more appropriate because data in discourse analysis (corpora) are usually sampled at the level of speakers/text, which guarantees their independence as cases in statistical analysis.

More generally, the assumption of independence of observations (which makes the use of the chi-squared test and the log-likelihood test in discourse analysis problematic) is one of the most important considerations in quantitative analysis. This involves not only the choice of an appropriate research design (see above) but also decisions about what gets included in the data. The idea is very simple: we want to count the same thing only once, otherwise we might be distorting or fabricating evidence. But what exactly constitutes the 'same thing'? In our example of the analysis of newspaper discourse, we need to collect articles of interest published in a particular period. However, how do we deal with the practice of recycling and repurposing of newspaper material? Figure 12.4 compares two texts (versions of the same story) published in two different Australian newspapers. The longer version (right) appears as a modified and extended version of the shorter text (left). Overall, the article appeared in three different versions in six different newspapers: *The Age* (438 words), *The Age online* (681 words), *Australian Financial Review* (656 words), *Brisbane Times* (681 words), *The Sydney Morning Herald* (681 words) and *WA Today* (681 words). These newspaper articles represent related types of linguistic output (similar versions of the text) intended for different types of audience. The basic tension in our analysis is whether we take the author/source perspective, in which case we should be counting the text only once, or whether we consider the audience perspective, in which case we sample all versions of the text and include them in our corpus. The decision, however, is not a statistical one; statistics can only inform us about the assumption we are making when using a particular quantitative procedure. Instead, the decision needs to be motivated by theoretical considerations about the construct – what we want to measure. When dealing with this or a similar type of situation, we thus need to make a principled decision on what to include/count based on the construct definition. This decision then needs to be clearly stated and justified in the research report.

12.3.1 Empirical analysis

Finally, the last step in the analytical process is empirical analysis. Scientific questions are empirical questions answered by reference to what the data has to say about the topic of our interest. Different aspects of this empirical analysis are described in the following sections of this chapter. At the most basic level, we need to provide a solid description of the data as demonstrated in Table 12.1 and Figure 12.1; the table and the graph represent different forms of data description. This type of description is the first step in the analysis providing an overview of the key tendencies in the data. Table 12.1 lists means and standard deviations for individual genres and registers. These are summary statistics of the central tendency in the data (means) and of the distribution of individual values relative to the mean (standard deviations). The mean and the standard deviation are calculated as follows:

$$\text{mean} = \frac{\text{sum of all values}}{\text{number of cases}} \qquad (1)$$

Australians are some of the hardest customers in the world to convince that Malaysia Airlines has left its safety problems in the past, Malaysia Airlines' new chief executive concedes.

In his first public outing since part of a wing believed to be from Flight MH370 was found on a remote island in the Indian Ocean last Wednesday, Christoph Mueller said Australia, Britain and China were three markets in which there had been "significant repercussions" for the airline from the disappearance of the Boeing 777 in March last year and the shooting down of another Malaysia Airlines flight, MH17 over Ukraine, four months later.

"In Australia it's easy to explain with all good *intentions*, but every mentioning of the search for 370 correlates with our demand," he said. "Our demand does not correlate with price any *longer*, but mentioning on social media - it's very adverse. It is very *regrettable*, but it's a fact."

It highlights the challenge ahead for Mr *Mueller* - a German who earned the nickname "The Terminator" during his time at Ireland's flag carrier Aer *Lingus* - in reshaping what he has described as a "technically bankrupt" airline.

Since taking the reins in May, he has ditched routes, begun cutting 6000 jobs from its 20,000-strong workforce and next month is set to unveil a new brand.

Mr Mueller would not be drawn on the discovery on Reunion Island in the Indian Ocean last week of a flaperon believed to be from MH370, saying he would not "participate in any speculation" about the search for the plane carrying 239 passengers and crew, including six Australians.

"There are investigators currently busy in all different parts of the world - I leave it to them to draw conclusions," he said in Sydney on Monday.

Malaysian authorities have confirmed the flaperon was from a Boeing 777. The wreckage was under forensic examination in Toulouse in southern France to determine whether it was from MH370.

Locals on Reunion Island had since found various other debris including a *suitcase*, but officials have been much more sceptical about whether they were from MH370.

Mr Mueller said MH370 and MH17 had triggered a "very looking forward debate" between the aviation industry and governments about gaps in the system such as aircraft tracking.

"Everyone has received their wake-up call," he said.

Malaysia Airlines will stop flying between Brisbane and Kuala Lumpur from Sunday, and reduce flights to Sydney and Melbourne this month from three times a day to two. It will also trim services to Adelaide and Perth. It is a major change from just before the loss of MH370 and MH17 when the airline boosted flights to Australia.

Australians are some of the hardest customers in the world to convince that Malaysia Airlines has left its safety problems in the past, Malaysia Airlines' new chief executive concedes.

In his first public outing since part of a wing believed to be from Flight MH370 was found on a remote island in the Indian Ocean last Wednesday, Christoph Mueller said Australia, Britain and China were three markets in which there had been "significant repercussions" for the airline from the disappearance of the Boeing 777 in March last year and the shooting down of another Malaysia Airlines flight, MH17 over Ukraine, four months later.

"In Australia it's easy to explain with all good *intentions* but every mentioning of the search for 370 correlates with our demand," he told Fairfax Media. "Our demand does not correlate with price any *longer* but mentioning on social media - it's very adverse. It is very *regrettable* but it's a fact."

It highlights the challenge ahead for Mr *Mueller*, a German who earned the nickname "The Terminator" during his time at Ireland's flag carrier Aer *Lingus*, in reshaping what he has described as a "technically bankrupt" airline.

Since taking the reins in May, he has ditched routes, begun cutting 6000 jobs from its 20,000-strong workforce and next month is set to unveil a new brand.

Mr Mueller would not be drawn on the discovery on Reunion Island in the Indian Ocean last week of a flaperon believed to be from MH370, saying he would not "participate in any speculation" about the search for the plane carrying 239 passengers and crew, including six Australians.

"There are investigators currently busy in all different parts of the world - I leave it to them to draw conclusions," he said in Sydney on Monday.

Malaysian authorities have confirmed the flaperon was from a Boeing 777. The wreckage was under forensic examination in Toulouse in southern France to determine whether it was from MH370.

Other debris

Locals on Reunion Island had since found various other debris including a *suit case*, but officials have been much more sceptical about whether they were from MH370.

Mr Mueller said MH370 and MH17 had triggered a "very looking forward debate" between the aviation industry and governments about gaps in the system such as aircraft tracking.

"Everyone has received their wake-up call," he said.

Malaysia Airlines will stop flying between Brisbane and Kuala Lumpur from Sunday, and reduce flights to Sydney and Melbourne this month from three times a day to two. It will also trim services to Adelaide and Perth. It is a major change from just before the *the* loss of MH370 and MH17 when the airline boosted flights to Australia by a third.

Mr Mueller said the airline's brand recognition, particularly in the Australian market, had "taken a severe hit".

"It's one of the reasons why we had to cut back our capacity in Australia," he said.

While declining to give specifics, Mr Mueller said the launch of a new company on September 1 was more than about simply "repainting" the airline, but involved installing a new management team, shareholding structure, revamping its product and setting up a new air-operator's licence.

More than a logo

"Brand is not just the name and the logo but is more what your airline stands for. We will embark on the idea that we provide value for money for our travellers," he said.

He admitted it was "a very very difficult" job but insisted he could turn around the financial fortunes of an airline that had lost money every year since 2010.

FIGURE 12.4 Recycling material in newspapers.

$$\text{standard deviation} = \sqrt{\frac{\text{sum of squared distances from the mean}}{\text{number of cases} - 1}} \quad (2)$$

For example, taking the first five values (relative frequencies of passives per 1,000) for newspaper texts from BE06 – 12.4, 13.8, 19.7, 24.9, 16.6 – we can calculate the mean as:

$$\text{mean} = \frac{12.4 + 13.8 + 19.7 + 24.9 + 16.6}{5} = 17.48 \quad (3)$$

The standard deviation (*SD*) will be calculated as:

$$SD = \sqrt{\frac{(12.4-17.48)^2+(13.8-17.48)^2+(19.7-17.48)^2+(24.9-17.48)^2+(16.6-17.48)^2}{5-1}} = 5.0 \quad (4)$$

The interpretation of the standard deviation is as follows: the smaller the *SD* is relative to the mean, the more homogeneous the group is. We can see that in this case, the mean is a fairly good representation of the central tendency in the group (genre/register) because the standard deviation is small relative to the mean. N.B. When reporting summary statistics, both the mean and the *SD* need to be included. If, on the other hand, *SD* is (almost) as large as the mean or larger, the mean is not a good representation of the group tendency because of the large amount of variation between texts; in this case, we can consider reporting the median (the middle value) instead (see Section 12.2).

In sum, when planning our study, we always need to think about the principled questions related to the research design. The research design is used to guide the study and make sure that the analytical techniques we choose are suitable for answering our research questions or testing our hypotheses.

12.4 How to categorise data? Inter-rater agreement

Categorising examples is one of the basic analytical strategies in discourse analysis. Categories, which in the analytical process need to be specified under construct definition (see Section 12.2), are typically fuzzy and open to interpretation (Lakoff 1987). Consider the examples in Table 12.2 below. These represent a random sample of concordance lines including the word *immigrants* from British newspaper discourse.

If we want to categorise broad attitudes (positive vs. negative) expressed towards immigrants in the British press we have to define what constitutes a positive and a negative attitude. We might be guided by semantic prosody (words with positive or negative connotations occurring around the word *immigrants,* see Partington 2004; Bednarek 2008) and other contextual features. For example, *immigrants* are often preceded by the adjective *illegal* (lines 1, 2, 6, 7, 8 and 10), which suggests a possibly negative framing of these contexts. However, is this a truly negative attitude expressed by the newspapers towards *immigrants* or simply a reflection of more general news values: newspapers focusing on negative aspects, problems and crises

TABLE 12.2 'Immigrants' in British newspaper discourse (BE06 corpus)

1	to give immigration officers the power to arrest illegal	immigrants,	people-traffickers and drug-smugglers are welcome. Unfortunately these plans are
2	Labour's failure to provide enough cells for the illegal	immigrants	and foreign criminals waiting to be deported from the
3	closing the stable door after the horse has bolted.	Immigrants	have come in though the back door and are
4	remains that France is a monocultural society and that	immigrants	(like his own family) are welcomed provided they see
5	the UK now has a mum from abroad and	immigrants	are putting the biggest strain on public services by
6	at Harmondsworth. He ordered a clearout of 150 illegal	immigrants	all awaiting removal from the UK from other detention
7	value for money.' The great migrant riot farce Illegal	immigrants	wreck their detention centre … They have to be moved
8	moved but prisons are full So 150 OTHER illegal	immigrants	will be freed from their centres to make room
9	Bishops? Could it be that their plea to welcome	immigrants	has resulted in their being silent lest they, too,
10	arrest. Blair's plan is to get them seizing illegal	immigrants,	drug smugglers and people traffickers. He also wants them

(Bednarek & Caple 2012)? So ultimately what is a truly negative attitude towards immigrants? Conversely, is it possible to clearly define contexts in which immigrants are construed in a positive light?

So, although the categorisation task might initially seem straightforward, in practice this rarely is the case. Most categories in discourse analysis can be considered a judgement variable, that is a variable that relies on the analyst's judgement and interpretation of the linguistic situation. When judgement variables are involved, it is important to double-code the data and compute an inter-rater agreement statistic in order to estimate how reliable the categorisation (coding) is. Ideally, all examples would be double-coded; however, in large datasets double-coding is usually done with a random sample of the data such as 20 per cent of all examples, which are categorised using the same scheme by two independent analysts. Different inter-rater agreement statistics are available (Brezina 2018: Ch 3). The most reliable one for categories in discourse analysis is Gwet's AC_1 (Gwet 2014). The idea behind inter-speaker agreement statistics is simple: we look at the general overlap between the two raters and subtract a portion of the agreement that could have been reached by chance alone. Gwet's AC_1 is calculated as follows:

$$AC_1 = \frac{\text{raw agreement} - \text{agreement by chance}}{1 - \text{agreement by chance}} \quad (5)$$

where agreement by chance is calculated as: 2 × chance of being categorised as X × chance of not being categorised as X.

Imagine that when categorising the attitudes (positive vs. negative) in examples in Table 12.2, two raters agreed in eight and disagreed in two cases. This is shown in Table 12.3. The raw agreement is 0.8 (8/10).

AC_1 in this situation would be calculated as follows:

$$AC_1 = \frac{0.8 - 0.32}{1 - 0.32} = 0.71 \qquad (6)$$

where agreement by chance was derived as follows:

$$\text{agreement by chance} = 2 \times \frac{4}{2 \times 10} \times \left(1 - \frac{4}{2 \times 10}\right) = 0.32$$

Note: In 4/(2 × 10), 4 is the number of positive ratings by both raters (2+2) and 2 × 10 is the number of ratings by both raters. 1 – 4/(2 × 10) is the complementary probability i.e. the probability of not being categorised as positive by chance.

The value of AC_1 in this case is relatively high (0.71). This shows a fair agreement between raters. Generally, AC_1 ranges from -1 (absolute disagreement) to 0 (the baseline for random agreement) to 1 (which shows absolute/perfect agreement). Krippendorff's (2012[1980]) recommends 0.67 and 0.8 as the cut-off points for agreement and very good agreement respectively.

In sum, categorisation of examples is one of the basic techniques of discourse analysis. Because it typically involves judgements by analysts, its robustness needs to be checked by calculating inter-rater agreement. For more options of inter-rater agreement statistics see Brezina 2018: Section 3.5. If the inter-rater agreement statistics shows fair or high agreement, we can carry on with the analysis. In the reverse case, the coding scheme needs to be modified and the categorisation of the data re-done until it reaches an acceptable level of agreement, which ensures greater reliability of the study as a whole. A practical note: Arguably, finding a second rater may present a challenge because manual coding of data is typically time consuming. However, given the importance of this procedure, researchers dealing with discourse analysis should be open to requests for double coding from colleagues – when double coding is adopted as standard in the discipline, the reciprocity of such requests will facilitate this procedure.

TABLE 12.3 'Immigrants' in British newspaper discourse – double coding of attitudes

Example	*Rater 1*	*Rater 2*	*Agreement*
1	negative	negative	YES
2	negative	negative	YES
3	negative	negative	YES
4	positive	positive	YES
5	negative	positive	NO
6	negative	negative	YES
7	negative	negative	YES
8	negative	negative	YES
9	positive	negative	NO
10	negative	negative	YES

12.5 How to capture meaning relations? Collocations and collocation networks

Discourse analysis provides a unique opportunity to examine connections between words and how these shape the meanings in the discourse. If two words habitually co-occur in text or discourse they create a close meaning association that frames the discourse in a particular way (Baker 2006). For example, in tabloid newspapers the words *flood* or *influx* often appear before the word *refugees*, thus creating a meaning association with a negative implication that suggests that there are far too many refugees and, like a large body of flowing water, they cannot be controlled (Gabrielatos & Baker 2008). We can identify co-occurrence of words statistically by focusing on the phenomenon called collocation. Collocations are habitual co-occurrences of words identified statistically using corpus analysis tools such as #LancsBox (Brezina et al. 2015)[1]; different corpus tools (CQPWeb, SketchEngine, WordSmith Tools etc.) can be used for collocation analysis. However, #LancsBox was specifically designed for the purpose of identification and visualisation of the collocational relationship. In practice, this means that we take a word of interest (node) around which the tool searches for collocates. Collocates can be listed in a table (see Table 12.4) or visualised as a collocation graph (see Figure 12.5), which also enables us to expand collocations into a network (collocation network) of second-, third-, fourth-order collocates (see Figure 12.6). Table 12.4 and Figure 12.5 show collocates of *war* based on the newspaper sub-corpus of BE06, which consists of over 175,000 running words. Table 12.4 displays statistical values of the collocation measure (MI score in this example, see Section 12.5.2) and the frequency of the co-occurrence of *war* and the collocates. Figure 12.5 displays the same type of information using visual means: the length of the lines that connect the collocates to the node (*war*) are inversely proportional to the strength of the collocation (MI score value): the stronger the association the closer the collocates are to the node. The intensity of the colour of the circles indicates the frequency information. As can be seen from Table 12.4, the strength of collocation as measured by the collocation measure and the frequency of co-occurrence are separate (although related) dimensions (see Section 12.5.2).

We can also look for multiple connections in discourse by means of creating a collocation network. A collocation network is a collocation graph with multiple levels of collocation displayed that shows complex relationships (associations and

TABLE 12.4 Collocates of 'war' in BE06 – newspapers

Collocate	*MI score*	*Frequency of co-occurrence*
Civil	9.9	18
Terror	9.8	6
Cold	8.9	5
Iraq	8.6	12
World	6.9	8
Could	5.2	5
Our	5.0	5

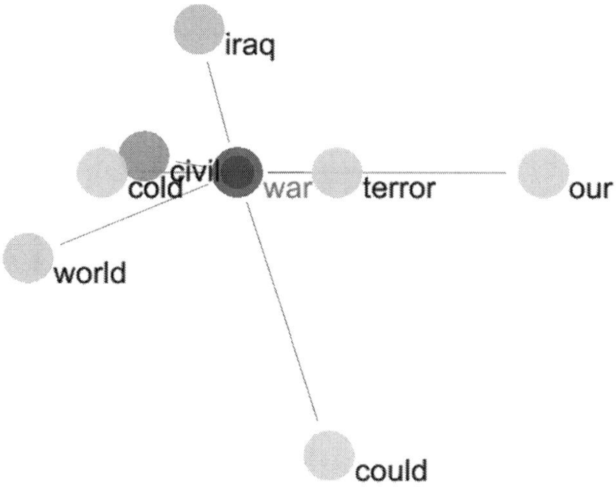

FIGURE 12.5 Collocates of 'war' in BE06 – newspapers.

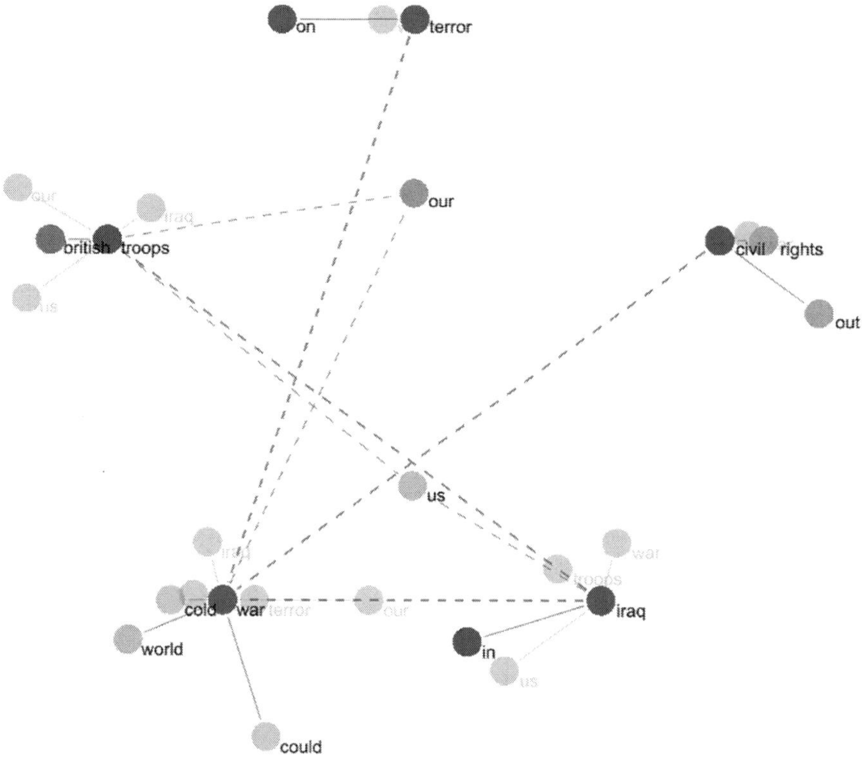

FIGURE 12.6 Collocation network: *war*, *terror*, *troops*, *Iraq* and *civil* in BE06 – newspapers.

cross-associations) between words of interest (Brezina et al. 2015; Phillips 1985). In discourse analysis, collocation networks are used as useful visual summaries of key meaning relationships in the data pointing to crucial aspects of the semantic structure of a text or corpus. The collocation network in Figure 12.6 shows the connection between the terms *war, terror, troops, Iraq* and *civil*. For example, we can see that apart from the direct associations with *war* (first-order collocates), which are listed and displayed in Table 12.4 and Figure 12.5, there are also indirect associations such as *troops* (second-order collocate via the connection with *Iraq*) and *British* (third-order collocate via the connection with *Iraq* and *troops*).

When identifying collocations, we have a number of statistical choices that influence the final result. We need to consider these carefully connecting the statistical decisions (operationalisation) to the construct we want to investigate (see Section 12.2). The basic statistical choices related to collocation (and collocation networks) involve the i) span, ii) collocation statistic (association measure) and iii) statistical and frequency threshold.

12.5.1 Statistical choices in collocation identification: span

The span is the window around the node (word of interest) in which we search for collocates. The larger the span, the broader perspective we take on word association because even more distant words from the node qualify as collocates. In discourse analysis, a symmetrical span of five words to the left and five words to the right of the node (abbreviated as 5L, 5R) can be recommended (e.g. Baker et al. 2013) but other options are also possible. For example, if we are interested in the adjectives that typically co-occur with the noun *time*, we could set the span to be 1L, 0R (one word to the left of the node and zero words to the right) because adjectives in English typically immediately precede the noun. A narrow span creates a more focused view on word co-occurrence but can lead to an omission of important meaning associations (think, for instance, of the phrase *long dreary time* in which only the second adjective will be captured by 1L, 0R span). A large span, on the other hand, can introduce noise into the collocation analysis, that is words that are not directly associated with the node such as words occurring across sentence and paragraph boundaries (... *metal cannulae could be inserted. To allow time for veins to recanalise* ...). It is important to remember that the span operates as a zoom helping us focus the analysis on the most relevant set of collocates as defined by the research question.

12.5.2 Statistical choices in collocation identification: collocation statistics

The second choice we need to make is related to the collocation statistic. There are many different options, each providing a different set of collocates. For example, Figure 12.7 shows collocates (in the form of a graph) of the word *war* in the BE06 newspaper sub-corpus based on four different collocation statistics (MI score, log likelihood, log Dice and Delta P); the span in each case is fixed to 5L, 5R. So, what is the best collocation measure to use? As Brezina et al. (2015) show, different collocation measures in discourse analysis highlight different aspects of the collocational relationship between words. MI score, which has been traditionally used in discourse analysis, highlights rare and unique combinations, often terms or compounds (e.g. *civil war, cold war*), which may stand out but are not necessarily representative (through frequent and repeated use) of the discourse as such. Log Dice, often used in lexicography (Rychlý 2008), compensates the low-frequency bias of the MI-score and identifies combinations of words which appear both uniquely in each other's company but also frequently in the discourse (*the war on* [something]). Delta P takes directionality of collocation into consideration producing two values for each collocational relationship: i) strength of attraction between the node and the collocate and ii) strength of attraction between the collocate and the node (Gries 2013); the Delta P graph in Figure 12.7. shows the node>collocate relationship. Log likelihood, a once popular measure, applies a statistical test, which,

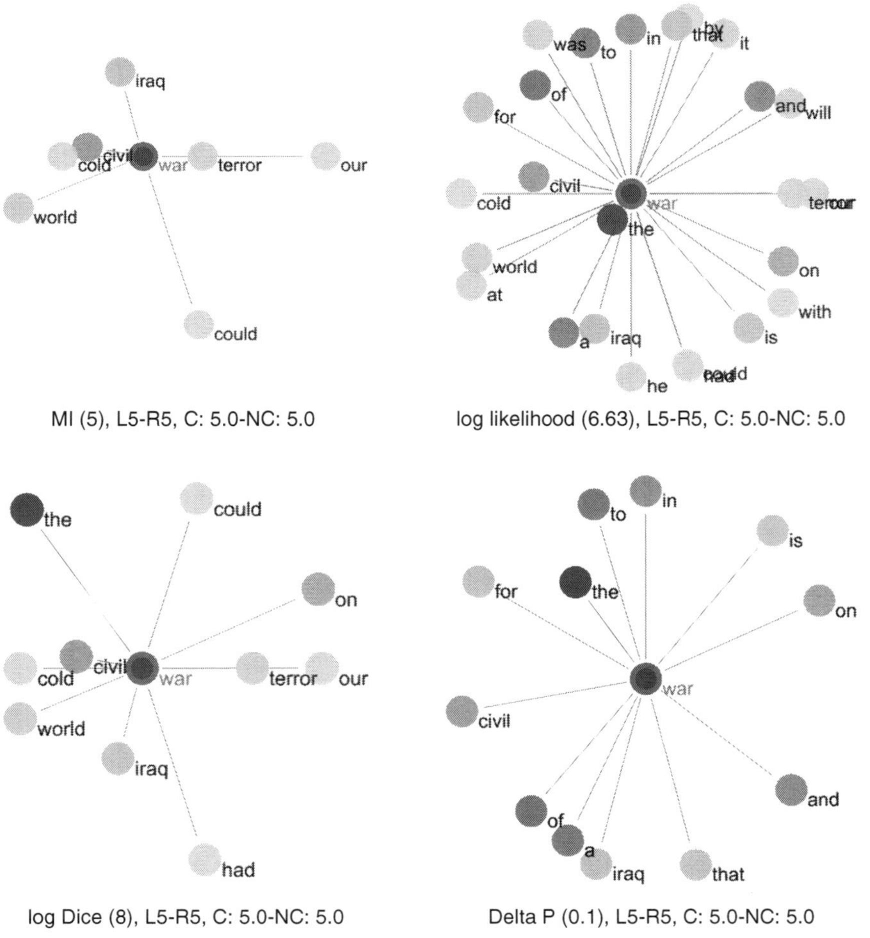

FIGURE 12.7 Collocates of war in BE06 – newspapers: MI score, log likelihood, log Dice and Delta.

however, is largely problematic and cannot be considered a valid test with a reliable *p*-value; although all collocates in the log-likelihood graph in Figure 12.7 are considered by the test to be statistically significant at the p<.01 level, this isn't based on statistically valid inference. Although (some) collocates identified by log likelihood may seem plausible, the measure itself lacks a principled basis and is best to be retired in the future. For more discussion of collocation measures and their implications for corpus linguistic research see Evert (2008) and Gablasova et al. (2017).

12.5.3 Statistical choices in collocation identification: threshold

Finally, we can also apply a variety of statistical and frequency thresholds which are used as filters that enable us to see only the most relevant collocates. Again, the application of thresholds involves statistical choices, which need to be clearly motivated. For example, if a combination of words (collocation) occurs only once in a one-million-word corpus, we probably wouldn't consider it frequent enough to be relevant for the analysis; one-off combinations often involve typos or represent very specific terms. With a collocation occurring multiple times (e.g. three, five, 10 etc. times), we have sufficient evidence that this collocation is not completely arbitrary. However, we still need to consider how typical this collocation is of the discourse as such. In this context, we need to look at the number of different texts in which the collocation occurs (does it appear only in one or two texts or is it evenly dispersed?). In practical terms, these questions can be addressed by using specialised tools such as #LancsBox and applying user-defined thresholds. One important thing that we need to realise is that there is no one definite set of collocates – different statistical procedures and threshold values highlight one set of collocates and downgrade another. For this reason, it is essential to always fully report the statistical choices involved in the identification of collocations. Brezina et al. (2015) propose a specific notation, Collocation Parameter Notation (CPN), to be used for accurate description of this procedure and replication of the results. Table 12.5 summarises the parameters in CPN.

As mentioned earlier in this section, collocations can be considered individually or can be combined into collocation networks. Collocation networks provide additional information about cross-association between different words in discourse (Phillips 1985; Brezina et al. 2015) and can thus serve as a useful summary of what a discourse is about. Brezina (2016) provides further examples of the use of collocation networks to identify prominent discourses in an online Q & A corpus based on Yahoo Answers!

TABLE 12.5 Collocation Parameters Notation (CPN)

Statistic ID	*Statistic name*	*Statistic cut-off value*	*L and R span*	*Minimum collocate freq. (C)*	*Minimum collocation freq. (NC)*	*Filter*
4b	MI2	3	L5-R5	5	1	function words removed

4b-MI2(3), L5-R5, C5-NC1; function words removed

12.6 How to compare different discourses? T-test and ANOVA

Using a comparative research design is a very common scientific procedure in which we compare two or more samples to establish whether there is a difference between them (see Duguid & Partington and Jaworska & Kinloch, this volume). In discourse analysis, this comparative design can be used, for example, to find out if there is a difference between two or more types of discourse appearing in newspapers, books, online forums etc. In this research design, the first step is to search for the frequencies of linguistic variables of interest in corpora representing the discourses we want to compare. As mentioned earlier (see Section 12.2), it is more appropriate to think of corpora as samples of individual texts (or transcripts of speech from individual speakers) than as large containers full of words. In this way, we can employ the individual text/speaker research design, where the frequencies of linguistic variables are counted in each text separately; this counting is performed automatically using tools such as #LancsBox, SketchEngine or CQPweb. The individual counts are then normalised to the same basis (e.g. per 1,000 words) to account for unequal length of texts and the relative (normalised) frequencies are compared using statistical tests such as the t-test and ANOVA or their non-parametric counterparts, the Mann-Whitney U and the Kruskal-Wallis test. Figure 12.8 shows the format of the data used as input for these tests.

More details about the tests (equations and principles of operation) can be found in Brezina (2018). Table 12.6 provides an overview of the most important aspects of the use of these tests directly relevant to discourse analysis.

The simplest option for the comparison of two groups e.g. genres/registers is the t-test. The t-test compares group means, taking into consideration the individual variation within each group, and evaluates if the two groups are likely to be sampled from the same underlying population. If this is the case, there is no statistically significant difference between the groups. This is indicated by a *p*-value (probability value, which the tests output), which is larger than 0.05. In the reverse case, where statistically significant difference is found, the *p*-value is smaller than 0.05. Although t-test assumes normal distribution of the linguistic variable in the underlying population – a bell-shaped curve (/\) that the frequencies of the linguistic variable should follow, the literature shows that it is robust against the violation of this assumption (Boneau 1960; Lumley et al. 2002); we therefore don't have

▲ File	Tokens	Frequency	Relative Frequency per 1000
BE_A01.txt	2004	4	1.996008
BE_A02.txt	1809	3	1.6583748
BE_A03.txt	2033	2	0.9837678
BE_A04.txt	1992	2	1.004016
BE_A05.txt	1919	6	3.1266284
BE_A06.txt	1933	7	3.621314
BE_A07.txt	1968	3	1.5243902
BE_A08.txt	1896	7	3.6919832
BE_A09.txt	2005	0	0.0
BE_A10.txt	2064	2	0.96899223
BE_A11.txt	2011	0	0.0
BE_A12.txt	1958	3	1.5321757
BE_A13.txt	1964	6	3.0549898

FIGURE 12.8 Output from #LancsBox.

TABLE 12.6 Comparison of four statistical tests suitable for individual text/speaker research design

Test	*T-test*	*ANOVA*	*Mann-Whitney U*	*Kruskal-Wallis*
No. of groups compared	2	2+	2	2+
Assumes underlying normal distribution of the linguistic variable in the population	YES	YES	NO	NO
Assumes independence of texts/speakers	YES	YES	YES	YES
Allows testing interaction between different explanatory variables (e.g. register and author's gender)	NO	YES	NO	NO
Effect size measure to report	Cohen's *d*	η^2	rank biserial correlation	-

to worry about the violation of this assumption too much. With more groups or more complex research designs (investigation of the interaction between explanatory variables) the ANOVA test can be used; ANOVA also uses mean values for each group, comparing within and between group variation taking individual texts/speakers into account. Simply put, the question we are asking when using the ANOVA test is this: Is there a larger difference between the groups (representing different registers, discourses etc.) than the difference between individual texts within each group? An alternative to comparing mean group values is to compare the sum of ranks per group. This can be done using non-parametric tests such as the Mann-Whitney U test or the Kruskal-Wallis test. Because these tests do not operate with the actual relative frequency values but first convert them to ranks, they do not make assumptions about the underlying distribution of the linguistic variable in the population; these tests are also more conservative, which means that they have less power to highlight smaller differences in groups than their parametric counterparts (t-test and ANOVA). In addition to the test statistics and *p*-values, appropriate effect size measures (see Table 12.6) should be reported. Effect sizes are (usually) standardised measures of the magnitude of the observed effect, which help us interpret the practical (linguistic/social) implications of what we observe in the data. For more information about effect sizes and their reporting see Cummings (2012) and Brezina (2018: chapter 8.4).

Finally, an interesting visual alternative to statistical testing is provided by an error bars plot with 95 per cent confidence intervals around the group mean values. Such a graph is displayed in Figure 12.9.

Although the graph in Figure 12.9 has some superficial similarities with the boxplot in Figure 12.1, the meaning of the display is very different. While the boxplot represents a description of the data in individual groups, the error bars plot indicates inferences beyond the samples (it is part of inferential statistics). For each group, the error bars show an interval within which the mean value for the group will likely appear in 95 per cent of the samples taken from the same population. In practice,

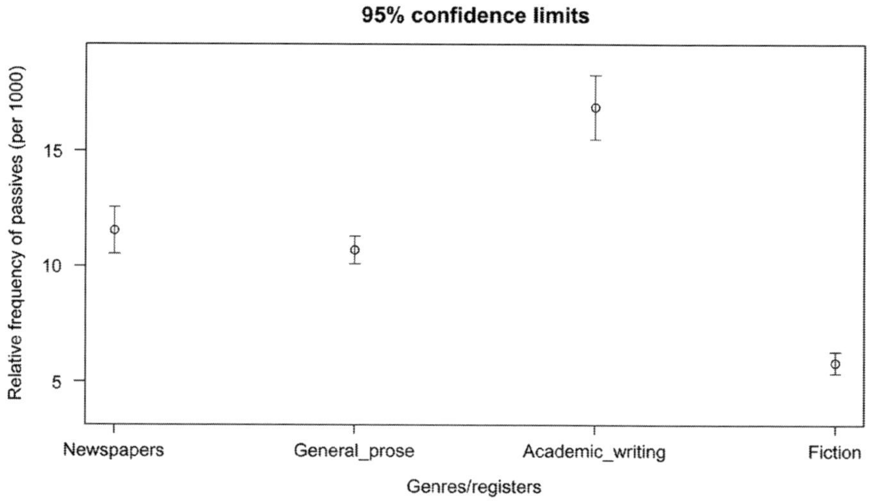

FIGURE 12.9 Passives in BE06.

non-overlapping error bars such as all genres/registers in Figure 12.9 with the exception of newspapers and general prose indicate statistically significant differences. Slightly overlapping bars can still be significant but large overlaps (e.g. newspapers and general fiction in Figure 12.9) signal a statistically non-significant result (Masson & Loftus 2003). The advantage of using this visual technique over the statistical test is the ability to immediately spot statistically significant differences between groups.

In sum, when comparing different discourses, we need to make statistical choices about the appropriate research design (whole corpus vs. individual texts/speakers design) as well as the specific statistical test. The individual texts/speakers design is to be preferred over the whole corpus design because it allows us to account for the variation between texts or speakers and thus capture more meaningfully the dynamics of discourse. We can also consider using a 95 per cent error bars plot as a visual alternative to a statistical test.

12.7 Conclusion

This chapter has outlined some of the statistical options that the analyst has when dealing with discourse data. Essentially, the process of quantitative analysis, if grounded in good statistical practice, can help address the issues of bias and partiality of discourse analysis. When we seek to answer the question of how typical or rare our observations are and whether we have enough evidence in the data to make certain claims we enter the realm of the scientific paradigm. The success of the analysis within this paradigm can be judged by how well the analysis captures essential aspects of the linguistic evidence present in the samples of discourse (corpora) which we investigate. However, statistical sophistication alone is not the goal of this pursuit. Statistics, although offering very important tools that help us understand the nature of the linguistic evidence, should always serve the data and not the other way around. The data, no matter how fuzzy and unruly, is our anchor to the reality and needs to be treated with respect. If the data does not support our theories, no matter how much we are convinced about the value of these theories, we need to state this clearly. Returning to the paradox described at the beginning of this chapter, we have to realise that the inherent fluidity, ambiguity and fuzziness of discourse offers a wonderful opportunity to explore the data from different perspectives using different methods; these perspectives can then be brought together via triangulation (Baker & Eckbert 2016), which provides a fuller picture of the complex linguistic and discourse reality than any single technique.

Acknowledgements

The writing of this chapter was supported by ESRC grants no. EP/P001559/1 and ES/K002155/1.

Note

1 #LancsBox is downloadable for free from http://corpora.lancs.ac.uk/lancsbox.

References

Abid, R. Z., Manan, S. A. & Rahman, Z. A. A. A. 2017. 'A flood of Syrians has slowed to a trickle': The use of metaphors in the representation of Syrian refugees in the online media news reports of host and non-host countries. *Discourse & Communication*, 11(2), 121–140.

Baker, P. 2006. *Using Corpora in Discourse Analysis*. London: Continuum.

Baker, P. & Egbert, J. (eds.) 2016. *Triangulating Methodological Approaches in Corpus Linguistic Research*. New York: Routledge.

Baker, P., Gabrielatos, C. & McEnery, T. 2013. *Discourse Analysis and Media Attitudes: The Representation of Islam in the British Press*. Cambridge: Cambridge University Press.

Bednarek, M. 2008. Semantic preference and semantic prosody re-examined. *Corpus Linguistics and Linguistic Theory*, 4(2), 119–139.

Bednarek, M. & Caple, H. 2012. *News Discourse*. London: Continuum.

Blommaert, J. 2005. Discourse: *A Critical Introduction*. Cambridge: Cambridge University Press.

Boneau, C.A. 1960. The effects of violations of assumptions underlying the t test. *Psychological Bulletin*, 57(1), 49.

Brezina, V. 2016. Collocation networks. In P. Baker & J. Egbert (eds.) *Triangulating Methodological Approaches in Corpus Linguistic Research*. New York: Routledge. pp. 90–107.

Brezina, V. 2018. *Statistics for Corpus Linguistics: A Practical Guide*. Cambridge: Cambridge University Press.

Brezina, V., McEnery, T. & Wattam, S. 2015. Collocations in context: A new perspective on collocation networks. *International Journal of Corpus Linguistics*, 20(2), 139–173.

Brezina V. & Meyerhoff M. 2014. Significant or random: A critical review of sociolinguistic generalisations based on large corpora. *International Journal of Corpus Linguistics*, 19: 1–28.

Cummings, G. 2012. *Understanding the New Statistics.* New York: Routledge.

Diggle, P. J. & Chetwynd, A. G. 2011. *Statistics and Scientific Method: An Introduction for Students and Researchers*. Oxford: Oxford University Press.

Evert, S. 2008. Corpora and collocations. In A. Lüdeling & M. Kytö (eds.) *Corpus Linguistics. An International Handbook*, Berlin: Mouton de Gruyter. pp. 1212–1248.

Fowler, R. 1991. *Language in the News: Discourse and Ideology in the Press.* London: Routledge.

Gablasova, D., Brezina, V. & McEnery, A. M. 2017. Collocations in corpus-based language learning research: identifying, comparing and interpreting the evidence. *Language Learning*, 67(1), 155–179.

Gabrielatos, C. & Baker, P. 2008. Fleeing, sneaking, flooding: A corpus analysis of discursive constructions of refugees and asylum seekers in the UK press, 1996–2005. *Journal of English linguistics*, 36(1), 5–38.

Gries, S. T. 2013. 50-something years of work on collocations: What is or should be next.... *International Journal of Corpus Linguistics*, 18(1), 137–166.

Gwet, K. L. 2014. *Handbook of Inter-Rater Reliability: The Definitive Guide to Measuring the Extent of Agreement among Raters*. Gaithersburg: Advanced Analytics, LLC.

Jacobi, C., van Atteveldt, W. & Welbers, K. 2016. Quantitative analysis of large amounts of journalistic texts using topic modelling. *Digital Journalism*, 4(1), 89–106.

Kilgarriff, A. 2005. Language is never, ever, ever, random. *Corpus linguistics and linguistic theory*, 1(2), 263–276.

Krippendorff, K. 2012 [1980]. *Content Analysis: An Introduction to Its Methodology*. London: Sage.

Lakoff, G. (1987). *Women, Fire, and Dangerous Things*. Chicago: University of Chicago Press.

Lijffijt, J., Nevalainen, T., Säily, T., Papapetrou, P., Puolamäki, K. & Mannila, H. 2016. Significance testing of word frequencies in corpora. *Digital Scholarship in the Humanities*, 31(2), 374–397.

Lumley, T., Diehr, P., Emerson, S. & Chen, L. 2002. The importance of the normality assumption in large public health data sets. *Annual Review of Public Health*, 23(1), 151–169.

Masson, M. E. & Loftus, G. R. 2003. Using confidence intervals for graphically based data interpretation. *Canadian Journal of Experimental Psychology/Revue canadienne de psychologie expérimentale*, 57(3), 203.

McEnery, T. & Baker, H. 2017. Corpus Linguistics and 17th-Century Prostitution: Computational Linguistics and History. London: Bloomsbury.

Michel, J. B., Shen, Y. K., Aiden, A. P., Veres, A., Gray, M. K., Pickett, J. P. & Pinker, S. 2011. Quantitative analysis of culture using millions of digitized books. *Science*, 331(6014), 176–182.

Oskamp, S. & Schultz, P. W. 2005. *Attitudes and Opinions*. New York: Psychology Press.

Partington, A. 2004. 'Utterly content in each other's company': Semantic prosody and semantic preference. *International Journal of Corpus Linguistics*, 9(1), 131–156.

Partington, A., Duguid, A. & Taylor, C. 2013. *Patterns and Meanings in Discourse: Theory and Practice in Corpus-Assisted Discourse Studies (CADS)* (Vol. 55). Amsterdam: John Benjamins.

Pechenick E.A., Danforth, C.M. & Dodds, P.S. 2015. Characterizing the Google Books corpus: Strong limits to inferences of socio-cultural and linguistic evolution. *PLoS ONE* 10(10), e0137041.

Phillips, M. 1985. *Aspects of Text Structure: An Investigation of the Lexical Organisation of Text.* Amsterdam: North-Holland.

Rayson, P., Leech, G. N. & Hodges, M. 1997. Social differentiation in the use of English vocabulary: Some analyses of the conversational component of the British National Corpus. *International Journal of Corpus Linguistics*, 2(1), 133–152.

Rychlý, P. 2008. A lexicographer-friendly association score. *Proceedings of Recent Advances in Slavonic Natural Language Processing, RASLAN*, 6–9.

13

CONCLUSION

Reflecting on reflective research

Paul Baker

13.1 Introduction

In this concluding chapter of the book I would like to address several aims. First, I try to outline what this book indicates about the current status of corpus-assisted, -based or -driven discourse analysis. Second, I use some of the points made in each of the chapters as a springboard for further reflection, making links through to my own experiences. Finally, I make some suggestions regarding how this kind of reflexivity in corpus-based discourse analysis could continue in ways that I think would be both interesting and productive for the field and its members.

The chapters in this book have addressed the kinds of questions that are sometimes asked at the end of conference presentations, the 'what about?' type of question, which points out an aspect of the approach that appears to have been overlooked, or what have been referred to as blind spots by Anna Marchi and Charlotte Taylor in Chapter 1 of this book. Such gaps do not mean that the research should be dismissed, and there are often plausible reasons why the researcher did not address every 'what about?' question. Even if such questions had been considered, we often do not have the resources to do everything we would like to, and we may not also have had the time or word count allocation to adequately outline the research that *was* done in its entirety. We often have to make choices about what to do or include and what gets left out, so we may favour a mainstream newspaper data source or a comparison which focusses on difference, because they are tried and tested techniques, at the expense of other options. It therefore suggests a maturing of the field of corpora and discourse studies that this book specifically addresses some of the 'what about?' questions. It could be seen as a plea for the implementation of plurality and depth in methodological thought and subsequently in practice, but at the very least it should raise awareness about some of the paths that could have been taken and get us to think about the consequences of the ones that we do take.

13.2 An impartial approach?

Corpus linguistics is sometimes seen as a more objective approach than other forms of linguistic analysis. Leech refers to it as approaching language study as a scientific method, referring to the principle of total accountability (Leech 1992: 112), which means that the findings from our analysis must be falsifiable (Popper 1959/2005) – we should have the means to identify any uses of language which go against our claims, and have convincingly attempted to do this. Our analysis should therefore draw on examples from the entirety of the corpus (e.g. by using randomised samples of concordance lines), without removing cases that do not support our hypotheses. As McEnery and Hardie (2012: 15–16) argue, we can only claim total accountability as far as the corpus itself, as it is a sample of language, and while efforts are made to ensure that the corpus is a representative sample, we cannot always be sure that we were successful. Thus, replicability is important – if the same results are achieved with the same or different data sets, then we have better evidence for 'total' accountability.

The adherence to the 'scientific method' within corpus linguistics has been used in arguments about its strength or even aspects of its superiority over other approaches, particularly qualitative ones. For example, I have referred to corpus linguistics as 'reducing bias' (Baker 2006: 10), whereas Mautner (2009: 34) has noted that 'large corpora can contribute to counteracting one of the most fundamental and persisting criticisms levelled against Critical Discourse Analysis (CDA), namely that it supposedly cherry-picks small and unrepresentative data samples in order to suit researchers' pre-conceived notions about hidden ideological meanings'.

However, as time has gone on, questions about the supposedly impartial nature of corpus linguistics have arisen. For example, in Baker (2012) I argued that while the keywords approach may itself be an objective, statistically derived way of identifying words that occur in a corpus more frequently than would be expected by chance, cherry-picking still tends to occur at different levels, e.g. in terms of the cut-off point for keyness which is first applied, and then in terms of which keywords from the resulting list are actually subjected to analysis and discussion (and the amount of time given over to each keyword). In this volume Jesse Egbert and Erin Schnur (Chapter 8) and Costas Gabrielatos (Chapter 11) address further issues around keyness including consideration of text dispersion, choice of statistic and reference corpora. And as Charlotte Taylor (Chapter 2) notes, keyness is usually used to identify difference (although the technique can be tweaked to show similarity). The problem is not that our techniques do not work properly, they are very good at what they do, but we have not always thought enough about the partial analytical picture that they can give.

This book thus demonstrates some of the potential pitfalls that discourse analysts who use corpora can encounter, as well as making useful suggestions relating to their avoidance. As Charlotte Taylor in Chapter 2 and Alison Duguid and Alan Partington in Chapter 3 have shown, the uniquely comparative nature of corpus linguistics means that we can get bogged down in difference, although some of the more well-known techniques that we use can be modified in order to identify similarities or absences. For example, as shown by Sylvia Jaworska and Karen Kinloch in Chapter 6, by engaging with multiple corpora we can determine what is missing from one corpus, or where the relative frequencies of a linguistic item are reasonably well-matched. Finding the solution is often not the most problematic aspect of corpus-based discourse analysis, we first need to know what the problems are, a point that this book extensively addresses.

As Chapter 5 implies, corpus linguists who engage in discourse analysis have a tendency to privilege certain text types or registers, at the expense of others. There are plausible reasons for this – at present it is easier to access mainstream newspapers online, and it could be argued that such news stories are widely read and influential. Alon Lischinsky in Chapter 4 uses erotic fiction as an example of a text type which is not widely engaged with (while Clyde Ancarno in Chapter 7 uses another overlooked text type, interviews), and it is hoped that corpus linguists will begin to engage more with fiction, for discourse purposes, rather than just for stylistic analyses. Sally Hunt's (2015) work on gender and agency in the Harry Potter book series is a nice example of what can be achieved, and indicates another type of overlooked text, that aimed at children – for it is children who are the most susceptible to discourse and it can be difficult to unlearn the discourses which are internalised at an early age. A fourth text type which tends to be overlooked is informal spoken interaction (as opposed to say a scripted political speech intended for a large audience). There are practical and ethical difficulties in collecting such large amounts of data, and it could be argued that political speeches are more 'important' in terms of telling us about discourse because of their mass reception and the power of the speaker. On the other hand, discourses which are referenced in the language of 'private' informal settings can also reveal something about the ways that ideologies trickle-down, circulate and spout back up, as well as giving us the potential to reveal a wider range of discourse positions that might be less easily articulated in a more public context. The recently created BNC2014 Corpus (McEnery et al. 2017) currently contains over 11 million words of transcribed private speech and has the potential to open up a great deal of research on the views of ordinary people on a range of topics.

Jesse Egbert and Erin Schnur (Chapter 8) make the important argument that, particularly for discourse-oriented research, corpora ought to consist of full texts rather than text samples, and that the texts themselves should be fully accessible with relevant metadata. When carrying out discourse analysis, a concordance table, while useful, can sometimes provide a narrow or even misleading interpretation (a point also made by Laurence Anthony in Chapter 10). For example, a series of concordance lines containing a collocational pair of social actor plus negative evaluative adjective may superficially reveal that a particular social group is repeatedly stereotyped in a disparaging way in a corpus. While this is clearly true, the story may be more complicated if we move beyond the few words of context that a typical concordance line gives in order to consider expanded concordance lines. We may now find that these negative representations occur within quotes, and some are being quoted by the author in order to be critical of them. The overall discourse-effect of some of the representations might be oppositional to our original interpretation. We could go further still by considering not just expanded concordance lines but whole texts. In such cases, we may want to consider the cases where a negative representation is quoted in a text but does not contain a clear evocation of author stance in relation to it. However, if we engage in more qualitative research of the texts in question, we may be able to make a few qualified interpretations about what the intended stance in regard to the quote might be. For example, a quote may be foregrounded or prioritised in various ways, appearing near the beginning of the text, or appearing as a lengthy quote. The same author may be quoted repeatedly at other points in the text or may be the only person whose perspective is quoted. Such practices might give clues to the way that the text creator wishes the quote to be viewed. However, a concordance table is unlikely to bring this kind of information to the forefront, especially if a text sample is used.

13.3 To be critical?

Perhaps the most important question we should be asking ourselves, at the start of the research, and throughout, all the way to its end and after its completion, is what is the *purpose* of this research? In other words, what do we hope to achieve by carrying it out? Not all discourse-related corpus research has a critical or social emancipatory aim behind it, and indeed a debate within the domain is the extent to which corpus methods release us from our political biases, whether this matters, and the extent to which we should explicitly outline and reflect upon our own 'positions' in relation to our research topic.

At the one extreme is the committed, caring CDA-oriented corpus researcher, who may have a vested interest in the topic they are studying – perhaps they (or persons close to them) belong to an oppressed or stigmatised social group. Even if there is not a personal connection, the researcher may be strongly motivated by issues of social justice, and they may bristle at unfairness, inequality and hatred when they encounter it in language texts. In such cases we often already have some evidence for the existence of a social problem, and want to examine how widespread the issue is and the different ways that it is substantiated. We expect to find something bad in other words.

My own research has sometimes been inspired by dismay at the capacity of people to treat others badly – the most marked example of this was when I read about the suicide of trans school teacher Lucy Meadows, who had been the subject of a pejorative newspaper article in a tabloid newspaper in 2012. Around the same time, a liberal broadsheet newspaper (which I largely respected) published articles by high-profile writers which were also hostile to trans people, inspiring me to want to learn more about why the topic provoked such a blanket negative reception, and to draw attention to the issue. The subsequent research (Baker 2014), which focussed on the representation of trans people in the UK press, aimed to provide a record of linguistic trends and to point out areas of reporting which could be better.

On the other hand, I have also engaged in research projects where I have had little background knowledge or personal or emotional investment at the start. For example, the RASIM project on immigration was collaborative, where other members of the research team were more familiar with the topic under consideration than I was at the outset. With my doctoral students, some have been assigned funding based on willingness to study certain topics, and while they were given leeway in the direction that they took, they too had little personal identification with that topic. The approaches described so far could be viewed as action research (Burr 1995: 162), aimed at inspiring some sort of social change, which does not stop at the publication of results. With our research on press representations of Islam for example, we worked with a media watchdog called Engage, as well as giving talks at the British House of Commons, a Labour party conference and mosques, where we advised audience members on how to complain about newspaper articles that contained the sorts of negative representations we outlined to them.

At the other extreme, there is the more dispassionate researcher who may not have a particular vested interest. They may have chosen a topic because other (perhaps non-corpus) studies have focussed on certain patterns and they wish to ascertain what a corpus approach would yield. They may have had the topic given to them by someone else. They may simply want to investigate a topic that nobody else has looked at or they may choose a topic in order to demonstrate the corpus method itself. With increasing pressures on academics to obtain funding, publish and generally justify their existence, the reasons behind a topic choice may not be especially lofty at times, responding in a somewhat circular manner to requirements to do the sort of things that academics do.

Such researchers are still perhaps likely to have hopes and expectations regarding what they will find but the hope might be for 'something interesting and unexpected' as opposed to 'evidence of bias'. They will instead aim to approach the analysis with an open mind and a commitment to being as objective as possible, acting more as an explorer – with an especial focus on uncovering findings which are not already known. This is perhaps more the stance taken by Partington's Corpus Assisted Discourse Studies (CADS).

To an extent these two positions could be seen as discourse-related iterations of the corpus-based/corpus-driven approach (Tognini-Bonelli 2001), of which McEnery and Hardie (2012: 150) have argued are more like imaginary positions, with most corpus research combining aspects of the two. Similarly, I would suggest that most people who engage in some combination of corpus linguistics and discourse analysis inhabit a moveable cline between political engagement and neutral objectivity. My own experience of starting a piece of research from the more dispassionate end of the scale is that usually, around the midway point, the analysis makes me more engaged with the topic or group under consideration. In other words, I start to care. In many cases, I think that once you begin researching the representation or discourse around a group or topic where you can identify misrepresentations or 'damaging' discourses (Sunderland 2004: 191), which can be linked to real-world consequences, then it is difficult for many people to not feel something.

There are dangers in trying to work at the extremes. The passionate critical researcher has a strong intuition that they will find offence in their corpus, and an overwhelming desire to 'prove' the existence of the offence, finding the texts or text producers guilty as charged. Their analysis may indeed be backed up with the existence of negative representations which are quantified, but they may overlook other aspects of the data which do not contribute towards an oppression narrative. Despite the claims about corpus approaches making us avoid cherry-picking data to suit our position, as noted above, it is still possible to cherry-pick from corpus data in various ways. And will such research really change anyone's mind? Partington (2015: 241–242) reminds us that:

> We should not forget when studying socio-political issues, including representations of groups in newspaper texts, that negativity is one of the principle news values (Galtung and Ruge, 1981). Wrongdoing makes the papers, normal good service rarely so. The corollary of this is that most social issues and groups will be spoken about more often in negative contexts than in positive ones. In studying media representations of events, issues and groups, we need to maintain the sensible distinction between negative representation meaning 'prejudiced representation' and negative representation meaning 'reporting of negative events'. The latter is what newspapers do for a living and by no means necessarily implies the former.

Bad news sells, and newspapers identify typical audiences and often pander to their prejudices, working within the attitudinal margins of what such audiences will tolerate. Most social groups do not come off well if a corpus of newspaper articles about them is analysed. And some of the other politically oriented text types that we want to look at critically may constitute 'easy targets'. A good number of people who post anonymously on online forums will be trolls and hold even more openly hateful opinions than journalists. Politicians will bend the truth as much as they can. We may not reveal much more than is obvious already from the analysis of such texts, and a lot of critical research can feel like it is preaching to the choir, with the danger of focussing on the more negative aspects of the corpus being that we expose what is sadly obvious rather than subtle.

Again, we should ask what the aims of our research are – is it to convince people from the oppositional side (or those who have no clear opinion) to change their mind and support calls for more accurate, fair or even kind representations of a group or topic? Longstanding political views can be difficult to sway and are not always influenced by rational argument or presentation of academic data, instead being driven by rhetorical fallacies or cognitive biases. Expertise is not always valued, as shown by the recent Brexit vote in the UK, where the Remain campaign was supported by a range of experts including economists, high-level politicians, trade union leaders, business leaders and academics, although still lost the vote, prompting Leave campaigner Michael Gove to say in a Sky News interview on 21 June 2017 that 'people in this country have had enough of experts'. Considering the current popular dislike of expertise, efforts from academics may not always convince (and I can attest to cases where my tables of numbers and concordances have not swayed people who hold opposing views to mine). Gove went on to argue that the experts had a vested interest in remaining in the UK, and there is a danger that people will see all forms of politically motivated research as partial, a point echoed by Partington, Duguid and Taylor (2013: 340):

> Research schools which perform discourse analysis with socio-political aims, critical discourse analysis being the foremost example, run a considerable risk of failing to meet Feynman's criteria of integrity. If researchers and teachers impose a priori a particular ideological perspective and then perhaps use the corpus simply as a source of material to support that perspective, then the chances are that very little that is new will be learned along the way. Researchers who work within the framework of CDA have stated that their form of research is more honest than others because they openly declare their political position. But such open declarations of stance are no more a guarantee of Popper-Feynman intellectual rigour and honesty than those of a politician or lawyer when they openly advocate their case …

On the other hand, the position of the exploratory, more objective researcher can also be questioned. It could be seen as idealistic (in a different way to the CDA approach) in that it believes itself to be above subjectivity. At best it might be viewed as fence-sitting, at worst as hiding an agenda. Post-structuralists would argue that the desire for objectivity is still a stance, still a form of bias in other words. An action-researcher might wonder why go to the trouble of doing the research if we don't hope to make some sort of positive impact on the world. But in an age of populist rejection of expertise, such an ambition can itself be scoffed at. And this takes us again back to the question I posed at the start of this section – what is the point of this research? To be fair, this question often is addressed in Introduction sections of journal articles, chapters or books, although I sometimes feel that it is superficially considered, or not always as honestly answered as it could be. It also tends to be addressed on a case-by-case basis, rather than the corpus and discourse community of scholars attempting to provide a more coherent and over-arching response to it. This is something which we could seek to address: why do CADS at all and should we realistically want or expect this kind of research to have any impact outside the rooms in an academic conference?

13.4 Triangulation

As noted in Chapter 1, several of the studies in this volume have used triangulation as a way of reducing partiality. This can involve the analysis of multiple corpora (Sylvia Jaworska and Karen Kinloch in Chapter 6), different semiotic modes within the same corpus (Helen Caple in Chapter 5) or different techniques of analysis (either multiple corpus methods or combining corpus methods with non-corpus methods). The overview of current work using corpus linguistics alongside other fields in Chapter 7 shows a broadening appeal of the methodology to academics working in history, economics, health, law, literature, organisational studies and political science, for example. And a few years ago we expanded the annual CASS Summer school at Lancaster to incorporate separate strands for researchers who want to use corpus methods in the humanities and social sciences.

We need to learn how to step outside the corpus more often as a way of making better interpretations and explanations. We could do well to learn from forms of analysis like the Discourse Historical Approach (Reisgl & Wodak 2001) which advocates a wide-ranging consideration of different sorts of context beyond the texts being analysed in order to provide a deeper understanding of findings. This triangulatory approach goes beyond linguistics to encompass many types of knowledge about the workings of societies, which then must be synthesised in some way: opinion polls, laws, linguistic etymologies, histories, cases of intertextuality, demographic information about populations etc. As linguists, used to working with language data, this may be a daunting task, especially as there are few guidelines on what sources of context are appropriate and how we should go about finding, interpreting and combining them into some sort of explanatory narrative (although see Flowerdew's 2014 edited collection on discourse in context).

As Baker and Egbert (2016) imply, triangulation can produce multiple sets of findings, many which will be unique, others which will overlap, providing a useful cross-check of results from more than one perspective, and a few which may contradict one another. What, if anything, are potential disadvantages or other issues around triangulation then? Triangulation is a wide-ranging term and most studies which employ it will usually do so in one dimension (e.g. multiple corpora or multiple modes or multiple analysts or multiple methods). So an initial question may involve decisions regarding which type(s) of triangulation could and should be carried out. Even accepting that triangulation itself is usually partial triangulation, there is an accompanying danger of trying to do too much with the result being a shallow or incoherent analysis. Particularly with combining a corpus method with other methods that the analyst is more familiar with, there may be over-reliance on the initial stages of a corpus analysis, such as reporting frequency tables, but then little of the actual qualitative legwork which goes into interpreting the reasons behind the frequencies and the ways that linguistic items are used in context.

We could advocate that to engage in corpus-based discourse analysis you need to be an academic polymath, having skills in academic writing, computer programming, statistics, specialist software use, linguistics, qualitative analyses and the kinds of contextual analysis involving the application of subjects like history, politics, economics and sociology to interpret and explain the patterns found. Such perfectly well-rounded people may exist but I have yet to meet any, and while it is a good idea to attempt to gain a basic grounding in as many relevant fields as possible, realistically, we may only be able to achieve mastery of a smaller number, necessitating a different approach.

Thus triangulation often requires expertise in multiple fields, and to be done well, it can involve the coordination of teams of researchers with different skillsets. Additionally, even if the analyses are carried out thoroughly, there are likely to be challenges in terms of providing a full account of all of the angles of the research within the word count limits of a journal article or 20-minute conference paper. Audiences for such pieces of research are also likely to be unfamiliar with one or more aspects of the paper, resulting in a higher chance of resistance or difficulties in finding the right publishing outlet for the research.

Triangulation is important then, but tricky, and some of our academic practices do not always facilitate its realisation. Authors, editors, publishers and conference organisers need to experiment with different ways of enabling triangulation to be foregrounded in corpus research. In Baker and Egbert (2016), when we presented the findings of 10 researchers on the same corpus, we structured the book so that information relevant to each piece of the research (such as the collection and structure of the corpus, and the general research questions) was at the start of the book and did not need to be repeated throughout. Other types of published triangulation research might require longer than usual chapters or articles. It would also be interesting for triangulation researchers to reflect on some of the more practical issues encountered such as good practice when building, working within or coordinating research teams, handling conflict, meeting word-count limits and engaging with different and multiple audiences.

13.5 Transparency

In Chapter 12, Vaclav Brezina argues that 'discourse analysis is often an exploratory approach, this is not a linear process but can be repeated multiple times'. A similar point is made by Clyde Ancarno in Chapter 7, relating to her experience of triangulatory research, when she refers to her description of her methods and methodologies as 'inevitably deceptive to some degree'. She is not alone. Perhaps the point is true of all fields of research but it could also be argued that it is something which corpus linguistics, as a collection of methods, and also a relatively new field, has to address. There are many variables – in terms of deciding what our corpus should look like, and what software and methods we should use and in what order. Sometimes it can feel like we are making our way in darkness, trying out different techniques until something works.

Over the last year I have had the following experience of doing research – I start with some corpus data and decide upon a methodology. The methodology is applied several times, either on different sub-corpora or to analyse different sets of features within the same corpus. I apply the methodology once, twice, three times. But the fourth time I stumble upon a better methodology – the results are better, more interesting, more convincing and provide a more complete answer to my research question. I am pleased with what I have found, something felt not quite right about the previous three iterations of the methodology, which had worked for an earlier project, but I had struggled to adapt it for this one. But now I realise, with a heavy heart, that I have to go backwards and redo the three earlier sets of analysis using the new methodology. The whole analysis takes twice as long as I had expected but I am happier with the end result. I wish that I had come up with the good methodology at the start, alas though, we often need to try something out and be uncomfortable with it before we can identify a better way. In other words, we don't always get it right at the first attempt.

Those first attempts are important but they are sometimes redacted from the research narrative we tell ourselves and others, in favour of a more straightforward version of events. And that is not good. As well as presenting the 'right' version of the methodology as the one that was first thought of, we sometimes take out research questions that were not answered and present research questions that were retro-fitted to the analysis as if they had been there from the beginning. PhD theses, which normally allow fledgling researchers to go into detail about methodology, are often better at providing an "honest" account of the research process, although it is ironic that subsequent research projects do not always take the time to tell the story of how the methodology was made. To an extent this is due to constraints beyond the researcher, to publish frequently, to publish short pieces of research in journals which are often more results-focussed, and to present a coherent narrative. But as Scott (2017) points out, the truth of many research projects is that it is more messy than the writing up process implies. Research is not a road, it is a maze. A piece of research can involve many dead-ends, back-tracks, side-steps and changes of track. Beyond the constraints mentioned above, there are other reasons not to reveal the extent of the tortuous journey – something of an Emperor's New Clothes effect, whereby we don't want to be the only one to admit that we didn't make it from A to B by the shortest possible route, and also, perhaps a concern that our readers don't actually care that much about the stop-over points C, D and E. Marchi and Taylor referred to the 'bottom-drawer effect' in Chapter 1, where researchers assign uninteresting research to a filing cabinet rather than publishing it, but there is perhaps a second drawer in the cabinet, where 'failed' research sits – comprising the dead-ends mentioned above, or worse still, research journeys that were simply abandoned at some point prior to completion. When Jesse Egbert and I published our corpus triangulation edited collection (Baker & Egbert 2016), which involved presenting 10 authors with the same corpus and research question, there were a number of additional authors who were given the data and at various points decided not to submit a completed chapter. These chapters were referred to briefly in the book but for each one there is potentially an interesting story, and perhaps lessons to be learnt.

Similarly, my own career has involved cases of research which never made it to print – ideas that were too ambitious, collaborations that didn't work out, findings that told me nothing new – all are absent from my CV. To my knowledge nobody has ever published a collection of 'failed corpus research'. Would anybody find such a book interesting? Illuminating? Even comforting? I wonder if we could collectively learn as much from our mistakes as our successes and perhaps we should worry less about our images. As a potential springboard from the current edited collection, it would be encouraging for us to be more open about the complexity of our research journeys, including discussion around 'failed research'.

13.6 Concluding remarks

As a relative latecomer to different linguistic methodologies (made possible by the widespread availability of large amounts of electronically formatted text and the specialised software to process them), I sometimes feel that corpus linguists engage in rather a lot of explanation and justification of their approach, compared to some of the older, more established approaches. The non-intuitive Latin-derived label *corpus* must be explained time and again, the pros and cons of the approach presented in bullet-pointed, referenced lists, the terms *collocation*, *concordance* and *keyword* must be outlined, and the method must then be *proven* to work, with a suitable short demonstration. Non-corpus audiences are approached with a degree of trepidation and at times it feels as if we are apologising for our new method, using sweet-talking phrases like 'it's a supplementary approach', 'it doesn't require you to be a computer or maths expert' and 'it can't do everything'. Lately, as demonstrated by Vaclav Brezina in Chapter 12, we have to set out our wares in an increasingly crowded barn, making it clear how we differ, overlap or are better than computational approaches or concepts like big data approaches, digital humanities, culturomics, topic modelling and sentiment analysis (the key difference here being that the other approaches are often not employed by linguists). Despite the rather repetitive nature of this kind of preparatory work, it has perhaps resulted in those working within corpus linguistics being particularly reflective on their method and the claims that are made about it. Or it may be the distinct combination of qualitative and quantitative techniques that has made us more apt to think about method *per se*. In any case, this book represents an important milestone in the development of corpus linguistics methods, and amply demonstrates the dedication with which we strive to improve our abilities as analysts.

As Marchi so aptly demonstrates in Chapter 9, with corpus-based approaches to discourse analysis there is (usually) no right answer, and so it is often a case of spending time at the start of a research project, thinking of the possible approaches one could take, what each one is likely to achieve, narrowing the approaches to a manageable set and then trying them out. The methodology we eventually employ may still be further down the line but we have to start somewhere. It is important that we do not view our methodology as being locked into place at the outset, but as a first step. The essays in this collection all point towards the importance of engaging with reflexivity, a form of self-aware thoughtfulness in other words. It is hoped that they will act as examples of good practice, helping to move our field as a whole towards more thorough, grounded and credible forms of analysis. This book is a promising start in that direction.

References

Baker, P. 2006. *Using Corpora in Discourse Analysis*. London: Continuum.

Baker, P. 2012. *Keywords: Signposts to objectivity?* Plenary talk given at Corpus Assisted Discourse Studies Conference, Bologna, 19 September 2012.

Baker, P. 2014. 'Bad wigs and screaming mimis': Using corpus-assisted techniques to carry out critical discourse analysis of the representation of trans people in the British press. In C. Hart & P. Cap (eds.) *Contemporary Critical Discourse Studies*. London: Bloomsbury. pp. 211–236.

Baker, P. & Egbert, J. (eds.) 2016. *Triangulating Methodological Approaches in Corpus-Linguistic Research*. London: Routledge.

Burr, V. 1995. *An Introduction to Social Constructionism*. London: Routledge.

Flowerdew, J. (ed.) 2014. *Discourse in Context(s)*. London: Bloomsbury.

Galtung, J & Ruge, M. 1981. Structuring and selecting news. In S. Cohen & J. Young (eds.) *The Manufacture of News: Social Problems, Deviance and the Mass Media*, 2nd ed. London: Constable. pp. 52–63.

Hunt, S. 2015. Representations of gender and agency in the Harry Potter series. In P. Baker, & T. McEnery (eds.) *Corpora and Discourse Studies: Integrating Discourse and Corpora*. London: Palgrave. pp. 266–284.

Leech, G. 1992. Corpora and theories of linguistic performance. In J. Svartvik (ed.) *Directions in Corpus Linguistics: Proceedings of the Nobel Symposium 82, Stockholm, 4–8 August 1991*. Berlin: Mouton de Gruyter. pp. 105–22.

Mautner, G. 2009. Corpora and Critical Discourse Analysis. In P. Baker (ed.) *Contemporary Corpus Linguistics*. London: Continuum. pp. 32–46.

McEnery, T. & Hardie, A. 2012. *Corpus Linguistics: Method, Theory and Practice*. Cambridge: Cambridge University Press.

McEnery, T., Love, R. & Brezina, V. 2017. Introduction: Compiling and analysing the Spoken British National Corpus 2014. *International Journal of Corpus Linguistics*, 22(3), 311–318.

Partington, A. 2015. Corpus-assisted comparative case studies of representations of the Arab world. In P. Baker & T. McEnery (eds.) *Corpora and Discourse Studies: Integrating Discourse and Corpora*. London: Palgrave. pp. 220–243.

Partington, A, Duguid, A. & Taylor, C. 2013. *Patterns and Meanings in Discourse: Theory and Practice in Corpus-Assisted Discourse Studies (CADS)*. Amsterdam: John Benjamins.

Popper, K. 1959. *The Logic of Scientific Discovery*. New York: Basic Books. Reprinted in 2005 by Taylor and Francis.

Reisigl, M. & Wodak, R. 2001. *Discourse and Discrimination: Rhetorics of Racism and Antisemitism*. London: Routledge.

Scott, M. 2017. *News Downloads and Aboutness*. Plenary talk given at Corpus Linguistics 2017 Conference. Birmingham UK. 26 July 2017.

Sunderland, J. 2004. *Gendered Discourses*. London: Palgrave Macmillan.

Tognini-Bonelli, E. 2001. *Corpus Linguistics at Work*. Amsterdam: John Benjamins.

INDEX